ON THE GENEALOGY OF MORALS
and
ECCE HOMO

ON THE GENEALOGY
OF MORALS

Translated by
WALTER KAUFMANN and R. J. HOLLINGDALE

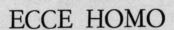

ECCE HOMO

Translated by
WALTER KAUFMANN

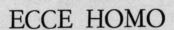

Edited, with Commentary,

by

WALTER KAUFMANN

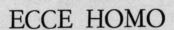

by

FRIEDRICH NIETZSCHE

VINTAGE BOOKS
A Division of Random House
NEW YORK

for

BARKLIE McKEE HENRY

1902–1966

A Note on This Edition

The translation of the *Genealogy of Morals* was done jointly with R. J. Hollingdale, author of *Nietzsche: The Man and His Philosophy* (University of Louisiana Press, 1965), but I alone bear the responsibility for the final version. The other translations in this volume, as well as the commentaries, involved no collaboration.

The commentaries, both on the *Genealogy* and on *Ecce Homo,* fall into three parts: an introduction, hundreds of footnotes, and an appendix. For the long appendix to the *Genealogy* I have translated most of the numerous aphorisms from his earlier works that Nietzsche refers to in the text. Nothing of this sort has been done before, but it should have been. For good measure, I have also included many aphorisms he did not cite. In the case of *Ecce Homo,* the appendix contains previously untranslated variants from Nietzsche's drafts.

All footnotes are mine, none are Nietzsche's.

In the original, almost every numbered section constitutes a single paragraph. Nietzsche used dashes and three dots to indicate breaks. I have largely dispensed with these devices and begun new paragraphs wherever that seemed helpful.

Of the two books offered here in a single volume, the *Genealogy* has long been considered one of Nietzsche's most important works. *Ecce Homo* has been appreciated very much less. May this edition lead to a better understanding of both works!

WALTER KAUFMANN

November 1, 1966

Acknowledgments

Ecce Homo is the tenth volume by Nietzsche that I have translated: the first four appeared in 1954; *Beyond Good and Evil* in 1966; and four more of his books as well as *The Will to Power* (a collection of his notes) in 1967. *Ecce Homo,* Nietzsche's last original work (*Nietzsche contra Wagner* consists of passages that Nietzsche selected from his earlier books) I left for the end; and because the book was intended to help the reader understand Nietzsche's thought, I have given it a more comprehensive and detailed commentary than any of the other works.

Jason Epstein's interest in this project was a necessary, although unfortunately not a sufficient, condition of its realization. I was sometimes unsure whether I ought to have undertaken this second series of six translations, but now I am glad that they are done.

It is a pleasure to give thanks once more to Berenice Hoffman for her unfailingly expert and gracious editorial queries and suggestions.

Stephen Watson helped me once again with the indices, and Sonia Volochova made scores of valuable additions to them.

George Brakas read the page proofs and called to my attention many points that were not as clear as, I hope, they are now.

My wife, Hazel, kept up my spirits.

WALTER KAUFMANN

CONTENTS

ON THE GENEALOGY OF MORALS

ECCE HOMO

ON THE
GENEALOGY OF MORALS

Editor's Introduction

1

Of all of Nietzsche's books, the *Genealogy of Morals* comes closest, at least in form, to Anglo-American philosophy: it consists of three inquiries, each self-contained and yet related to the other two. Even those who suppose, erroneously, that *Beyond Good and Evil* is a book for browsing, a collection of aphorisms that may be read in any order whatever, generally recognize that the *Genealogy* comprises three essays. Moreover, all three essays deal with morality, a subject close to the heart of British and American philosophy; and Nietzsche's manner is much more sober and single-minded than usual.

Yet it should be noted that the title page is followed by these words: "A Sequel to My Last Book, *Beyond Good and Evil,* Which It Is Meant to Supplement and Clarify." [1] In other words, Nietzsche did not suppose that the *Genealogy* could be readily understood by itself, and in the final section of the preface he explained emphatically at some length that he presupposed not only a passing acquaintance with his earlier books but actually a rather close study of them.

Moreover, Nietzsche refers the reader, especially (but not only) in the preface, to a large number of specific passages in his earlier works. It is easy to resent all this as tedious and self-important—and to misunderstand the book and Nietzsche's philosophy generally. It is fashionable to read hastily, as if, for example, one knew all about Nietzsche's contrast of master and slave morality before one had even begun to read him. But if one reads snippets here and there, projecting ill-founded preconceptions into the gaps, one is apt to misconstrue Nietzsche's moral philosophy completely—as Loeb and Leopold did when, as youngsters, they supposed that a brutal and senseless murder would prove them masters. Similar misunderstandings mar many academic interpretations;

---

[1] *Dem letztveröffentlichten* "Jenseits von Gut und Böse" *zur Ergänzung und Verdeutlichung beigegeben.*

but professors naturally react differently: they feel outraged by Nietzsche and do violence, on a different level, to *him*.

To understand Nietzsche's conceptions of master and slave morality, one should read *Beyond Good and Evil,* section 260, and *Human, All-Too-Human,* section 45—and keep in mind the title of our book, which deals with the *origins* of morality. Nietzsche distinguishes moralities that originated in ruling classes from moralities that originated among the oppressed.

Unfortunately, some of the aphoristic material in his earlier works to which Nietzsche refers us is not easy to come by, and the larger part of it has never been translated adequately. Most of these aphorisms have therefore been included in the present volume, in new translations. And some commentary, in the form of footnotes, may not be supererogatory.

The extent of such a commentary poses insoluble problems: if there is too little of it, students may feel that they get no help where they need it; if there is too much, it becomes an affront to the reader's knowledge and intelligence and a monument of pedantry. No mean can possibly be right for all.

At the end of his Preface Nietzsche says that it won't do simply to read an aphorism, one must also decipher it; and he claims that his whole third inquiry is a paradigm case of a commentary on a single aphorism. Taking my cue from this suggestion, I have selected one exceptionally interesting section in the third essay and given it a much more detailed commentary than the rest of the book: section 24, which deals with the intellectual conscience and with truth. But this is not to suggest that this section is self-contained; on the contrary, the argument is continued in the following section—and so is the commentary.

2

The title of our book is ambiguous, but it is clear which meaning Nietzsche intended. *Zur Genealogie der Moral* could mean "Toward a (literally, "Toward the") Genealogy of Morals" (or Morality); it could also mean—and does mean—"On the Genealogy of Morals." How can one tell?

There is one, and only one, sure way. In many of Nietzsche's books, the aphorisms or sections have brief titles; and several of these (about two dozen) begin with the word *Zur*. So do a great many of his notes, including more than two dozen of those included in the posthumous collection, *The Will to Power*. In the case of the notes, to be sure, the titles were sometimes added by Peter Gast, Nietzsche's worshipful friend and editor; but even titles contributed by Gast have some evidential value, as he had presumably acquired some feeling for Nietzsche's usage.

The upshot: In no title does Nietzsche's *Zur* or *Zum* clearly mean "Toward," and he used *Zur* again and again in contexts in which "Toward" makes no sense at all, and "On" is the only possible meaning; for example, the heading of section 381, in the fifth book of *The Gay Science*—published in 1887 as was the *Genealogy of Morals*—reads: *Zur Frage der Verständlichkeit*, "On the Question of Being Understandable." To be sure, if that same phrase were found in Heidegger, one would not hesitate to translate it, "toward the question of understandability": Heidegger is always on the way toward the point from which it may be possible some day to ask a question. But not Nietzsche. It is not enough to know the language; one must also acquire some feeling for an author. Toward the latter end, an excellent prescription would be to read Nietzsche "On the Question of Being Understandable"; and this aphorism is included in the present volume.

3

Speaking of intelligibility: why does Nietzsche use the French word *ressentiment*? First of all, the German language lacks any close equivalent to the French term. That alone would be sufficient excuse for Nietzsche, though perhaps not for a translator, who could use "resentment."

Secondly, Nietzsche's emergence from the influence of Wagner, who extolled everything Germanic and excoriated the French, was marked by an attitude more Francophile than that of any other major German writer—at least since Leibniz (1646–1716), who preferred to write in French. Nietzsche saw himself as the heir of the French *moralistes* and as a "good European."

In 1805 Hegel wrote to Johann Heinrich Voss, who had translated Homer into German dactylic hexameters: "I should like to say of my aspirations that I shall try to teach philosophy to speak German." [2] Avoiding Greek, Latin, and French terms, Hegel created an involved German terminology, devising elaborate locutions that make his prose utterly forbidding. And a little over a century later, Heidegger tried to do much the same thing. Yet Hegel was assuredly wrong when he went on to say, in the next sentence of his letter: "Once that is accomplished, it will be infinitely more difficult to give shallowness the appearance of profound speech." On the contrary. Nothing serves as well as obscurity to make shallowness look profound.

Modern readers who do not know foreign languages may wonder whether Nietzsche's abundant use of French phrases, and occasionally also of Latin, Greek, and Italian (sometimes he uses English words, too) does not make for obscurity. If it does, this is obscurity of an altogether different kind and easily removed—by a brief footnote, for example. Nietzsche likes brevity as much as he likes being a good European; and he hates nationalism as much as he hates saying approximately, at great length, what can be said precisely, in one word.

One is tempted to add that the kind of obscurantism he abominated involves irremediable ambiguities which lead to endless discussion, while his terms, whether German or foreign, are unequivocal. That is true up to a point—but not quite. Nietzsche had an almost pathological weakness for one particular kind of ambiguity, which, to be sure, is not irremediable: he loved words and phrases that mean one thing out of context and almost the opposite in the context he gives them. He loved language as poets do and relished these "revaluations." All of them involve a double meaning, one exoteric and one esoteric, one—to put it crudely—wrong, and the other right. The former is bound to lead astray hasty readers, browsers, and that rapidly growing curse of our time—the non-readers who do not realize that galloping consumption is a disease.

The body of knowledge keeps increasing at incredible speed,

---

[2] The letter is lost, but three drafts have survived. The quotation is from the final draft, May 1805. See Kaufmann's *Hegel* (Garden City, N.Y., Anchor Books, 1966), Chapter VII, p. 316.

but the literature of nonknowledge grows even faster. Books multiply like mushrooms, or rather like toadstools—mildew would be still more precise—and even those who read books come perforce to depend more and more on knowledge *about* books, writers, and, if at all possible—for this is the intellectual, or rather the nonintellectual, equivalent of a bargain—*movements*. As long as one knows about existentialism, one can talk about a large number of authors without having actually read their books.

Nietzsche diagnosed this disease in its early stages, long before it had reached its present proportions—yet wrote in a manner that insured his being misunderstood by the kind of reader and nonreader he despised. Why? He gave reasons more than once; for example, in *Beyond Good and Evil*, sections 30, 40, 230, 270, 278, 289, and 290, and in the aforementioned section 381 of *The Gay Science*. And I have attempted a different sort of explanation in an essay on "Philosophy versus Poetry." [3]

The *Genealogy* contains several examples of misleading slogans, but *ressentiment* is actually not one of them. That term is univocal, but—to ask this once more—why couldn't we substitute "resentment" for it in an English translation? Apart from the fact that something of the flavor of Nietzsche's style and thought would be lost, this is a point at which Nietzsche succeeded in teaching psychology to speak—Nietzschean. His conception of *ressentiment* constitutes one of his major contributions to psychology—and helps to illuminate the widespread misunderstanding of Nietzsche.

To begin with the first point: At the beginning of his own lengthy essay on "[The role of] *Ressentiment* in the Construction of Moralities," [4] Max Scheler says: "Among the exceedingly few discoveries made in recent times concerning the origin of moral value judgments, Friedrich Nietzsche's discovery of *ressentiment* as the source of such value judgments is the most profound, even if his more specific claim that Christian morality and in particular Chris-

---

[3] Chapter 14 of *From Shakespeare to Existentialism* (Boston, Mass., Beacon Press, 1959; rev. ed., Garden City, N.Y., Doubleday Anchor Books, 1960).
[4] "Das Ressentiment im Aufbau der Moralen" in *Vom Umsturz der Werte* (collapse of values), Leipzig, Der Neue Geist Verlag, 1915; 2nd ed., 1919, vol. I, pp. 43–236.

tian love are the finest 'flower of resssentiment' should turn out to be false." [5]

Scheler, one of the outstanding German philosophers of the first quarter of the twentieth century, converted to Roman Catholicism and persuaded some of his disciples to follow his example—but later abandoned Christianity as well as all theism. In the essay on *ressentiment* he argued: "We believe that Christian values are particularly prone to being reinterpreted into values of *ressentiment* and have also been understood that way particularly often, but that the *core of Christian ethics did not grow on the soil of ressentiment.* Yet we also believe that the *core of bourgeois morality,* which since the thirteenth century has begun more and more to supersede Christian morality until it attained its supreme achievement in the French Revolution, does have its roots in *ressentiment.*" Even where he disagreed with Nietzsche, Scheler emphasized that he considered Nietzsche's account singularly profound and worthy of the most serious consideration.[6]

Readers ready to jump to the conclusion that Nietzsche confounded true Christianity with its bourgeois misinterpretation while Scheler obviously understood Christianity far better should ponder Scheler's footnote: "The possible unity of style of warlike and Christian morality is demonstrated in detail in my book *Der Genius des Krieges und der deutsche Krieg* (The genius of war and the German war), 1915." [7] To be sure, most Christians in England, France, and the United States felt the same way in 1915, but the question remains whether Scheler's reading of Christianity was not designed to be heard gladly in the twentieth century, around 1915, when the essay on *ressentiment,* too, appeared. In any case, this essay does not compare in originality and importance with Nietzsche's *Genealogy,* but it deserves mention as an attempt to develop Nietzsche's ideas, and it shows how the term *ressentiment* has become established.

Nietzsche's conception of *ressentiment* also throws light on

---

[5] *Ibid.,* p. 49. Both here and on p. 106 Scheler claims erroneously that Nietzsche used the phrase in single quotes in *Genealogy,* essay I, section 8.

[6] *Ibid.,* pp. 106f.

[7] *Ibid.,* p. 143.

the reception of his ideas. By way of contrast, consider Max Weber, perhaps the greatest sociologist of the century, and certainly *one* of the greatest. Weber's sociology of religion owes a great deal to Nietzsche's *Genealogy*. But why is it generally recognized that Weber was by no means an anti-Semite, although he found the clue to the Jewish religion in the alleged fact that the Jews were a pariah people, while Nietzsche's comments on slave morality and the slave rebellion in morals have so often been considered highly offensive and tinged by anti-Semitism? (Nietzsche's many references to anti-Semitism are invariably scathing: see the indices in this volume.) Could it be that a scholar is given the benefit of every doubt so long as he does not have the presumption to write well?

To write about Nietzsche "scholars" with the lack of inhibition with which *they* have written about Nietzsche, mixing moralistic denunciations with attempts at psychiatric explanations, would be utterly unthinkable. Why? The answer is clearly not that Nietzsche really was an inferior scholar and did eventually become insane. Most Nietzsche "scholars" cannot hold a candle to his learning or originality, and the closer they are to meriting psychological explanations, the worse it would be to offer any.

Could the reason for the disparity in treatment be that Nietzsche is dead? We are in no danger of hurting his feelings or his career; and he cannot hit back. He is no longer a member of the family; he has left us and is fair game. But Max Weber is dead, too; yet he is still treated as a member of the guild. Clearly, there must be another reason. Nietzsche wrote too well and was too superior. That removed him from the immunity of our community, quite as much as the commission of a crime. But where the transgression has been spiritual or intellectual, and those offended are the intellectual community, the revenge, too, is intellectual. The pent-up resentment against fellow members of the community—sloppy scholars and writers as well as those who excite envy—all this rancor that cannot be vented against living colleagues, at least not in print, may be poured out against a few great scapegoats.

There are many reasons for Nietzsche's being one of the great scapegoats of all time. During World War I British intellectuals

found it convenient to contribute to the war effort by denouncing a
German intellectual of stature whom one could discuss in print
without losing a lot of time reading him—and Nietzsche had said
many nasty things about the British.[8] Henceforth Nietzsche was a
marked man, and World War II contributed its share to this type of
disgraceful literature. But there are even more such studies in German—which is scarcely surprising. After all, Nietzsche said far
more wicked things—incomparably more and worse—about the
Germans than he ever did about the British. And as the literature
shows us beyond a doubt: Christian scholars also needed outlets
for their rancor. For all that, it would be wrong to think in terms of
any strict tit-for-tat, as if each group the dead man had offended
then felt justified in hitting back once he was dead. Once it was
established that this writer was a scapegoat, *anybody* was allowed
to play and vent his own *ressentiment* on him, no matter what its
source.

Apart from these considerations, Nietzsche's reception cannot
be understood. To be sure, reactions of *that* sort do not exhaust
this story. There is also Nietzsche's influence on Rilke and German
poetry, on Thomas Mann and the German novel, on Karl Jaspers
and German philosophy, on Gide and Malraux, Sartre and Camus,
Freud and Buber, Shaw and Yeats. But to understand that, one
only has to read them—and him.

4

One final word about the contents and spirit of the *Genealogy*.
All three inquiries deal with the origins of moral phenomena, as the
title of the book indicates. The first essay, which contrasts "Good
and Evil" with "Good and Bad," juxtaposes master and slave morality; the second essay considers "guilt," the "bad conscience,"
and related matters; and the third, ascetic ideals. The most common misunderstanding of the book is surely to suppose that Nietzsche considers slave morality, the bad conscience, and ascetic
ideals evil; that he suggests that mankind would be better off if only

---

[8] To give at least one example, consider Ernest Barker's Oxford pamphlet on
Nietzsche and Treitschke (London, Oxford University Press, 1914).

these things had never appeared; and that in effect he glorifies unconscionable brutes.

Any such view is wrong in detail and can be refuted both by considering in context the truncated quotations that have been adduced to buttress it and by citing a large number of other passages. I have tried to do this in my book on *Nietzsche*,[9] and this is not the place to repeat the demonstration. But this sort of misinterpretation involves not only hundreds of particular misreadings, it also involves a misreading of the *Genealogy* and, even more generally, of Nietzsche's attitude toward history and the world. In conclusion, something needs to be said about that.

The *Genealogy* is intended as a supplement and clarification of *Beyond Good and Evil*. And while that title suggests an attempt to rise above the slave morality that contrasts good and evil, it also signifies a very broad attack on *"the faith in opposite values."* [10] Decidedly, it is not Nietzsche's concern in the *Genealogy* to tell us that master morality is good, while slave morality is evil; or to persuade us that the bad conscience and ascetic ideals are bad, while a brutish state antedating both phenomena is good. Of course, it is his plan to open new perspectives and to make us see what he discusses in unwonted, different ways. If you are bent on using terms like good and bad, you might say that he tries to show us, among other things, how moral valuations, phenomena, and ideals that are usually not questioned have their bad or dark side. Ordinarily, we see the foreground only; Nietzsche seeks to show us the background.

In a nutshell: when Nietzsche has shown us the dark side of the bad conscience, he says, "The bad conscience is an illness, there is no doubt about that, but an illness as pregnancy is an illness" (II, section 19). His love of fate, his *amor fati*, should not be forgotten. The second chapter of *Ecce Homo* ends: "My formula for greatness in a human being is *amor fati*: that one wants

---

9 Princeton University Press, 1950; rev. ed., Meridian Books, 1956; 3rd rev. ed., Princeton University Press and Vintage Books, 1968.

10 Section 2. For a list of other sections that illuminate the title of the book, see section 4 of the Preface to my translation of *Beyond Good and Evil*, with commentary (New York, Vintage Books, 1966), p. xv.

nothing to be different, not forward, not backward, not in all eternity. Not merely to bear what is necessary, still less conceal it—all idealism is mendaciousness in the face of what is necessary—but *love* it."

In the imagery of the first chapter of *Zarathustra,* it is not Nietzsche's intention to malign or to glorify either the camel or the lion—either the ascetic "spirit that would bear much, and kneels down like a camel" or the blond beast. Indeed, Zarathustra is eloquent in his praise of the camel, and it is plain that much of his description fits Nietzsche himself, who was certainly no stranger to ascetic ideals. But the point is that both camel and lion represent mere stages in the development of the spirit; and insofar as Nietzsche feels dissatisfied with both, it is because he would not have us settle for either: he wants us to climb higher—which, however, cannot be done without passing through these stages. And what lies beyond? What is the goal? Here we return to the image of pregnancy: the third stage is represented by the child. "The child is innocence and forgetting, a new beginning, a game, a self-propelled wheel, a first movement, a sacred 'Yes.' For the game of creation, my brothers, a sacred 'Yes' is needed."

Without acquiring a bad conscience, without learning to be profoundly dissatisfied with ourselves, we cannot envisage higher norms, a new state of being, self-perfection. Without ascetic ideals, without self-control and cruel self-discipline, we cannot attain that self-mastery which Nietzsche ever praises and admires. But to settle down with a nagging bad conscience, to remain an ascetic and mortify oneself, is to fall short of Nietzsche's "Dionysian" vision. What he celebrates is neither the camel nor the lion but the creator.

"*Goethe* . . . fought the mutual extraneousness of reason, senses, feeling, and will . . . he disciplined himself into wholeness, he *created* himself. . . . Such a spirit who has *become free* stands amid the cosmos with a joyous and trusting fatalism, in the *faith* . . . that all is redeemed and affirmed in the whole—*he does not negate any more.* Such a faith, however, is the highest of all possible faiths: I have baptized it with the name of *Dionysus.*" [11]

---

[11] *Twilight of the Idols,* section 49 (*The Portable Nietzsche,* translated, with an introduction, prefaces, and notes, by Walter Kaufmann, New York, The Viking Press, 1954; paperback edition, 1958, pp. 553f.).

ON THE
GENEALOGY OF MORALS

A Polemic[1]

---

[1] *Eine Streitschrift.*

Preface

1

We are unknown to ourselves, we men of knowledge—and with good reason. We have never sought ourselves—how could it happen that we should ever *find* ourselves? It has rightly been said: "Where your treasure is, there will your heart be also";[1] *our* treasure is where the beehives of our knowledge are. We are constantly making for them, being by nature winged creatures and honey-gatherers of the spirit; there is one thing alone we really care about from the heart—"bringing something home." Whatever else there is in life, so-called "experiences"—which of us has sufficient earnestness for them? Or sufficient time? Present experience has, I am afraid, always found us "absent-minded": we cannot give our hearts to it—not even our ears! Rather, as one divinely preoccupied and immersed in himself into whose ear the bell has just boomed with all its strength the twelve beats of noon suddenly starts up and asks himself: "what really was that which just struck?" so we sometimes rub our ears *afterward* and ask, utterly surprised and disconcerted, "what really was that which we have just experienced?" and moreover: "who *are* we really?" and, afterward as aforesaid, count the twelve trembling bell-strokes of our experience, our life, our *being*—and alas! miscount them.—So we are necessarily strangers to ourselves, we do not comprehend ourselves, we *have* to misunderstand ourselves, for us the law "Each is furthest from himself" applies to all eternity—we are not "men of knowledge" with respect to ourselves.

2

My ideas on the *origin* of our moral prejudices—for this is the subject of this polemic—received their first, brief, and provisional

---

[1] Matthew 6:21.

expression in the collection of aphorisms that bears the title *Human, All-Too-Human. A Book for Free Spirits*. This book was begun in Sorrento during a winter when it was given to me to pause as a wanderer pauses and look back across the broad and dangerous country my spirit had traversed up to that time. This was in the winter of 1876–77; the ideas themselves are older. They were already in essentials the same ideas that I take up again in the present treatises—let us hope the long interval has done them good, that they have become riper, clearer, stronger, more perfect! *That* I still cleave to them today, however, that they have become in the meantime more and more firmly attached to one another, indeed entwined and interlaced with one another, strengthens my joyful assurance that they might have arisen in me from the first not as isolated, capricious, or sporadic things but from a common root, from a *fundamental will* of knowledge, pointing imperiously into the depths, speaking more and more precisely, demanding greater and greater precision. For this alone is fitting for a philosopher. We have no right to *isolated* acts of any kind: we may not make isolated errors or hit upon isolated truths. Rather do our ideas, our values, our yeas and nays, our ifs and buts, grow out of us with the necessity with which a tree bears fruit—related and each with an affinity to each, and evidence of *one* will, *one* health, *one* soil, *one* sun.—Whether *you* like them, these fruits of ours?—But what is that to the trees! What is that to *us,* to us philosophers!

3

Because of a scruple peculiar to me that I am loth to admit to—for it is concerned with *morality,* with all that has hitherto been celebrated on earth as morality—a scruple that entered my life so early, so uninvited, so irresistibly, so much in conflict with my environment, age, precedents, and descent that I might almost have the right to call it my *"a priori"*—my curiosity as well as my suspicions were bound to halt quite soon at the question of where our good and evil really *originated*. In fact, the problem of the origin of evil pursued me even as a boy of thirteen: at an age in which you have "half childish trifles, half God in your heart," [2] I

---

[2] Goethe's *Faust,* lines 3781f.

devoted to it my first childish literary trifle, my first philosophical effort—and as for the "solution" of the problem I posed at that time, well, I gave the honor to God, as was only fair, and made him the *father* of evil. Was *that* what my *"a priori"* demanded of me? that new immoral, or at least unmoralistic *"a priori"* and the alas! so anti-Kantian, enigmatic "categorical imperative" which spoke through it and to which I have since listened more and more closely, and not merely listened?

Fortunately I learned early to separate theological prejudice from moral prejudice and ceased to look for the origin of evil *behind* the world. A certain amount of historical and philological schooling, together with an inborn fastidiousness of taste in respect to psychological questions in general, soon transformed my problem into another one: under what conditions did man devise these value judgments good and evil? *and what value do they themselves possess?* Have they hitherto hindered or furthered human prosperity? Are they a sign of distress, of impoverishment, of the degeneration of life? Or is there revealed in them, on the contrary, the plenitude, force, and will of life, its courage, certainty, future?

Thereupon I discovered and ventured divers answers; I distinguished between ages, peoples, degrees of rank among individuals; I departmentalized my problem; out of my answers there grew new questions, inquiries, conjectures, probabilities—until at length I had a country of my own, a soil of my own, an entire discrete, thriving, flourishing world, like a secret garden the existence of which no one suspected.—Oh how *fortunate* we are, we men of knowledge, provided only that we know how to keep silent long enough!

4

The first impulse to publish something of my hypotheses concerning the origin of morality was given me by a clear, tidy, and shrewd—also precocious—little book in which I encountered distinctly for the first time an upside-down and perverse species of genealogical hypothesis, the genuinely *English* type, that attracted me—with that power of attraction which everything contrary, everything antipodal possesses. The title of the little book was *The*

Origin of the Moral Sensations; its author Dr. Paul Rée; the year in which it appeared 1877. Perhaps I have never read anything to which I would have said to myself No, proposition by proposition, conclusion by conclusion, to the extent that I did to this book: yet quite without ill-humor or impatience. In the above-mentioned work, on which I was then engaged, I made opportune and inopportune reference to the propositions of that book, not in order to refute them—what have I to do with refutations!—but, as becomes a positive spirit, to replace the improbable with the more probable, possibly one error with another. It was then, as I have said, that I advanced for the first time those genealogical hypotheses to which this treatise is devoted—ineptly, as I should be the last to deny, still constrained, still lacking my own language for my own things and with much backsliding and vacillation. One should compare in particular what I say in *Human, All-Too-Human,* section 45, on the twofold prehistory of good and evil (namely, in the sphere of the noble and in that of the slaves); likewise, section 136, on the value and origin of the morality of asceticism; likewise, sections 96 and 99 and volume II, section 89, on the "morality of mores," that much older and more primitive species of morality which differs *toto caelo*[3] from the altruistic mode of evaluation (in which Dr. Rée, like all English moral genealogists, sees moral evaluation *as such*); likewise, section 92, *The Wanderer,* section 26, and *Dawn,* section 112, on the origin of justice as an agreement between two approximately equal powers (equality as the presupposition of all compacts, consequently of all law); likewise *The Wanderer,* sections 22 and 33, on the origin of punishment, of which the aim of intimidation is neither the essence nor the source (as Dr. Rée thinks—it is rather only introduced, under certain definite circumstances, and always as an incidental, as something added).[4]

---

[3] Diametrically: literally, by the whole heavens.

[4] Nietzsche always gives page references to the first editions. I have substituted section numbers, which are the same in all editions and translations; and in an appendix most of the sections cited are offered in my translations.

For Nietzsche's relation to Rée, see Rudolph Binion, *Frau Lou,* Princeton, N.J., Princeton University Press, 1968.

5

Even then my real concern was something much more important than hypothesis-mongering, whether my own or other people's, on the origin of morality (or more precisely: the latter concerned me solely for the sake of a goal to which it was only one means among many). What was at stake was the *value* of morality—and over this I had to come to terms almost exclusively with my great teacher Schopenhauer, to whom that book of mine, the passion and the concealed contradiction of that book, addressed itself as if to a contemporary (—for that book, too, was a "polemic"). What was especially at stake was the value of the "unegoistic," the instincts of pity, self-abnegation, self-sacrifice, which Schopenhauer had gilded, deified, and projected into a beyond for so long that at last they became for him "value-in-itself," on the basis of which he *said No* to life and to himself. But it was against precisely *these* instincts that there spoke from me an ever more fundamental mistrust, an ever more corrosive skepticism! It was precisely here that I saw the *great* danger to mankind, its sublimest enticement and seduction—but to what? to nothingness?—it was precisely here that I saw the beginning of the end, the dead stop, a retrospective weariness, the will turning *against* life, the tender and sorrowful signs of the ultimate illness: I understood the ever spreading morality of pity that had seized even on philosophers and made them ill, as the most sinister symptom of a European culture that had itself become sinister, perhaps as its by-pass to a new Buddhism? to a Buddhism for Europeans? to—*nihilism?*

For this overestimation of and predilection for pity on the part of modern philosophers is something new: hitherto philosophers have been at one as to the *worthlessness* of pity. I name only Plato, Spinoza, La Rochefoucauld and Kant—four spirits as different from one another as possible, but united in one thing: in their low estimation of pity.

6

This problem of the *value* of pity and of the morality of pity (—I am opposed to the pernicious modern effeminacy of feeling—) seems at first to be merely something detached, an isolated question mark; but whoever sticks with it and *learns* how to ask questions here will experience what I experienced—a tremendous new prospect opens up for him, a new possibility comes over him like a vertigo, every kind of mistrust, suspicion, fear leaps up, his belief in morality, in all morality, falters—finally a new demand becomes audible. Let us articulate this *new demand:* we need a *critique* of moral values, *the value of these values themselves must first be called in question*—and for that there is needed a knowledge of the conditions and circumstances in which they grew, under which they evolved and changed (morality as consequence, as symptom, as mask, as tartufferie, as illness, as misunderstanding; but also morality as cause, as remedy, as stimulant, as restraint, as poison), a knowledge of a kind that has never yet existed or even been desired. One has taken the *value* of these "values" as given, as factual, as beyond all question; one has hitherto never doubted or hesitated in the slightest degree in supposing "the good man" to be of greater value than "the evil man," of greater value in the sense of furthering the advancement and prosperity of man in general (the future of man included). But what if the reverse were true? What if a symptom of regression were inherent in the "good," likewise a danger, a seduction, a poison, a narcotic, through which the present was possibly living *at the expense of the future?* Perhaps more comfortably, less dangerously, but at the same time in a meaner style, more basely?— So that precisely morality would be to blame if the *highest power and splendor* actually possible to the type man was never in fact attained? So that precisely morality was the danger of dangers?

7

Let it suffice that, after this prospect had opened up before me, I had reasons to look about me for scholarly, bold, and industrious comrades (I am still looking). The project is to traverse with quite novel questions, and as though with new eyes, the enormous, distant, and so well hidden land of morality—of morality that has actually existed, actually been lived; and does this not mean virtually to *discover* this land for the first time?

If I considered in this connection the above-mentioned Dr. Rée, among others, it was because I had no doubt that the very nature of his inquiries would compel him to adopt a better method for reaching answers. Have I deceived myself in this? My desire, at any rate, was to point out to so sharp and disinterested an eye as his a better direction in which to look, in the direction of an actual *history of morality,* and to warn him in time against gazing around haphazardly in the blue after the English fashion. For it must be obvious which color is a hundred times more vital for a genealogist of morals than blue: namely *gray,* that is, what is documented, what can actually be confirmed and has actually existed, in short the entire long hieroglyphic record, so hard to decipher, of the moral past of mankind!

This was unknown to Dr. Rée; but he had read Darwin—so that in his hypotheses, and after a fashion that is at least entertaining, the Darwinian beast and the ultramodern unassuming moral milksop who "no longer bites" politely link hands, the latter wearing an expression of a certain good-natured and refined indolence, with which is mingled even a grain of pessimism and weariness, as if all these things—the problems of morality—were really not worth taking quite so seriously. But to me, on the contrary, there seems to be nothing *more* worth taking seriously, among the rewards for it being that some day one will perhaps be allowed to take them *cheerfully.* For cheerfulness—or in my own language *gay science*—is a reward: the reward of a long, brave, industrious, and subterranean seriousness, of which, to be sure, not everyone is capable. But on the day we can say with all our hearts, "Onwards!

our old morality too is part *of the comedy!*" we shall have discovered a new complication and possibility for the Dionysian drama of "The Destiny of the Soul"—and one can wager that the grand old eternal comic poet of our existence will be quick to make use of it!

8

If this book is incomprehensible to anyone and jars on his ears, the fault, it seems to me, is not necessarily mine. It is clear enough, assuming, as I do assume, that one has first read my earlier writings and has not spared some trouble in doing so: for they are, indeed, not easy to penetrate.[5] Regarding my *Zarathustra,* for example, I do not allow that anyone knows that book who has not at some time been profoundly wounded and at some time profoundly delighted by every word in it; for only then may he enjoy the privilege of reverentially sharing in the halcyon element out of which that book was born and in its sunlight clarity, remoteness, breadth, and certainty. In other cases, people find difficulty with the aphoris-

---

[5] See also the end of Nietzsche's Preface to the new edition of *The Dawn,* written in the fall of 1886: ". . . to read *well,* that means reading slowly, deeply, with consideration and caution . . ." The last four words do not adequately render *rück- und vorsichtig,* which can also mean, looking backward and forward—i.e., with a regard for the context, including also the writer's earlier and later works. Cf. *Beyond Good and Evil,* my note on section 250.

Yet Arthur Danto voices a very common assumption when he says on the first page of the first chapter of his *Nietzsche as Philosopher* (New York, Macmillan, 1965): "No one of them [i.e., Nietzsche's books] presupposes an acquaintance with any other . . . his writings may be read in pretty much any order, without this greatly impeding the comprehension of his ideas." This is as wrong as Danto's claim on the same page that "it would be difficult even for a close reader to tell the difference between those works he [Nietzsche] saw through the press [e.g., the *Genealogy*] and those [*sic*] pieced together by his editors [i.e., *The Will to Power*]." Indeed, Danto, like most readers, approaches Nietzsche as if "any given aphorism or essay might as easily have been placed in one volume as in another"; he bases his discussions on short snippets, torn from their context, and frequently omits phrases without indicating that he has done so; and he does not bother to consider all or most of the passages that are relevant to the topics he discusses.

This is one of the few books in English that deal with Nietzsche as a philosopher, and Danto's standing as a philosopher inspires confidence; but his account of Nietzsche's moral and epistemological ideas unfortunately depends on this untenable approach. See also the first footnote to the second essay, below.

tic form: this arises from the fact that today this form is *not taken seriously enough*. An aphorism, properly stamped and molded, has not been "deciphered" when it has simply been read; rather, one has then to begin its *exegesis,* for which is required an art of exegesis. I have offered in the third essay of the present book an example of what I regard as "exegesis" in such a case—an aphorism is prefixed to this essay, the essay itself is a commentary on it. To be sure, one thing is necessary above all if one is to practice reading as an *art* in this way, something that has been unlearned most thoroughly nowadays—and therefore it will be some time before my writings are "readable"—something for which one has almost to be a cow and in any case *not* a "modern man": *rumination*.

Sils-Maria, Upper Engadine,
July 1887

First Essay
"Good and Evil," "Good and Bad"

1

These English psychologists, whom one has also to thank for the only attempts hitherto to arrive at a history of the origin of morality—they themselves are no easy riddle; I confess that, as living riddles, they even possess one essential advantage over their books —*they are interesting!* These English psychologists—what do they really want? One always discovers them voluntarily or involuntarily at the same task, namely at dragging the *partie honteuse*[1] of our inner world into the foreground and seeking the truly effective and directing agent, that which has been decisive in its evolution, in just that place where the intellectual pride of man would least *desire* to find it (in the *vis inertiae*[2] of habit, for example, or in forgetfulness, or in a blind and chance mechanistic hooking-together of ideas, or in something purely passive, automatic, reflexive, molecular, and thoroughly stupid)—what is it really that always drives these psychologists in just *this* direction? Is it a secret, malicious, vulgar, perhaps self-deceiving instinct for belittling man? Or possibly a pessimistic suspicion, the mistrustfulness of disappointed idealists grown spiteful and gloomy? Or a petty subterranean hostility and rancor toward Christianity (and Plato) that has perhaps not even crossed the threshold of consciousness? Or even a lascivious taste for the grotesque, the painfully paradoxical, the questionable and absurd in existence? Or finally—something of each of them, a little vulgarity, a little gloominess, a little anti-Christianity, a little itching and need for spice?

But I am told they are simply old, cold, and tedious frogs, creeping around men and into men as if in their own proper ele-

---

[1] Shame.
[2] Inertia.

ment, that is, in a *swamp*. I rebel at that idea; more, I do not believe it; and if one may be allowed to hope where one does not know, then I hope from my heart they may be the reverse of this—that these investigators and microscopists of the soul may be fundamentally brave, proud, and magnanimous animals, who know how to keep their hearts as well as their sufferings in bounds and have trained themselves to sacrifice all desirability to truth, *every* truth, even plain, harsh, ugly, repellent, unchristian, immoral truth.—For such truths do exist.—

2

All respect then for the good spirits that may rule in these historians of morality! But it is, unhappily, certain that the *historical spirit* itself is lacking in them, that precisely all the good spirits of history itself have left them in the lurch! As is the hallowed custom with philosophers, the thinking of all of them is *by nature* unhistorical; there is no doubt about that. The way they have bungled their moral genealogy comes to light at the very beginning, where the task is to investigate the origin of the concept and judgment "good." "Originally"—so they decree—"one approved unegoistic actions and called them good from the point of view of those to whom they were done, that is to say, those to whom they were *useful;* later one *forgot* how this approval originated and, simply because unegoistic actions were always *habitually* praised as good, one also felt them to be good—as if they were something good in themselves." One sees straightaway that this primary derivation already contains all the typical traits of the idiosyncrasy of the English psychologists—we have "utility," "forgetting," "habit," and finally "error," all as the basis of an evaluation of which the higher man has hitherto been proud as though it were a kind of prerogative of man as such. This pride *has* to be humbled, this evaluation disvalued: has that end been achieved?

Now it is plain to me, first of all, that in this theory the source of the concept "good" has been sought and established in the wrong place: the judgment "good" did *not* originate with those to whom "goodness" was shown! Rather it was "the good" themselves, that is to say, the noble, powerful, high-stationed and high-minded, who felt and established themselves and their actions as good, that is, of the first rank, in contradistinction to all the low, low-minded, common and plebeian. It was out of this *pathos of distance*[1] that they first seized the right to create values and to coin names for values: what had they to do with utility! The viewpoint of utility is as remote and inappropriate as it possibly could be in face of such a burning eruption of the highest rank-ordering, rank-defining value judgments: for here feeling has attained the antithesis of that low degree of warmth which any calculating prudence, any calculus of utility, presupposes—and not for once only, not for an exceptional hour, but for good. The pathos of nobility and distance, as aforesaid, the protracted and domineering fundamental total feeling on the part of a higher ruling order in relation to a lower order, to a "below"—*that* is the origin of the antithesis "good" and "bad." (The lordly right of giving names extends so far that one should allow oneself to conceive the origin of language itself as an expression of power on the part of the rulers: they say "this *is* this and this," they seal every thing and event with a sound and, as it were, take possession of it.) It follows from this origin that the word "good" was definitely *not* linked from the first and by necessity to "unegoistic" actions, as the superstition of these genealogists of morality would have it. Rather it was only when aristocratic value judgments *declined* that the whole antithesis "egoistic" "unegoistic" obtruded itself more and more on the human conscience—it is, to speak in my own language, the *herd instinct* that through this antithesis at last gets its word (and its *words*) in. And even then it was a long time before that instinct attained such dominion that moral evaluation was actually stuck and halted at this antithesis (as, for example, is the case in contemporary Europe: the prejudice that takes "moral," "unegoistic," *"désintéressé"* as concepts of equivalent value already rules today with the force of a "fixed idea" and brain-sickness).

---

[1] Cf. *Beyond Good and Evil,* section 257.

3

In the second place, however: quite apart from the historical untenability of this hypothesis regarding the origin of the value judgment "good," it suffers from an inherent psychological absurdity. The utility of the unegoistic action is supposed to be the source of the approval accorded it, and this source is supposed to have been *forgotten*—but how is this forgetting *possible?* Has the utility of such actions come to an end at some time or other? The opposite is the case: this utility has rather been an everyday experience at all times, therefore something that has been underlined again and again: consequently, instead of fading from consciousness, instead of becoming easily forgotten, it must have been impressed on the consciousness more and more clearly. How much more reasonable is that opposing theory (it is not for that reason more true—) which Herbert Spencer,[1] for example, espoused: that the concept "good" is essentially identical with the concept "useful," "practical," so that in the judgments "good" and "bad" mankind has summed up and sanctioned precisely its *unforgotten* and *unforgettable* experiences regarding what is useful-practical and what is harmful-impractical. According to this theory, that which has always proved itself useful is good: therefore it may claim to be "valuable in the highest degree," "valuable in itself." This road to an explanation is, as aforesaid, also a wrong one, but at least the explanation is in itself reasonable and psychologically tenable.

4

The signpost to the *right* road was for me the question: what was the real etymological significance of the designations for "good" coined in the various languages? I found they all led back to the *same conceptual transformation*—that everywhere "noble," "aristocratic" in the social sense, is the basic concept from which

---

[1] Herbert Spencer (1820–1903) was probably the most widely read English philosopher of his time. He applied the principle of evolution to many fields, including sociology and ethics.

"good" in the sense of "with aristocratic soul," "noble," "with a soul of a high order," "with a privileged soul" necessarily developed: a development which always runs parallel with that other in which "common," "plebeian," "low" are finally transformed into the concept "bad." The most convincing example of the latter is the German word *schlecht* [bad] itself: which is identical with *schlicht* [plain, simple]—compare *schlechtweg* [plainly], *schlechterdings* [simply]—and orginally designated the plain, the common man, as yet with no inculpatory implication and simply in contradistinction to the nobility. About the time of the Thirty Years' War, late enough therefore, this meaning changed into the one now customary.[1]

With regard to a moral genealogy this seems to me a *fundamental* insight; that it has been arrived at so late is the fault of the retarding influence exercised by the democratic prejudice in the modern world toward all questions of origin. And this is so even in the apparently quite objective domain of natural science and physiology, as I shall merely hint here. But what mischief this prejudice is capable of doing, especially to morality and history, once it has been unbridled to the point of hatred is shown by the notorious case of Buckle;[2] here the *plebeianism* of the modern spirit, which is of English origin, erupted once again on its native soil, as violently as a mud volcano and with that salty, noisy, vulgar eloquence with which all volcanos have spoken hitherto.—

5

With regard to *our* problem, which may on good grounds be called a *quiet* problem and one which fastidiously directs itself to few ears, it is of no small interest to ascertain that through those words and roots which designate "good" there frequently still shines the most important nuance by virtue of which the noble felt themselves to be men of a higher rank. Granted that, in the

---

[1] Cf. *Dawn,* section 231, included in the present volume.
[2] Henry Thomas Buckle (1821–1862), English historian, is known chiefly for his *History of Civilization* (1857ff.). The suggestion in the text is developed more fully in section 876 of *The Will to Power.*

majority of cases, they designate themselves simply by their superiority in power (as "the powerful," "the masters," "the commanders") or by the most clearly visible signs of this superiority, for example, as "the rich," "the possessors" (this is the meaning of *arya;* and of corresponding words in Iranian and Slavic). But they also do it by a *typical character trait:* and this is the case that concerns us here. They call themselves, for instance, "the truthful"; this is so above all of the Greek nobility, whose mouthpiece is the Megarian poet Theognis.[1] The root of the word coined for this, *esthlos,*[2] signifies one who *is,* who possesses reality, who is actual, who is true; then, with a subjective turn, the true as the truthful: in this phase of conceptual transformation it becomes a slogan and catchword of the nobility and passes over entirely into the sense of "noble," as distinct from the *lying* common man, which is what

---

[1] Nietzsche's first publication, in 1867 when he was still a student at the University of Leipzig, was an article in a leading classical journal, *Rheinisches Museum,* on the history of the collection of the maxims of Theognis ("Zur Geschichte der Theognideischen Spruchsammlung"). Theognis of Megara lived in the sixth century B.C.

[2] Greek: good, brave. Readers who are not classical philologists may wonder as they read this section how well taken Nietzsche's points about the Greeks are. In this connection one could obviously cite a vast literature, but in this brief commentary it will be sufficient to quote Professor Gerald F. Else's monumental study *Aristotle's Poetics: The Argument* (Cambridge, Mass., Harvard University Press, 1957), a work equally notable for its patient and thorough scholarship and its spirited defense of some controversial interpretations. On the points at issue here, Else's comments are not, I think, controversial; and that is the reason for citing them here.

"The dichotomy is mostly taken for granted in Homer: there are not many occasions when the heaven-wide gulf between heroes and commoners even has to be mentioned.[30] [30 Still, one finds 'good' (*esthloi*) and 'bad' (*kakoi*) explicitly contrasted a fair number of times: B366, Z489, I319, . . .] In the . . . seventh and sixth centuries, on the other hand, the antithesis grows common. In Theognis it amounts to an obsession . . . Greek thinking begins with and for a long time holds to the proposition that mankind is divided into 'good' and 'bad,' and these terms are quite as much social, political, and economic as they are moral. . . . The dichotomy is absolute and exclusive for a simple reason: it began as the aristocrats' view of society and reflects their idea of the gulf between themselves and the 'others.' In the minds of a comparatively small and close-knit group like the Greek aristocracy there are only two kinds of people, 'we' and 'they'; and of course 'we' are the good people, the proper, decent, good-looking, right-thinking ones, while 'they' are the rascals, the poltroons, the good-for-nothings . . . Aristotle knew and sympathized with this older aristocratic, 'practical' ideal, not as superior to the contemplative, but at least as next best to it" (p. 75).

Theognis takes him to be and how he describes him—until finally, after the decline of the nobility, the word is left to designate nobility of soul and becomes as it were ripe and sweet. In the word *kakos*,[3] as in *deilos*[4] (the plebeian in contradistinction to the *agathos*[5]), cowardice is emphasized: this perhaps gives an indication in which direction one should seek the etymological origin of *agathos*, which is susceptible of several interpretations. The Latin *malus*[6] (beside which I set *melas*[7]) may designate the common man as the dark-colored, above all as the black-haired man (*"hic niger est"*[8]—"), as the pre-Aryan occupant of the soil of Italy who was distinguished most obviously from the blond, that is Aryan, conqueror race by his color; Gaelic, at any rate, offers us a precisely similar case— *fin* (for example in the name *Fin-Gal*), the distinguishing word for nobility, finally for the good, noble, pure, orginally meant the blond-headed, in contradistinction to the dark, black-haired aboriginal inhabitants.

The Celts, by the way, were definitely a blond race; it is wrong to associate traces of an essentially dark-haired people which appear on the more careful ethnographical maps of Germany with any sort of Celtic origin or blood-mixture, as Virchow[9] still does: it is rather the *pre-Aryan* people of Germany who emerge in these places. (The same is true of virtually all Europe: the suppressed race has gradually recovered the upper hand again, in coloring, shortness of skull, perhaps even in the intellectual and social in-

---

[3] Greek: bad, ugly, ill-born, mean, craven.

[4] Greek: cowardly, worthless, vile, wretched.

[5] Greek: good, well-born, gentle, brave, capable.

[6] Bad.

[7] Greek: black, dark.

[8] Quoted from Horace's *Satires*, I.4, line 85: "He that backbites an absent friend . . . and cannot keep secrets, is black, O Roman, beware!" *Niger*, originally "black," also came to mean unlucky and, as in this quotation, wicked. Conversely, *candidus* means white, bright, beautiful, pure, guileless, candid, honest, happy, fortunate. And in *Satires*, I.5, 41, Horace speaks of "the whitest souls earth ever bore" (*animae qualis neque candidiores terra tulit*).

[9] Rudolf Virchow (1821–1902) was one of the greatest German pathologists, as well as a liberal politician, a member of the German Reichstag (parliament), and an opponent of Bismarck.

stincts: who can say whether modern democracy, even more modern anarchism and especially that inclination for *"commune,"* for the most primitive form of society, which is now shared by all the socialists of Europe, does not signify in the main a tremendous *counterattack*—and that the conqueror and *master race,*[10] the Aryan, is not succumbing physiologically, too?

I believe I may venture to interpret the Latin *bonus*[11] as "the warrior," provided I am right in tracing *bonus* back to an earlier *duonus*[12] (compare *bellum = duellum = duen-lum,* which seems to me to contain *duonus*). Therefore *bonus* as the man of strife, of dissention (*duo*), as the man of war: one sees what constituted the "goodness" of a man in ancient Rome. Our German *gut* [good] even: does it not signify "the godlike," the man of "godlike race"? And is it not identical with the popular (originally noble) name of the Goths? The grounds for this conjecture cannot be dealt with here.—

6

To this rule that a concept denoting political superiority always resolves itself into a concept denoting superiority of soul it is not necessarily an exception (although it provides occasions for exceptions) when the highest caste is at the same time the *priestly* caste and therefore emphasizes in its total description of itself a predicate that calls to mind its priestly function. It is then, for example, that "pure" and "impure" confront one another for the first time as designations of station; and here too there evolves a "good" and a "bad" in a sense no longer referring to station. One should be warned, moreover, against taking these concepts "pure" and "impure" too ponderously or broadly, not to say symbolically: all the concepts of ancient man were rather at first

---

[10] For a detailed discussion both of this concept and of Nietzsche's attitude toward the Jews and anti-Semitism, see Kaufmann's *Nietzsche,* Chapter 10: "The Master-Race."

[11] Good.

[12] Listed in Harper's Latin Dictionary as the old form of *bonus,* with the comment: "for *duonus,* cf. *bellum.*" And *duellum* is identified as an early and poetic form of *bellum* (war).

incredibly uncouth, coarse, external, narrow, straightforward, and altogether *unsymbolical* in meaning to a degree that we can scarcely conceive. The "pure one" is from the beginning merely a man who washes himself, who forbids himself certain foods that produce skin ailments, who does not sleep with the dirty women of the lower strata, who has an aversion to blood—no more, hardly more! On the other hand, to be sure, it is clear from the whole nature of an essentially priestly aristocracy why antithetical valuations could in precisely this instance soon become danger-ously deepened, sharpened, and internalized; and indeed they finally tore chasms between man and man that a very Achilles of a free spirit would not venture to leap without a shudder. There is from the first something *unhealthy* in such priestly aristocracies and in the habits ruling in them which turn them away from action and alternate between brooding and emotional explosions, habits which seem to have as their almost invariable consequence that intestinal morbidity and neurasthenia which has afflicted priests at all times; but as to that which they themselves devised as a remedy for this morbidity—must one not assert that it has ultimately proved itself a hundred times more dangerous in its effects than the sickness it was supposed to cure? Mankind itself is still ill with the effects of this priestly naïveté in medicine! Think, for example, of certain forms of diet (abstinence from meat), of fasting, of sexual continence, of flight "into the wilderness" (the Weir Mitchell isola-tion cure[1]—without, to be sure, the subsequent fattening and over-feeding which constitute the most effective remedy for the hysteria induced by the ascetic ideal): add to these the entire antisensualis-tic metaphysic of the priests that makes men indolent and overre-fined, their autohypnosis in the manner of fakirs and Brahmins —Brahma used in the shape of a glass knob and a fixed idea—and finally the only-too-comprehensible satiety with all this, together with the radical cure for it, *nothingness* (or God—the desire for a *unio mystica* with God is the desire of the Buddhist for nothing-ness, Nirvana—and no more!). For with the priests *everything* be-comes more dangerous, not only cures and remedies, but also arro-

---

[1] The cure developed by Dr. Silas Weir Mitchell (1829–1914, American) consisted primarily in isolation, confinement to bed, dieting, and massage.

gance, revenge, acuteness, profligacy, love, lust to rule, virtue, disease—but it is only fair to add that it was on the soil of this *essentially dangerous* form of human existence, the priestly form, that man first became *an interesting animal,* that only here did the human soul in a higher sense acquire *depth* and become *evil*—and these are the two basic respects in which man has hitherto been superior to other beasts!

7

One will have divined already how easily the priestly mode of valuation can branch off from the knightly-aristocratic and then develop into its opposite; this is particularly likely when the priestly caste and the warrior caste are in jealous opposition to one another and are unwilling to come to terms. The knightly-aristocratic value judgments presupposed a powerful physicality, a flourishing, abundant, even overflowing health, together with that which serves to preserve it: war, adventure, hunting, dancing, war games, and in general all that involves vigorous, free, joyful activity. The priestly-noble mode of valuation presupposes, as we have seen, other things: it is disadvantageous for it when it comes to war! As is well known, the priests are the *most evil enemies*—but why? Because they are the most impotent. It is because of their impotence that in them hatred grows to monstrous and uncanny proportions, to the most spiritual and poisonous kind of hatred. The truly great haters in world history have always been priests; likewise the most ingenious[1] haters: other kinds of spirit [2] hardly come into consideration when compared with the spirit of priestly vengefulness. Human history would be altogether too stupid a thing without the spirit that the impotent have introduced into it—let us take at once the most notable example. All that has been done on earth against "the noble," "the powerful," "the masters," "the rulers," fades into nothing compared with what the *Jews* have done against them; the Jews, that priestly people, who in opposing their enemies and conquerors were ultimately satisfied with nothing less than a radical

---

[1] *Geistreich.*
[2] *Geist.*

revaluation of their enemies' values, that is to say, an act of the *most spiritual revenge*. For this alone was appropriate to a priestly people, the people embodying the most deeply repressed [3] priestly vengefulness. It was the Jews who, with awe-inspiring consistency, dared to invert the aristocratic value-equation (good = noble = powerful = beautiful = happy = beloved of God) and to hang on to this inversion with their teeth, the teeth of the most abysmal hatred (the hatred of impotence), saying "the wretched alone are the good; the poor, impotent, lowly alone are the good; the suffering, deprived, sick, ugly alone are pious, alone are blessed by God, blessedness is for them alone—and you, the powerful and noble, are on the contrary the evil, the cruel, the lustful, the insatiable, the godless to all eternity; and you shall be in all eternity the unblessed, accursed, and damned!" . . . One knows *who* inherited this Jewish revaluation . . . In connection with the tremendous and immeasurably fateful initiative provided by the Jews through this most fundamental of all declarations of war, I recall the proposition I arrived at on a previous occasion (*Beyond Good and Evil*, section 195)[4]—that with the Jews there begins *the slave revolt in morality:* that revolt which has a history of two thousand years behind it and which we no longer see because it—has been victorious.

8

But you do not comprehend this? You are incapable of seeing something that required two thousand years to achieve victory?— There is nothing to wonder at in that: all *protracted* things are hard to see, to see whole. *That,* however, is what has happened: from the trunk of that tree of vengefulness and hatred, Jewish hatred— the profoundest and sublimest kind of hatred, capable of creating ideals and reversing values, the like of which has never existed on earth before—there grew something equally incomparable, a *new love,* the profoundest and sublimest kind of love—and from what other trunk could it have grown?

---

[3] *Zurückgetretensten.*

[4] See my commentary on that section in *Beyond Good and Evil* (New York, Vintage Books, 1966), section 195, note 11.

One should not imagine it grew up as the denial of that thirst for revenge, as the opposite of Jewish hatred! No, the reverse is true! That love grew out of it as its crown, as its triumphant crown spreading itself farther and farther into the purest brightness and sunlight, driven as it were into the domain of light and the heights in pursuit of the goals of that hatred—victory, spoil, and seduction— by the same impulse that drove the roots of that hatred deeper and deeper and more and more covetously into all that was profound and evil. This Jesus of Nazareth, the incarnate gospel of love, this "Redeemer" who brought blessedness and victory to the poor, the sick, and the sinners—was he not this seduction in its most un- canny and irresistible form, a seduction and bypath to precisely those *Jewish* values and new ideals? Did Israel not attain the ulti- mate goal of its sublime vengefulness precisely through the bypath of this "Redeemer," this ostensible opponent and disintegrator of Israel? Was it not part of the secret black art of truly *grand* politics of revenge, of a farseeing, subterranean, slowly advancing, and premeditated revenge, that Israel must itself deny the real instrument of its revenge before all the world as a mortal enemy and nail it to the cross, so that "all the world," namely all the opponents of Israel, could unhesitatingly swallow just this bait? And could spiritual subtlety imagine any *more dangerous* bait than this? Any- thing to equal the enticing, intoxicating, overwhelming, and under- mining power of that symbol of the "holy cross," that ghastly para- dox of a "God on the cross," that mystery of an unimaginable ultimate cruelty and self-crucifixion of God *for the salvation of man?*

What is certain, at least, is that *sub hoc signo*[1] Israel, with its vengefulness and revaluation of all values, has hitherto triumphed again and again over all other ideals, over all *nobler* ideals.——

9

"But why are you talking about *nobler* ideals! Let us stick to the facts: the people have won—or 'the slaves' or 'the mob' or 'the herd' or whatever you like to call them—if this has happened

---

[1] Under this sign.

through the Jews, very well! in that case no people ever had a more world-historic mission. 'The masters' have been disposed of; the morality of the common man has won. One may conceive of this victory as at the same time a blood-poisoning (it has mixed the races together)—I shan't contradict; but this in-toxication has undoubtedly been *successful*. The 'redemption' of the human race (from 'the masters,' that is) is going forward; everything is visibly becoming Judaized, Christianized, mob-ized (what do the words matter!). The progress of this poison through the entire body of mankind seems irresistible, its pace and tempo may from now on even grow slower, subtler, less audible, more cautious—there is plenty of time.— To this end, does the church today still have any *necessary* role to play? Does it still have the right to exist? Or could one do without it? *Quaeritur*.[2] It seems to hinder rather than hasten this progress. But perhaps that is its usefulness.— Certainly it has, over the years, become something crude and boorish, something repellent to a more delicate intellect, to a truly modern taste. Ought it not to become at least a little more refined?— Today it alienates rather than seduces.— Which of us would be a free spirit if the church did not exist? It is the church, and not its poison, that repels us.— Apart from the church, we, too, love the poison.—"

This is the epilogue of a "free spirit" to my speech; an honest animal, as he has abundantly revealed, and a democrat, moreover; he had been listening to me till then and could not endure to listen to my silence. For at this point I have much to be silent about.

10

The slave revolt in morality begins when *ressentiment*[1] itself becomes creative and gives birth to values: the *ressentiment* of natures that are denied the true reaction, that of deeds, and compensate themselves with an imaginary revenge. While every noble morality develops from a triumphant affirmation of itself, slave morality from the outset says No to what is "outside," what is "different," what is "not itself"; and *this* No is its creative deed. This inversion of the value-positing eye—this *need* to direct one's

---

[2] One asks.

[1] Resentment. The term is discussed above, in section 3 of the Introduction.

view outward instead of back to oneself—is of the essence of *ressentiment:* in order to exist, slave morality always first needs a hostile external world; it needs, physiologically speaking, external stimuli in order to act at all—its action is fundamentally reaction.

The reverse is the case with the noble mode of valuation: it acts and grows spontaneously, it seeks its opposite only so as to affirm itself more gratefully and triumphantly—its negative concept "low," "common," "bad" is only a subsequently-invented pale, contrasting image in relation to its positive basic concept—filled with life and passion through and through—"we noble ones, we good, beautiful, happy ones!" When the noble mode of valuation blunders and sins against reality, it does so in respect to the sphere with which it is *not* sufficiently familiar, against a real knowledge of which it has indeed inflexibly guarded itself: in some circumstances it misunderstands the sphere it despises, that of the common man, of the lower orders; on the other hand, one should remember that, even supposing that the affect of contempt, of looking down from a superior height, *falsifies* the image of that which it despises, it will at any rate still be a much less serious falsification than that perpetrated on its opponent—*in effigie* of course—by the submerged hatred, the vengefulness of the impotent. There is indeed too much carelessness, too much taking lightly, too much looking away and impatience involved in contempt, even too much joyfulness, for it to be able to transform its object into a real caricature and monster.

One should not overlook the almost benevolent nuances that the Greek nobility, for example, bestows on all the words it employs to distinguish the lower orders from itself; how they are continuously mingled and sweetened with a kind of pity, consideration, and forbearance, so that finally almost all the words referring to the common man have remained as expressions signifying "unhappy," "pitiable" (campore *deilos,*[2] *deilaios,*[3] *ponēros,*[4] *mochthēros,*[5] the

---

[2] All of the footnoted words in this section are Greek. The first four mean *wretched,* but each has a separate note to suggest some of its other connotations. *Deilos:* cowardly, worthless, vile.

[3] Paltry.

[4] Oppressed by toils, good for nothing, worthless, knavish, base, cowardly.

[5] Suffering hardship, knavish.

last two of which properly designate the common man as work-slave and beast of burden)—and how on the other hand "bad," "low," "unhappy" have never ceased to sound to the Greek ear as one note with a tone-color in which "unhappy" preponderates: this as an inheritance from the ancient nobler aristocratic mode of evaluation, which does not belie itself even in its contempt (—philologists should recall the sense in which *oïzyros,*[6] *anolbos,*[7] *tlēmōn,*[8] *dystychein,*[9] *xymphora*[10] are employed). The "well-born" *felt* themselves to be the "happy"; they did not have to establish their happiness artificially by examining their enemies, or to persuade themselves, *deceive* themselves, that they were happy (as all men of *ressentiment* are in the habit of doing); and they likewise knew, as rounded men replete with energy and therefore *necessarily* active, that happiness should not be sundered from action—being active was with them necessarily a part of happiness (whence *eu prattein*[11] takes its origin)—all very much the opposite of "happiness" at the level of the impotent, the oppressed, and those in whom poisonous and inimical feelings are festering, with whom it appears as essentially narcotic, drug, rest, peace, "sabbath," slackening of tension and relaxing of limbs, in short *passively.*

While the noble man lives in trust and openness with himself (*gennaios*[12] "of noble descent" underlines the nuance "upright" and probably also "naïve"), the man of *ressentiment* is neither upright nor naïve nor honest and straightforward with himself. His soul *squints*; his spirit loves hiding places, secret paths and back doors, everything covert entices him as *his* world, *his* security, *his* refreshment; he understands how to keep silent, how not to forget, how to wait, how to be provisionally self-deprecating and humble. A race of such men of *ressentiment* is bound to become eventually *cleverer* than any noble race; it will also honor cleverness to a far greater degree: namely, as a condition of existence of the first im-

---

[6] Woeful, miserable, toilsome; wretch.
[7] Unblest, wretched, luckless, poor.
[8] Wretched, miserable.
[9] To be unlucky, unfortunate.
[10] Misfortune.
[11] To do well in the sense of faring well.
[12] High-born, noble, high-minded.

portance; while with noble men cleverness can easily acquire a subtle flavor of luxury and subtlety—for here it is far less essential than the perfect functioning of the regulating *unconscious* instincts or even than a certain imprudence, perhaps a bold recklessness whether in the face of danger or of the enemy, or that enthusiastic impulsiveness in anger, love, reverence, gratitude, and revenge by which noble souls have at all times recognized one another. *Ressentiment* itself, if it should appear in the noble man, consummates and exhausts itself in an immediate reaction, and therefore does not *poison*: on the other hand, it fails to appear at all on countless occasions on which it inevitably appears in the weak and impotent.

To be incapable of taking one's enemies, one's accidents, even one's misdeeds seriously for very long—that is the sign of strong, full natures in whom there is an excess of the power to form, to mold, to recuperate and to forget (a good example of this in modern times is Mirabeau,[13] who had no memory for insults and vile actions done him and was unable to forgive simply because he—forgot). Such a man shakes off with a *single* shrug many vermin that eat deep into others; here alone genuine "love of one's enemies" is possible—supposing it to be possible at all on earth. How much reverence has a noble man for his enemies!—and such reverence is a bridge to love.— For he desires his enemy for himself, as his mark of distinction; he can endure no other enemy than one in whom there is nothing to despise and *very much* to honor! In contrast to this, picture "the enemy" as the man of *ressentiment* conceives him—and here precisely is his deed, his creation: he has conceived "the evil enemy," *"the Evil One,"* and this in fact is his basic concept, from which he then evolves, as an afterthought and pendant, a "good one"—himself!

11

This, then, is quite the contrary of what the noble man does, who conceives the basic concept "good" in advance and spontaneously out of himself and only then creates for himself an idea of

---

[13] Honoré Gabriel Riqueti, Comte de Mirabeau (1749–1791), was a celebrated French Revolutionary statesman and writer.

"bad"! This "bad" of noble origin and that "evil" out of the caul-
dron of unsatisfied hatred—the former an after-production, a side
issue, a contrasting shade, the latter on the contrary the original
thing, the beginning, the distinctive *deed* in the conception of a
slave morality—how different these words "bad" and "evil" are,
although they are both apparently the opposite of the same concept
"good." But it is *not* the same concept "good": one should ask
rather precisely *who* is "evil" in the sense of the morality of *ressentiment*. The answer, in all strictness, is: *precisely* the "good
man" of the other morality, precisely the noble, powerful man, the
ruler, but dyed in another color, interpreted in another fashion, seen
in another way by the venomous eye of *ressentiment*.

Here there is one thing we shall be the last to deny: he who
knows these "good men" only as enemies knows only *evil enemies*, and the same men who are held so sternly in check *inter
pares*[1] by custom, respect, usage, gratitude, and even more by mutual suspicion and jealousy, and who on the other hand in their
relations with one another show themselves so resourceful in consideration, self-control. delicacy, loyalty, pride, and friendship—
once they go outside, where the strange, the *stranger* is found, they
are not much better than uncaged beasts of prey. There they savor
a freedom from all social constraints, they compensate themselves
in the wilderness for the tension engendered by protracted confinement and enclosure within the peace of society, they go *back* to the
innocent conscience of the beast of prey, as triumphant monsters
who perhaps emerge from a disgusting[2] procession of murder, arson, rape, and torture, exhilarated and undisturbed of soul, as if it
were no more than a students' prank, convinced they have provided
the poets with a lot more material for song and praise. One cannot
fail to see at the bottom of all these noble races the beast of prey,
the splendid *blond beast*[3] prowling about avidly in search of spoil

---

[1] Among equals.

[2] *Scheusslichen.*

[3] This is the first appearance in Nietzsche's writings of the notorious "blond
beast." It is encountered twice more in the present section; a variant appears
in section 17 of the second essay; and then the *blonde Bestie* appears once
more in *Twilight*, "The 'Improvers' of Mankind," section 2 (*Portable Nietzsche*, p. 502). That is all. For a detailed discussion of these passages see

and victory; this hidden core needs to erupt from time to time, the animal has to get out again and go back to the wilderness: the Roman, Arabian, Germanic, Japanese nobility, the Homeric heroes, the Scandinavian Vikings—they all shared this need.

It is the noble races that have left behind them the concept "barbarian" wherever they have gone; even their highest culture betrays a consciousness of it and even a pride in it (for example, when Pericles says to his Athenians in his famous funeral oration "our boldness has gained access to every land and sea, everywhere raising imperishable monuments to its goodness *and wickedness*"). This "boldness" of noble races, mad, absurd, and sudden in its expression, the incalculability, even incredibility of their undertakings—Pericles specially commends the *rhathymia*[4] of the Athenians—

Kaufmann's *Nietzsche*, Chapter 7, section III: ". . . The 'blond beast' is not a racial concept and does not refer to the 'Nordic race' of which the Nazis later made so much. Nietzsche specifically refers to Arabs and Japanese . . . —and the 'blondness' presumably refers to the beast, the lion."

Francis Golffing, in his free translation of the *Genealogy*, deletes the blond beast three times out of four; only where it appears the second time in the original text, he has "the blond Teutonic beast." This helps to corroborate the myth that the blondness refers to the Teutons. Without the image of the lion, however, we lose not only some of Nietzsche's poetry as well as any chance to understand one of his best known coinages; we also lose an echo of the crucial first chapter of *Zarathustra*, where the lion represents the second stage in "The Three Metamorphoses" of the spirit—above the obedient camel but below the creative child (*Portable Nietzsche*, pp. 138f.).

Arthur Danto has suggested that if lions were black and Nietzsche had written "Black Beast," the expression would "provide support for African instead of German nationalists" (*Nietzsche as Philosopher*, New York, Macmillan, 1965, p. 170). Panthers *are* black and magnificent animals, but anyone calling Negroes black beasts and associating them with "a disgusting procession of murder, arson, rape, and torture," adding that "the animal has to get out again and go back to the wilderness," and then going on to speak of "their hair-raising cheerfulness and profound joy in all destruction," would scarcely be taken to "provide support for . . . nationalists." On the contrary, he would be taken for a highly prejudiced critic of the Negro.

No other German writer of comparable stature has been a more extreme critic of German nationalism than Nietzsche. For all that, it is plain that in this section he sought to describe the behavior of the ancient Greeks and Romans, the Goths and the Vandals, not that of nineteenth-century Germans.

[4] Thucydides, 2.39. In *A Historical Commentary on Thucydides*, vol. II (Oxford, Clarendon Press, 1956; corrected imprint of 1966), p. 118, A. W. Gomme comments on this word: "in its original sense, 'ease of mind,' 'without anxiety' . . . But ease of mind can in certain circumstances become

their indifference to and contempt for security, body, life, comfort,
their hair-raising[5] cheerfulness and profound joy in all destruction,
in all the voluptuousness of victory and cruelty—all this came together, in the minds of those who suffered from it, in the image of
the "barbarian," the "evil enemy," perhaps as the "Goths," the
"Vandals." The deep and icy mistrust the German still arouses today whenever he gets into a position of power is an echo of that
inextinguishable horror with which Europe observed for centuries
that raging of the blond Germanic beast (although between the old
Germanic tribes and us Germans there exists hardly a conceptual
relationship, let alone one of blood).

I once drew attention to the dilemma in which Hesiod found
himself when he concocted his succession of cultural epochs and
sought to express them in terms of gold, silver, and bronze: he
knew no way of handling the contradiction presented by the glori-
ous but at the same time terrible and violent world of Homer except by dividing one epoch into two epochs, which he then placed
one behind the other—first the epoch of the heroes and demigods
of Troy and Thebes, the form in which that world had survived in
the memory of the noble races who were those heroes' true descendants; then the bronze epoch, the form in which that same
world appeared to the descendants of the downtrodden, pillaged,
mistreated, abducted, enslaved: an epoch of bronze, as aforesaid,
hard, cold, cruel, devoid of feeling or conscience, destructive and
bloody.

Supposing that what is at any rate believed to be the "truth"
really is true, and the *meaning of all culture* is the reduction of the
beast of prey "man" to a tame and civilized animal, a *domestic
animal,* then one would undoubtedly have to regard all those instincts of reaction and *ressentiment* through whose aid the noble
races and their ideals were finally confounded and overthrown as
the actual *instruments of culture*; which is not to say that the *bear-
ers* of these instincts themselves represent culture. Rather is the
reverse not merely probable—no! today it is *palpable!* These bear-

---

carelessness, remissness, frivolity: Demosthenes often accused the Athenians
of *rhathymia* . . ."
[5] *Entsetzliche.*

ers of the oppressive instincts that thirst for reprisal, the descendants of every kind of European and non-European slavery, and especially of the entire pre-Aryan populace—they represent the *regression* of mankind! These "instruments of culture" are a disgrace to man and rather an accusation and counterargument against "culture" in general! One may be quite justified in continuing to fear the blond beast at the core of all noble races and in being on one's guard against it: but who would not a hundred times sooner fear where one can also admire than *not* fear but be permanently condemned to the repellent sight of the ill-constituted, dwarfed, atrophied, and poisoned? [6] And is that not *our* fate? What today constitutes *our* antipathy to "man"?—for we *suffer* from man, beyond doubt.

Not fear; rather that we no longer have anything left to fear in man; that the maggot[7] "man" is swarming in the foreground; that the "tame man," the hopelessly mediocre and insipid[8] man, has already learned to feel himself as the goal and zenith, as the meaning of history, as "higher man"—that he has indeed a certain right to feel thus, insofar as he feels himself elevated above the surfeit of ill-constituted, sickly, weary and exhausted people of which Europe is beginning to stink today, as something at least relatively well-constituted, at least still capable of living, at least affirming life.

12

At this point I cannot suppress a sigh and a last hope. What is it that I especially find utterly unendurable? That I cannot cope with, that makes me choke and faint? Bad air! Bad air! The ap-

---

[6] If the present section is not clear enough to any reader, he might turn to *Zarathustra*'s contrast of the *overman* and the *last man* (Prologue, sections 3–5) and, for good measure, read also the first chapter or two of Part One. Then he will surely see how Aldous Huxley's *Brave New World* and George Orwell's *1984*—but especially the former—are developments of Nietzsche's theme. Huxley, in his novel, uses Shakespeare as a foil; Nietzsche, in the passage above, Homer.

[7] *Gewürm* suggests wormlike animals; *wimmelt* can mean swarm or crawl but is particularly associated with maggots—in a cheese, for example.

[8] *Unerquicklich.*

proach of some ill-constituted thing; that I have to smell the entrails of some ill-constituted soul!

How much one is able to endure: distress, want, bad weather,
sickness, toil, solitude. Fundamentally one can cope with everything else, born as one is to a subterranean life of struggle; one
emerges again and again into the light, one experiences again and
again one's golden hour of victory—and then one stands forth as
one was born, unbreakable, tensed, ready for new, even harder,
remoter things, like a bow that distress only serves to draw tauter.

But grant me from time to time—if there are divine goddesses
in the realm beyond good and evil—grant me the sight, but *one*
glance of something perfect, wholly achieved, happy, mighty, triumphant, something still capable of arousing fear! Of a man who justi-
fies *man*, of a complementary and redeeming lucky hit on the part
of man for the sake of which one may still *believe in man!*

For this is how things are: the diminution and leveling of European man constitutes *our* greatest danger, for the sight of him
makes us weary.— We can see nothing today that wants to grow
greater, we suspect that things will continue to go down, down, to
become thinner, more good-natured, more prudent, more comfortable, more mediocre, more indifferent, more Chinese, more Christian—there is no doubt that man is getting "better" all the time.

Here precisely is what has become a fatality for Europe—together with the fear of man we have also lost our love of him, our
reverence for him, our hopes for him, even the will to him. The
sight of man now makes us weary—what is nihilism today if it is
not *that*?— We are weary *of man*.

13

But let us return: the problem of the *other* origin of the
"good," of the good as conceived by the man of *ressentiment*, demands its solution.

That lambs dislike great birds of prey does not seem strange:
only it gives no ground for reproaching these birds of prey for bearing off little lambs. And if the lambs say among themselves: "these
birds of prey are evil; and whoever is least like a bird of prey, but

rather its opposite, a lamb—would he not be good?" there is no reason to find fault with this institution of an ideal, except perhaps that the birds of prey might view it a little ironically and say: "*we* don't dislike them at all, these good little lambs; we even love them: nothing is more tasty than a tender lamb."

To demand of strength that it should *not* express itself as strength, that it should *not* be a desire to overcome, a desire to throw down, a desire to become master, a thirst for enemies and resistances and triumphs, is just as absurd as to demand of weakness that it should express itself as strength. A quantum of force is equivalent to a quantum of drive, will, effect—more, it is nothing other than precisely this very driving, willing, effecting, and only owing to the seduction of language (and of the fundamental errors of reason that are petrified in it) which conceives and misconceives all effects as conditioned by something that causes effects, by a "subject," can it appear otherwise. For just as the popular mind separates the lightning from its flash and takes the latter for an *action*, for the operation of a subject called lightning, so popular morality also separates strength from expressions of strength, as if there were a neutral substratum behind the strong man, which was *free* to express strength or not to do so. But there is no such substratum; there is no "being" behind doing, effecting, becoming; "the doer" is merely a fiction added to the deed—the deed is everything. The popular mind in fact doubles the deed; when it sees the lightning flash, it is the deed of a deed: it posits the same event first as cause and then a second time as its effect. Scientists do no better when they say "force moves," "force causes," and the like— all its coolness, its freedom from emotion notwithstanding, our entire science still lies under the misleading influence of language and has not disposed of that little changeling, the "subject" (the atom, for example, is such a changeling, as is the Kantian "thing-in-itself"); no wonder if the submerged, darkly glowering emotions of vengefulness and hatred exploit this belief for their own ends and in fact maintain no belief more ardently than the belief that *the strong man is free* to be weak and the bird of prey to be a lamb— for thus they gain the right to make the bird of prey *accountable* for being a bird of prey.

When the oppressed, downtrodden, outraged exhort one another with the vengeful cunning of impotence: "let us be different from the evil, namely good! And he is good who does not outrage, who harms nobody, who does not attack, who does not requite, who leaves revenge to God, who keeps himself hidden as we do, who avoids evil and desires little from life, like us, the patient, humble, and just"—this, listened to calmly and without previous bias, really amounts to no more than: "we weak ones are, after all, weak; it would be good if we did nothing *for which we are not strong enough*"; but this dry matter of fact, this prudence of the lowest order which even insects possess (posing as dead, when in great danger, so as not to do "too much"), has, thanks to the counterfeit and self-deception of impotence, clad itself in the ostentatious garb of the virtue of quiet, calm resignation, just as if the weakness of the weak—that is to say, their *essence,* their effects, their sole ineluctable, irremovable reality—were a voluntary achievement, willed, chosen, a *deed,* a *meritorious* act. This type of man *needs* to believe in a neutral independent "subject," prompted by an instinct for self-preservation and self-affirmation in which every lie is sanctified. The subject (or, to use a more popular expression, the *soul*) has perhaps been believed in hitherto more firmly than anything else on earth because it makes possible to the majority of mortals, the weak and oppressed of every kind, the sublime self-deception that interprets weakness as freedom, and their being thus-and-thus as a *merit.*

14

Would anyone like to take a look into the secret of how *ideals are made* on earth? Who has the courage?— Very well! Here is a point we can see through into this dark workshop. But wait a moment or two, Mr. Rash and Curious: your eyes must first get used to this false iridescent light.— All right! Now speak! What is going on down there? Say what you see, man of the most perilous kind of inquisitiveness—now I am the one who is listening.—

—"I see nothing, but I hear the more. There is a soft, wary, malignant muttering and whispering coming from all the corners and nooks. It seems to me one is lying; a saccharine sweetness clings to every sound. Weakness is being lied into something *meritorious*, no doubt of it—so it is just as you said"—

—Go on!

—"and impotence which does not requite into 'goodness of heart'; anxious lowliness into 'humility'; subjection to those one hates into 'obedience' (that is, to one of whom they say he commands this subjection—they call him God). The inoffensiveness of the weak man, even the cowardice of which he has so much, his lingering at the door, his being ineluctably compelled to wait, here acquire flattering names, such as 'patience,' and are even called virtue itself; his inability for revenge is called unwillingness to revenge, perhaps even forgiveness ('for *they* know not what they do—we alone know what *they* do!'). They also speak of 'loving one's enemies'— and sweat as they do so."

—Go on!

—"They are miserable, no doubt of it, all these mutterers and nook counterfeiters, although they crouch warmly together—but they tell me their misery is a sign of being chosen by God; one beats the dogs one likes best; perhaps this misery is also a preparation, a testing, a schooling, perhaps it is even more—something that will one day be made good and recompensed with interest, with huge payments of gold, no! of happiness. This they call 'bliss.' "

—Go on!

—"Now they give me to understand that they are not merely better than the mighty, the lords of the earth whose spittle they have to lick (*not* from fear, not at all from fear! but because God has commanded them to obey the authorities)[1]—that they are not merely better but are also 'better off,' or at least will be better off someday. But enough! enough! I can't take any more. Bad air! Bad air! This workshop where *ideals are manufactured*—it seems to me it stinks of so many lies."

—No! Wait a moment! You have said nothing yet of the masterpiece of these black magicians, who make whiteness, milk, and innocence of every blackness—haven't you noticed their perfection

---

[1] Allusion to Romans 13:1–2.

of refinement, their boldest, subtlest, most ingenious, most mendacious artistic stroke? Attend to them! These cellar rodents full of vengefulness and hatred—what have they made of revenge and hatred? Have you heard these words uttered? If you trusted simply to their words, would you suspect you were among men of *ressentiment?* . . .

—"I understand; I'll open my ears again (oh! oh! oh! and *close* my nose). Now I can really hear what they have been saying all along: 'We good men—*we are the just*'—what they desire they call, not retaliation, but 'the triumph of *justice';* what they hate is not their enemy, no! they hate 'injustice,' they hate 'godlessness'; what they believe in and hope for is not the hope of revenge, the intoxication of sweet revenge (—'sweeter than honey' Homer called it), but the victory of God, of the *just* God, over the godless; what there is left for them to love on earth is not their brothers in hatred but their 'brothers in love,' as they put it, all the good and just on earth."

—And what do they call that which serves to console them for all the suffering of life—their phantasmagoria of anticipated future bliss?

—"What? Do I hear aright? They call that 'the Last Judgment,' the coming of *their* kingdom, of the 'Kingdom of God'—meanwhile, however, they live 'in faith,' 'in love,' 'in hope.' "

—Enough! Enough!

15

In faith in what? In love of what? In hope of what?— These weak people—some day or other *they* too intend to be the strong, there is no doubt of that, some day *their* "kingdom" too shall come—they term it "the kingdom of God," of course, as aforesaid: for one is so very humble in all things! To experience *that* one needs to live a long time, beyond death—indeed one needs eternal life, so as to be eternally indemnified in the "kingdom of God" for this earthly life "in faith, in love, in hope." Indemnified for what? How indemnified?

Dante, I think, committed a crude blunder when, with a terror-inspiring ingenuity, he placed above the gateway of his hell the inscription "I too was created by eternal love"—at any rate, there would be more justification for placing above the gateway to the Christian Paradise and its "eternal bliss" the inscription "I too was created by eternal *hate*"—provided a truth may be placed above the gateway to a lie! For *what* is it that constitutes the bliss of this Paradise?

We might even guess, but it is better to have it expressly described for us by an authority not to be underestimated in such matters, Thomas Aquinas, the great teacher and saint. *"Beati in regno coelesti,"* he says, meek as a lamb, *"videbunt poenas damnatorum, ut beatitudo illis magis complaceat."* [1] Or if one would like to hear it in a stronger key, perhaps from the mouth of a triumphant Church Father, adjuring his Christians to avoid the cruel pleasures of the public games—but why? "For the faith offers us much more"—he says, *De Spectaculis,* chs. 29f.—*"something much stronger;* thanks to the Redemption, quite other joys are at our command; in place of athletes we have our martyrs; if we crave blood, we have the blood of Christ . . . But think of what awaits us on the day of his return, the day of his triumph!"—and then he goes on, the enraptured visionary.[2] *"At enim supersunt alia spectacula, ille ultimus et per-*

---

[1] The blessed in the kingdom of heaven will see the punishments of the damned, *in order that their bliss be more delightful for them.*—To be precise, what we find in *Summa Theologiae,* III, *Supplementum,* Q. 94, Art. 1, is this: "In order that the bliss of the saints may be more delightful for them and that they may render more copious thanks to God for it, it is given to them to see perfectly the punishment of the damned." *Ut beatitudo sanctorum eis magis complaceat, et de ea uberiores gratias Deo agant, datur eis ut poenam impiorum perfecte intueantur.*

[2] Nietzsche quotes Tertullian in the original Latin. This footnote offers, first, an English translation, and then some discussion.

"Yes, and there are other sights: that last day of judgment, with its everlasting issues; that day unlooked for by the nations, the theme of their derision, when the world hoary with age, and all its many products, shall be consumed in one great flame! How vast a spectacle then bursts upon the eye! *What there excites my admiration? what my derision? Which sight gives me joy? which rouses me to exultation?*—as I see so many illustrious monarchs, whose reception into the heavens was publicly announced, groaning now in the lowest darkness with great Jove himself, and those, too, who bore witness of their exultation; governors of provinces, too, who persecuted the Christian name, in fires more fierce than those with which in the days of their pride they raged against the followers of Christ. What world's wise men besides,

petuus judicii dies, ille nationibus insperatus, ille derisus, cum tanta saeculi vetustas et tot ejus nativitates uno igne haurientur. Quae tunc spectaculi latitudo! **Quid admirer! Quid rideam! Ubi gaudeam! Ubi exultem,** *spectans tot et tantos* **reges,** *qui in coelum recepti nuntiabantur, cum ipso Jove et ipsis suis testibus in imis tenebris congemescentes! Item praesides"* (the provincial governors) *"persecutores dominici nominis saevioribus quam ipsi flammis saevierunt insultantibus contra Christianos liquescentes! Quos praeterea sapientes illos philosophos coram discipulis suis una conflagrantibus erubescentes, quibus nihil ad deum pertinere suadebant, quibus animas aut nullas aut non in pristina corpora redituras affirmabant! Etiam poëtas non ad Rhadamanti nec ad Minois, sed ad inopinati Christi tribunal palpitantes! Tunc magis tragoedi audiendi, magis*

---

the very philosophers, in fact, who taught their followers that God had no concern in aught that is sublunary, and were wont to assure them that either they had no souls, or that they would never return to the bodies which at death they had left, now covered with shame before the poor deluded ones, as one fire consumes them! Poets also, trembling not before the judgment-seat of Rhadamanthus or Minos, but of the unexpected Christ! I shall have a better opportunity then of hearing the tragedians, louder-voiced in their own calamity; of viewing the play-actors, much more 'dissolute' [another translation has "much lither of limb"] in the dissolving flame; of looking upon the charioteer, all glowing in his chariot of fire; of beholding the wrestlers, not in their gymnasia, but tossing in the fiery billows; unless even then I shall not care to attend to such ministers of sin, in my eager wish rather to fix a gaze *insatiable* on those whose fury vented itself against the Lord. 'This,' I shall say, 'this is that carpenter's or hireling's son, that Sabbath-breaker, that Samaritan and devil-possessed! This is He whom you purchased from Judas! [*Quaestuaria* means prostitute, not carpenter: see Nietzsche's parenthesis above.] This is He whom you struck with reed and fist, whom you contemptuously spat upon, to whom you gave gall and vinegar to drink! This is He whom His disciples secretly stole away, that it might be said He had risen again, or the gardener abstracted, that his lettuces might come to no harm from the crowds of visitants!' What quaestor or priest in his munificence will bestow on you the favour of seeing and *exulting in such things as these?* And yet even now we in a measure have them *by faith* in the picturings of imagination. But what are the things which eye has not seen, ear has not heard, and which have not so much as dimly dawned upon the human heart? Whatever they are, they are nobler, I believe, than circus, and both theatres, and every race-course." [Translation by the Rev. S. Thelwall.] There are two standard translations of Tertullian's *De Spectaculis*. One is by the Rev. S. Thelwall in *The Ante-Nicene Fathers: Translations of The Writings of the Fathers down to A.D. 325,* edited by the Rev. Alexander Roberts, D.D. and James Donaldson, LL.D., in volume III: *Latin Christianity: Its Founder, Tertullian* (American Reprint of the Edinburgh Edition, Grand Rapids, Mich., Wm. B. Eerd-

scilicet vocales" (in better voice, yet worse screamers) *"in sua propria calamitate; tunc histriones cognoscendi, solutiores multo per ignem; tunc spectandus auriga in flammea rota totus rubens, tunc xystici contemplandi non in gymnasiis, sed in igne jaculati, nisi quod ne tunc quidem illos velim vivos, ut qui malim ad eos potius conspectum* **insatiabilem** *conferre, qui in dominum desaevierunt. 'Hic est ille,' dicam, 'fabri aut quaestuariae filius' "* (what follows, and especially this term for the mother of Jesus, which is found in the Talmud, shows that from here on Tertullian is referring to the Jews), *" 'sabbati destructor, Samarites et daemonium habens. Hic est, quem a Juda redemistis, hic est ille arundine et colaphis diverberatus, sputamentis dedecoratus, felle et aceto potatus. Hic est, quem clam discentes subripuerunt, ut resurrexisse dicatur vel hor-*

---

mans Publishing Company, 1957). The other translation is by Rudolph Arbesmann, O.S.A., Ph.D., Fordham University, in *The Fathers of the Church: A New Translation*, in the volume entitled *Tertullian: Disciplinary, Moral and Ascetical Works* (New York, Fathers of the Church, Inc., 1959, Imprimatur Francis Cardinal Spellman).

In the former edition we are told in a footnote to the title that although there has been some dispute as to whether the work was written before or after Tertullian's "lapse" from orthodoxy to Montanism, "a work so colourless that doctors can disagree about even its shading, must be regarded as practically orthodox. Exaggerated expressions are but the characteristics of the author's genius. We find the like in all writers of strongly marked individuality. Neander dates this treatise *circa* A.D. 197." And in a footnote to the last sentence quoted by Nietzsche, which concludes the last chapter of the treatise, we read: "This concluding chapter, which Gibbon delights to censure, because its fervid rhetoric so fearfully depicts the punishments of Christ's enemies, 'appears to Dr. Neander to contain a beautiful specimen of lively faith and Christian confidence.' "

In the latter edition we are informed that *"De Spectaculis* is one of Tertullian's most interesting and original works" (p. 38). And chapter 30, which Nietzsche quotes almost in its entirety, omitting only the first four lines, is introduced by a footnote that begins (and it continues in the same vein): "Tertullian gives here a colorful description of the millennium, picturing the feverish expectation of an early return of Christ . . ."

It is noteworthy that the Protestant edition finds the work "so colourless," while the Roman Catholic edition considers it "colorful"—and neither of them evinces any sensitivity to what outraged Nietzsche or Gibbon.

Edward Gibbon's comments are found in Chapter XV of *The History of The Decline and Fall of the Roman Empire:* "The condemnation of the wisest and most virtuous of the Pagans, on account of their ignorance or disbelief of the divine truth, seems to offend the reason and the humanity of the present age. But the primitive church, whose faith was of a much firmer consistence, delivered over, without hesitation, to eternal torture the far

tulanus detraxit, ne lactucae suae frequentia commeantium laede-
rentur.' Ut talia spectes, **ut talibus exultes,** *quis tibi praetor aut*
consul aut guaestor aut sacerdos de sua liberalitate praestabit? Et
tamen haec jam habemus quodammodo **per fidem** *spiritu imaginante*
repraesentata. Ceterum qualia illa sunt, quae nec oculus vidit nec
auris audivit nec in cor hominis ascenderunt?" (1 Cor. 2,9.) *"Credo*
circo et utraque cavea" (first and fourth rank or, according to others, the comic and tragic stage) *"et omni stadio gratiora."* —**Per**
fidem: thus is it written.

16

Let us conclude. The two *opposing* values "good and bad,"
"good and evil" have been engaged in a fearful struggle on earth
for thousands of years; and though the latter value has certainly
been on top for a long time, there are still places where the struggle
is as yet undecided. One might even say that it has risen ever higher
and thus become more and more profound and spiritual: so that
today there is perhaps no more decisive mark of a *"higher nature,"*
a more spiritual nature, than that of being divided in this sense and
a genuine battleground of these opposed values.[1]

The symbol of this struggle, inscribed in letters legible across
all human history, is "Rome against Judea, Judea against Rome":
—there has hitherto been no greater event than *this* struggle, *this*
question, *this* deadly contradiction. Rome felt the Jew to be something like anti-nature itself, its antipodal monstrosity as it were: in

---

greater part of the human species. . . . These rigid sentiments, which had
been unknown to the ancient world, appear to have infused a spirit of bitter-
ness into a system of love and harmony. . . . The Christians, who, in this
world, found themselves oppressed by the power of the Pagans, were sometimes seduced by resentment and spiritual pride to delight in the prospect of
their future triumph. 'You are fond of spectacles,' exclaims the stern Tertullian; 'except the greatest of all spectacles, the last and eternal judgment of the
universe. How shall I admire, how laugh . . .' "

[1] This remark which recalls *Beyond Good and Evil,* section 200, is entirely
in keeping with the way in which the contrast of master and slave morality is
introduced in *Beyond Good and Evil,* section 260; and it ought not to be
overlooked. It sheds a good deal of light not only on this contrast but also
on Nietzsche's *amor fati,* his love of fate. Those who ignore all this material
are bound completely to misunderstand Nietzsche's moral philosophy.

Rome the Jew stood *"convicted* of hatred for the whole human race"; and rightly, provided one has a right to link the salvation and future of the human race with the unconditional dominance of aristocratic values, Roman values.

How, on the other hand, did the Jews feel about Rome? A thousand signs tell us; but it suffices to recall the Apocalypse of John, the most wanton of all literary outbursts that vengefulness has on its conscience. (One should not underestimate the profound consistency of the Christian instinct when it signed this book of hate with the name of the disciple of love, the same disciple to whom it attributed that amorous-enthusiastic Gospel: there is a piece of truth in this, however much literary counterfeiting might have been required to produce it.) For the Romans were the strong and noble, and nobody stronger and nobler has yet existed on earth or even been dreamed of: every remnant of them, every inscription gives delight, if only one divines *what* it was that was there at work. The Jews, on the contrary, were the priestly nation of *ressentiment par excellence*, in whom there dwelt an unequaled popular-moral genius: one only has to compare similarly gifted nations —the Chinese or the Germans, for instance—with the Jews, to sense which is of the first and which of the fifth rank.[2]

Which of them has won *for the present,* Rome or Judea? But there can be no doubt: consider to whom one bows down in Rome itself today, as if they were the epitome of all the highest values— and not only in Rome but over almost half the earth, everywhere that man has become tame or desires to become tame: *three Jews,* as is known, and *one Jewess* (Jesus of Nazareth, the fisherman Peter, the rug weaver Paul, and the mother of the aforementioned Jesus, named Mary). This is very remarkable: Rome has been defeated beyond all doubt.

There was, to be sure, in the Renaissance an uncanny and glittering reawakening of the classical ideal, of the noble mode of evaluating all things; Rome itself, oppressed by the new superimposed Judaized Rome that presented the aspect of an ecumenical

---

[2] Having said things that can easily be misconstrued as grist to the mill of the German anti-Semites, Nietzsche goes out of his way, as usual, to express his admiration for the Jews and his disdain for the Germans.

synagogue and was called the "church," stirred like one awakened from seeming death: but Judea immediately triumphed again, thanks to that thoroughly plebeian (German and English) *ressentiment* movement called the Reformation, and to that which was bound to arise from it, the restoration of the church—the restoration too of the ancient sepulchral repose of classical Rome.

With the French Revolution, Judea once again triumphed over the classical ideal, and this time in an even more profound and decisive sense: the last political noblesse in Europe, that of the *French* seventeenth and eighteenth century, collapsed beneath the popular instincts of *ressentiment*—greater rejoicing, more uproarious enthusiasm had never been heard on earth! To be sure, in the midst of it there occurred the most tremendous, the most unexpected thing: the ideal of antiquity itself stepped *incarnate* and in unheard-of splendor before the eyes and conscience of mankind— and once again, in opposition to the mendacious slogan of *ressentiment*, "supreme rights of the majority," in opposition to the will to the lowering, the abasement, the leveling and the decline and twilight of mankind, there sounded stronger, simpler, and more insistently than ever the terrible and rapturous counterslogan "supreme rights of the few"! Like a last signpost to the *other* path, Napoleon appeared, the most isolated and late-born man there has even been, and in him the problem of the *noble ideal as such* made flesh— one might well ponder *what* kind of problem it is: Napoleon, this synthesis of the *inhuman* and *superhuman*.

17

Was that the end of it? Had that greatest of all conflicts of ideals been placed *ad acta*[1] for all time? Or only adjourned, indefinitely adjourned?

Must the ancient fire not some day flare up much more terribly, after much longer preparation? More: must one not desire it with all one's might? even will it? even promote it?

Whoever begins at this point, like my readers, to reflect and

---

[1] Disposed of.

pursue his train of thought will not soon come to the end of it—reason enough for me to come to an end, assuming it has long since been abundantly clear what my *aim* is, what the aim of that dangerous slogan is that is inscribed at the head of my last book *Beyond Good and Evil*.— At least this does *not* mean "Beyond Good and Bad."——

Note.[2] I take the opportunity provided by this treatise to express publicly and formally a desire I have previously voiced only in occasional conversation with scholars; namely, that some philosophical faculty might advance *historical* studies *of morality* through a series of academic prize-essays—perhaps this present book will serve to provide a powerful impetus in this direction. In case this idea should be implemented, I suggest the following question: it deserves the attention of philologists and historians as well as that of professional philosophers:

"What light does linguistics, and especially the study of etymology, throw on the history of the evolution of moral concepts?"

On the other hand, it is equally necessary to engage the interest of physiologists and doctors in these problems (of the *value* of existing evaluations); it may be left to academic philosophers to act as advocates and mediators in this matter too, after they have on the whole succeeded in the past in transforming the originally so reserved and mistrustful relations between philosophy, physiology, and medicine into the most amicable and fruitful exchange. Indeed, every table of values, every "thou shalt" known to history or ethnology, requires first a *physiological* investigation and interpretation, rather than a psychological one; and every one of them needs a critique on the part of medical science. The question: what is the *value* of this or that table of values and "morals"? should be viewed from the most divers perspectives; for the problem "value *for what?*" cannot be examined too subtly. Something, for example, that possessed obvious value in relation to the longest possible survival of a race (or to the enhancement of its power of adapta-

---

[2] *Anmerkung.*

tion to a particular climate or to the preservation of the greatest number) would by no means possess the same value if it were a question, for instance, of producing a stronger type. The well-being of the majority and the well-being of the few are opposite viewpoints of value: to consider the former *a priori* of higher value may be left to the naïveté of English biologists.— *All* the sciences have from now on to prepare the way for the future task of the philosophers: this task understood as the solution of the *problem of value,* the determination of the *order of rank among values.*

Second Essay
"Guilt," "Bad Conscience,"[1]
and the Like

1

To breed an animal *with the right to make promises*—is not this the paradoxical task that nature has set itself in the case of man? is it not the real problem regarding man?

That this problem has been solved to a large extent must seem all the more remarkable to anyone who appreciates the strength of the opposing force, that of *forgetfulness*. Forgetting is no mere *vis inertiae*[2] as the superficial imagine; it is rather an active and in the strictest sense positive faculty of repression,[3] that is responsible for the fact that what we experience and absorb enters our consciousness as little while we are digesting it (one might call the process "inpsychation") as does the thousandfold process, involved in physical nourishment—so-called "incorporation." To close the doors and windows of consciousness for a time; to remain undisturbed by the noise and struggle of our underworld of utility organs working with and against one another; a little quietness, a little *tabula rasa*[4] of

---

[1] *Schlechtes Gewissen* is no technical term but simply the common German equivalent of "bad conscience." Danto's translation "bad consciousness" (*Nietzsche as Philosopher*, New York, Macmillan, 1965, pp. 164 and 180) is simply wrong: *Gewissen*, like conscience, and unlike the French *conscience*, cannot mean consciousness.

There are many mistranslations in Danto's *Nietzsche*. Another one, though relatively unimportant, is of some interest and relevant to the *Genealogy: Schadenfreude*—a German word for which there is no English equivalent—is not quite "the wicked pleasure in the beholding of suffering" (p. 181) or "in the sheer spectacle of suffering: in fights, executions, . . . bullbaiting, cockfights, and the like" (p. 174). In such contexts the word is utterly out of place: it signifies the petty, mischievous delight felt in the discomfiture of another human being.

[2] *Inertia.*

[3] *Positives Hemmungsvermögen.*

[4] Clean slate.

the consciousness, to make room for new things, above all for the
nobler functions and functionaries, for regulation, foresight, pre-
meditation (for our organism is an oligarchy)—that is the purpose
of active forgetfulness, which is like a doorkeeper, a preserver of
psychic order, repose, and etiquette: so that it will be immediately
obvious how there could be no happiness, no cheerfulness, no
hope, no pride, no *present,* without forgetfulness. The man in
whom this apparatus of repression is damaged and ceases to function properly may be compared (and more than merely compared) with a dyspeptic—he cannot "have done" with anything.

Now this animal which needs to be forgetful, in which forgetting represents a force, a form of *robust* health, has bred in itself an
opposing faculty, a memory, with the aid of which forgetfulness is
abrogated in certain cases—namely in those cases where promises
are made. This involves no mere passive inability to rid oneself of
an impression, no mere indigestion through a once-pledged word
with which one cannot "have done," but an active *desire* not to rid
oneself, a desire for the continuance of something desired once, a
real *memory of the will*: so that between the original "I will," "I
shall do this" and the actual discharge of the will, its *act,* a world of
strange new things, circumstances, even acts of will may be inter-
posed without breaking this long chain of will. But how many
things this presupposes! To ordain the future in advance in this
way, man must first have learned to distinguish necessary events
from chance ones, to think causally, to see and anticipate distant
eventualities as if they belonged to the present, to decide with certainty what is the goal and what the means to it, and in general be
able to calculate and compute. Man himself must first of all have
become *calculable, regular, necessary,* even in his own image of
himself, if he is to be able to stand security for *his own future,*
which is what one who promises does!

2

This precisely is the long story of how *responsibility* originated. The task of breeding an animal with the right to make promises evidently embraces and presupposes as a preparatory task that

one first *makes* men to a certain degree necessary, uniform, like among like, regular, and consequently calculable. The tremendous labor of that which I have called "morality of mores" (*Dawn,* sections 9, 14, 16)[1]—the labor performed by man upon himself during the greater part of the existence of the human race, his entire *prehistoric* labor, finds in this its meaning, its great justification, notwithstanding the severity, tyranny, stupidity, and idiocy involved in it: with the aid of the morality of mores and the social straitjacket, man was actually *made* calculable.

If we place ourselves at the end of this tremendous process, where the tree at last brings forth fruit, where society and the morality of custom at last reveal *what* they have simply been the means to: then we discover that the ripest fruit is the *sovereign individual,* like only to himself, liberated again from morality of custom, autonomous and supramoral (for "autonomous" and "moral" are mutually exclusive),[2] in short, the man who has his own independent, protracted will and the *right to make promises—* and in him a proud consciousness, quivering in every muscle, of *what* has at length been achieved and become flesh in him, a consciousness of his own power and freedom, a sensation of mankind come to completion. This emancipated individual, with the actual *right* to make promises, this master of a *free* will, this sovereign man—how should he not be aware of his superiority over all those who lack the right to make promises and stand as their own guarantors, of how much trust, how much fear, how much reverence he arouses—he *"deserves"* all three—and of how this mastery over

---

[1] See also *Human, All-Too-Human,* section 96; *Mixed Opinions and Maxims,* section 89; and *The Dawn,* section 18, all of which are included in the present volume. *Dawn,* section 16, is included in *The Portable Nietzsche,* p. 76. The German phrase is *die Sittlichkeit der Sitte,* the morality of mores.

[2] The parenthetical statement is the contrary of Kant's view. When it was written, it must have struck most readers as paradoxical, but in the twentieth century it is apt to seem *less* paradoxical than Kant's view. *The Lonely Crowd* (by David Riesman, with Nathan Glazer and Reuel Denney; New Haven, Conn.: Yale University Press, 1950) has popularized a Nietzschean, non-Kantian conception of the autonomous individual, who is contrasted with the tradition-directed (Nietzsche's morality of mores), the inner-directed (Kant, for example), and the other-directed (Nietzsche's "last man").

himself also necessarily gives him mastery over circumstances, over nature, and over all more short-willed and unreliable creatures? The "free" man, the possessor of a protracted and unbreakable will, also possesses his *measure of value*: looking out upon others from himself, he honors or he despises; and just as he is bound to honor his peers, the strong and reliable (those with the *right* to make promises)—that is, all those who promise like sovereigns, reluctantly, rarely, slowly, who are chary of trusting, whose trust is a mark of *distinction*, who give their word as something that can be relied on because they know themselves strong enough to maintain it in the face of accidents, even "in the face of fate"—he is bound to reserve a kick for the feeble windbags who promise without the right to do so, and a rod for the liar who breaks his word even at the moment he utters it. The proud awareness of the extraordinary privilege of *responsibility*, the consciousness of this rare freedom, this power over oneself and over fate, has in his case penetrated to the profoundest depths and become instinct, the dominating instinct. What will he call this dominating instinct, supposing he feels the need to give it a name? The answer is beyond doubt: this sovereign man calls it his *conscience*.

3

His conscience?— It is easy to guess that the concept of "conscience" that we here encounter in its highest, almost astonishing, manifestation, has a long history and variety of forms behind it. To possess the right to stand security for oneself and to do so with pride, thus to possess also the *right to affirm oneself*—this, as has been said, is a ripe fruit, but also a *late* fruit: how long must this fruit have hung on the tree, unripe and sour! And for a much longer time nothing whatever was to be seen of any such fruit: no one could have promised its appearance, although everything in the tree was preparing for and growing toward it!

"How can one create a memory for the human animal? How can one impress something upon this partly obtuse, partly flighty mind, attuned only to the passing moment, in such a way that it will stay there?"

One can well believe that the answers and methods for solving this primeval problem were not precisely gentle; perhaps indeed there was nothing more fearful and uncanny in the whole prehistory of man than his *mnemotechnics.* "If something is to stay in the memory it must be burned in: only that which never ceases to *hurt* stays in the memory"—this is a main clause of the oldest (unhappily also the most enduring) psychology on earth. One might even say that wherever on earth solemnity, seriousness, mystery, and gloomy coloring still distinguish the life of man and a people, something of the terror that formerly attended all promises, pledges, and vows on earth is *still effective:* the past, the longest, deepest and sternest past, breathes upon us and rises up in us whenever we become "serious." Man could never do without blood, torture, and sacrifices when he felt the need to create a memory for himself; the most dreadful sacrifices and pledges (sacrifices of the first-born among them), the most repulsive mutilations (castration, for example), the cruelest rites of all the religious cults (and all religions are at the deepest level systems of cruelties)—all this has its origin in the instinct that realized that pain is the most powerful aid to mnemonics.

In a certain sense, the whole of asceticism belongs here: a few ideas are to be rendered inextinguishable, ever-present, unforgetable, "fixed," with the aim of hypnotising the entire nervous and intellectual system with these "fixed ideas"—and ascetic procedures and modes of life are means of freeing these ideas from the competition of all other ideas, so as to make them "unforgettable." The worse man's memory has been, the more fearful has been the appearance of his customs; the severity of the penal code provides an especially significant measure of the degree of effort needed to overcome forgetfulness and to impose a few primitive demands of social existence as *present realities* upon these slaves of momentary affect and desire.

We Germans certainly do not regard ourselves as a particularly cruel and hardhearted people, still less as a particularly frivolous one, living only for the day; but one has only to look at our former codes of punishments to understand what effort it costs on this earth to breed a "nation of thinkers" (which is to say, *the* nation in Europe in which one still finds today the maximum of trust, seriousness, lack of taste, and matter-of-factness—and with these qualities one has the right to breed every kind of European mandarin). These Germans have employed fearful means to acquire a memory, so as to master their basic mob-instinct and its brutal coarseness. Consider the old German punishments; for example, stoning (the sagas already have millstones drop on the head of the guilty), breaking on the wheel (the most characteristic invention and speciality of the German genius in the realm of punishment!), piercing with stakes, tearing apart or trampling by horses ("quartering"), boiling of the criminal in oil or wine (still employed in the fourteenth and fifteenth centuries), the popular flaying alive ("cutting straps"), cutting flesh from the chest, and also the practice of smearing the wrongdoer with honey and leaving him in the blazing sun for the flies. With the aid of such images and procedures one finally remembers five or six "I will not's," in regard to which one had given one's *promise* so as to participate in the advantages of society—and it was indeed with the aid of this kind of memory that one at last came "to reason"! Ah, reason, seriousness, mastery over the affects, the whole somber thing called reflection, all these prerogatives and showpieces of man: how dearly they have been bought! how much blood and cruelty lie at the bottom of all "good things"!

4

But how did that other "somber thing," the consciousness of guilt, the "bad conscience," come into the world?— And at this point we return to the genealogists of morals. To say it again—or haven't I said it yet?—they are worthless. A brief span of experience that is merely one's own, merely modern; no knowledge or will to knowledge of the past; even less of historical instinct, of that "second sight" needed here above all—and yet they undertake history of morality: it stands to reason that their results stay at a more than respectful distance from the truth. Have these genealogists of morals had even the remotest suspicion that, for example, the major moral concept *Schuld* [guilt] has its origin in the very material concept

Schulden [debts]?[1] Or that punishment, as requital, evolved quite independently of any presupposition concerning freedom or non-freedom of the will?—to such an extent, indeed, that a *high* degree of humanity had to be attained before the animal "man" began even to make the much more primitive distinctions between "intentional," "negligent," "accidental," "accountable," and their opposites and to take them into account when determining punishments. The idea, now so obvious, apparently so natural, even unavoidable, that had to serve as the explanation of how the sense of justice ever appeared on earth—"the criminal deserves punishment *because* he could have acted differently"—is in fact an extremely late and subtle form of human judgment and inference: whoever transposes it to the beginning is guilty of a crude misunderstanding of the psychology of more primitive mankind. Throughout the greater part of human history punishment was *not* imposed *because* one held the wrong-doer responsible for his deed, thus *not* on the presupposition that only the guilty one should be punished: rather, as parents still punish their children, from anger at some harm or injury, vented on the one who caused it—but this anger is held in check and modified by the idea that every injury has its *equivalent* and can actually be paid back, even if only through the *pain* of the culprit. And whence did this primeval, deeply rooted, perhaps by now ineradicable idea draw its power—this idea of an equivalence between injury and pain? I have already divulged it: in the contractual relationship between *creditor* and *debtor,* which is as old as the idea of "legal subjects" and in turn points back to the fundamental forms of buying, selling, barter, trade, and traffic.

---

[1] The German equivalent of "guilt" is *Schuld;* and the German for "debt(s)" is *Schuld(en).* "Innocent" is *unschuldig;* "debtor" is *Schuldner;* and so forth. This obviously poses problems for an English translation of this essay; but once the point has been clearly stated, no misunderstandings need result. Nietzsche's claims obviously do not *depend* on the double meaning of a German word; nor are they weakened by the fact that in English there are two different words, one derived from an Anglo-Saxon root, the other from Latin.

5

When we contemplate these contractual relationships, to be sure, we feel considerable suspicion and repugnance toward those men of the past who created or permitted them. This was to be expected from what we have previously noted. It was here that *promises* were made; it was here that a memory had to be *made* for those who promised; it is here, one suspects, that we shall find a great deal of severity, cruelty, and pain. To inspire trust in his promise to repay, to provide a guarantee of the seriousness and sanctity of his promise, to impress repayment as a duty, an obligation upon his own conscience, the debtor made a contract with the creditor and pledged that if he should fail to repay he would substitute something else that he "possessed," something he had control over; for example, his body, his wife, his freedom, or even his life (or, given certain religious presuppositions, even his bliss after death, the salvation of his soul, ultimately his peace in the grave: thus it was in Egypt, where the debtor's corpse found no peace from the creditor even in the grave—and among the Egyptians such peace meant a great deal). Above all, however, the creditor could inflict every kind of indignity and torture upon the body of the debtor; for example, cut from it as much as seemed commensurate with the size of the debt—and everywhere and from early times one had exact evaluations, *legal* evaluations, of the individual limbs and parts of the body from this point of view, some of them going into horrible and minute detail. I consider it as an advance, as evidence of a freer, more generous, *more Roman* conception of law when the Twelve Tables of Rome decreed it a matter of indifference how much or how little the creditor cut off in such cases: *"si plus minusve secuerunt, ne fraude esto."* [1]

Let us be clear as to the logic of this form of compensation: it is strange enough. An equivalence is provided by the creditor's receiving, in place of a literal compensation for an injury (thus in place of money, land, possessions of any kind), a recompense in the

---

[1] If they have secured more or less, let that be no crime.

form of a kind of *pleasure*—the pleasure of being allowed to vent his power freely upon one who is powerless, the voluptuous pleasure *"de faire le mal pour le plaisir de le faire,"* [2] the enjoyment of violation. This enjoyment will be the greater the lower the creditor stands in the social order, and can easily appear to him as a most delicious morsel, indeed as a foretaste of higher rank. In "punishing" the debtor, the creditor participates in a *right of the masters:* at last he, too, may experience for once the exalted sensation of being allowed to despise and mistreat someone as "beneath him"— or at least, if the actual power and administration of punishment has already passed to the "authorities," to *see* him despised and mistreated. The compensation, then, consists in a warrant for and title to cruelty.—

6

It was in *this* sphere then, the sphere of legal obligations, that the moral conceptual world of "guilt," "conscience," "duty," "sacredness of duty" had its origin: its beginnings were, like the beginnings of everything great on earth, soaked in blood thoroughly and for a long time. And might one not add that, fundamentally, this world has never since lost a certain odor of blood and torture? (Not even in good old Kant: the categorical imperative smells of cruelty.) It was here, too, that that uncanny intertwining of the ideas "guilt and suffering" was first effected—and by now they may well be inseparable. To ask it again: to what extent can suffering balance debts or guilt? [3] To the extent that to *make* suffer was in the highest degree pleasurable, to the extent that the injured party exchanged for the loss he had sustained, including the displeasure caused by the loss, an extraordinary counterbalancing pleasure: that of *making* suffer—a genuine *festival,* something which, as aforesaid, was prized the more highly the more violently it contrasted with the rank and social standing of the creditor. This is offered only as a conjecture; for the depths of such subterranean things are difficult to fathom, besides being painful; and whoever clumsily interposes

[2] Of doing evil for the pleasure of doing it.
[3] "Debts or guilt": *"Schulden."*

the concept of "revenge" does not enhance his insight into the matter but further veils and darkens it (—for revenge merely leads us back to the same problem: "how can making suffer constitute a compensation?").

It seems to me that the delicacy and even more the tartuffery of tame domestic animals (which is to say modern men, which is to say us) resists a really vivid comprehension of the degree to which *cruelty* constituted the great festival pleasure of more primitive men and was indeed an ingredient of almost every one of their pleasures; and how naïvely, how innocently their thirst for cruelty manifested itself, how, as a matter of principle, they posited "disinterested malice" (or, in Spinoza's words, *sympathia malevolens*) as a *normal* quality of man—and thus as something to which the conscience cordially *says Yes!* A more profound eye might perceive enough of this oldest and most fundamental festival pleasure of man even in our time; in *Beyond Good and Evil,* section 229[4] (and earlier in *The Dawn,* sections 18, 77, 113)[5] I pointed cautiously to the ever-increasing spiritualization and "deification" of cruelty which permeates the entire history of higher culture (and in a significant sense actually constitutes it). In any event, it is not long since princely weddings and public festivals of the more magnificent kind were unthinkable without executions, torturings, or perhaps an auto-da-fé, and no noble household was without creatures upon whom one could heedlessly vent one's malice and cruel jokes. (Consider, for instance, Don Quixote at the court of the Duchess. Today we read *Don Quixote* with a bitter taste in our mouths, almost with a feeling of torment, and would thus seem very strange and incomprehensible to its author and his contemporaries: they read it with the clearest conscience in the world as the most cheerful of books, they laughed themselves almost to death over

---

[4] Nietzsche, as usual, furnishes a page reference to the first edition—in this instance, pp. 117ff., which would take us to the middle of section 194 and the following section(s); and German editors, down to Karl Schlechta, give the equivalent page reference. But 117 is plainly a misprint for 177, which takes us to section 229—beyond a doubt, the passage Nietzsche means.

[5] Section 18 is included in the present volume; section 113 is quoted and analyzed in Kaufmann's *Nietzsche,* Chapter 6, section II. Both repay reading in connection with the passage above, to avoid misunderstanding.

it). To see others suffer does one good, to make others suffer even more: this is a hard saying but an ancient, mighty, human, all-too-human principle to which even the apes might subscribe; for it has been said that in devising bizarre cruelties they anticipate man and are, as it were, his "prelude." Without cruelty there is no festival: thus the longest and most ancient part of human history teaches—and in punishment there is so much that is *festive!*—

7

With this idea, by the way, I am by no means concerned to furnish our pessimists with more grist for their discordant and creaking mills of life-satiety. On the contrary, let me declare expressly that in the days when mankind was not yet ashamed of its cruelty, life on earth was more cheerful than it is now that pessimists exist. The darkening of the sky above mankind has deepened in step with the increase in man's feeling of shame *at man.* The weary pessimistic glance, mistrust of the riddle of life, the icy No of disgust with life—these do not characterize the most *evil* epochs of the human race: rather do they first step into the light of day as the swamp weeds they are when the swamp to which they belong comes into being—I mean the morbid softening and moralization through which the animal "man" finally learns to be ashamed of all his instincts. On his way to becoming an "angel" (to employ no uglier word) man has evolved that queasy stomach and coated tongue through which not only the joy and innocence of the animal but life itself has become repugnant to him—so that he sometimes holds his nose in his own presence and, with Pope Innocent the Third, disapprovingly catalogues his own repellent aspects ("impure begetting, disgusting means of nutrition in his mother's womb, baseness of the matter out of which man evolves, hideous stink, secretion of saliva, urine, and filth").

Today, when suffering is always brought forward as the principal argument *against* existence, as the worst question mark, one does well to recall the ages in which the opposite opinion prevailed because men were unwilling to refrain from *making* suffer and saw in it an enchantment of the first order, a genuine seduction *to* life.

Perhaps in those days—the delicate may be comforted by this thought—pain did not hurt as much as it does now; at least that is the conclusion a doctor may arrive at who has treated Negroes (taken as representatives of prehistoric man—) for severe internal inflammations that would drive even the best constituted European to distraction—in the case of Negroes they do *not* do so. (The curve of human susceptibility to pain seems in fact to take an extraordinary and almost sudden drop as soon as one has passed the upper ten thousand or ten million of the top stratum of culture; and for my own part, I have no doubt that the combined suffering of all the animals ever subjected to the knife for scientific ends is utterly negligible compared with *one* painful night of a single hysterical bluestocking.) Perhaps the possibility may even be allowed that this joy in cruelty does not really have to have died out: if pain hurts more today, it simply requires a certain sublimation and subtilization, that is to say it has to appear translated into the imaginative and psychical and adorned with such innocent names that even the tenderest and most hypocritical conscience is not suspicious of them ("tragic pity" is one such name; *"les nostalgies de la croix"* [6] is another).

What really arouses indignation against suffering is not suffering as such but the senselessness of suffering: but neither for the Christian, who has interpreted a whole mysterious machinery of salvation into suffering, nor for the naïve man of more ancient times, who understood all suffering in relation to the spectator of it or the causer of it, was there any such thing as *senseless* suffering. So as to abolish hidden, undetected, unwitnessed suffering from the world and honestly to deny it, one was in the past virtually compelled to invent gods and genii of all the heights and depths, in short something that roams even in secret, hidden places, sees even in the dark, and will not easily let an interesting painful spectacle pass unnoticed. For it was with the aid of such inventions that life then knew how to work the trick which it has always known how to work, that of justifying itself, of justifying its "evil." Nowadays it might require other auxiliary inventions (for example, life as a

---

[6] The nostalgia of the cross.

riddle, life as an epistemological problem). "Every evil the sight of which edifies a god is justified": thus spoke the primitive logic of feeling—and was it, indeed, only primitive? The gods conceived of as the friends of *cruel* spectacles—oh how profoundly this ancient idea still permeates our European humanity! Merely consult Calvin and Luther. It is certain, at any rate, that the *Greeks* still knew of no tastier spice to offer their gods to season their happiness than the pleasures of cruelty. With what eyes do you think Homer made his gods look down upon the destinies of men? What was at bottom the ultimate meaning of Trojan Wars and other such tragic terrors? There can be no doubt whatever: they were intended as *festival plays* for the gods; and, insofar as the poet is in these matters of a more "godlike" disposition than other men, no doubt also as festival plays for the poets.

It was in the same way that the moral philosophers of Greece later imagined the eyes of God looking down upon the moral struggle, upon the heroism and self-torture of the virtuous: the "Herakles of duty" was on a stage and knew himself to be; virtue without a witness was something unthinkable for this nation of actors. Surely, that philosophers' invention, so bold and so fateful, which was then first devised for Europe, the invention of "free will," of the absolute spontaneity of man in good and in evil, was devised above all to furnish a right to the idea that the interest of the gods in man, in human virtue, *could never be exhausted*. There must never be any lack of real novelty, of really unprecedented tensions, complications, and catastrophies on the stage of the earth: the course of a completely deterministic world would have been predictable for the gods and they would have quickly grown weary of it—reason enough for those *friends of the gods,* the philosophers, not to inflict such a deterministic world on their gods! The entire mankind of antiquity is full of tender regard for "the spectator," as an essentially public, essentially visible world which cannot imagine happiness apart from spectacles and festivals.— And, as aforesaid, even in great *punishment* there is so much that is festive!

8

To return to our investigation: the feeling of guilt, of personal obligation, had its origin, as we saw, in the oldest and most primitive personal relationship, that between buyer and seller, creditor and debtor: it was here that one person first encountered another person, that one person first *measured himself* against another. No grade of civilization, however low, has yet been discovered in which something of this relationship has not been noticeable. Setting prices, determining values, contriving equivalences, exchanging—these preoccupied the earliest thinking of man to so great an extent that in a certain sense they constitute thinking *as such*: here it was that the oldest kind of astuteness developed; here likewise, we may suppose, did human pride, the feeling of superiority in relation to other animals, have its first beginnings. Perhaps our word "man" (*manas*) still expresses something of precisely *this* feeling of self-satisfaction: man designated himself as the creature that measures values, evaluates and measures, as the "valuating animal as such."

Buying and selling, together with their psychological appurtenances, are older even than the beginnings of any kind of social forms of organization and alliances: it was rather out of the most rudimentary form of personal legal rights that the budding sense of exchange, contract, guilt, right, obligation, settlement, first *transferred* itself to the coarsest and most elementary social complexes (in their relations with other similar complexes), together with the custom of comparing, measuring, and calculating power against power. The eye was now focused on this perspective; and with that blunt consistency characteristic of the thinking of primitive mankind, which is hard to set in motion but then proceeds inexorably in the same direction, one forthwith arrived at the great generalization, "everything has its price; *all* things can be paid for"—the oldest and naïvest moral canon of *justice,* the beginning of all "good-naturedness," all "fairness," all "good will," all "objectivity" on earth. Justice on this elementary level is the good will among parties of approximately equal power to come to terms with one another, to reach an "understanding" by means of a settlement —and to *compel* parties of lesser power to reach a settlement among themselves.—

9

Still retaining the criteria of prehistory (this prehistory is in any case present in all ages or may always reappear)[1]: the community, too, stands to its members in that same vital basic relation, that of the creditor to his debtors. One lives in a community, one enjoys the advantages of a communality (oh what advantages! we sometimes underrate them today), one dwells protected, cared for, in peace and trustfulness, without fear of certain injuries and hostile acts to which the man *outside,* the "man without peace," is exposed—a German will understand the original connotations of *Elend*[2]—since one has bound and pledged oneself to the community precisely with a view to injuries and hostile acts. What will happen *if this pledge is broken?* The community, the disappointed creditor, will get what repayment it can, one may depend on that. The direct harm caused by the culprit is here a minor matter; quite apart from this, the lawbreaker is above all a "breaker," a breaker of his contract and his word *with the whole* in respect to all the benefits and comforts of communal life of which he has hitherto had a share. The lawbreaker is a debtor who has not merely failed to make good the advantages and advance payments bestowed upon him but has actually attacked his creditor: therefore he is not only deprived henceforth of all these advantages and benefits, as is fair—he is also reminded *what these benefits are really worth.* The wrath of the disappointed creditor, the community, throws him back again into the savage and outlaw state against which he has hitherto been protected: it thrusts him away—and now every kind of hostility may be vented upon him. "Punishment" at this level of civilization is simply a copy, a *mimus,* of the normal attitude toward a hated, disarmed, prostrated enemy, who has lost not only every right and protection, but all hope of quarter as well; it is thus

---

[1] A prophetic parenthesis.
[2] Misery. Originally, exile.

the rights of war and the victory celebration of the *vae victis!*[3] in all their mercilessness and cruelty—which explains why it is that war itself (including the warlike sacrificial cult) has provided all the *forms* that punishment has assumed throughout history.

10

As its power increases, a community ceases to take the individual's transgressions so seriously, because they can no longer be considered as dangerous and destructive to the whole as they were formerly: the malefactor is no longer "set beyond the pale of peace" and thrust out; universal anger may not be vented upon him as unrestrainedly as before—on the contrary, the whole from now on carefully defends the malefactor against this anger, especially that of those he has directly harmed, and takes him under its protection. A compromise with the anger of those directly injured by the criminal; an effort to localize the affair and to prevent it from causing any further, let alone a general, disturbance; attempts to discover equivalents and to settle the whole matter (*compositio*); above all, the increasingly definite will to treat every crime as in some sense *dischargeable,* and thus at least to a certain extent to *isolate* the criminal and his deed from one another—these traits become more and more clearly visible as the penal law evolves. As the power and self-confidence of a community increase, the penal law always becomes more moderate; every weakening or imperiling of the former brings with it a restoration of the harsher forms of the latter. The "creditor" always becomes more humane to the extent that he has grown richer; finally, how much injury he can endure without suffering from it becomes the actual *measure* of his wealth. It is not unthinkable that a society might attain such a *consciousness of power* that it could allow itself the noblest luxury possible to it—letting those who harm it go *unpunished.* "What are my parasites to me?" it might say. "May they live and prosper: I am strong enough for that!"

The justice which began with, "everything is dischargeable,

---

[3] Woe to the losers!

everything must be discharged," ends by winking and letting those incapable of discharging their debt go free: it ends, as does every good thing on earth, by *overcoming itself*.[1] This self-overcoming of justice: one knows the beautiful name it has given itself—*mercy;* it goes without saying that mercy remains the privilege of the most powerful man, or better, his—beyond the law.[2]

11

Here a word in repudiation of attempts that have lately been made to seek the origin of justice in quite a different sphere— namely in that of *ressentiment*. To the psychologists first of all, presuming they would like to study *ressentiment* close up for once, I would say: this plant blooms best today among anarchists and anti-Semites—where it has always bloomed, in hidden places, like the violet, though with a different odor. And as like must always produce like, it causes us no surprise to see a repetition in such circles of attempts often made before—see above, section 14—to sanctify

---

[1] *Sich selbst aufhebend.* And in the next sentence *Selbstaufhebung* has been translated as self-overcoming. Similarly, *aufzuheben* in the middle of section 13, below, and *aufgehoben* in section 8 of the third essay have been rendered "overcome." See also III, section 27, with note. *Aufheben* is a very troublesome word, though common in ordinary German. Literally, it means "pick up"; but it has two derivative meanings that are no less common: "cancel" and "preserve" or "keep." Something picked up is no longer there, but the point of picking it up may be to keep it. Hegel made much of this term; his use of it is explained and discussed in Walter Kaufmann, *Hegel* (Garden City, N.Y., Doubleday, 1965; Garden City, N.Y., Doubleday Anchor Books, 1966), section 34—and a comparison of Hegel and Nietzsche on this point may be found in Kaufmann's *Nietzsche,* Chapter 8, section II.

[2] The theme sounded here is one of the central motifs of Nietzsche's philosophy. Cf. *Dawn,* section 202: ". . . Let us eliminate the concept of *sin* from the world—and let us soon dispatch the concept of *punishment* after it! May these exiled monsters live somewhere else henceforth and not among men— if they insist on living and will not perish of disgust with themselves! . . . Shouldn't we be mature enough yet for the opposite view? Shouldn't we be able to say yet: every 'guilty' person is sick?— No, the hour for that has not yet come. As yet the physicians are lacking above all . . . As yet no thinker has had the courage of measuring the health of a society and of individuals according to how many parasites they can stand . . ." (See *The Portable Nietzsche,* pp. 85–88.) Cf. also *Zarathustra* II, "On the Tarantulas": *"That man be delivered from revenge,* that is for me the bridge to the highest hope . . ." (*ibid.,* p. 211). Many other pertinent passages are cited in Kaufmann, *Nietzsche,* Chapter 12, sections II and V.

revenge[1] under the name of *justice*[2]—as if justice were at bottom
merely a further development of the feeling of being aggrieved—
and to rehabilitate not only revenge but all *reactive* affects in general. To the latter as such I would be the last to raise any objection: in respect to the entire biological problem (in relation to
which the value of these affects has hitherto been underrated) it
even seems to me to constitute a *service*. All I draw attention to is
the circumstance that it is the spirit of *ressentiment* itself out of
which this new nuance of scientific fairness (for the benefit of hatred, envy, jealousy, mistrust, rancor, and revenge) proceeds. For
this "scientific fairness" immediately ceases and gives way to accents of deadly enmity and prejudice once it is a question of dealing
with another group of affects, affects that, it seems to me, are of
even greater biological value than those reactive affects and consequently deserve even more to be *scientifically* evaluated and esteemed: namely, the truly *active* affects, such as lust for power,
avarice, and the like. (E. Dühring:[3] *The Value of Life; A Course
in Philosophy;* and, fundamentally, *passim.*)

So much against this tendency in general: as for Dühring's
specific proposition that the home of justice is to be sought in the
sphere of the reactive feelings, one is obliged for truth's sake to
counter it with a blunt antithesis: the *last* sphere to be conquered
by the spirit of justice is the sphere of the reactive feelings! When it
really happens that the just man remains just even toward those
who have harmed him (and not merely cold, temperate, remote,
indifferent: being just is always a *positive* attitude), when the exalted, clear objectivity, as penetrating as it is mild, of the eye of
justice and *judging* is not dimmed even under the assault of personal injury, derision, and calumny, this is a piece of perfection
and supreme mastery on earth—something it would be prudent not
to expect or to *believe* in too readily. On the average, a small dose

---

[1] *Rache.*

[2] *Gerechtigkeit.*

[3] Eugen Dühring (1833–1901), a prolific German philosopher and political
economist, was among other things an impassioned patriot and anti-Semite
and hated the cosmopolitan Goethe and the Greeks. He is remembered
chiefly as the butt of polemical works by Karl Marx and Friedrich Engels
and of scattered hostile remarks in Nietzsche's writings.

of aggression, malice, or insinuation certainly suffices to drive the blood into the eyes—and fairness out of the eyes—of even the most upright people. The active, aggressive, arrogant man is still a hundred steps closer to justice than the reactive man; for he has absolutely no need to take a false and prejudiced view of the object before him in the way the reactive man does and is bound to do. For that reason the aggressive man, as the stronger, nobler, more courageous, has in fact also had at all times a *freer* eye, a *better* conscience on his side: conversely, one can see who has the invention of the "bad conscience" on his conscience—the man of *ressentiment!*

Finally, one only has to look at history: in which sphere has the entire administration of law[4] hitherto been at home—also the need for law? In the sphere of reactive men, perhaps? By no means: rather in that of the active, strong, spontaneous, aggressive. From a historical point of view, law represents on earth—let it be said to the dismay of the above-named agitator (who himself once confessed: "the doctrine of revenge is the red thread of justice that runs through all my work and efforts")—the struggle *against* the reactive feelings, the war conducted against them on the part of the active and aggressive powers who employed some of their strength to impose measure and bounds upon the excesses of the reactive pathos and to compel it to come to terms. Wherever justice is practiced and maintained one sees a stronger power seeking a means of putting an end to the senseless raging of *ressentiment* among the weaker powers that stand under it (whether they be groups or individuals)—partly by taking the object of *ressentiment* out of the hands of revenge, partly by substituting for revenge the struggle against the enemies of peace and order, partly by devising and in some cases imposing settlements, partly by elevating certain equivalents for injuries into norms to which from then on *ressentiment* is once and for all directed. The most decisive act, however, that the supreme power performs and accomplishes against the predominance of grudges and rancor—it always takes this action as soon as it is in any way strong enough to do so—is the institution of *law,*[5] the imperative declaration of what in general counts as permitted,

---

4 *Recht.*
5 *Gesetz.*

as just,[6] in its eyes, and what counts as forbidden, as unjust:[7] once
it has instituted the law, it treats violence and capricious acts on the
part of individuals or entire groups as offenses against the law, as
rebellion against the supreme power itself, and thus leads the feelings of its subjects away from the direct injury caused by such
offenses; and in the long run it thus attains the reverse of that
which is desired by all revenge that is fastened exclusively to the
viewpoint of the person injured: from now on the eye is trained to
an ever more *impersonal* evaluation of the deed, and this applies
even to the eye of the injured person himself (although last of all,
as remarked above).

"Just" and "unjust" exist, accordingly, only after the institution of the law (and *not,* as Dühring would have it, after the perpe-
tration of the injury). To speak of just or unjust *in itself* is quite
senseless; *in itself,* of course, no injury, assault, exploitation, destruction can be "unjust," since life operates *essentially,* that is in
its basic functions, through injury, assault, exploitation, destruction
and simply cannot be thought of at all without this character. One
must indeed grant something even more unpalatable: that, from the
highest biological standpoint, legal conditions can never be other
than *exceptional conditions,* since they constitute a partial restric-
tion of the will of life, which is bent upon power, and are subordi-
nate to its total goal as a single means: namely, as a means of
creating *greater* units of power. A legal order thought of as sovereign and universal, not as a means in the struggle between power-
complexes but as a means of *preventing* all struggle in general—
perhaps after the communistic cliché of Dühring, that every will
must consider every other will its equal—would be a principle *hostile to life,* an agent of the dissolution and destruction of man, an
attempt to assassinate the future of man, a sign of weariness, a
secret path to nothingness.—

12

Yet a word on the origin and the purpose of punishment—two
problems that are separate, or ought to be separate: unfortunately,

---

[6] *Recht.*
[7] *Unrecht.*

they are usually confounded. How have previous genealogists of morals set about solving these problems? Naïvely, as has always been their way: they seek out some "purpose" in punishment, for example, revenge or deterrence, then guilelessly place this purpose at the beginning as *causa fiendi*[1] of punishment, and—have done. The "purpose of law," however, is absolutely the last thing to employ in the history of the origin of law: on the contrary, there is for historiography of any kind no more important proposition than the one it took such effort to establish but which really *ought to be* established now: the cause of the origin of a thing and its eventual utility, its actual employment and place in a system of purposes, lie worlds apart; whatever exists, having somehow come into being, is again and again reinterpreted to new ends, taken over, transformed, and redirected by some power superior to it; all events in the organic world are a subduing, a *becoming master,* and all subduing and becoming master involves a fresh interpretation, an adaptation through which any previous "meaning" and "purpose" are necessarily obscured or even obliterated. However well one has understood the *utility* of any physiological organ (or of a legal institution, a social custom, a political usage, a form in art or in a religious cult), this means nothing regarding its origin: however uncomfortable and disagreeable this may sound to older ears—for one had always believed that to understand the demonstrable purpose, the utility of a thing, a form, or an institution, was also to understand the reason why it originated—the eye being made for seeing, the hand being made for grasping.

Thus one also imagined that punishment was devised for punishing. But purposes and utilities are only *signs* that a will to power has become master of something less powerful and imposed upon it the character of a function; and the entire history of a "thing," an organ, a custom can in this way be a continuous sign-chain of ever new interpretations and adaptations whose causes do not even have to be related to one another but, on the contrary, in some cases succeed and alternate with one another in a purely chance fashion. The "evolution" of a thing, a custom, an organ is thus by no means its *progressus* toward a goal, even less a logical *progressus* by the

---

[1] The cause of the origin.

shortest route and with the smallest expenditure of force—but a succession of more or less profound, more or less mutually independent processes of subduing, plus the resistances they encounter, the attempts at transformation for the purpose of defense and reaction, and the results of successful counteractions. The form is fluid, but the "meaning" is even more so.

The case is the same even within each individual organism: with every real growth in the whole, the "meaning" of the individual organs also changes; in certain circumstances their partial destruction, a reduction in their numbers (for example, through the disappearance of intermediary members) can be a sign of increasing strength and perfection. It is not too much to say that even a partial *diminution of utility,* an atrophying and degeneration, a loss of meaning and purposiveness—in short, death—is among the conditions of an actual *progressus,* which always appears in the shape of a will and way to *greater power* and is always carried through at the expense of numerous smaller powers. The magnitude of an "advance" can even be measured by the mass of things that had to be sacrificed to it; mankind in the mass sacrificed to the prosperity of a single *stronger* species of man—that *would* be an advance.

I emphasize this major point of historical method all the more because it is in fundamental opposition to the now prevalent instinct and taste which would rather be reconciled even to the absolute fortuitousness, even the mechanistic senselessness of all events than to the theory that in all events a *will to power* is operating. The democratic idiosyncrasy which opposes everything that dominates and wants to dominate, the modern *misarchism*[2] (to coin an ugly word for an ugly thing) has permeated the realm of the spirit and disguised itself in the most spiritual forms to such a degree that today it has forced its way, has acquired the *right* to force its way into the strictest, apparently most objective sciences; indeed, it seems to me to have already taken charge of all physiology and theory of life—to the detriment of life, as goes without saying, since it has robbed it of a fundamental concept, that of *activity.* Under the influence of the above-mentioned idiosyncrasy, one

---

[2] Hatred of rule or government.

places instead "adaptation" in the foreground, that is to say, an activity of the second rank, a mere reactivity; indeed, life itself has been defined as a more and more efficient inner adaptation to external conditions (Herbert Spencer[3]). Thus the essence of life, its *will to power,* is ignored; one overlooks the essential priority of the spontaneous, aggressive, expansive, form-giving forces that give new interpretations and directions, although "adaptation" follows only after this; the dominant role of the highest functionaries within the organism itself in which the will to life appears active and form-giving is denied. One should recall what Huxley[4] reproached Spencer with—his "administrative nihilism": but it is a question of rather *more* than mere "administration."

13

To return to our subject, namely *punishment,* one must distinguish two aspects: on the one hand, that in it which is relatively *enduring,* the custom, the act, the "drama," a certain strict sequence of procedures; on the other, that in it which is *fluid,* the meaning, the purpose, the expectation associated with the performance of such procedures. In accordance with the previously developed major point of historical method, it is assumed without further ado that the procedure itself will be something older, earlier than its employment in punishment, that the latter is *projected* and interpreted *into* the procedure (which has long existed but been employed in another sense), in short, that the case is *not* as has hitherto been assumed by our naïve genealogists of law and morals, who have one and all thought of the procedure as *invented* for the purpose of punishing, just as one formerly thought of the hand as invented for the purpose of grasping.

As for the other element in punishment, the fluid element, its

---

[3] On Spencer, see the note in section 3 of the first essay, above.

[4] Thomas Henry Huxley (1825–95), the English biologist and writer, fought tirelessly for the acceptance of Darwinism. In 1869 he coined the word *agnosticism,* which Spencer took over from him. Aldous Huxley (1894–1963), the author of *Brave New World* (1932), and Julian Huxley (born 1897), the biologist, are T. H. Huxley's grandsons.

"meaning," in a very late condition of culture (for example, in modern Europe) the concept "punishment" possesses in fact not *one* meaning but a whole synthesis of "meanings": the previous history of punishment in general, the history of its employment for the most various purposes, finally crystallizes into a kind of unity that is hard to disentangle, hard to analyze and, as must be emphasized especially, totally *indefinable*. (Today it is impossible to say for certain *why* people are really punished: all concepts in which an entire process is semiotically concentrated elude definition; only that which has no history is definable.[1]) At an earlier stage, on the contrary, this synthesis of "meanings" can still be disentangled, as well as changed; one can still perceive how in each individual case the elements of the synthesis undergo a shift in value and rearrange themselves accordingly, so that now this, now that element comes to the fore and dominates at the expense of the others; and under certain circumstances one element (the purpose of deterrence perhaps) appears to overcome all the remaining elements.

To give at least an idea of how uncertain, how supplemental, how accidental "the meaning" of punishment is, and how one and the same procedure can be employed, interpreted, adapted to ends that differ fundamentally, I set down here the pattern that has emerged from consideration of relatively few chance instances I have noted. Punishment as a means of rendering harmless, of preventing further harm. Punishment as recompense to the injured party for the harm done, rendered in any form (even in that of a compensating affect). Punishment as the isolation of a disturbance of equilibrium, so as to guard against any further spread of the disturbance. Punishment as a means of inspiring fear of those who determine and execute the punishment. Punishment as a kind of repayment for the advantages the criminal has enjoyed hitherto (for example, when he is employed as a slave in the mines). Punishment as the expulsion of a degenerate element (in some cases, of an entire branch, as in Chinese law: thus as a means of preserving the purity of a race or maintaining a social type). Punishment as a festival, namely as the rape and mockery of a finally defeated enemy. Punishment as the making of a memory, whether for him

---

[1] A superb epigram that expresses a profound insight. Cf. *The Wanderer and His Shadow*, section 33, included in the present volume, p. 179.

who suffers the punishment—so-called "improvement"—or for those who witness its execution. Punishment as payment of a fee stipulated by the power that protects the wrongdoer from the excesses of revenge. Punishment as a compromise with revenge in its natural state when the latter is still maintained and claimed as a privilege by powerful clans. Punishment as a declaration of war and a war measure against an enemy of peace, of the law, of order, of the authorities, whom, as a danger to the community, as one who has broken the contract that defines the conditions under which it exists, as a rebel, a traitor, and breaker of the peace, one opposes with the means of war.—

14

This list is certainly not complete; it is clear that punishment is overdetermined [1] by utilities of all kinds. All the more reason, then, for deducting from it a *supposed* utility that, to be sure, counts in the popular consciousness as the most essential one—belief in punishment, which for several reasons is tottering today, always finds its strongest support in this. Punishment is supposed to possess the value of awakening the *feeling of guilt* in the guilty person; one seeks in it the actual *instrumentum* of that psychical reaction called "bad conscience," "sting of conscience." Thus one misunderstands psychology and the reality of things even as they apply today: how much more as they applied during the greater part of man's history, his prehistory!

It is precisely among criminals and convicts that the sting of conscience is extremely rare; prisons and penitentiaries are *not* the kind of hotbed in which this species of gnawing worm is likely to flourish: all conscientious observers are agreed on that, in many cases unwillingly enough and contrary to their own inclinations. Generally speaking, punishment makes men hard and cold; it concentrates; it sharpens the feeling of alienation; it strengthens the power of resistance. If it happens that punishment destroys the vital energy and brings about a miserable prostration and self-abasement, such a result is certainly even less pleasant than the

---

[1] *Überladen.*

usual effects of punishment—characterized by dry and gloomy seriousness.

If we consider those millennia *before* the history of man, we may unhesitatingly assert that it was precisely through punishment that the development of the feeling of guilt was most powerfully *hindered*—at least in the victims upon whom the punitive force was vented. For we must not underrate the extent to which the sight of the judicial and executive procedures prevents the criminal from considering his deed, the type of his action *as such,* reprehensible: for he sees exactly the same kind of actions practiced in the service of justice and approved of and practiced with a good conscience: spying, deception, bribery, setting traps, the whole cunning and underhand art of police and prosecution, plus robbery, violence, defamation, imprisonment, torture, murder, practiced as a matter of principle and without even emotion to excuse them, which are pronounced characteristics of the various forms of punishment—all of them therefore actions which his judges in no way condemn and repudiate *as such,* but only when they are applied and directed to certain particular ends.

The "bad conscience," this most uncanny and most interesting plant of all our earthly vegetation, did *not* grow on this soil; indeed, during the greater part of the past the judges and punishers themselves were *not at all* conscious of dealing with a "guilty person." But with an instigator of harm, with an irresponsible piece of fate. And the person upon whom punishment subsequently descended, again like a piece of fate, suffered no "inward pain" other than that induced by the sudden appearance of something unforeseen, a dreadful natural event, a plunging, crushing rock that one cannot fight.

15

This fact once came insidiously into the mind of Spinoza (to the vexation of his interpreters, Kuno Fischer,[1] for example, who

---

[1] Kuno Fischer (1824–1907), professor at Heidelberg, made a great reputation with a ten-volume history of modern philosophy that consists of imposing monographs on selected modern philosophers. One of the volumes is devoted to Spinoza.

make a real *effort* to misunderstand him on this point), when one afternoon, teased by who knows what recollection, he mused on the question of what really remained to him of the famous *morsus conscientiae*[2]—he who had banished good and evil to the realm of human imagination and had wrathfully defended the honor of his "free" God against those blasphemers who asserted that God effected all things *sub ratione boni*[3] ("but that would mean making God subject to fate and would surely be the greatest of all absurdities"). The world, for Spinoza, had returned to that state of innocence in which it had lain before the invention of the bad conscience: what then had become of the *morsus conscientiae?*

"The opposite of *gaudium*," [4] he finally said to himself—"a sadness accompanied by the recollection of a past event that flouted all of our expectations." *Eth.III, propos. XVIII, schol. I.*

II. Mischief-makers overtaken by punishments have for thousands of years felt in respect of their "transgressions" *just as Spinoza did:* "here something has unexpectedly gone wrong," *not:* "I ought not to have done that." They submitted to punishment as one submits to an illness or to a misfortune or to death, with that stout-hearted fatalism without rebellion through which the Russians, for example, still have an advantage over us Westerners in dealing with life.

If there existed any criticism of the deed in those days, it was prudence that criticized the deed: the actual *effect* of punishment must beyond question be sought above all in a heightening of prudence, in an extending of the memory, in a will henceforth to go to work more cautiously, mistrustfully, secretly, in the insight that one is definitely too weak for many things, in a kind of improvement in self-criticism. That which can in general be attained through punishment, in men and in animals, is an increase of fear, a heightening of prudence, mastery of the desires: thus punishment *tames* men, but it does not make them "better"—one might with more justice assert the opposite. ("Injury makes one prudent," says the proverb: insofar as it makes one prudent it also makes one bad. Fortunately, it frequently makes people stupid.)

---

[2] Sting of conscience.
[3] For a good reason.
[4] Joy.

16

At this point I can no longer avoid giving a first, provisional statement of my own hypothesis concerning the origin of the "bad conscience": it may sound rather strange and needs to be pondered, lived with, and slept on for a long time. I regard the bad conscience as the serious illness that man was bound to contract under the stress of the most fundamental change he ever experienced—that change which occurred when he found himself finally enclosed within the walls of society and of peace. The situation that faced sea animals when they were compelled to become land animals or perish was the same as that which faced these semi-animals, well adapted to the wilderness, to war, to prowling, to adventure: suddenly all their instincts were disvalued and "suspended." From now on they had to walk on their feet and "bear themselves" whereas hitherto they had been borne by the water: a dreadful heaviness lay upon them. They felt unable to cope with the simplest undertakings; in this new world they no longer possessed their former guides, their regulating, unconscious and infallible drives: they were reduced to thinking, inferring, reckoning, co-ordinating cause and effect, these unfortunate creatures; they were reduced to their "consciousness," their weakest and most fallible organ! I believe there has never been such a feeling of misery on earth, such a leaden discomfort—and at the same time the old instincts had not suddenly ceased to make their usual demands! Only it was hardly or rarely possible to humor them: as a rule they had to seek new and, as it were, subterranean gratifications.

All instincts that do not discharge themselves outwardly *turn inward*—this is what I call the *internalization*[1] of man: thus it was that man first developed what was later called his "soul." The entire inner world, originally as thin as if it were stretched between two membranes, expanded and extended itself, acquired depth, breadth, and height, in the same measure as outward discharge was *inhibited*. Those fearful bulwarks with which the political organiza-

---

[1] *Verinnerlichung.* Cf. Freud.

tion protected itself against the old instincts of freedom—punishments belong among these bulwarks—brought about that all those instincts of wild, free, prowling man turned backward *against man himself.* Hostility, cruelty, joy in persecuting, in attacking, in change, in destruction—all this turned against the possessors of such instincts: *that* is the origin of the "bad conscience."

The man who, from lack of external enemies and resistances and forcibly confined to the oppressive narrowness and punctiliousness of custom, impatiently lacerated, persecuted, gnawed at, assaulted, and maltreated himself; this animal that rubbed itself raw against the bars of its cage as one tried to "tame" it; this deprived creature, racked with homesickness for the wild, who had to turn himself into an adventure, a torture chamber, an uncertain and dangerous wilderness—this fool, this yearning and desperate prisoner became the inventor of the "bad conscience." But thus began the gravest and uncanniest illness, from which humanity has not yet recovered, man's suffering *of man, of himself*—the result of a forcible sundering from his animal past, as it were a leap and plunge into new surroundings and conditions of existence, a declaration of war against the old instincts upon which his strength, joy, and terribleness had rested hitherto.

Let us add at once that, on the other hand, the existence on earth of an animal soul turned against itself, taking sides against itself, was something so new, profound, unheard of, enigmatic, contradictory, *and pregnant with a future* that the aspect of the earth was essentially altered. Indeed, divine spectators were needed to do justice to the spectacle that thus began and the end of which is not yet in sight—a spectacle too subtle, too marvelous, too paradoxical to be played senselessly unobserved on some ludicrous planet! From now on, man is *included* among the most unexpected and exciting lucky throws in the dice game of Heraclitus' "great child," be he called Zeus or chance; he gives rise to an interest, a tension, a hope, almost a certainty, as if with him something were announcing and preparing itself, as if man were not a goal but only a way, an episode, a bridge, a great promise.—

17

Among the presuppositions of this hypothesis concerning the origin of the bad conscience is, first, that the change referred to was not a gradual or voluntary one and did not represent an organic adaptation to new conditions but a break, a leap, a compulsion, an ineluctable disaster which precluded all struggle and even all *ressentiment*. Secondly, however, that the welding of a hitherto unchecked and shapeless populace into a firm form was not only instituted by an act of violence but also carried to its conclusion by nothing but acts of violence—that the oldest "state" thus appeared as a fearful tyranny, as an oppressive and remorseless machine, and went on working until this raw material of people and semi-animals was at last not only thoroughly kneaded and pliant but also *formed*.

I employed the word "state": it is obvious what is meant— some pack of blond beasts of prey,[1] a conqueror and master race which, organized for war and with the ability to organize, unhesitatingly lays its terrible claws upon a populace perhaps tremendously superior in numbers but still formless and nomad. That is after all how the "state" began on earth: I think that sentimentalism which would have it begin with a "contract" has been disposed of. He who can command, he who is by nature "master," he who is violent in act and bearing—what has he to do with contracts! One does not reckon with such natures; they come like fate, without reason, consideration, or pretext; they appear as lightning appears, too terrible, too sudden, too convincing, too "different" even to be hated. Their work is an instinctive creation and imposition of forms; they are the most involuntary, unconscious artists there are —wherever they appear something new soon arises, a ruling structure that *lives*, in which parts and functions are delimited and co-

---

[1] *Irgendein Rudel blonder Raubtiere, eine Eroberer- und Herren-Rasse:* Francis Golffing, in his translation, spirits away both the blond beasts of prey and the master race by rendering these words "a pack of savages, a race of conquerors." Cf. section 11 of the first essay, above, with its three references to the *blonde Bestie,* and note 3 of section 11. See also Kaufmann's *Nietzsche,* Chapter 10, "The Master-Race."

ordinated, in which nothing whatever finds a place that has not first
been assigned a "meaning" in relation to the whole. They do not
know what guilt, responsibility, or consideration are, these born
organizers; they exemplify that terrible artists' egoism that has the
look of bronze and knows itself· justified to all eternity in its
"work," like a mother in her child. It is not in *them* that the "bad
conscience" developed, that goes without saying—but it would not
have developed *without them*, this ugly growth, it would be lacking
if a tremendous quantity of freedom had not been expelled from
the world, or at least from the visible world, and made as it were
latent under their hammer blows and artists' violence. This *instinct
for freedom* forcibly made latent—we have seen it already—this
instinct for freedom pushed back and repressed, incarcerated
within and finally able to discharge and vent itself only on itself:
that, and that alone, is what the *bad conscience* is in its beginnings.

18

One should guard against thinking lightly of this phenomenon
merely on account of its initial painfulness and ugliness. For fundamentally it is the same active force that is at work on a grander
scale in those artists of violence and organizers who build states,
and that here, internally, on a smaller and pettier scale, directed
backward, in the "labyrinth of the breast," to use Goethe's expression, creates for itself a bad conscience and builds negative ideals
—namely, the *instinct for freedom* (in my language: the will to
power); only here the material upon which the form-giving and
ravishing nature of this force vents itself is man himself, his whole
ancient animal self—and *not,* as in that greater and more obvious
phenomenon, some *other* man, *other* men. This secret self-ravish-
ment, this artists' cruelty, this delight in imposing a form upon oneself as a hard, recalcitrant, suffering material and in burning a will,
a critique, a contradiction, a contempt, a No into it, this uncanny,
dreadfully joyous labor of a soul voluntarily at odds with itself that
makes itself suffer out of joy in making suffer—eventually this entire *active* "bad conscience"—you will have guessed it—as the
womb of all ideal and imaginative phenomena, also brought to light

an abundance of strange new beauty and affirmation, and perhaps beauty itself.— After all, what would be "beautiful" if the contradiction had not first become conscious of itself, if the ugly had not first said to itself: "I am ugly"?

This hint will at least make less enigmatic the enigma of how contradictory concepts such as *selflessness, self-denial, self-sacrifice* can suggest an ideal, a kind of beauty; and one thing we know henceforth—I have no doubt of it—and that is the nature of the *delight* that the selfless man, the self-denier, the self-sacrificer feels from the first: this delight is tied to cruelty.

So much for the present about the origin of the moral value of the "unegoistic," about the soil from which this value grew: only the bad conscience, only the will to self-maltreatment provided the conditions for the *value* of the unegoistic.—

19

The bad conscience is an illness, there is no doubt about that, but an illness as pregnancy is an illness.[1] Let us seek out the conditions under which this illness has reached its most terrible and most sublime height; we shall see what it really was that thus entered the world. But for that one needs endurance—and first of all we must go back again to an earlier point of view.

The civil-law relationship between the debtor and his creditor, discussed above, has been interpreted in an, historically speaking, exceedingly remarkable and dubious manner into a relationship in which to us modern men it seems perhaps least to belong: namely into the relationship between the present generation and its ancestors.

Within the original tribal community—we are speaking of primeval times—the living generation always recognized a juridical duty toward earlier generations, and especially toward the earliest, which founded the tribe (and by no means a merely sentimental obligation: there are actually reasons for denying the existence of the latter for the greater part of human history). The conviction

---

[1] Cf. pp. 10 ff. and 520 f.

reigns that it is only through the sacrifices and accomplishments of the ancestors that the tribe *exists*—and that one has to *pay them back* with sacrifices and accomplishments: one thus recognizes a *debt* that constantly grows greater, since these forebears never cease, in their continued existence as powerful spirits, to accord the tribe new advantages and new strength. In vain, perhaps? But there is no "in vain" for these rude and "poor-souled" ages. What can one give them in return? Sacrifices (initially as food in the coarsest sense), feasts, music, honors; above all, obedience—for all customs, as works of the ancestors, are also their statutes and commands: can one ever give them enough? This suspicion remains and increases; from time to time it leads to a wholesale sacrifice, something tremendous in the way of repayment to the "creditor" (the notorious sacrifice of the first-born, for example; in any case blood, human blood).

The *fear* of the ancestor and his power, the consciousness of indebtedness to him, increases, according to this kind of logic, in exactly the same measure as the power of the tribe itself increases, as the tribe itself grows ever more victorious, independent, honored, and feared. By no means the other way round! Every step toward the decline of a tribe, every misfortune, every sign of degeneration, of coming disintegration always *diminishes* fear of the spirit of its founder and produces a meaner impression of his cunning, foresight, and present power. If one imagines this rude kind of logic carried to its end, then the ancestors of the *most powerful* tribes are bound eventually to grow to monstrous dimensions through the imagination of growing fear and to recede into the darkness of the divinely uncanny and unimaginable: in the end the ancestor must necessarily be transfigured into a *god*. Perhaps this is even the origin of gods, an origin therefore out of *fear!* . . . And whoever should feel obliged to add, "but out of piety also!" would hardly be right for the greater part of the existence of man, his prehistory. To be sure, he would be quite right for the *intermediate* age, in which the noble tribes developed—who indeed paid back their originators, their ancestors (heroes, gods) with interest all the qualities that had become palpable in themselves, the *noble* qualities. We shall take another look later at the ennoblement of the

gods (which should not be confused with their becoming "holy");
let us first of all follow to its end the course of this whole development of the consciousness of guilt.

20

History shows that the consciousness of being in debt[1] to the
deity did not by any means come to an end together with the organization of communities on the basis of blood relationship. Even as
mankind inherited the concepts "good and bad" from the tribal
nobility (along with its basic psychological propensity to set up
orders of rank), it also inherited, along with the tribal and family
divinities, the burden of still unpaid debts and of the desire to be
relieved of them. (The transition is provided by those numerous
slave and dependent populations who, whether through compulsion
or through servility and mimicry, adapted themselves to their masters' cult of the gods: this inheritance then overflows from them in
all directions.) The guilty feeling of indebtedness[2] to the divinity
continued to grow for several millennia—always in the same measure as the concept of God and the feeling for divinity increased on
earth and was carried to the heights. (The entire history of ethnic
struggle, victory, reconciliation, fusion, everything that precedes
the definitive ordering of rank of the different national elements in
every great racial synthesis, is reflected in the confused genealogies
of their gods, in the sagas of the gods' struggles, victories, and reconciliations; the advance toward universal empires is always also
an advance toward universal divinities; despotism with its triumph
over the independent nobility always prepares the way for some
kind of monotheism.)

The advent of the Christian God, as the maximum god attained so far, was therefore accompanied by the maximum feeling
of guilty indebtedness[3] on earth. Presuming we have gradually entered upon the *reverse* course, there is no small probability that
with the irresistible decline of faith in the Christian God there is

---

[1] *Schulden zu haben.*

[2] *Das Schuldgefühl.*

[3] *Des Schuldgefühls.*

now also a considerable decline in mankind's feeling of guilt;[4] indeed, the prospect cannot be dismissed that the complete and definitive victory of atheism might free mankind of this whole feeling of guilty indebtedness[5] toward its origin, its *causa prima*.[6] Atheism and a kind of *second innocence*[7] belong together.—

<h2 style="text-align:center">21</h2>

So much for a first brief preliminary on the connection of the concepts "guilt" and "duty" with religious presuppositions: I have up to now deliberately ignored the moralization of these concepts (their pushing back into the conscience; more precisely, the involvement of the *bad* conscience with the concept of god); and at the end of the last section I even spoke as if this moralization had not taken place at all, and as if these concepts were now necessarily doomed since their presupposition, the faith in our "creditor," [1] in God, had disappeared. The reality is, to a fearful degree, otherwise.

The moralization of the concepts guilt and duty, their being pushed back into the *bad* conscience, actually involves an attempt to *reverse* the direction of the development described above, or at least to bring it to a halt: the *aim* now is to preclude pessimistically, once and for all, the prospect of a final discharge; the *aim* now is to make the glance recoil disconsolately from an iron impossibility; the *aim* now is to turn back the concepts "guilt" and "duty"—back against whom? There can be no doubt: against the "debtor" first of all, in whom from now on the bad conscience is firmly rooted, eating into him and spreading within him like a polyp, until at last the irredeemable debt gives rise to the conception of irredeemable penance, the idea that it cannot be discharged (*"eternal* punishment"). Finally, however, they are turned back against the "creditor," too: whether we think of the *causa prima* of

---

4 *Schuldbewusstseins.*

5 *Gefühl, Schulden . . . zu haben.*

6 First cause.

7 *Unschuld.*

1 *Der Glaube an unsern "Gläubiger":* the creed in our "creditor"—or: that one credits our "creditor."

man, the beginning of the human race, its primal ancestor who is from now on burdened with a curse ("Adam," "original sin," "unfreedom of the will"), or of nature from whose womb mankind arose and into whom the principle of evil is projected from now on ("the diabolizing of nature"), or of existence in general, which is now considered *worthless as such* (nihilistic withdrawal from it, a desire for nothingness or a desire for its antithesis, for a different mode of being, Buddhism and the like)—suddenly we stand before the paradoxical and horrifying expedient that afforded temporary relief for tormented humanity, that stroke of genius on the part of Christianity: God himself sacrifices himself for the guilt of mankind, God himself makes payment to himself, God as the only being who can redeem man from what has become unredeemable for man himself—the creditor sacrifices himself for his debtor, out of *love* (can one credit that?), out of love for his debtor!—

22

You will have guessed *what* has really happened here, *beneath* all this: that will to self-tormenting, that repressed cruelty of the animal-man made inward and scared back into himself, the creature imprisoned in the "state" so as to be tamed, who invented the bad conscience in order to hurt himself after the *more natural* vent for this desire to hurt had been blocked—this man of the bad conscience has seized upon the presupposition of religion so as to drive his self-torture to its most gruesome pitch of severity and rigor. Guilt before *God:* this thought becomes an instrument of torture to him. He apprehends in "God" the ultimate antithesis of his own ineluctable animal instincts; he reinterprets these animal instincts themselves as a form of guilt before God (as hostility, rebellion, insurrection against the "Lord," the "father," the primal ancestor and origin of the world); he stretches himself upon the contradiction "God" and "Devil"; he ejects from himself all his denial of himself, of his nature, naturalness, and actuality, in the form of an affirmation, as something existent, corporeal, real, as God, as the holiness of God, as God the Judge, as God the Hangman, as the beyond, as eternity, as torment without end, as hell, as the immeasurability of punishment and guilt.

In this psychical cruelty there resides a madness of the will which is absolutely unexampled: the *will* of man to find himself guilty and reprehensible to a degree that can never be atoned for; his *will* to think himself punished without any possibility of the punishment becoming equal to the guilt; his *will* to infect and poison the fundamental ground of things with the problem of punishment and guilt so as to cut off once and for all his own exit from this labyrinth of "fixed ideas"; his *will* to erect an ideal—that of the "holy God"—and in the face of it to feel the palpable certainty of his own absolute unworthiness. Oh this insane, pathetic beast—man! What ideas he has, what unnaturalness, what paroxysms of nonsense, what *bestiality of thought* erupts as soon as he is prevented just a little from being a *beast in deed!*

All this is interesting, to excess, but also of a gloomy, black, unnerving sadness, so that one must forcibly forbid oneself to gaze too long into these abysses. Here is *sickness,* beyond any doubt, the most terrible sickness that has ever raged in man; and whoever can still bear to hear (but today one no longer has ears for this!) how in this night of torment and absurdity there has resounded the cry of *love,* the cry of the most nostalgic rapture, of redemption through *love,* will turn away, seized by invincible horror.— There is so much in man that is hideous!— Too long, the earth has been a madhouse!—

23

This should dispose once and for all of the question of how the "holy God" originated.

That the conception of gods *in itself* need not lead to the degradation of the imagination that we had to consider briefly, that there are *nobler* uses for the invention of gods than for the self-crucifixion and self-violation of man in which Europe over the past millennia achieved its distinctive mastery—that is fortunately revealed even by a mere glance at the *Greek gods,* those reflections of noble and autocratic men, in whom *the animal* in man felt deified and did *not* lacerate itself, did *not* rage against itself! For the longest time these Greeks used their gods precisely so as to ward off the "bad conscience," so as to be able to rejoice in their freedom of

soul—the very opposite of the use to which Christianity put its
God. They went *very far* in this direction, these splendid and lion-
hearted children; and no less an authority than the Homeric Zeus
himself occasionally gives them to understand that they are making
things too easy for themselves. "Strange!" he says once—the case
is that of Aegisthus, a *very* bad case—

> *Strange how these mortals so loudly complain of the gods!*
> We alone produce evil, *they say; yet themselves*
> *Make themselves wretched through folly, even counter to fate.*[1]

Yet one can see and hear how even this Olympian spectator
and judge is far from holding a grudge against them or thinking ill
of them on that account: "how *foolish* they are!" he thinks when
he observes the misdeeds of mortals—and "foolishness," "folly," a
little "disturbance in the head," this much even the Greeks of the
strongest, bravest age conceded of themselves as the reason for
much that was bad and calamitous—foolishness, *not* sin! do you
grasp that?

Even this disturbance in the head, however, presented a problem: "how is it possible? how could it actually have happened to
heads such as *we* have, we men of aristocratic descent, of the best
society, happy, well-constituted, noble, and virtuous?"—thus noble
Greeks asked themselves for centuries in the face of every incomprehensible atrocity or wantonness with which one of their kind
had polluted himself. "He must have been deluded by a *god*," they
concluded finally, shaking their heads . . . This expedient is *typical* of the Greeks . . . In this way the gods served in those days to
justify man to a certain extent even in his wickedness, they served
as the originators of evil—in those days they took upon themselves, not the punishment but, what is *nobler,* the guilt.[2]

---

[1] *Odyssey,* I, line 32ff.

[2] Cf. *Ecce Homo,* Chapter I, section 5, and Sartre's play *The Flies,* which
was decisively influenced by Nietzsche, as I have shown in "Nietzsche Between Homer and Sartre: Five Treatments of the Orestes Story" (*Revue Internationale de Philosophie,* LXVII, 1964, pp. 50–73).

24

I end up with three question marks; that seems plain. "What are you really doing, erecting an ideal or knocking one down?" I may perhaps be asked.

But have you ever asked yourselves sufficiently how much the erection of *every* ideal on earth has cost? How much reality has had to be misunderstood and slandered, how many lies have had to be sanctified, how many consciences disturbed, how much "God" sacrificed every time? If a temple is to be erected *a temple must be destroyed:* that is the law—let anyone who can show me a case in which it is not fulfilled!

We modern men are the heirs of the conscience-vivisection and self-torture[3] of millennia: this is what we have practiced longest, it is our distinctive art perhaps, and in any case our subtlety in which we have acquired a refined taste. Man has all too long had an "evil eye" for his natural inclinations, so that they have finally become inseparable from his "bad conscience." An attempt at the reverse would *in itself* be possible—but who is strong enough for it?—that is, to wed the bad conscience to all the *unnatural* inclinations, all those aspirations to the beyond, to that which runs counter to sense, instinct, nature, animal, in short all ideals hitherto, which are one and all hostile to life and ideals that slander the world. To whom should one turn today with *such* hopes and demands?

One would have precisely the *good* men against one; and, of course, the comfortable, the reconciled, the vain, the sentimental, the weary.

What gives greater offense, what separates one more fundamentally, than to reveal something of the severity and respect with which one treats oneself? And on the other hand—how accommodating, how friendly all the world is toward us as soon as we act as all the world does and "let ourselves go" like all the world!

---

[3] *Selbsttierquälerei: Tierquälerei* really means cruelty to animals or, literally, animal torture; hence Nietzsche's coinage suggests that this kind of self-torture involves mortification of the animal nature of man.

The attainment of this goal would require a *different* kind of spirit from that likely to appear in this present age: spirits strengthened by war and victory, for whom conquest, adventure, danger, and even pain have become needs; it would require habituation to the keen air of the heights, to winter journeys, to ice and mountains in every sense; it would require even a kind of sublime wickedness, an ultimate, supremely self-confident mischievousness in knowledge that goes with great health; it would require, in brief and alas, precisely this *great health!*

Is this even possible today?— But some day, in a stronger age than this decaying, self-doubting present, he must yet come to us, the *redeeming* man of great love and contempt, the creative spirit whose compelling strength will not let him rest in any aloofness or any beyond, whose isolation is misunderstood by the people as if it were flight *from* reality—while it is only his absorption, immersion, penetration *into* reality, so that, when he one day emerges again into the light, he may bring home the *redemption* of this reality: its redemption from the curse that the hitherto reigning ideal has laid upon it. This man of the future, who will redeem us not only from the hitherto reigning ideal but also from that which was bound to grow out of it, the great nausea, the will to nothingness, nihilism; this bell-stroke of noon and of the great decision that liberates the will again and restores its goal to the earth and his hope to man; this Antichrist and antinihilist; this victor over God and nothingness—*he must come one day.*—

25

But what am I saying? Enough! Enough! At this point it behooves me only to be silent; or I shall usurp that to which only one younger, "heavier with future," and stronger than I has a right— that to which only *Zarathustra* has a right, *Zarathustra the godless.*—

Third Essay
What Is the Meaning of Ascetic Ideals?

> Unconcerned, mocking, violent—thus wisdom wants *us:* she is a woman and always loves only a warrior.
>
> *Thus Spoke Zarathustra*[1]

1

What is the meaning of ascetic ideals?— In the case of artists they mean nothing or too many things; in the case of philosophers and scholars something like a sense and instinct for the most favorable preconditions of higher spirituality; in the case of women at best one *more* seductive charm, a touch of *morbidezza* in fair flesh, the angelic look of a plump pretty animal; in the case of the physiologically deformed and deranged (the *majority* of mortals) an attempt to see themselves as "too good" for this world, a saintly form of debauch, their chief weapon in the struggle against slow pain and boredom; in the case of priests the distinctive priestly faith, their best instrument of power, also the "supreme" license for power; in the case of saints, finally, a pretext for hibernation, their *novissima gloriae cupido,*[2] their repose in nothingness ("God"), their form of madness. *That* the ascetic ideal has meant so many things to man, however, is an expression of the basic fact of the human will, its *horror vacui*:[3] *it needs a goal*—and it will rather will *nothingness* than *not* will.— Am I understood? . . . Have I been understood?

---

[1] "On Reading and Writing" (*Portable Nietzsche,* p. 153).

[2] Newest lust for glory.

[3] Horror of a vacuum.

. . . *"Not at all, my dear sir!"*—Then let us start again, from the beginning.

2

What is the meaning of ascetic ideals?— Or, to take an individual case that I have often been asked about: what does it mean, for example, when an artist like Richard Wagner pays homage to chastity in his old age? In a certain sense, to be sure, he had always done this: but only in the very end in an ascetic sense. What is the meaning of this change of "sense," this radical reversal of sense?— for that is what it was: Wagner leaped over into his opposite. What does it mean when an artist leaps over into his opposite?

Here, if we are disposed to pause a moment at this question, we are at once reminded of what was perhaps the finest, strongest, happiest, *most courageous* period of Wagner's life: the period during which he was deeply concerned with the idea of Luther's wedding. Who knows upon what chance events it depended that instead of this wedding music we possess today *Die Meistersinger?* And how much of the former perhaps still echoes in the latter? But there can be no doubt that "Luther's Wedding" would also have involved a praise of chastity. And also a praise of sensuality, to be sure— and this would have seemed to be quite in order, quite "Wagnerian."

For there is no necessary antithesis between chastity and sensuality;[1] every good marriage, every genuine love affair, transcends this antithesis. Wagner would have done well, I think, to have brought this *pleasant* fact home once more to his Germans by means of a bold and beautiful Luther comedy, for there have always been and still are many slanderers of sensuality among the Germans; and perhaps Luther performed no greater service than to have had the courage of his *sensuality* (in those days it was called, delicately enough, "evangelical freedom"). But even in those cases in which this antithesis between chastity and sensuality really ex-

---

[1] This paragraph as well as section 3 was included with some revisions in *Nietzsche contra Wagner,* in the chapter "Wagner as the Apostle of Chastity" (*Portable Nietzsche,* pp. 673–75).

ists, there is fortunately no need for it to be a tragic antithesis. At least this holds good for all those well-constituted, joyful mortals who are far from regarding their unstable equilibrium between "animal and angel" as necessarily an argument against existence— the subtlest and brightest among them have even found in it, like Goethe and Hafiz, one *more* stimulus to life. It is precisely such "contradictions" that seduce one to existence . . . On the other hand, it is only too clear that when swine who have come to grief are finally induced to worship chastity—and there are such swine! —they will see and worship in it only their antithesis, the antithesis of failed swine—and one can imagine with what tragic zeal and grunting they will do so!—that embarrassing and superfluous antithesis which Richard Wagner at the end of his life unquestionably intended to set to music and put upon the stage. *But why?* as one might reasonably ask. For what were swine to him, what are they to us?—

3

This does not, of course, help us to avoid asking this other question, what that male (yet so unmanly) "country simpleton" was to him, that poor devil and nature boy Parsifal, whom he finally made into a Catholic by such captious means—what? was this Parsifal meant *seriously?* For one might be tempted to suppose the reverse, even to desire it—that the Wagnerian *Parsifal* was intended as a joke, as a kind of epilogue and satyr play with which the tragedian Wagner wanted to take leave of us, also of himself, above all *of tragedy* in a fitting manner worthy of himself, namely with an extravagance of wanton parody of the tragic itself, of the whole gruesome earthly seriousness and misery of his previous works, of the *crudest form,* overcome at long last, of the anti-nature of the ascetic ideal. This, to repeat, would have been worthy of a great tragedian, who, like every artist, arrives at the ultimate pinnacle of his greatness only when he comes to see himself and his art *beneath* him—when he knows how to *laugh* at himself.

Is Wagner's *Parsifal* his secret laughter of superiority at himself, the triumph of his ultimate artist's freedom and artist's transcendence? One could wish that it were, to repeat again; for what would a *seriously-intended Parsifal* be? Must one really see in him (as someone once put it to me) "the product of an insane hatred of knowledge, spirit, and sensuality"? A curse on the senses and the spirit in a *single* breath of hatred? An apostacy and return to morbid Christian and obscurantist ideals? And ultimately a self-negation, a self-cancellation on the part of an artist who had hitherto aimed with all the power of his will at the reverse, at the *highest spiritualization and sensualization* of his art? And not of his art only; of his life, too.

One should recall how enthusiastically Wagner at one time followed in the footsteps of the philosopher Feuerbach:[1] Feuerbach's cry of "healthy sensuality"—that sounded in the thirties and forties, to Wagner as to many other Germans (they called themselves the *"young* Germans"), like a cry of redemption. Did he at last come to *learn otherwise?* For at least it seems that he finally had the will to *teach otherwise.* And not only from the stage with the trumpets of *Parsifal;* in the murky writings of his last years, as unfree as they are perplexed, there are a hundred passages that betray a secret wish and will, a despairing, unsure, unacknowledged will to preach nothing other than reversion, conversion, denial, Christianity, medievalism, and to say to his disciples "it is no good! seek salvation elsewhere!" Even the "blood of the Redeemer" is invoked in one place.—

4

In such a case as this, embarrassing in many ways, my view is—and it is a *typical* case—that one does best to separate an artist from his work, not taking him as seriously as his work. He is, after all, only the precondition of his work, the womb, the soil, sometimes the dung and manure on which, out of which, it grows—and

---

[1] Ludwig Feuerbach (1804–1872) was the outstanding "Young" (left-wing) Hegelian philosopher who tried to transform theology into anthropology. His influence on Karl Marx was considerable, but Marx and Engels took sharp issue with him. Feuerbach's book, *Das Wesen des Christentums* (1841) was translated into English by George Eliot as *The Essence of Christianity* (1853, 2nd ed., 1881), and is still considered a classic of humanism.

therefore in most cases something one must forget if one is to enjoy the work itself. Insight into the origin of a work concerns the physiologists and vivisectionists of the spirit; never the aesthetic man, the artist!

The poet and creator of *Parsifal* could no more be spared a deep, thorough, even frightful identification with and descent into medieval soul-conflicts, a hostile separation from all spiritual height, severity, and discipline, a kind of intellectual *perversity* (if I may be pardoned the word), than can a pregnant woman be spared the repellent and bizarre aspects of pregnancy—which, as aforesaid, must be *forgotten* if one is to enjoy the child.

One should guard against confusion through psychological *contiguity*, to use a British term,[1] a confusion to which an artist himself is only too prone: as if he himself were what he is able to represent, conceive, and express. The fact is that *if* he were it, he would not represent, conceive, and express it: a Homer would not have created an Achilles nor a Goethe a Faust if Homer had been an Achilles or Goethe a Faust. Whoever is completely and wholly an artist is to all eternity separated from the "real," the actual; on the other hand, one can understand how he may sometimes weary to the point of desperation of the eternal "unreality" and falsity of his innermost existence—and that then he may well attempt what is most forbidden him, to lay hold of actuality, for once actually to *be*. With what success? That is easy to guess.

It is the *typical velleity* of the artist: the same velleity to which the aged Wagner fell victim and for which he had to pay so high and fateful a price (it cost him those of his friends who were valuable). Finally, however, quite apart from this velleity, who would not wish for Wagner's own sake that he had taken leave of us and of his art *differently,* not with a *Parsifal* but in a more triumphant manner, more self-confident, more Wagnerian—less misleading, less ambiguous in relation to his over-all intentions, less Schopenhauerian, less nihilistic?

---

[1] Nietzsche uses the English term. The allusion is to David Hume.

5

What, then, is the meaning of ascetic ideals? In the case of an artist, as we see, *nothing whatever!* . . . Or so many things it amounts to nothing whatever!

Let us, first of all, eliminate the artists: they do not stand nearly independently enough in the world and *against* the world for their changing valuations to deserve attention *in themselves!* They have at all times been valets of some morality, philosophy, or religion; quite apart from the fact that they have unfortunately often been all-too-pliable courtiers of their own followers and patrons, and cunning flatterers of ancient or newly arrived powers. They always need at the very least protection, a prop, an established authority: artists never stand apart; standing alone is contrary to their deepest instincts.

Thus Richard Wagner, for example, used the philosopher Schopenhauer, when the latter's "time had come," as his herald and protection: who would regard it as even thinkable that he would have had the *courage* for the ascetic ideal without the prop provided by Schopenhauer's philosophy, without the authority of Schopenhauer which had gained *ascendancy* in Europe during the seventies? (Let us leave out of account whether in the *new* Germany an artist could have existed who lacked the milk of pious, *Reichs*-pious sentiments).

Here we have arrived at the more serious question: what does it mean when a genuine *philosopher* pays homage to the ascetic ideal, a genuinely independent spirit like Schopenhauer, a man and knight of a steely eye who had the courage to be himself, who knew how to stand alone without first waiting for heralds and signs from above?

Let us here consider straightaway the remarkable and for many kinds of men even fascinating attitude Schopenhauer adopted toward *art:* for it was obviously for the sake of this that Richard Wagner *initially* went over to Schopenhauer (persuaded, as one knows, by a poet, by Herwegh[1]), and did so to such an extent that

---

[1] Georg Herwegh, 1817–1875.

there exists a complete theoretical contradiction between his earlier and his later aesthetic creed—the former set down, for example, in *Opera and Drama,* the latter in the writings he published from 1870 onward. Specifically, he ruthlessly altered—and this is perhaps most astonishing—his judgment as to the value and status of *music:* what did he care that he had formerly made of music a means, a medium, a "woman" who required a goal, a man, in order to prosper—namely, drama! He grasped all at once that with the Schopenhauerian theory and innovation *more* could be done *in majorem musicae gloriam*[2]—namely, with the theory of the *sovereignty* of music as Schopenhauer conceived it: music set apart from all the other arts, the independent art as such, *not* offering images of phenomenality, as the other arts did, but speaking rather the language of the will itself, directly out of the "abyss" as its most authentic, elemental, nonderivative revelation. With this extraordinary rise in the value of music that appeared to follow from Schopenhauerian philosophy, the value of *the musician* himself all at once went up in an unheard-of manner, too: from now on he became an oracle, a priest, indeed more than a priest, a kind of mouthpiece of the "in itself" of things, a telephone from the beyond—henceforth he uttered not only music, this ventriloquist of God—he uttered metaphysics: no wonder he one day finally uttered *ascetic ideals*.

6

Schopenhauer made use of the Kantian version of the aesthetic problem—although he certainly did not view it with Kantian eyes. Kant thought he was honoring art when among the predicates of beauty he emphasized and gave prominence to those which establish the honor of knowledge: impersonality and universality. This is not the place to inquire whether this was essentially a mistake; all I wish to underline is that Kant, like all philosophers, instead of envisaging the aesthetic problem from the point of view of the artist (the creator), considered art and the beautiful purely from that of the "spectator," and unconsciously introduced the

---

[2] For the greater glory of music.

"spectator" into the concept "beautiful." It would not have been so bad if this "spectator" had at least been sufficiently familiar to the philosophers of beauty—namely, as a great *personal* fact and experience, as an abundance of vivid authentic experiences, desires, surprises, and delights in the realm of the beautiful! But I fear that the reverse has always been the case; and so they have offered us, from the beginning, definitions in which, as in Kant's famous definition of the beautiful, a lack of any refined first-hand experience reposes in the shape of a fat worm of error. "That is beautiful," said Kant,[1] "which gives us pleasure *without interest*." Without interest! Compare with this definition one framed by a genuine "spectator" and artist—Stendhal, who once called the beautiful *une promesse de bonheur*.[2] At any rate he *rejected* and repudiated the one point about the aesthetic condition which Kant had stressed: *le désintéressement*. Who is right, Kant or Stendhal?

If our aestheticians never weary of asserting in Kant's favor that, under the spell of beauty, one can *even* view undraped female statues "without interest," one may laugh a little at their expense: the experiences of *artists* on this ticklish point are more "interesting," and Pygmalion was in any event *not* necessarily an "unaesthetic man." Let us think the more highly of the innocence of our aestheticians which is reflected in such arguments; let us, for example, credit it to the honor of Kant that he should expatiate on the peculiar properties of the sense of touch with the naïveté of a country parson!

And here we come back to Schopenhauer, who stood much closer to the arts than Kant and yet did not free himself from the spell of the Kantian definition: how did that happen? The circumstance is remarkable enough: he interpreted the term "without interest" in an extremely personal way, on the basis of one of his most regular experiences. Of few things does Schopenhauer speak with greater assurance than he does of the effect of aesthetic contemplation: he says of it that it counteracts *sexual* "interestedness," like lupulin and camphor; he never wearied of glorifying *this* liberation from the

---

[1] *Critique of Judgment* (1790), sections 1–5.
[2] A promise of happiness.

"will" as the great merit and utility of the aesthetic condition. Indeed, one might be tempted to ask whether his basic conception of
"will and representation," the thought that redemption from the
"will" could be attained only through "representation," did not
originate as a generalization from this sexual experience. (In all
questions concerning Schopenhauer's philosophy, by the way, one
should never forget that it was the conception of a young man
of twenty-six; so that it partakes not only of the specific qualities of
Schopenhauer, but also of the specific qualities of that period of
life.) Listen, for instance, to one of the most explicit of the countless passages he has written in praise of the aesthetic condition
(*World as Will and Representation,* I, p. 231 [3]); listen to the tone,
the suffering, the happiness, the gratitude expressed in such words.

"This is the painless condition that Epicurus praised as the
highest good and the condition of the gods; for a moment we are
delivered from the vile urgency of the will; we celebrate the Sabbath of the penal servitude of volition; the wheel of Ixion stands
still!"

What vehemence of diction! What images of torment and long
despair! What an almost pathological antithesis between "a moment" and the usual "wheel of Ixion," "penal servitude of volition," and "vile urgency of the will!"— But even if Schopenhauer
was a hundred times right in his own case, what insight does that
give us into the nature of the beautiful? Schopenhauer described
one effect of the beautiful, its calming effect on the will—but is this
a regular effect? Stendhal, as we have seen, a no less sensual but
more happily constituted person than Schopenhauer, emphasizes
another effect of the beautiful: "the beautiful *promises* happiness";
to him the fact seems to be precisely that the beautiful *arouses the
will* ("interestedness"). And could one not finally urge against
Schopenhauer himself that he was quite wrong in thinking himself a
Kantian in this matter, that he by no means understood the Kantian definition of the beautiful in a Kantian sense—that he, too,
was pleased by the beautiful from an "interested" viewpoint, even
from the very strongest, most personal interest: that of a tortured

---

[3] Ed. Julius Frauenstädt; i.e., Book III, section 38.

man who gains release from his torture?— And, to return to our first question, "what does it *mean* when a philosopher pays homage to the ascetic ideal?"—here we get at any rate a first indication: he wants *to gain release from a torture.*—

7

Let us not become gloomy as soon as we hear the word "torture": in this particular case there is plenty to offset and mitigate that word—even something to laugh at. Above all, we should not underestimate the fact that Schopenhauer, who treated sexuality as a personal enemy (including its tool, woman, that *"instrumentum diaboli"* [1]), *needed* enemies in order to keep in good spirits; that he loved bilious, black-green words, that he scolded for the sake of scolding, out of passion; that he would have become ill, become a *pessimist* (for he was not one, however much he desired it), if deprived of his enemies, of Hegel, of woman, of sensuality and the whole will to existence, to persistence. Without these, Schopenhauer would *not* have persisted, one may wager on that; he would have run away: but his enemies held him fast, his enemies seduced him ever again to existence; his anger was, just as in the case of the Cynics of antiquity, his balm, his refreshment, his reward, his specific against disgust, his *happiness*. So much in regard to what is most personal in the case of Schopenhauer; on the other hand, there is also something typical in him—and here we finally come back to our problem.

As long as there are philosophers on earth, and wherever there have been philosophers (from India to England, to take the antithetical poles of philosophical endowment), there unquestionably exists a peculiar philosophers' irritation at and rancor against sensuality: Schopenhauer is merely its most eloquent and, if one has ears for this, most ravishing and delightful expression. There also exists a peculiar philosophers' prejudice and affection in favor of the whole ascetic ideal; one should not overlook that. Both, to repeat, pertain to the type; if both are lacking in a philosopher,

---

[1] Instrument of the devil.

then—one can be sure of it—he is always only a "so-called" philosopher. What does that *mean?* For this fact has to be interpreted: *in itself* it just stands there, stupid to all eternity, like every "thing-in-itself."

Every animal—therefore *la bête philosophe,*[2] too—instinctively strives for an optimum of favorable conditions under which it can expend all its strength and achieve its maximal feeling of power; every animal abhors, just as instinctively and with a subtlety of discernment that is "higher than all reason," every kind of intrusion or hindrance that obstructs or could obstruct this path to the optimum (I am *not* speaking of its path to happiness, but its path to power, to action, to the most powerful activity, and in most cases actually its path to unhappiness). Thus the philosopher abhors *marriage,* together with that which might persuade to it—marriage being a hindrance and calamity on his path to the optimum. What great philosopher hitherto has been married? Heraclitus, Plato, Descartes, Spinoza, Leibniz, Kant, Schopenhauer—they were not; more, one cannot even *imagine* them married. A married philosopher belongs *in comedy,* that is my proposition—and as for that exception, Socrates[3]—the malicious Socrates, it would seem, married *ironically,* just to demonstrate *this* proposition.

Every philosopher would speak as Buddha did when he was told of the birth of a son: "Rahula has been born to me, a fetter has been forged for me" (Rahula here means "a little demon"); every "free spirit" would experience a thoughtful moment, supposing he had previously experienced a thoughtless one, of the kind that once came to the same Buddha—"narrow and oppressive," he thought to himself, "is life in a house, a place of impurity; freedom lies in leaving the house": "thinking thus, he left the house." Ascetic ideals reveal so many bridges to *independence* that a philosopher is bound to rejoice and clap his hands when he hears the story of all those resolute men who one day said No to all servitude and went into some *desert:* even supposing they were merely strong asses and quite the reverse of a strong spirit.

What, then, is the meaning of the ascetic ideal in the case of a

---

[2] The philosophical animal.

[3] Socrates appears in Aristophanes' comedy *The Clouds.*

philosopher? My answer is—you will have guessed it long ago: the philosopher sees in it an optimum condition for the highest and boldest spirituality and smiles—he does *not* deny "existence," he rather affirms *his* existence and *only* his existence, and this perhaps to the point at which he is not far from harboring the impious wish: *pereat mundus, fiat philosophia, fiat philosophus,* **fiam!** [4]—

8

As you see, they are not unbiased witnesses and judges of the *value* of the ascetic ideal, these philosophers! They think of *themselves*—what is "the saint" to them! They think of what *they* can least do without: freedom from compulsion, disturbance, noise, from tasks, duties, worries; clear heads; the dance, leap, and flight of ideas; good air, thin, clear, open, dry, like the air of the heights through which all animal being becomes more spiritual and acquires wings; repose in all cellar regions; all dogs nicely chained up; no barking of hostility and shaggy-haired rancor; no gnawing worm of injured ambition; undemanding and obedient intestines, busy as windmills but distant; the heart remote, beyond, heavy with future, posthumous—all in all, they think of the ascetic ideal as the cheerful asceticism of an animal become fledged and divine, floating above life rather than in repose.

The three great slogans of the ascetic ideal are familiar: poverty, humility, chastity. Now take a close look at the lives of all the great, fruitful, inventive spirits: you will always encounter all three to a certain degree. *Not,* it goes without saying, as though these constituted their "virtues"—what has this kind of man to do with virtues!—but as the most appropriate and natural conditions of their *best* existence, their *fairest* fruitfulness. It is quite possible that their dominating spirituality had first to put a check on an unrestrained and irritable pride or a wanton sensuality, or that it perhaps had a hard job to maintain its will to the "desert" against a love of luxury and refinement or an excessive liberality of heart and hand. But it did it, precisely because it was the dominating

---

[4] Let the world perish, but let there be philosophy, the philosopher, *me!*

instinct whose demands prevailed against those of all the other instincts—it continues to do it; if it did not do it, it would not dominate. There is thus nothing of "virtue" in this.

The *desert,* incidentally, that I just mentioned, where the
strong, independent spirits withdraw and become lonely—oh, how
different it looks from the way educated people imagine a desert!—
for in some cases they themselves are this desert, these educated
people. And it is certain that no actor of the spirit could possibly
endure life in it—for them it is not nearly romantic or Syrian
enough, not nearly enough of a stage desert! To be sure, there is no
lack of camels[1] in it; but that is where the similarity ends. A voluntary obscurity perhaps; an avoidance of oneself; a dislike of noise,
honor, newspapers, influence; a modest job, an everyday job, something that conceals rather than exposes one; an occasional association with harmless, cheerful beasts and birds whose sight is re-
freshing; mountains for company, but not dead ones, mountains
with *eyes* (that is, with lakes); perhaps even a room in a full, utterly commonplace hotel, where one is certain to go unrecognized
and can talk to anyone with impunity—that is what "desert" means
here: oh, it is lonely enough, believe me! When Heraclitus with-
drew into the courtyards and colonnades of the great temple of
Artemis, this was a worthier "desert," I admit: why do we *lack*
such temples? (Perhaps we do *not* lack them: I just recall my most
beautiful study—the Piazza di San Marco, in spring of course, and
morning also, the time between ten and twelve.) That which Heraclitus avoided, however, is still the same as that which *we* shun
today: the noise and democratic chatter of the Ephesians, their
politics, their latest news of the "Empire" [2] (the Persian, you understand), their market business of "today"—for we philosophers need
to be spared *one* thing above all: everything to do with "today."
We reverence what is still, cold, noble, distant, past, and in general
everything in the face of which the soul does not have to defend
itself and wrap itself up—what one can speak to without speaking
aloud.

One should listen to how a spirit sounds when it speaks: every

---

[1] Here used in the sense of silly asses, which is common in German.
[2] *Reich.*

spirit has its own sound and loves its own sound. That one, over there, for example, must be an agitator, that is to say, a hollow head, a hollow pot: whatever goes into him comes back out of him dull and thick, heavy with the echo of great emptiness. This fellow usually speaks hoarsely: has he perhaps *thought* himself hoarse? That might be possible—ask any physiologist—but whoever thinks in *words* thinks as an orator and not as a thinker (it shows that fundamentally he does not think facts, nor factually, but only in relation to facts; that he is really thinking of *himself* and his listeners). A third person speaks importunately, he comes too close to us, he breathes on us—involuntarily we close our mouths, although it is a book through which he is speaking to us: the sound of his style betrays the reason: he has no time to waste, he has little faith in himself, he must speak today or never. A spirit that is sure of itself, however, speaks softly; it seeks concealment, it keeps people waiting.

A philosopher may be recognized by the fact that he avoids three glittering and loud things: fame, princes, and women—which is not to say they do not come to him. He shuns light that is too bright: that is why he shuns his age and its "day." In this he is like a shadow: the lower his sun sinks the bigger he becomes. As for his "humility," he endures a certain dependence and eclipse, as he endures the darkness: more, he is afraid of being distracted by lightning, he shies away from the unprotected isolation of abandoned trees upon which any bad weather can vent its moods, any mood its bad weather. His "maternal" instinct, the secret love of that which is growing in him, directs him toward situations in which he is relieved of the necessity of thinking *of himself;* in the same sense in which the instinct of the *mother* in woman has hitherto generally kept woman in a dependent situation. Ultimately they ask for little enough, these philosophers: their motto is "he who possesses is possessed"—*not,* as I must say again and again, from virtue, from a laudable will to contentment and simplicity, but because their supreme lord demands this of them, prudently and inexorably: he is concerned with one thing alone, and assembles and saves up everything—time, energy, love, and interest—only for that one thing.

This kind of man does not like to be disturbed by enmities, nor by friendships; he easily forgets and easily despises. He thinks it in bad taste to play the martyr; "to *suffer* for truth"—he leaves that to the ambitious and the stage heroes of the spirit and to anyone else who has the time for it (the philosophers themselves have something to *do* for the truth). They use big words sparingly; it is said that they dislike the very word "truth": it sounds too grandiloquent.

As for the "chastity" of philosophers, finally, this type of spirit clearly has its fruitfulness somewhere else than in children; perhaps it also has the survival of its name elsewhere, its little immortality (philosophers in ancient India expressed themselves even more immodestly: "why should he desire progeny whose soul is the world?"). There is nothing in this of chastity from any kind of ascetic scruple or hatred of the senses, just as it is not chastity when an athlete or jockey abstains from women: it is rather the will of their dominating instinct, at least during their periods of great pregnancy. Every artist knows what a harmful effect intercourse has in states of great spiritual tension and preparation; those with the greatest power and the surest instincts do not need to learn this by experience, by unfortunate experience—their "maternal" instinct ruthlessly disposes of all other stores and accumulations of energy, of animal vigor, for the benefit of the evolving work: the greater energy then *uses up* the lesser.

Now let us interpret the case of Schopenhauer, discussed above, in the light of these remarks: the sight of the beautiful obviously had upon him the effect of releasing the *chief energy* of his nature (the energy of contemplation and penetration), so that this exploded and all at once became the master of his consciousness. This should by no means preclude the possibility that the sweetness and plenitude peculiar to the aesthetic state might be derived precisely from the ingredient of "sensuality" (just as the "idealism" of adolescent girls derives from this source)—so that sensuality is not overcome by the appearance of the aesthetic condition, as Schopenhauer believed, but only transfigured and no longer enters consciousness as sexual excitement. (I shall return to this point on another occasion, in connection with the still more delicate problems of the *physiology of aesthetics*,[3] which is practically untouched and unexplored so far.)

9

We have seen how a certain asceticism, a severe and cheerful continence with the best will, belongs to the most favorable conditions of supreme spirituality, and is also among its most natural consequences: hence it need be no matter for surprise that philosophers have always discussed the ascetic ideal with a certain fondness. A serious examination of history actually reveals that the bond between philosophy and the ascetic ideal is even much closer and stronger. One might assert that it was only on the leading-strings of this ideal that philosophy learned to take its first small steps on earth—alas, so clumsily, so unwillingly, so ready to fall on its face and lie on its belly, this timid little toddler and mollycoddle with shaky legs!

Philosophy began as all good things begin: for a long time it lacked the courage for itself; it was always looking round to see if someone would come and help it; yet it was afraid of all who looked at it. Draw up a list of the various propensities and virtues of the philosopher—his bent to doubt, his bent to deny, his bent to suspend judgment (his "ephectic" bent), his bent to analyze, his bent to investigate, seek, dare, his bent to compare and balance, his will to neutrality and objectivity, his will to every *"sine ira et studio"*:[1] is it not clear that for the longest time all of them contravened the basic demands of morality and conscience (not to speak of *reason* quite generally, which Luther liked to call "Mistress Clever, the clever whore")—that if a philosopher *had* been

---

[3] Nietzsche did not live to publish an essay on this subject, but pertinent material may be found in his next two books, *The Case of Wagner* (1888; English translation by Walter Kaufmann, published in the same volume with *The Birth of Tragedy,* New York, Vintage Books, 1967) and *Twilight of the Idols,* "Skirmishes of an Untimely Man," section 8ff., 19ff., and 47ff. (*Portable Nietzsche,* pp. 518ff.). See also *Nietzsche contra Wagner* (*ibid.*) and the sections on "The Will to Power as Art" in *The Will to Power,* ed. Kaufmann (New York, Random House, 1967).

[1] Without anger or affection; i.e., impartial(ity).

conscious of what he was, he would have been compelled to feel himself the embodiment of *"nitimur in vetitum"* [2]—and consequently *guarded* against "feeling himself," against becoming conscious of himself?

It is, to repeat, no different with all the good things of which we are proud today; measured even by the standards of the ancient Greeks, our entire modern way of life, insofar as it is not weakness but power and consciousness of power, has the appearance of sheer *hubris*[3] and godlessness: for the longest time it was precisely the reverse of those things we hold in honor today that had a good conscience on its side and God for its guardian. Our whole attitude toward nature, the way we violate her with the aid of machines and the heedless inventiveness of our technicians and engineers, is *hubris;* our attitude toward God as some alleged spider of purpose and morality behind the great captious web of causality, is *hubris* —we might say, with Charles the Bold when he opposed Louis XI, *"je combats l'universelle araignée";*[4] our attitude toward *ourselves* is *hubris,* for we experiment with ourselves in a way we would never permit ourselves to experiment with animals and, carried away by curiosity, we cheerfully vivisect our souls: what is the "salvation" of the soul to us today? Afterward we cure ourselves: sickness is instructive, we have no doubt of that, even more instructive than health—*those who make sick* seem even more necessary to us today than any medicine men or "saviors." We violate ourselves nowadays, no doubt of it, we nutcrackers of the soul, ever questioning and questionable, as if life were nothing but cracking nuts; and thus we are bound to grow day-by-day more questionable, *worthier* of asking questions;[5] perhaps also worthier—of living?

All good things were formerly bad things; every original sin has turned into an original virtue. Marriage, for example, seemed for a long time a transgression against the rights of the community;

---

[2] We strive for the forbidden: *Ovid's Amores,* III, 4, 17. Cf. *Beyond Good and Evil,* section 227.

[3] Overweening pride—often ascribed to the heroes of Greek tragedies.

[4] I fight the universal spider.

[5] *Fragwürdiger,* würdiger *zu fragen.*

one had to make reparation for being so immodest as to claim a woman for oneself (hence, for example, the *jus primae noctis*,[6] which in Cambodia is still the prerogative of the priests, those guardians of all "hallowed customs"). The gentle, benevolent, conciliatory, and compassionate feelings—eventually so highly valued that they almost constitute "the eternal values"—were opposed for the longest time by self-contempt: one was ashamed of mildness as one is today ashamed of hardness (cf. *Beyond Good and Evil*, section 260). Submission to *law:* how the consciences of noble tribes all over the earth resisted the abandonment of vendetta and were loath to bow before the power of the law! "Law" was for a long time a *vetitum*,[7] an outrage, an innovation; it was characterized by violence—it *was* violence to which one submitted, feeling ashamed of oneself. Every smallest step on earth has been paid for by spiritual and physical torture: this whole point of view, "that not only every progressive step, no! every step, movement, and change has required its countless martyrs," sounds utterly strange to us today—I called attention to it in *The Dawn*, section 18.

"Nothing has been bought more dearly," I say there, "than the modicum of human reason and feeling of freedom that are now our pride. It is this pride, however, that makes it almost impossible for us today to empathize with that vast era of the 'morality of mores' [8] which preceded 'world history' as the truly decisive history that determined the character of mankind: when suffering was everywhere counted as a virtue, cruelty as a virtue, dissembling as a virtue, revenge as a virtue, slander of reason as a virtue, and when on the other hand well-being was counted as a danger, thirst for knowledge as a danger, peace as a danger, pity as a danger, being pitied as a disgrace, work as a disgrace, madness as divine, *change* as the very essence of immorality[9] and pregnant with disaster."

---

[6] The right of the first night.

[7] Something forbidden, or a prohibition.

[8] *Sittlichkeit der Sitte:* see Nietzsche's Preface, section 4.

[9] *Das Unsittliche . . . an sich: an sich* (in itself, the very essence of) and *überall* (everywhere) are not found in *The Dawn* but added by Nietzsche in the *Genealogy*. Where morality is identified with the traditional *mores* or customs, change is *eo ipso* immoral.

10

In the same book (section 42) it is explained under what valuation, what *oppression* of valuation, the earliest race of contemplative men had to live: when not feared, they were despised. Contemplation first appeared on earth in disguise, in ambiguous form, with an evil heart and often an anxious head: there is no doubt of that. The inactive, brooding, unwarlike element in the instincts of contemplative men long surrounded them with a profound mistrustfulness: the only way of dispelling it was to arouse a decided *fear* of oneself. And the ancient Brahmins, for instance, knew how to do this! The earliest philosophers knew how to endow their existence and appearance with a meaning, a basis and background, through which others might come to *fear* them: more closely considered, they did so from an even more fundamental need, namely, so as to fear and reverence themselves. For they found all the value judgments within them turned *against* them, they had to fight down every kind of suspicion and resistance against "the philosopher in them." As men of frightful ages, they did this by using frightful means: cruelty toward themselves, inventive self-castigation—this was the principal means these power-hungry hermits and innovators of ideas required to overcome the gods and tradition in themselves, so as to be able to *believe* in their own innovations. I recall the famous story of King Vishvamitra, who through millennia of self-torture acquired such a feeling of power and self-confidence that he endeavored to build a *new heaven*—the uncanny symbol of the most ancient and most recent experience of philosophers on earth: whoever has at some time built a "new heaven" has found the power to do so only in his *own hell*.

Let us compress the facts into a few brief formulas: to begin with, the philosophic spirit always had to use as a mask and cocoon the *previously established* types of the contemplative man—priest, sorcerer, soothsayer, and in any case a religious type—in order to be able to *exist at all: the ascetic ideal* for a long time served the philosopher as a form in which to appear, as a precondition of existence—he had to *represent* it so as to be able to be a philosopher; he had to *believe* in it in order to be able to represent it. The peculiar, withdrawn attitude of the philosopher, world-denying, hostile to life, suspicious of the senses, freed from sensuality, which has been maintained down to the most modern times and has become virtually the *philosopher's pose par excellence*—it is above all a result of the emergency conditions under which philosophy arose and survived at all; for the longest time philosophy would not have been *possible at all* on earth without ascetic wraps and cloak, without an ascetic self-misunderstanding. To put it vividly: the *ascetic priest* provided until the most modern times the repulsive and gloomy caterpillar form in which alone the philosopher could live and creep about.

Has all this really *altered?* Has that many-colored and dangerous winged creature, the "spirit" which this caterpillar concealed, really been unfettered at last and released into the light, thanks to a sunnier, warmer, brighter world? Is there sufficient pride, daring, courage, self-confidence available today, sufficient will of the spirit, will to responsibility, *freedom of will,* for "the philosopher" to be henceforth—*possible* on earth?—

11

Only now that we behold the *ascetic priest* do we seriously come to grips with our problem: what is the meaning of the ascetic ideal?—only now does it become "serious": we are now face to face with the actual *representative of seriousness.* "What is the meaning of all seriousness?"—this even more fundamental question may perhaps be trembling on our lips at this point: a question for physiologists, of course, but one which we must still avoid for the moment. The ascetic priest possessed in this ideal not only his faith but also his will, his power, his interest. His *right* to exist stands or falls with that ideal: no wonder we encounter here a terrible antagonist—supposing we are antagonists of that ideal—one who fights for his existence against those who deny that ideal.

On the other hand, it is inherently improbable that so interested an attitude toward our problem will benefit it: the ascetic priest will hardly provide the best defense of his ideal, just as a woman who tries to defend "woman as such" usually fails—and he certainly will not be the most objective judge of this controversy. Far from fearing he will confute us—this much is already obvious —we shall have to help him defend himself against us.

The idea at issue here is the *valuation* the ascetic priest places on our life: he juxtaposes it (along with what pertains to it: "nature," "world," the whole sphere of becoming and transitoriness) with a quite different mode of existence which it opposes and excludes, *unless* it turn against itself, *deny itself:* in that case, the case of the ascetic life, life counts as a bridge to that other mode of existence. The ascetic treats life as a wrong road on which one must finally walk back to the point where it begins, or as a mistake that is put right by deeds—that we *ought* to put right: for he *demands* that one go along with him; where he can he compels acceptance of *his* evaluation of existence.

What does this mean? So monstrous a mode of valuation stands inscribed in the history of mankind not as an exception and curiosity, but as one of the most widespread and enduring of all phenomena. Read from a distant star, the majuscule script of our earthly existence would perhaps lead to the conclusion that the earth was the distinctively *ascetic planet,* a nook of disgruntled, arrogant, and offensive creatures filled with a profound disgust at themselves, at the earth, at all life, who inflict as much pain on themselves as they possibly can out of pleasure in inflicting pain— which is probably their only pleasure. For consider how regularly and universally the ascetic priest appears in almost every age; he belongs to no one race; he prospers everywhere; he emerges from every class of society. Nor does he breed and propagate his mode of valuation through heredity: the opposite is the case—broadly speaking, a profound instinct rather forbids him to propagate. It must be a necessity of the first order that again and again promotes the growth and prosperity of this *life-inimical* species—it must indeed be in the *interest of life itself* that such a self-contradictory type does not die out. For an ascetic life is a self-contradiction: here rules a *ressentiment* without equal, that of an insatiable instinct and power-will that wants to become master not over something in life but over life itself, over its most profound, powerful, and basic conditions; here an attempt is made to employ force to block up the wells of force; here physiological well-being itself is viewed askance, and especially the outward expression of this well-being, beauty and joy; while pleasure is felt and *sought* in ill-constitutedness, decay, pain, mischance, ugliness, voluntary deprivation, self-mortification, self-flagellation, self-sacrifice. All this is in the highest degree paradoxical: we stand before a discord that *wants* to be discordant, that *enjoys* itself in this suffering and even grows more self-confident and triumphant the more its own presupposition, its physiological capacity for life, *decreases.* "Triumph in the ultimate agony": the ascetic ideal has always fought under this hyperbolic sign; in this enigma of seduction, in this image of torment and delight, it recognized its brightest light, its salvation, its ultimate victory. *Crux, nux, lux*[1]—for the ascetic ideal these three are one.—

12

Suppose such an incarnate will to contradiction and antinaturalness is induced to *philosophize:* upon what will it vent its innermost contrariness? Upon what is felt most certainly to be real and actual: it will look for error precisely where the instinct of life most unconditionally posits truth. It will, for example, like the ascetics of the Vedanta philosophy, downgrade physicality to an illusion; likewise pain, multiplicity, the entire conceptual antithesis "subject" and "object"—errors, nothing but errors! To renounce belief in one's ego, to deny one's own "reality"—what a triumph! not merely over the senses, over appearance, but a much higher kind of triumph, a violation and cruelty against *reason*—a voluptuous pleasure that reaches its height when the ascetic self-contempt and self-mockery of reason declares: *"there is a realm of truth and being, but reason is excluded from it!"*

---

[1] Cross, nut, light. In one of Nietzsche's notebooks we find this sketch for a title:

Nux et Crux
A Philosophy for Good Teeth

(Erich Podach, *Ein Blick in Notizbücher Nietzsches,* Heidelberg, Wolfgang Rothe, 1963, p. 163 and errata slip).

(Incidentally, even in the Kantian concept of the "intelligible character of things" something remains of this lascivious ascetic discord that loves to turn reason against reason: for "intelligible character" signifies in Kant that things are so constituted that the intellect comprehends just enough of them to know that for the intellect they are—*utterly incomprehensible*.)

But precisely because we seek knowledge, let us not be ungrateful to such resolute reversals of accustomed perspectives and valuations with which the spirit has, with apparent mischievousness and futility, raged against itself for so long: to see differently in this way for once, to *want* to see differently, is no small discipline and preparation of the intellect for its future "objectivity"—the latter understood not as "contemplation without interest" (which is a nonsensical absurdity), but as the ability *to control* one's Pro and Con and to dispose of them, so that one knows how to employ a *variety* of perspectives and affective interpretations in the service of knowledge.

Henceforth, my dear philosophers, let us be on guard against the dangerous old conceptual fiction that posited a "pure, will-less, painless, timeless knowing subject"; let us guard against the snares of such contradictory concepts as "pure reason," "absolute spirituality," "knowledge in itself": these always demand that we should think of an eye that is completely unthinkable, an eye turned in no particular direction, in which the active and interpreting forces, through which alone seeing becomes seeing *something,* are supposed to be lacking; these always demand of the eye an absurdity and a nonsense. There is *only* a perspective seeing, *only* a perspective "knowing"; and the *more* affects we allow to speak about one thing, the *more* eyes, different eyes, we can use to observe one thing, the more complete will our "concept" of this thing, our "objectivity," be.[1] But to eliminate the will altogether, to suspend each and every affect, supposing we were capable of this—what would that mean but to *castrate* the intellect?—

---

[1] This passage throws a great deal of light on Nietzsche's perspectivism and on his style and philosophical method.

13

But let us return to our problem. It will be immediately obvious that such a self-contradiction as the ascetic appears to represent, "life *against* life," is, physiologically considered and not merely psychologically, a simple absurdity. It can only be *apparent;* it must be a kind of provisional formulation, an interpretation and psychological misunderstanding of something whose real nature could not for a long time be understood or described *as it really was*—a mere word inserted into an old *gap* in human knowledge. Let us replace it with a brief formulation of the facts of the matter: *the ascetic ideal springs from the protective instinct of a degenerating life* which tries by all means to sustain itself and to fight for its existence; it indicates a partial physiological obstruction and exhaustion against which the deepest instincts of life, which have remained intact, continually struggle with new expedients and devices. The ascetic ideal is such an expedient; the case is therefore the opposite of what those who reverence this ideal believe: life wrestles in it and through it with death and *against* death; the ascetic ideal is an artifice for the *preservation* of life.

That this ideal acquired such power and ruled over men as imperiously as we find it in history, especially wherever the civilization and taming of man has been carried through, expresses a great fact: the *sickliness* of the type of man we have had hitherto, or at least of the tamed man, and the physiological struggle of man against death (more precisely: against disgust with life, against exhaustion, against the desire for the "end"). The ascetic priest is the incarnate desire to be different, to be in a different place, and indeed this desire at its greatest extreme, its distinctive fervor and passion; but precisely this power of his desire is the chain that holds him captive so that he becomes a tool for the creation of more favorable conditions for being here and being man—it is precisely this *power* that enables him to persuade to existence the whole herd of the ill-constituted, disgruntled, underprivileged, unfortunate, and all who suffer of themselves, by instinctively going before them as their shepherd. You will see my point: this ascetic priest, this ap-

parent enemy of life, this *denier*—precisely he is among the greatest *conserving* and yes-creating[1] forces of life.

Where does it come from, this sickliness? For man is more
sick, uncertain, changeable, indeterminate than any other animal,
there is no doubt of that—he is *the* sick animal: how has that come
about? Certainly he has also dared more, done more new things,
braved more and challenged fate more than all the other animals
put together: he, the great experimenter with himself, discontented
and insatiable, wrestling with animals, nature, and gods for ultimate dominion—he, still unvanquished, eternally directed toward
the future, whose own restless energies never leave him in peace, so
that his future digs like a spur into the flesh of every present—how
should such a courageous and richly endowed animal not also be
the most imperiled, the most chronically and profoundly sick of all
sick animals?

Man has often had enough; there are actual epidemics of having had enough (as around 1348, at the time of the dance of
death); but even this nausea, this weariness, this disgust with himself—all this bursts from him with such violence that it at once
becomes a new fetter. The No he says to life brings to light, as if by
magic, an abundance of tender Yeses; even when he *wounds* himself, this master of destruction, of self-destruction—the very
wound itself afterward compels him *to live.*—

14

The more normal sickliness becomes among men—and we cannot deny its normality—the higher should be the honor accorded
the rare cases of great power of soul and body, man's *lucky hits;*
the more we should protect the well-constituted from the worst
kind of air, the air of the sickroom. Is this done?

The sick represent the greatest danger for the healthy; it is *not*

---

[1] *Dieser Verneinende . . . und Ja-schaffende:* cf. Goethe, *Faust,* lines 1335ff.,
where Mephistopheles calls himself: "The spirit that negates [*verneint*]" and
"part of that force which would / Do evil evermore, and yet creates the
good." In the next paragraph, the portrait of "the great experimenter" brings
to mind Goethe's Faust.

the strongest but the weakest who spell disaster for the strong. Is this known?

Broadly speaking, it is not fear of man that we should desire to see diminished; for this fear compels the strong to be strong, and occasionally terrible—it *maintains* the well-constituted type of man. What is to be feared, what has a more calamitous effect than any other calamity, is that man should inspire not profound fear but profound *nausea;* also not great fear but great *pity.* Suppose these two were one day to unite, they would inevitably beget one of the uncanniest monsters: the "last will" of man, his will to nothingness, nihilism. And indeed a great deal points to this union. Whoever can smell not only with his nose but also with his eyes and ears, scents almost everywhere he goes today something like the air of madhouses and hospitals—I am speaking, of course, of the cultural domain, of every kind of "Europe" on this earth. The *sick* are man's greatest danger; *not* the evil, *not* the "beasts of prey." Those who are failures from the start, downtrodden, crushed—it is they, the *weakest,* who must undermine life among men, who call into question and poison most dangerously our trust in life, in man, and in ourselves. Where does one not encounter that veiled glance which burdens one with a profound sadness, that inward-turned glance of the born failure which betrays how such a man speaks to himself—that glance which is a sigh! "If only I were someone else," sighs this glance: "but there is no hope of that. I am who I am: how could I ever get free of myself? And yet—I *am sick of myself!"*

It is on such soil, on swampy ground, that every weed, every poisonous plant grows, always so small, so hidden, so false, so saccharine. Here the worms of vengefulness and rancor swarm; here the air stinks of secrets and concealment; here the web of the most malicious of all conspiracies is being spun constantly—the conspiracy of the suffering against the well-constituted and victorious, here the aspect of the victorious is *hated.* And what mendaciousness is employed to disguise that this hatred is hatred! What a display of grand words and postures, what an art of "honest" calumny! These failures: what noble eloquence flows from their lips! How much sugary, slimy, humble submissiveness swims in their eyes! What do

they really want? At least to *represent* justice, love, wisdom, superiority—that is the ambition of the "lowest," the sick. And how
skillfull such an ambition makes them! Admire above all the forg-
er's skill with which the stamp of virtue, even the ring, the golden-
sounding ring of virtue, is here counterfeited. They monopolize virtue, these weak, hopelessly sick people, there is no doubt of it: "we
alone are the good and just," they say, "we alone are *homines
bonae voluntatis.*" [1] They walk among us as embodied reproaches,
as warnings to us—as if health, well-constitutedness, strength,
pride, and the sense of power were in themselves necessarily vicious things for which one must pay some day, and pay bitterly:
how ready they themselves are at bottom to *make* one pay; how
they crave to be *hangmen*. There is among them an abundance of
the vengeful disguised as judges, who constantly bear the word
"justice" in their mouths like poisonous spittle, always with pursed
lips, always ready to spit upon all who are not discontented but go
their way in good spirits. Nor is there lacking among them that
most disgusting species of the vain, the mendacious failures whose
aim is to appear as "beautiful souls" and who bring to market their
deformed sensuality, wrapped up in verses and other swaddling
clothes, as "purity of heart": the species of moral masturbaters and
"self-gratifiers." The will of the weak to represent *some* form of
superiority, their instinct for devious paths to tyranny over the
healthy—where can it not be discovered, this will to power of the
weakest!

The sick woman especially: no one can excel her in the wiles
to dominate, oppress, and tyrannize. The sick woman spares nothing, living or dead; she will dig up the most deeply buried things
(the Bogos say: "woman is a hyena").

Examine the background of every family, every organization,
every commonwealth: everywhere the struggle of the sick against
the healthy—a silent struggle as a rule, with petty poisons, with
pinpricks, with sly long-suffering expressions, but occasionally also
with that invalid's Phariseeism of *loud* gestures that likes best to
pose as "noble indignation." This hoarse, indignant barking of sick

---

[1] Men of good will.

dogs, this rabid mendaciousness and rage of "noble" Pharisees, penetrates even the hallowed halls of science (I again remind readers who have ears for such things of that Berlin apostle of revenge, Eugen Dühring, who employs moral mumbo-jumbo more indecently and repulsively than anyone else in Germany today: Dühring, the foremost moral bigmouth today—unexcelled even among his own ilk, the anti-Semites).

They are all men of *ressentiment*, physiologically unfortunate and worm-eaten, a whole tremulous realm of subterranean revenge, inexhaustible and insatiable in outbursts against the fortunate and happy[2] and in masquerades of revenge and pretexts for revenge: when would they achieve the ultimate, subtlest, sublimest triumph of revenge? Undoubtedly if they succeeded in *poisoning the consciences* of the fortunate with their own misery, with all misery, so that one day the fortunate began to be ashamed of their good fortune and perhaps said one to another: "it is disgraceful to be fortunate: *there is too much misery!*"

But no greater or more calamitous misunderstanding is possible than for the happy, well-constituted, powerful in soul and body, to begin to doubt their *right to happiness* in this fashion. Away with this "inverted world"! Away with this shameful emasculation of feeling! That the sick should *not* make the healthy sick—and this is what such an emasculation would involve—should surely be our supreme concern on earth; but this requires above all that the healthy should be *segregated* from the sick, guarded even from the sight of the sick, that they may not confound themselves with the sick. Or is it their task, perhaps, to be nurses or physicians? [3]

But no worse misunderstanding and denial of *their* task can be imagined: the higher *ought* not to degrade itself to the status of an

---

[2] "Fortunate and happy": *die Glücklichen.* In the next sentence the word is rendered "the fortunate," and *Glück* as "good fortune"; but in the next paragraph "happy" and "happiness" have been used, as Nietzsche evidently means both.

[3] Cf. Goethe's letter to Frau von Stein, June 8, 1787: "Also, I must say myself, I think it true that humanity will triumph eventually, only I fear that at the same time the world will become a large hospital and each will become the other's humane nurse." In a letter to Rée, April 17, 1877, Nietzsche writes, "each the other's 'humane nurse.'"

instrument of the lower, the pathos of distance *ought* to keep their tasks eternally separate! Their right to exist, the privilege of the full-toned bell over the false and cracked, is a thousand times greater: they alone are our *warranty* for the future, they alone are *liable* for the future of man. The sick can never have the ability or obligation to do what *they* can do, what *they* ought to do: but if they are to be able to do what *they* alone ought to do, how can they at the same time be physicians, consolers, and "saviors" of the sick?

And therefore let us have fresh air! fresh air! and keep clear of the madhouses and hospitals of culture! And therefore let us have good company, *our* company! Or solitude, if it must be! But away from the sickening fumes of inner corruption and the hidden rot of disease! . . . So that we may, at least for a while yet, guard ourselves, my friends, against the two worst contagions that may be reserved just for us—against the *great nausea at man!* against *great pity for man!* [4]

15

If one has grasped in all its profundity—and I insist that precisely this matter requires *profound* apprehension and comprehension—how it cannot be the task of the healthy to nurse the sick and to make them well, then one has also grasped one further necessity —the necessity of doctors and nurses *who are themselves sick;* and now we understand the meaning of the ascetic priest and grasp it with both hands.

We must count the ascetic priest as the predestined savior, shepherd, and advocate of the sick herd: only thus can we understand his tremendous historical mission. *Dominion over the suffering* is his kingdom, that is where his instinct directs him, here he possesses his distinctive art, his mastery, his kind of happiness. He

---

[4] The dangers of the great nausea and the great pity are among the central motifs of *Thus Spoke Zarathustra*. The theme of nausea is introduced in the chapter "On the Rabble" in Part Two and is encountered again and again in later chapters. Another chapter in Part Two bears the title "On the Pitying," and the whole of Part Four, which bears a motto from that chapter, is cast in the form of a story: having overcome his nausea at the end of Part Three, Zarathustra's final temptation is pity.

must be sick himself, he must be profoundly related to the sick—
how else would they understand each other?—but he must also be
strong, master of himself even more than of others, with his will to
power intact, so as to be both trusted and feared by the sick, so as
to be their support, resistance, prop, compulsion, taskmaster, ty-
rant, and god. He has to defend his herd—against whom? Against
the healthy, of course, and also against envy of the healthy; he
must be the natural opponent *and despiser* of all rude, stormy, unbridled, hard, violent beast-of-prey health and might. The priest is
the first form of the more *delicate* animal that despises more readily than it hates. He will not be spared war with the beasts of prey,
a war of cunning (of the "spirit") rather than one of force, as goes
without saying; to fight it he will under certain circumstances need
to evolve a virtually new type of preying animal out of himself, or
at least he will need to *represent* it—a new kind of animal ferocity
in which the polar bear, the supple, cold, and patient tiger, and not
least the fox seem to be joined in a unity at once enticing and
terrifying. If need compels him, he will walk among the other
beasts of prey with bearlike seriousness and feigned superiority,
venerable, prudent, and cold, as the herald and mouthpiece of
more mysterious powers, determined to sow this soil with misery,
discord, and self-contradiction wherever he can and, only too certain of his art, to dominate the *suffering* at all times. He brings
salves and balm with him, no doubt; but before he can act as a
physician he first has to wound; when he then stills the pain of the
wound *he at the same time infects the wound*—for that is what he
knows to do best of all, this sorcerer and animal-tamer, in whose
presence everything healthy necessarily grows sick, and everything
sick tame.

Indeed, he defends his sick herd well enough, this strange
shepherd—he also defends it against itself, against the baseness,
spite, malice, and whatever else is natural to the ailing and sick and
smolders within the herd itself; he fights with cunning and severity
and in secret against anarchy and ever-threatening disintegration
within the herd, in which the most dangerous of all explosives, *ressentiment,* is constantly accumulating. So to detonate this explosive
that it does not blow up herd and herdsman is his essential art, as it

is his supreme utility; if one wanted to express the value of the priestly existence in the briefest formula it would be: the priest *alters the direction* of *ressentiment*.

For every sufferer instinctively seeks a cause for his suffering; more exactly, an agent; still more specifically, a *guilty* agent who is susceptible to suffering—in short, some living thing upon which he can, on some pretext or other, vent his affects, actually or in effigy: for the venting of his affects represents the greatest attempt on the part of the suffering to win relief, *anaesthesia*—the narcotic he cannot help desiring to deaden pain of any kind. This alone, I surmise, constitutes the actual physiological cause of *ressentiment*, vengefulness, and the like: a desire to *deaden pain by means of affects*. This cause is usually sought, quite wrongly in my view, in defensive retaliation, a mere reactive protective measure, a "reflex movement" set off by sudden injury or peril, such as even a beheaded frog still makes to shake off a corrosive acid. But the difference is fundamental: in the one case, the desire is to prevent any further injury, in the other it is to *deaden,* by means of a more violent emotion of any kind, a tormenting, secret pain that is becoming unendurable, and to drive it out of consciousness at least for the moment: for that one requires an affect, as savage an affect as possible, and, in order to excite that, any pretext at all. "Someone or other must be to blame for my feeling ill"—this kind of reasoning is common to all the sick, and is indeed held the more firmly the more the real cause of their feeling ill, the physiological cause, remains hidden. (It may perhaps lie in some disease of the *nervus sympathicus,* or in an excessive secretion of bile, or in a deficiency of potassium sulphate and phosphate in the blood, or in an obstruction in the abdomen which impedes the blood circulation, or in degeneration of the ovaries, and the like).

The suffering are one and all dreadfully eager and inventive in discovering occasions for painful affects; they enjoy being mistrustful and dwelling on nasty deeds and imaginary slights; they scour the entrails of their past and present for obscure and questionable occurrences that offer them the opportunity to revel in tormenting suspicions and to intoxicate themselves with the poison of their own malice: they tear open their oldest wounds, they bleed from

long-healed scars, they make evildoers out of their friends, wives,
children, and whoever else stands closest to them.[1] "I suffer: someone must be to blame for it"—thus thinks every sickly sheep. But
his shepherd, the ascetic priest, tells him: "Quite so, my sheep!
someone must be to blame for it: but you yourself are this someone, you alone are to blame for it—*you alone are to blame for
yourself!*"—This is brazen and false enough: but one thing at least
is achieved by it, the direction of *ressentiment* is *altered.*

16

You will guess what, according to my idea, the curative instinct of life has at least *attempted* through the ascetic priest, and
why it required for a time the tyranny of such paradoxical and
paralogical concepts as "guilt," "sin," "sinfulness," "depravity,"
"damnation": to render the sick to a certain degree *harmless,* to
work the self-destruction of the incurable, to direct the *ressentiment* of the less severely afflicted sternly back upon themselves
("one thing is needful")—and in this way to *exploit* the bad instincts of all sufferers for the purpose of self-discipline, self-surveil-
lance, and self-overcoming.

It goes without saying that a "medication" of this kind, a mere
affect medication, cannot possibly bring about a real cure of sickness in a physiological sense; we may not even suppose that the
instinct of life contemplates or intends any sort of cure. A kind of
concentration and organization of the sick on one side (the word
"church" is the most popular name for it), a kind of provisional
safeguarding of the more healthily constituted, the more fully

---

[1] The most striking illustration of this sentence is found in Dostoevsky's
Notes from Underground—and on February 23, 1887, not quite nine
months before the publication of the *Genealogy,* Nietzsche wrote Overbeck
about his accidental discovery of Dostoevsky in a bookstore, where he had
chanced upon a French translation of that work: "my joy was extraordinary"
(*Portable Nietzsche,* pp. 454f.). In 1888 he wrote in section 45 of *Twilight
of the Idols:* "The testimony of Dostoevsky is relevant to this problem—Dostoevsky, the only psychologist, incidentally, from whom I had something to
learn; he ranks among the most beautiful strokes of fortune in my life, even
more than my discovery of Stendhal. . . ." (*ibid.,* p. 549; cf. also pp. 601
and 603). See also note 8, section 24, below.

achieved, on the other, and the creation of a *chasm* between healthy and sick—for a long time that was all! And it was much! *very much!*

(It is plain that in this essay I proceed on a presupposition that I do not first have to demonstrate to readers of the kind I need: that man's "sinfulness" is not a fact, but merely the interpretation of a fact, namely of physiological depression—the latter viewed in a religio-moral perspective that is no longer binding on us.— That someone *feels* "guilty" or "sinful" is no proof that he is right, any more than a man is healthy merely because he feels healthy. Recall the famous witch trials: the most acute and humane judges were in no doubt as to the guilt of the accused; the "witches" *themselves did not doubt it*—and yet there was no guilt. — To express this presupposition in a more general form: I consider even "psychological pain" to be not a fact but only an interpretation—a causal interpretation—of facts that have hitherto defied exact formulation—too vague to be scientifically serious—a fat word replacing a very thin question mark. When someone cannot get over a "psychological pain," that is *not* the fault of his "psyche" but, to speak crudely, more probably even that of his belly (speaking crudely, to repeat, which does not mean that I want to be heard crudely or understood crudely—). A strong and well-constituted man digests his experiences (his deeds and misdeeds included) as he digests his meals, even when he has to swallow some tough morsels. If he cannot get over an experience and have done with it, this kind of indigestion is as much physiological as is the other—and often in fact merely a consequence of the other.— With such a conception one can, between ourselves, still be the sternest opponent of all materialism.—)

17

But is he really a *physician,* this ascetic priest?—We have seen why it is hardly permissible to call him a physician, however much he enjoys feeling like a "savior" and letting himself be reverenced as a "savior." He combats only the suffering itself, the discomfiture of the sufferer, *not* its cause, *not* the real sickness: this must be our most fundamental objection to priestly medication.

But if one adopts the only perspective known to the priest, it is not easy to set bounds to one's admiration of how much he has seen, sought, and found under this perspective. The *alleviation* of suffering, "consolation" of every kind—here lies his genius; how inventively he has gone about his task of consolation, how boldly and unscrupulously he has selected the means for it! Christianity in particular may be called a great treasure house of ingenious means of consolation: it offers such a collection of refreshments, palliatives, and narcotics; it risks so much that is most dangerous and audacious; it has displayed such refinement and subtlety, such southern subtlety, in guessing what stimulant affects will overcome, at least for a time, the deep depression, the leaden exhaustion, the black melancholy of the physiologically inhibited. For we may generalize: the main concern of all great religions has been to fight a certain weariness and heaviness grown to epidemic proportions.

One may assume in advance the probability that from time to time and in certain parts of the earth a *feeling of physiological inhibition* is almost bound to seize on large masses of people, though, owing to their lack of physiological knowledge, they do not diagnose it as such: its "cause" and remedy are sought and tested only in the psychological-moral domain (this is my most general formula for what is usually called a *"religion"*). Such a feeling of inhibition can have the most various origins: perhaps it may arise from the crossing of races too different from one another (or of classes—classes always also express differences of origin and race: European *"Weltschmerz,"* [1] the "pessimism" of the nineteenth century, is essentially the result of an absurdly precipitate mixing of classes); or from an injudicious emigration—a race introduced into a climate for which its powers of adaptation are inadequate (the case of the Indians in India); or from the aftereffects of age and exhaustion in the race (Parisian pessimism from 1850 onward); or from an incorrect diet (the alcoholism of the Middle Ages; the absurdity of the *vegetarians* who, to be sure, can invoke

---

[1] Sentimental sorrow over the world's woes.

the authority of Squire Christopher in Shakespeare);[2] or from degeneration of the blood, malaria, syphilis, and the like (German depression after the Thirty Years' War, which infected half of Germany with vile diseases and thus prepared the ground for German servility, German pusillanimity). In every such case a grand *struggle against the feeling of displeasure* is attempted; let us briefly examine its principal forms and methods. (I here ignore altogether, as seems reasonable, *the philosophers'* struggle against this feeling, which is usually waged at the same time: it is interesting enough but too absurd, too practically ineffective, too much the work of web-spinners and idlers—as when pain is proved to be an error, in the naïve supposition that pain is *bound* to vanish as soon as the error in it is recognized; but behold! it refuses to vanish . . .)

This dominating sense of displeasure is combatted, *first,*[3] by means that reduce the feeling of life in general to its lowest point. If possible, will and desire are abolished altogether; all that produces affects and "blood" is avoided (abstinence from salt: the hygienic regimen of the fakirs); no love; no hate; indifference; no revenge; no wealth; no work; one begs; if possible, no women, or as little as possible; in spiritual matters, Pascal's principle *il faut s'abêtir"* [4] is applied. The result, expressed in moral-psychological terms, is "selflessness," "sanctification"; in physiological terms: hypnotization—the attempt to win for man an approximation to what in certain animals is *hibernation,* in many tropical plants *estivation,* the minimum metabolism at which life will still subsist without really entering consciousness. An astonishing amount of human energy has been expended to this end—has it been in vain?

---

[2] Nietzsche uses the English word "vegetarians." The reference to *Junker Christoph,* who is mentioned once more later in this section, is presumably intended to allude to *The Taming of the Shrew.* "She eat no meat today, nor none shall eat" (IV. 2, line 200) is, of course, said by Petruchio, and in the accepted version of the play Christopher Sly, the drunken tinker who is made to believe that he is a lord, appears only in the "Induction" (or Prologue) and in one subsequent comment. But in *The Taming of A* (sic) *Shrew* (1594), which slightly antedates the accepted version and is attributed to Shakespeare by a few scholars, the characters introduced in the Induction make comments from time to time throughout the play.

[3] The *second* strategy is introduced at the beginning of section 18.

[4] One must make oneself stupid: in the famous passage in the *Pensées* in which Pascal's wager is found.

There can be no doubt that these *sportsmen*[5] of "sanctity"
who proliferate in almost all ages and all peoples have in fact discovered a real release from that which they combated with such
rigorous *training: in countless cases they have really freed* themselves from that profound physiological depression by means of
their system of hypnotics, which thus counts among the most universal facts of ethnology. Nor is there any ground for considering
this program of starving the body and the desires as necessarily a
symptom of lunacy (as a certain clumsy kind of beef-eating "free
spirits" and Squire Christopher are wont to do). But it is certainly
capable of opening the way to all kinds of spiritual disturbances, to
"an inner light" for instance, as with the Hesychasts of Mount
Athos,[6] to auditory and visual hallucinations, to voluptuous inun-
dations and ecstasies of sensuality (the case of St. Theresa). It
goes without saying that the interpretation which those subject to
these states have placed upon them has always been as enthusiastic
and false as possible; but we should not overlook the note of utterly
convinced gratitude that finds expression in the very *will* to offer
that kind of interpretation. The supreme state, *redemption* itself,
total hypnotization and repose at last achieved, is always accounted the mystery as such for whose expression even the supreme symbols are inadequate, as entry and return into the ground
of things, as liberation from all illusion, as "knowledge," as "truth,"
as "being," as release from all purpose, all desire, all action, as a
state beyond even good and evil. "Good and evil," says the Buddhist—"both are fetters: the Perfect One became master over
both"; "what is done and what is not done," says the believer of the
Vedanta, "give him no pain; as a sage, he shakes good and evil
from himself; no deed can harm his kingdom; he has gone beyond
both good and evil": this idea is common to all of India, Hindu
and Buddhist. (Neither in the Indian nor in the Christian conception is this "redemption" *attainable* through virtue, through moral
improvement, however highly they may esteem the value of virtue

---

[5] Nietzsche uses the English word; also "training" later in the same sentence
and in some later passages.
[6] A sect of mystics that originated among the monks on Mount Athos in the
fourteenth century.

as a means of hypnotization: one should remember this—here they are true to the facts. To have remained *true* in this may perhaps be regarded as the finest piece of realism in the three great religions, which are in other respects so steeped in moralization. "For the man of knowledge there are no duties."

"Redemption cannot be attained through an *increase* in virtue; for redemption consists in being one with Brahma, in whom no increase in perfection is possible; nor through a *decrease* in faults:. for Brahma, with whom to be one constitutes redemption, is eternally pure." These are passages from the commentary of Shankara, quoted by the first European *expert* in Indian philosophy, my friend Paul Deussen.[7]) Let us therefore honor "redemption" as it appears in the great religions. But it is not easy for us to take seriously the high valuation placed on *deep sleep* by these people, so weary of life that they are too weary even to dream—deep sleep, that is, as an entry into Brahma, as an *achieved unio mystica* with God.

"When he is completely asleep"—it says in the oldest and most venerable "scripture"—"and perfectly at rest, so that he no longer dreams, then, dearly beloved, he is united with What Is, he has entered into himself—embraced by the cognitive self, he is no longer conscious of what is without or within. Over this bridge come neither day nor night, nor death, nor suffering, nor good works, nor evil works."

"In deep sleep," say the faithful of this deepest of the three great religions, "the soul rises out of the body, enters into the supreme light and thus steps forth in its real form: there it is the supreme spirit itself that walks about, joking and playing and amusing itself, whether with women or with carriages or with friends; there it thinks no more of this appendage of a body to which the *prana* (the breath of life) is harnessed like a beast to a cart."

Nonetheless, we must bear in mind here, as in the case of

---

[7] Paul Deussen (1845–1919) translated sixty Upanishads into German, wrote pioneering works on the Vedanta and on Indian philosophy generally, as well as a multi-volume history of philosophy—and *Erinnerungen an Friedrich Nietzsche* (Leipzig, Brockhaus, 1901: "Reminiscences of Friedrich Nietzsche").

"redemption," that, although it is arrayed in Oriental exaggeration, what is expressed is merely the same appraisal as that of the clear, cool, Hellenically cool, but suffering Epicurus: the hypnotic sense of nothingness, the repose of deepest sleep, in short *absence of suffering*—sufferers and those profoundly depressed will count this as the supreme good, as the value of values; they are *bound* to accord it a positive value, to experience it as *the* positive as such. (According to the same logic of feeling, all pessimistic religions call nothingness *God*.)

18

Much more common than this hypnotic muting of all sensitivity, of the capacity to feel pain—which presupposes rare energy and above all courage, contempt for opinion, "intellectual stoicism"—is a different *training* against states of depression which is at any rate easier: *mechanical activity*. It is beyond doubt that this regimen alleviates an existence of suffering to a not inconsiderable degree: this fact is today called, somewhat dishonestly, "the blessings of work." The alleviation consists in this, that the interest of the sufferer is directed entirely away from his suffering—that activity, and nothing but activity, enters consciousness, and there is consequently little room left in it for suffering: for the chamber of human consciousness is *small!*

Mechanical activity and what goes with it—such as absolute regularity, punctilious and unthinking obedience, a mode of life fixed once and for all, fully occupied time, a certain permission, indeed training for "impersonality," for self-forgetfulness, for *"incuria sui"* [1]—: how thoroughly, how subtly the ascetic priest has known how to employ them in the struggle against pain! When he was dealing with sufferers of the lower classes, with work-slaves or prisoners (or with women—who are mostly both at once, work-slaves and prisoners), he required hardly more than a little ingenuity in name-changing and rebaptizing to make them see benefits and a relative happiness in things they formerly hated: the slave's

---

[1] Lack of care of self.

discontent with his lot was at any rate *not* invented by the priest.

An even more highly valued means of combating depression is the prescribing of a *petty pleasure* that is easily attainable and can be made into a regular event; this medication is often employed in association with the previous one. The most common form in which pleasure is thus prescribed as a curative is that of the pleasure of *giving* pleasure (doing good, giving, relieving, helping, encouraging, consoling, praising, rewarding); by prescribing "love of the neighbor," the ascetic priest prescribes fundamentally an excitement of the strongest, most life-affirming drive, even if in the most cautious doses— namely, of the *will to power*. The happiness of "slight superiority," involved in all doing good, being useful, helping, and rewarding, is the most effective means of consolation for the physiologically inhibited, and widely employed by them when they are well advised: otherwise they hurt one another, obedient, of course, to the same basic instinct.

When one looks for the beginnings of Christianity in the Roman world, one finds associations for mutual aid, associations for the poor, for the sick, for burial, evolved among the lowest strata of society, in which this major remedy for depression, petty pleasure produced by mutual helpfulness, was consciously employed: perhaps this was something new in those days, a real discovery? The "will to mutual aid," to the formation of a herd, to "community," to "congregation," called up in this way is bound to lead to fresh and far more fundamental outbursts of that will to power which it has, even if only to a small extent, aroused: the *formation of a herd* is a significant victory and advance in the struggle against depression. With the growth of the community, a new interest grows for the individual, too, and often lifts him above the most personal element in his discontent, his aversion to *himself* (Geulincx's *"despectio sui"*).[2] All the sick and sickly instinctively strive after a herd organization as a means of shaking off their dull displeasure and feeling of weakness: the ascetic priest divines this instinct and furthers it; wherever there are herds, it is the instinct of weakness that has willed the herd and the prudence of the priest

---

[2] Self-contempt. Arnold Geulincx (1624–1669) was a Belgian philosopher.

that has organized it. For one should not overlook this fact: the
strong are as naturally inclined to *separate* as the weak are to *con-
gregate;* if the former unite together, it is only with the aim of an
aggressive collective action and collective satisfaction of their will
to power, and with much resistance from the individual conscience;
the latter, on the contrary, *enjoy* precisely this coming together—
their instinct is just as much satisfied by this as the instinct of the
born "masters" (that is, the solitary, beast-of-prey species of man)
is fundamentally irritated and disquieted by organization. The
whole of history teaches that every oligarchy conceals the lust for
tyranny; every oligarchy constantly trembles with the tension each
member feels in maintaining control over this lust. (So it was in
Greece, for insance: Plato bears witness to it in a hundred passages—and he knew his own kind—*and* himself . . .)

19

The means employed by the ascetic priest that we have discovered up to now—the general muting of the feeling of life, mechanical activity, the petty pleasure, above all "love of one's neighbor," herd organization, the awakening of the communal feeling of
power through which the individual's discontent with himself is
drowned in his pleasure in the prosperity of the community—these
are, by modern standards, his *innocent* means in the struggle with
displeasure; let us now turn to the more interesting means, the
"guilty" ones. They all involve one thing: some kind of an *orgy of
feeling*—employed as the most effective means of deadening dull,
paralyzing, protracted pain; hence priestly inventiveness in thinking through this single question—*"how* can one produce an orgy of
feeling?"—has been virtually inexhaustible.

This sounds harsh; obviously it would sound more pleasant
and be more ingratiating if I said: "the ascetic priest has at all
times made use of the *enthusiasm* that lies in all strong affects."
But why stroke the effeminate ears of our modern weaklings? Why
should *we* give way even one step to their tartuffery of words? For
us psychologists this would constitute a tartuffery in *deed,* quite
apart from the fact that it would nauseate us. For if a psychologist

today has *good taste* (others might say, integrity) it consists in resistance to the shamefully *moralized* way of speaking which has gradually made all modern judgments of men and things slimy.[1] One should not deceive oneself in this matter: the most distinctive feature of modern souls and modern books is not lying but their inveterate *innocence* in moralistic mendaciousness. To have to rediscover this "innocence" everywhere—this constitutes perhaps the most disgusting job among all the precarious tasks a psychologist has to tackle today; it is a part of *our* great danger—it is a path that may lead precisely *us* toward great nausea.

I have no doubt for *what* sole *purpose* modern books (if they last, which we fortunately have little reason to fear, and if there will one day be a posterity with a more severe, harder, *healthier* taste)—for what purpose *everything* modern will serve this posterity: as an emetic—and that on account of its moral mawkishness and falseness, its innermost feminism that likes to call itself "idealism" and at any rate believes it is idealism. Our educated people of today, our "good people," do not tell lies—that is true; but that is *not* to their credit! A real lie, a genuine, resolute, "honest" lie (on whose value one should consult Plato) would be something far too severe and potent for them: it would demand of them what one *may* not demand of them, that they should open their eyes to themselves, that they should know how to distinguish "true" and "false" in themselves. All they are capable of is a *dishonest* lie; whoever today accounts himself a "good man" is utterly incapable of confronting any matter except with *dishonest mendaciousness*—a mendaciousness that is abysmal but innocent, truehearted, blue-

---

[1] Here as much as anywhere Freud is Nietzsche's great heir who did more than anyone else to change the style of the twentieth century. Freud's insistence on using the term "sexual" rather than "erotic" is a case in point; so is his stubborn insistence on the crucial importance of sexual factors. This was indeed influenced by the time and place in which he lived, as his critics have long claimed—but not in the sense intended by them: rather, he fought against the slimy idealism of the age. And he was quick to suspect, not without reason, that erstwhile followers who developed more ingratiating variations on his theories were guilty of "tartuffery in *deed*" and not merely in words. He seems to have felt—and this is at any rate one of Nietzsche's central motifs—that a cleansing of the atmosphere and a radical change in tone were indispensable presuppositions of major scientific advances in psychology.

eyed, and virtuous. These "good men"—they are one and all moralized to the very depths and ruined and botched to all eternity as
far as honesty is concerned: who among them could endure a
single *truth* "about man"? Or, put more palpably: who among
them could stand a *true* biography?

A couple of pointers: Lord Byron wrote a number of very
personal things about himself, but Thomas Moore was "too good"
for them: he burned his friend's papers.[2] Dr. Gwinner, Schopenhauer's executor, is said to have done the same:[3] for Schopenhauer, too, had written a few things about himself and perhaps
against himself (*eis heauton*[4]). The solid American, Thayer, Beethoven's biographer, suddenly called a halt to his work: at some
point or other in this venerable and naïve life he could no longer
take it.[5]

Moral: what prudent man would write a single honest word
about himself today?—he would have to be a member of the Order
of Holy Foolhardiness to do so. We are promised an autobiography
of Richard Wagner: who doubts that it will be a *prudent* autobiography?

Let us finally mention that ludicrous horror aroused in Germany by the Catholic priest Janssen with his incomparably artless
and innocuous picture of the Reformation movement. What would
happen if someone were to describe this movement *differently,* if a
real psychologist were to describe a real Luther, not with the
moralistic simplicity of a country parson, not with the sickly and
discreet bashfulness of a Protestant historian, but, say, with the

---

[2] Thomas Moore (1779–1852) was an Irish poet. A brief account of the episode mentioned here may be found in the article on Moore in the Encyclopaedia Britannica, 11th ed.

[3] Wilhelm von Gwinner (1825–1917) was a German jurist and civil servant
(Stadtgerichtsrat in Frankfurt a. M., and later Konsistorialpräsident). As
Schopenhauer's executor, he did indeed destroy his autobiographical papers
—and then published three biographical studies of Schopenhauer: *Arthur
Schopenhauer aus persönlichem Umgang dargestellt* (1862: "A. S. as seen at
first hand"), *Schopenhauer und seine Freunde* (1863: "S. and his friends"),
and *Schopenhauers Leben* (1878: "S.'s life").

[4] About, or against, himself.

[5] The most scholarly edition of the *Life of Beethoven* by Alexander Wheelock
Thayer (1817–1897) is that revised and edited by Elliot Forbes (2 volumes,
Princeton, N.J., Princeton University Press, 1964).

intrepidity of a Taine, out of *strength of soul* and not out of a prudent indulgence toward strength? [6] (The Germans, incidentally, have finally produced a beautiful example of the classical type of the latter—they may well claim him as one of their own and be proud of him: Leopold Ranke,[7] that born classical *advocatus* of every *causa fortior*,[8] that most prudent of all prudent "realists.")

20

But my point will have been taken—there is reason enough, is there not, for us psychologists nowadays to be unable to shake off a certain mistrust *of ourselves*.

Probably, we, too, are still "too good" for our job; probably, we, too, are still victims of and prey to this moralized contemporary taste and ill with it, however much we think we despise it—probably it infects even *us*. What was the warning that diplomat gave his colleagues? "Let us above all mistrust our first impulses, gentlemen!" he said; *"they are almost always good."*— Thus should every psychologist, too, address his colleagues today.

And with that we return to our problem, which in fact demands a certain severity of us, especially a certain mistrust of "first impulses." *The ascetic ideal employed to produce orgies of feeling* —whoever recalls the preceding essay will anticipate from these nine words the essence of what is now to be shown. To wrench the human soul from its moorings, to immerse it in terrors, ice, flames, and raptures to such an extent that it is liberated from all petty displeasure, gloom, and depression as by a flash of lightning: what paths lead to *this* goal? And which of them do so most surely?

Fundamentally, every great affect has this power, provided it explodes suddenly: anger, fear, voluptuousness, revenge, hope, triumph, despair, cruelty; and the ascetic priest has indeed pressed into his service indiscriminately the *whole* pack of savage hounds in man and let loose now this one and now that, always with the

---

[6] Again, it was Freud who did more than anyone else to change the tone and standards of biography—including discussions of Luther.

[7] Perhaps the most renowned German historian of his time (1795–1886).

[8] Stronger cause.

same end in view: to awaken men from their slow melancholy, to
hunt away, if only for a time, their dull pain and lingering misery,
and always under cover of a religious interpretation and "justification." Every such orgy of feeling has to be *paid* for afterward, that
goes without saying—it makes the sick sicker; and that is why this
kind of cure for pain is, by modern standards, "guilty." Yet, to be
fair, one must insist all the more that it was employed *with a good
conscience,* that the ascetic priest prescribed it in the profoundest
faith in its utility, indeed indispensability—and even that he was
often almost shattered by the misery he had caused; one must also
add that the violent physiological revenge taken by such excesses,
including even mental disturbances, does not really confute the
sense of this kind of medication, which, as has been shown above,
does *not* aim at curing the sickness but at combating the depression
by relieving and deadening its displeasure. This is one way of attaining that end.

The chief trick the ascetic priest permitted himself for making
the human soul resound with heart-rending, ecstatic music of all
kinds was, as everyone knows, the exploitation of the *sense of guilt.*
Its origin has been briefly suggested in the preceding essay—as a
piece of animal psychology, no more: there we encountered the
sense of guilt in its raw state, so to speak. It was only in the hands
of the priest, that artist in guilt feelings, that it achieved form—oh,
what a form! "Sin"—for this is the priestly name for the animal's
"bad conscience" (cruelty directed backward)—has been the
greatest event so far in the history of the sick soul: we possess in it
the most dangerous and fateful artifice of religious interpretation.
Man, suffering from himself in some way or other but in any case
physiologically like an animal shut up in a cage, uncertain why or
wherefore, thirsting for reasons—reasons relieve—thirsting, too,
for remedies and narcotics, at last takes counsel with one who
knows hidden things, too—and behold! he receives a hint, he receives from his sorcerer, the ascetic priest, the *first* hint as to the
"cause" of his suffering: he must seek it in *himself,* in some *guilt,* in
a piece of the past, he must understand his suffering as a *punishment.*

He has heard, he has understood, this unfortunate: from now

on he is like a hen imprisoned by a chalk line. He can no longer get out of this chalk circle: the invalid has been transformed into "the sinner."

For two millennia now we have been condemned to the sight of this new type of invalid, "the sinner"—shall it always be so?—everywhere one looks there is the hypnotic gaze of the sinner, always fixed on the same object (on "guilt" as the *sole* cause of suffering); everywhere the bad conscience, that "abominable beast," as Luther called it; everywhere the past regurgitated, the fact distorted, the "jaundiced eye" for all action; everywhere the *will* to misunderstand suffering made the content of life, the reinterpretation of suffering as feelings of guilt, fear, and punishment; everywhere the scourge, the hair shirt, the starving body, contrition; everywhere the sinner breaking himself on the cruel wheel of a restless, morbidly lascivious conscience; everywhere dumb torment, extreme fear, the agony of the tortured heart, convulsions of an unknown happiness, the cry for "redemption." The old depression, heaviness, and weariness were indeed *overcome* through this system of procedures; life again became *very* interesting: awake, everlastingly awake, sleepless, glowing, charred, spent and yet not weary—thus was the man, "the sinner," initiated into *this* mystery. This ancient mighty sorcerer in his struggle with displeasure, the ascetic priest—he had obviously won, *his* kingdom had come: one no longer protested *against* pain, one *thirsted* for pain; *"more* pain! *more* pain!" the desire of his disciples and initiates has cried for centuries. Every painful orgy of feeling, everything that shattered, bowled over, crushed, enraptured, transported; the secrets of the torture chamber, the inventiveness of hell itself—all were henceforth discovered, divined, and exploited, all stood in the service of the sorcerer, all served henceforward to promote the victory of his ideal, the ascetic ideal.— "My kingdom is not of *this* world"—he continued to say, as before: but did he still have the right to say it?

Goethe claimed there were only thirty-six tragic situations: one could guess from that, if one did not know it anyway, that Goethe was no ascetic priest. He—knows more.—

21

It would be pointless to indulge in criticism of *this* kind of priestly medication, the "guilty" kind. Who would want to maintain that such orgies of feeling as the ascetic priest prescribed for his sick people (under the holiest names, as goes without saying, and convinced of the holiness of his ends) ever *benefited* any of them? At least we should be clear on the meaning of the word "benefit." If one intends it to convey that such a system of treatment has *improved* men, I shall not argue: only I should have to add what "improved" signifies to me—the same thing as "tamed," "weakened," "discouraged," "made refined," "made effete," "emasculated" (thus almost the same thing as *harmed*.) But when such a system is chiefly applied to the sick, distressed, and depressed, it invariably makes them *sicker,* even if it does "improve" them; one need only ask psychiatrists[1] what happens to patients who are methodically subjected to the torments of repentance, states of contrition, and fits of redemption. One should also consult history: wherever the ascetic priest has prevailed with this treatment, sickness has spread in depth and breadth with astonishing speed. What has always constituted its "success"? A shattered nervous system added to any existing illness—and this on the largest as on the smallest scale, in individuals as in masses.

In the wake of repentance and redemption *training* we find tremendous epileptic epidemics, the greatest known to history, such as the St. Vitus' and St. John's dances of the Middle Ages; as another aftereffect we encounter terrible paralyses and protracted states of depression, which sometimes transform the temperament of a people or a city (Geneva, Basel) once and for all into its opposite; here we may also include the witch-hunt hysteria, something related to somnambulism (there were eight great epidemic outbreaks of this between 1564 and 1605 alone); we also find in its wake those death-seeking mass deliria whose dreadful cry *"evviva la morte!"* [2] was heard all over Europe, interspersed now

---

[1] *Irrenärzte:* we probably ought to think of physicians working in lunatic asylums, as psychiatrists in the twentieth-century sense did not exist in 1887.

[2] Long live death!

with voluptuous idiosyncrasies, now with rages of destruction; and the same alternation of affects, accompanied by the same intermissions and somersaults, is to be observed even today whenever the ascetic doctrine of sin again achieves a grand success. (The religious neurosis *appears* as a form of evil; there is no doubt about that. What is it? *Quaeritur.*[3]) Broadly speaking, the ascetic ideal and its sublimely moral cult, this most ingenious, unscrupulous, and dangerous systematization of all the means for producing orgies of feeling under the cover of holy intentions, has inscribed itself in a fearful and unforgettable way in the entire history of man—and unfortunately *not only* in his history.

I know of hardly anything else that has had so destructive an effect upon the *health* and racial strength of Europeans as this ideal; one may without any exaggeration call it *the true calamity* in the history of European health. The only thing that can be compared with its influence is the specifically Teutonic influence: I mean the alcoholic poisoning of Europe, which has hitherto gone strictly in step with the political and racial hegemony of the Teutons (wherever they infused their blood they also infused their vice).— Third in line would be syphilis—*magno sed proxima intervallo.*[4]

22

The ascetic priest has ruined psychical health wherever he has come to power; consequently he has also ruined taste *in artibus et litteris*[1]—he is still ruining it. "Consequently?" I hope I shall be granted this "consequently"; at any rate, I don't want to bother to prove it. Just one pointer: it concerns the basic book of Christian literature, its model, its "book in itself." Even in the midst of Graeco-Roman splendor, which was also a splendor of books, in the face of an ancient literary world that had not yet eroded and been ruined, at a time when one could still read some books for whose possession one would nowadays exchange half of some national literatures, the simplicity and vanity of Christian agitators—

[3] That is the question.
[4] After a great interval, though next.
[1] In arts and letters.

they are called Church Fathers—had the temerity to declare: *"we, too, have a classical literature, we have no need of that of the Greeks";* and saying this they pointed proudly to books of legends, letters of apostles, and apologetic tracts, rather as the English "Salvation Army" today employs similar literature in its struggle against Shakespeare and other "pagans."

I do not like the "New Testament," that should be plain; I find it almost disturbing that my taste in regard to this most highly esteemed and overestimated work should be so singular (I have the taste of two millennia *against* me): but there it is! "Here I stand, I cannot do otherwise" [2]— I have the courage of my bad taste. The *Old* Testament—that is something else again: all honor to the Old Testament! I find in it great human beings, a heroic landscape, and something of the very rarest quality in the world, the incomparable naïveté of the *strong heart;* what is more, I find a people. In the New one, on the other hand, I find nothing but petty sectarianism, mere rococo of the soul, mere involutions, nooks, queer things, the air of the conventicle, not to forget an occasional whiff of bucolic mawkishness that belongs to the epoch (*and* to the Roman province) and is not so much Jewish as Hellenistic. Humility and self-importance cheek-by-jowl; a garrulousness of feeling that almost stupefies; impassioned vehemence, not passion; embarrassing gesticulation; it is plain that there is no trace of good breeding. How can one make such a fuss about one's little lapses as these pious little men do! Who gives a damn? Certainly not God. Finally, they even want "the crown of eternal life," these little provincial people; but for what? to what purpose? Presumption can go no further. An "immortal" Peter: who could stand him? Their ambition is laughable: people of *that* sort regurgitating their most private affairs, their stupidities, sorrows, and petty worries, as if the Heart of Being were obliged to concern itself with them; they never grow tired of involving God himself in even the pettiest troubles they have got themselves into. And the appalling taste of this perpetual familiarity with God! This Jewish and not merely Jewish obtrusiveness of pawing and nuzzling God!

---

[2] Luther's famous words at the Diet of Worms.

There are despised little "pagan nations" in eastern Asia from whom these first Christians could have learned something important, some *tact* in reverence; as Christian missionaries witness, these nations do not even utter the name of their god. This seems to me delicate enough; it is certainly too delicate not only for "*first*" Christians: to see the full contrast, one should recall Luther, for instance, that "most eloquent" and presumptuous peasant Germany has ever produced, and the tone he preferred when conversing with God. Luther's attack on the mediating saints of the church (and especially on "the devil's sow, the pope") was, beyond any doubt, fundamentally the attack of a lout who could not stomach the *good etiquette* of the church, that reverential etiquette of the hieratic taste which permits only the more initiated and silent into the holy of holies and closes it to louts. Here of all places the louts were to be kept from raising their voices; but Luther, the peasant, wanted it altogether different: this arrangement was not *German* enough for him: he wanted above all to speak directly, to speak himself, to speak "informally" with his God.— Well, he did it.

It is easy to see that the ascetic ideal has never and nowhere been a school of good taste, even less of good manners—at best it was a school of hieratic manners: that is because its very nature includes something that is the deadly enemy of all good manners— lack of moderation, dislike of moderation; it itself is a *"non plus ultra."* [3]

23

The ascetic ideal has not only ruined health and taste, it has also ruined a third, fourth, fifth, sixth thing as well—I beware of enumerating everything (I'd never finish). It is my purpose here to bring to light, not what this ideal has *done,* but simply what it *means;* what it indicates; what lies hidden behind it, beneath it, in it; of what it is the provisional, indistinct expression, overlaid with question marks and misunderstandings. And it is only in pursuit of

---

[3] Ultimate extreme.

this end that I could not spare my readers a glance at its monstrous and calamitous effects, to prepare them for the ultimate and most terrifying aspect of the question concerning the meaning of this ideal. What is the meaning of the *power* of this ideal, the monstrous nature of its power? Why has it been allowed to flourish to this extent? Why has it not rather been resisted? The ascetic ideal expresses a will: *where* is the opposing will that might express an *opposing ideal*? The ascetic ideal has a *goal*—this goal is so universal that all the other interests of human existence seem, when compared with it, petty and narrow; it interprets epochs, nations, and men inexorably with a view to this one goal; it permits no other interpretation, no other goal; it rejects, denies, affirms, and sanctions solely from the point of view of *its* interpretation (and has there ever been a system of interpretation more thoroughly thought through?); it submits to no power, it believes in its own predominance over every other power, in its absolute *superiority of rank* over every other power—it believes that no power exists on earth that does not first have to receive a meaning, a right to exist, a value, as a tool of the ascetic ideal, as a way and means to *its* goal, to *one* goal.— Where is the match of this closed system of will, goal, and interpretation? Why has it not found its match?— Where is the *other* "*one* goal"?

But they tell me it is *not* lacking, it has not merely waged a long and successful fight against this ideal, it has already conquered this ideal in all important respects: all of modern *science*[1] is supposed to bear witness to that—modern science which, as a genuine philosophy of reality, clearly believes in itself alone, clearly possesses the courage for itself and the will to itself, and has up to now survived well enough without God, the beyond, and the virtues of denial. Such noisy agitators' chatter, however, does not impress me: these trumpeters of reality are bad musicians, their voices obviously do *not* come from the depths, the abyss of the scientific

---

[1] *Wissenschaft* does not refer only, or primarily, to the natural sciences, and when Nietzsche refers to scholars later in this section he is by no means changing the subject. It seems best to call attention to this while using "science" to translate *Wissenschaft*. Cf. Part Six, "We Scholars" (*Wir Gelehrten*, sections 204–13) in *Beyond Good and Evil*.

conscience does *not* speak through them—for today the scientific conscience is an abyss—the word "science" in the mouths of such trumpeters is simply an indecency, an abuse, and a piece of impudence. The truth is precisely the opposite of what is asserted here: science today has absolutely *no* belief in itself, let alone an ideal above it—and where it still inspires passion, love, ardor, and *suffering* at all, it is not the opposite of the ascetic ideal but rather *the latest and noblest form of it*. Does that sound strange to you?

Today there are plenty of modest and worthy laborers[2] among scholars, too, who are happy in their little nooks; and because they are happy there, they sometimes demand rather immodestly that one ought to be content with things today, generally—especially in the domain of science, where so much that is useful remains to be done. I am not denying that; the last thing I want is to destroy the pleasure these honest workers take in their craft: for I approve of their work. But that one works rigorously in the sciences and that there are contented workers certainly does *not* prove that science as a whole possesses a goal, a will, an ideal, or the passion of a great faith. The opposite is the case, to repeat: where it is not the latest expression of the ascetic ideal—and the exceptions are too rare, noble, and atypical to refute the general proposition—science today is a *hiding place* for every kind of discontent, disbelief, gnawing worm, *despectio sui,* bad conscience—it is the unrest of the *lack* of ideals, the suffering from the *lack* of any great love, the discontent in the face of involuntary contentment.

Oh, what does science not conceal today! how much, at any rate, is it *meant* to conceal! The proficiency of our finest scholars, their heedless industry, their heads smoking day and night, their very craftsmanship—how often the real meaning of all this lies in the desire to keep something hidden from oneself! Science as a means of self-narcosis: *do you have experience of that?*

Whoever associates with scholars knows that one occasionally wounds them to the marrow with some harmless word; one incenses one's scholarly friends just when one means to honor them,

---

[2] *Braves und bescheidnes Arbeitervolk:* the following remarks about these laborers (where the English text speaks of "workers" the original again has *Arbeiter*) should be compared with *Beyond Good and Evil,* section 211.

one can drive them beside themselves merely because one has been
too coarse to realize with whom one was really dealing—with
sufferers who refuse to admit to themselves what they are, with
drugged and heedless men who fear only one thing: *regaining consciousness*.—

24

And now look, on the other hand, at those rarer cases of
which I spoke, the last idealists left among philosophers and scholars: are they perhaps the desired *opponents* of the ascetic ideal, the
counteridealists? Indeed, they *believe* they are, these "unbelievers"
(for that is what they are, one and all); they are so serious on this
point, so passionate about it in word and gesture, that the faith[1]
that they are opponents of this ideal seems to be the last remnant of
faith they have left—but does this mean that their faith is *true*?

We "men of knowledge" have gradually come to mistrust believers of all kinds; our mistrust has gradually brought us to make
inferences the reverse of those of former days: wherever the
strength of a faith is very prominently displayed, we infer a certain
weakness of demonstrability, even the *improbability* of what is believed. We, too, do not deny that faith "makes blessed": that is
precisely *why* we deny that faith *proves* anything—a strong faith
that makes blessed raises suspicion against that which is believed;
it does not establish "truth," it establishes a certain probability—of
deception. What is the situation in the present case?

These Nay-sayers and outsiders of today who are unconditional on one point[2]—their insistence on intellectual cleanliness;
these hard, severe, abstinent, heroic spirits who constitute the

---

[1] In German there is a single word for belief and faith, *Glaube*. To believe is
glauben; unbelievers, *Ungläubige*. In the translation, "faith" is called for
rather than belief; for Nietzsche emphasizes the unconditional and religious
character of the faith he discusses.

 The ideas expressed here are developed further in *The Antichrist*, sections 50ff. (*Portable Nietzsche*, pp. 631ff.)

 See also Kaufmann's *Nietzsche*, Chapter 12, section III (about ten pages
on "Faith versus Reason"). Most of the relevant passages, from the *Dawn*
on, are cited there.

[2] This unconditional attitude, this refusal to question one point, is what
seems objectionable to Nietzsche.

honor of our age; all these pale atheists, anti-Christians,[3] immoralists, nihilists; these skeptics, ephectics,[4] *hectics* of the spirit (they are all hectics in some sense or other); these last idealists of knowledge in whom alone the intellectual conscience dwells and is incarnate today[5]—they certainly believe they are as completely liber-

---

[3] *Antichristen* could also mean Antichrists; and when Nietzsche, a year later, entitled one of his last books *Der Antichrist* he plainly meant *The Antichrist*: the content of that book makes that clear, nor can there be any doubt about his wish at that time to be as provocative as possible. In the last sentence of section 5 of the Preface, which Nietzsche had added to the new edition of *The Birth of Tragedy* in 1886, the year before, the grammatical form no less than the meaning makes it clear that "the Antichrist" is meant. The enumeration in the text above raises the question whether the critique Nietzsche offers is not applicable to himself: after all, he had also called himself an immoralist both in *Beyond Good and Evil*, section 32, and in the Preface added to the new edition of *The Dawn* (section 4); and in *Ecce Homo*, the following year, he several times called himself "the first immoralist." Nevertheless, the plural in the text above and the whole "feel" of the passage make "anti-Christians" the more plausible reading. For all that, the points just mentioned color the tone: the men he speaks of are plainly very close to him.

[4] In section 9 above, Nietzsche explained the "ephectic bent": it is the propensity to suspend judgment. The primary denotation of the next word, "hectics," is consumptive.

[5] This, from Nietzsche, is high praise indeed. Cf., e.g., *The Gay Science*, section 2: "*The Intellectual Conscience.*— . . . *By far the most lack an intellectual conscience* . . . I mean: *by far the most* do not find it contemptible to believe this or that and to live according to it, *without* first having become conscious of the last and surest reasons pro and con, and without even taking the trouble to consider such reasons afterward; the most gifted men and the most noble women still belong to these 'by far the most.' Yet what is good-heartedness, refinement, and genius to me, when the human being who has these virtues tolerates slack feelings in his faith and judgments, and when the demand for certainty is not to him the inmost craving and the deepest need—that which distinguishes the higher from the lower men. . . . *Not to question,* not to tremble with the craving and the joy of questioning . . . that is what I feel to be *contemptible* . . ."

Nietzsche never renounced these views. See, e.g., one of his very last works, *The Antichrist* (section 50; *Portable Nietzsche*, p. 632): "At every step one has to wrestle for truth; one has had to surrender for it almost everything to which the heart, to which our love, our trust in life, cling otherwise. That requires greatness of soul: the service of truth is the hardest service. What does it mean, after all, to have *integrity* in matters of the spirit? That one is severe against one's heart, that one despises 'beautiful sentiments,' that one makes of every Yes and No a matter of conscience. Faith makes blessed: consequently it lies."

Nietzsche's objection to those "in whom alone the intellectual conscience dwells and is incarnate today" is that there is "one point" they refuse to question; that there is one "beautiful sentiment" they still permit themselves. As Nietzsche puts it a few lines later: "they still have faith in truth."

ated from the ascetic ideal as possible, these "free, *very* free
spirits"; and yet, to disclose to them what they themselves cannot
see—for they are too close to themselves: this ideal is precisely
their ideal, too; they themselves embody it today and perhaps they
alone; they themselves are its most spiritualized product, its most
advanced front-line troops and scouts, its most captious, tender,
intangible form of seduction—if I have guessed any riddles, I wish
that *this* proposition might show it!— They are far from being *free*
spirits: *for they still have faith in truth.*

When the Christian crusaders in the Orient encountered the
invincible order of Assassins,[6] that order of free spirits *par excellence,* whose lowest ranks followed a rule of obedience the like of
which no order of monks ever attained, they obtained in some way
or other a hint concerning that symbol and watchword reserved for
the highest ranks alone as their *secretum*: "Nothing is true, everything is permitted."— Very well, *that* was *freedom* of spirit; in *that*
way the faith in truth itself was *abrogated.*[7]

Has any European, any Christian free spirit ever strayed into
this proposition and into its labyrinthine consequences? has one of
them ever known the Minotaur of this cave *from experience?*— I
doubt it;[8] more, I know better: nothing is more foreign to these

---

[6] An Islamic sect, founded in the eleventh century. "As for the initiated, they
knew the worthlessness of positive religion and morality; they believed in
nothing . . ." (Encyclopaedia Britannica, 11th ed.)

[7] The striking slogan is plainly neither Nietzsche's coinage nor his motto. It
is a quotation on which he comments, contrasting it with the unquestioning
faith in the truth that characterizes so many so-called free spirits.

[8] The Assassins' slogan is often mistaken for Nietzsche's coinage and derived
from Dostoevsky; e.g., by Danto: it "must surely be a paraphrase of the
Russian novelist he so admired" (*op. cit.,* p. 193).

In Dostoevsky's *Brothers Karamazov* we encounter the idea that, if
mankind lost the belief in God and immortality, "everything would be permitted." But what matters to Nietzsche in this section is the first half of his
quotation, "nothing is true," which has no parallel in Dostoevsky. Moreover,
the quotation from *The Brothers* is not particularly profound: it "works" in
its context in the novel but expresses no great insight, taken by itself.

Incidentally, Nietzsche never read *The Brothers* (originally serialized
in Russia in 1879–80); and this novel was not translated into French until
1888, in a mutilated version. On March 7, 1887, Nietzsche wrote Gast that
he had read, first, *L'Esprit souterrain* (translated, 1886: *Notes from Underground*); then *La maison des morts* (tr., 1886: *The House of the Dead*);
finally, *Humiliés et offensés* (tr., 1884: *The Injured and the Insulted*—the

men who are unconditional about *one* thing, these *so-called* "free spirits," than freedom and liberation in this sense; in no respect are they more rigidly bound;[9] it is precisely in their faith in truth that they are more rigid and unconditional than anyone. I know all this from too close up perhaps:[10] that venerable philosopher's abstinence to which such a faith commits one; that intellectual stoicism which ultimately refuses not only to affirm but also to deny; that *desire* to halt before the factual, the *factum brutum;* that fatalism of *"petits faits"* (*ce petit faitalisme,*[11] as I call it) through which French scholarship nowadays tries to establish a sort of moral superiority over German scholarship; that general renunciation of all interpretation (of forcing, adjusting, abbreviating, omitting, padding, inventing, falsifying, and whatever else is of the *essence* of interpreting)—all this expresses, broadly speaking, as much ascetic virtue as any denial of sensuality (it is at bottom only a particular mode of this denial). That which *constrains* these men, however, this unconditional will to truth, is *faith in the ascetic ideal itself*, even if as an unconscious imperative—don't be deceived about that —it is the faith in a *metaphysical* value, the absolute value of *truth*, sanctioned and guaranteed by this ideal alone (it stands or falls with this ideal).

Strictly speaking, there is no such thing as science "without any presuppositions"; this thought does not bear thinking through,

first of Dostoevsky's novels to be translated into French). On October 14, 1888, Nietzsche wrote Gast: "The French have produced a stage version of Dostoevsky's main novel." This was *Le Crime et le châtiment* (tr., 1884: *Crime and Punishment*). Cf. F. W. J. Hemmings, *The Russian Novel in France, 1884–1914* (New York, Oxford University Press, 1950), especially p. 241. See also the note on section 15 above.

Finally, see section 602 of *The Will to Power,* probably written in 1884: ". . . 'Everything is false! Everything is permitted!' . . ."

[9] Nietzsche returns to his objection.

[10] Is Nietzsche here referring to himself? Without ruling out the possibility that he also had some first-hand experience of the attitude he goes on to describe—at least as a possibility—I find the portrait very different from him. On the other hand, "that intellectual stoicism which ultimately refuses not only to affirm but also to deny"—and not only this trait—seems as close to Nietzsche's best friend, Franz Overbeck (professor of church history at Basel, and an unbeliever), as it seems remote from Nietzsche's own spirit.

[11] The pun is less felicitous in English: small facts (the small factalism, as I call it).

it is paralogical: a philosophy, a "faith," must always be there first of all, so that science can acquire from it a direction, a meaning, a limit, a method, a *right* to exist. (Whoever has the opposite notion, whoever tries, for example, to place philosophy "on a strictly scientific basis," first needs to stand not only philosophy but truth itself *on its head*—the grossest violation of decency possible in relation to two such venerable females!) There is no doubt of it—and here I cite the fifth book of my *Gay Science* (section 344[12]):

"The truthful man, in the audacious and ultimate sense presupposed by the faith in science, *thereby affirms another world* than that of life, nature, and history; and insofar as he affirms this 'other world,' does this not mean that he has to deny its antithesis, this world, *our* world? . . . It is still a *metaphysical faith* that underlies our faith in science—and we men of knowledge of today, we godless men and anti-metaphysicians, we, too, still derive *our* flame from the fire ignited by a faith millennia old, the Christian faith, which was also Plato's, that God is truth, that truth is *divine*.—But what if this belief is becoming more and more unbelievable, if nothing turns out to be divine any longer unless it be error, blindness, lies—if God himself turns out to be our *longest lie?"*

At this point it is necessary to pause and take careful stock. Science itself henceforth *requires* justification (which is not to say that there is any such justification).[13] Consider on this question both the earliest and most recent philosophers: they are all oblivious of how much the will to truth itself first requires justification; here there is a lacuna in every philosophy—how did this come about? Because the ascetic ideal has hitherto *dominated* all philosophy, because truth was posited as being, as God, as the highest court of appeal—because truth was not *permitted* to be a problem

---

[12] In the following quotation, the three dots mark Nietzsche's omission of a few words (about one line) from the text he quotes. Most of section 344 will be found in the *Portable Nietzsche,* pp. 448–50. See also Kaufmann's *Nietzsche,* Chapter 12, section III.

[13] Neither is it to say that no justification is possible. The point is that the problem has to be considered in all seriousness. Even as it is naïve to suppose that we *know* what is good and what is evil—and it is Nietzsche's intent to show us how problematic morality is—it is also naïve to overlook that the justification of science poses a problem.

at all. Is this "permitted" understood?— From the moment faith in the God of the ascetic ideal is denied, a *new problem arises:* that of the *value* of truth.

The will to truth requires a critique—let us thus define our own task—the value of truth must for once be experimentally *called into question.*[14]

(Whoever feels that this has been stated too briefly should read the section of the *Gay Science* entitled "To What Extent We, Too, Are Still Pious" (section 344), or preferably the entire fifth book of that work, as well as the Preface to *The Dawn.*)

25

No! Don't come to me with science when I ask for the natural antagonist of the ascetic ideal, when I demand: "where is the opposing will expressing the *opposing ideal?*" Science is not nearly self-reliant enough to be that; it first requires in every respect an ideal of value, a value-creating power, in the *service* of which it could *believe* in itself—it never creates values. Its relation to the ascetic ideal is by no means essentially antagonistic; it might even be said to represent the driving force in the latter's inner development. It opposes and fights, on closer inspection, not the ideal itself but only its exteriors, its guise and masquerade, its temporary dogmatic hardening and stiffening, and by denying what is exoteric in this ideal, it liberates what life is in it. This pair, science and the ascetic ideal, both rest on the same foundation—I have already indicated it: on the same overestimation of truth (more exactly: on the same belief that truth is inestimable and cannot be criticized). Therefore they are *necessarily* allies, so that if they are to be fought they can only be fought and called in question together. A depreciation of the ascetic ideal unavoidably involves a depreciation of science: one must keep one's eyes and ears open to this fact!

(*Art*—to say it in advance, for I shall some day return to this subject at greater length—art, in which precisely the *lie* is sanctified and the *will to deception* has a good conscience, is much more

---

[14] This is the conclusion to which Nietzsche has been working up.

fundamentally opposed to the ascetic ideal than is science: this was instinctively sensed by Plato, the greatest enemy of art Europe has yet produced. Plato versus Homer: that is the complete, the genuine antagonism—there the sincerest advocate of the "beyond," the great slanderer of life; here the instinctive deifier, the *golden* nature.[1] To place himself in the service of the ascetic ideal is therefore the most distinctive *corruption* of an artist that is at all possible; unhappily, also one of the most common forms of corruption, for nothing is more easily corrupted than an artist.)

Physiologically, too, science rests on the same foundation as the ascetic ideal: a certain *impoverishment of life* is a presupposition of both of them—the affects grown cool, the tempo of life slowed down, dialectics in place of instinct, seriousness imprinted on faces and gestures (seriousness, the most unmistakable sign of a labored metabolism, of struggling, laborious life). Observe the ages in the history of people when the scholar steps into the foreground: they are ages of exhaustion, often of evening and decline; overflowing energy, certainty of life and of the *future,* are things of the past. A predominance of mandarins always means something is wrong; so do the advent of democracy, international courts in place of war, equal rights for women, the religion of pity, and whatever other symptoms of declining life there are. (Science posed as a problem; what is the meaning of science?—cf. the Preface[2] to *The Birth of Tragedy.*)

---

[1] We return to a problem posed in Nietzsche's first book, *The Birth of Tragedy:* the relation of art and science. There it was the contrast of tragedy and Socratism that served as a point of departure; here "Plato versus Homer" sums up the problem. Nietzsche still finds Socratism and the unquestioned faith in a life devoted to scientific inquiry problematic. But he is as far as ever from contempt for the life of inquiry: after all, was not this the life he himself chose, clinging to it in spite of his doctors' advice to read and write less?

Here we should recall the symbol of the "artistic Socrates" that Nietzsche introduced near the end of section 14 of *The Birth.* He clearly does not cast his lot with either Plato or Homer. He is a philosopher *and* a poet—in his *concerns* much more a philosopher, but in his loving transfiguration of the language closer to the poets—and he does not denigrate this world in favor of another. He wants to celebrate this world, though, like Homer, he is anything but blind to its suffering. And not only *The Birth of Tragedy* is relevant to Nietzsche's theme here; *The Gay Science* is, too; e.g., section 327, which will be found in this volume.

[2] Added in 1886 to the new edition.

No! this "modern science"—let us face this fact!—is the *best* ally the ascetic ideal has at present, and precisely because it is the most unconscious, involuntary, hidden, and subterranean ally! They have played the same game up to now, the "poor in spirit" and the scientific opponents of this ideal (one should not think, by the way, that they are their opposites, the *rich* in spirit perhaps— they are *not;* I have called them the hectics[3] of the spirit). As for the famous *victories* of the latter, they undoubtedly are victories— but over what? The ascetic ideal has decidedly not been conquered: if anything, it became stronger, which is to say, more elusive, more spiritual, more captious, as science remorselessly detached and broke off wall upon wall, external additions that had coarsened its appearance. Does anyone really believe that the defeat of theological astronomy represented a defeat for that ideal?

Has man perhaps become *less desirous* of a transcendent solution to the riddle of his existence, now that this existence appears more arbitrary, beggarly, and dispensable in the *visible* order of things? Has the self-belittlement of man, his *will* to self-belittlement, not progressed irresistibly since Copernicus? Alas, the faith in the dignity and uniqueness of man, in his irreplaceability in the great chain of being,[4] is a thing of the past—he has become an *animal,* literally and without reservation or qualification, he who was, according to his old faith, almost God ("child of God," "God-man").

Since Copernicus, man seems to have got himself on an inclined plane—now he is slipping faster and faster away from the center into—what? into nothingness? into a *"penetrating sense of his nothingness"?* [5] Very well! hasn't this been the straightest route to—the *old* ideal?

All science (and by no means only astronomy, on the humiliating and degrading effect of which Kant made the noteworthy confession: "it destroys my importance" . . .), all science, natural as well as *unnatural*—which is what I call the self-critique of knowledge—has at present the object of dissuading man from his

---

[3] Section 24 above.

[4] *Rangabfolge der Wesen.*

[5] Here Nietzsche makes use of material included in section 1 of the posthumous edition of *The Will to Power.*

former respect for himself, as if this had been nothing but a piece of bizarre conceit. One might even say that its own pride, its own austere form of stoical ataraxy, consists in sustaining this hard-won *self-contempt* of man as his ultimate and most serious claim to self-respect (and quite rightly, indeed: for he that despises is always one who "has not forgotten how to respect" . . .) Is this really to *work against* the ascetic ideal? Does one still seriously believe (as theologians imagined for a while) that Kant's *victory* over the dogmatic concepts of theology ("God," "soul," "freedom," "immortality") damaged that ideal?—it being no concern of ours for the present whether Kant ever had any intention of doing such a thing. What is certain is that, since Kant, transcendentalists of every kind have once more won the day—they have been emancipated from the theologians: what joy!— Kant showed them a secret path by which they may, on their own initiative and with all scientific respectability, from now on follow their "heart's desire."

In the same vein: who could hold it against the agnostics if, as votaries of the unknown and mysterious as such, they now worship the *question mark itself* as God? (Xaver Doudan[6] once spoke of the *ravages* worked by *"l'habitude d'admirer l'inintelligible au lieu de rester tout simplement dans l'inconnu";*[7] he thought the ancients had avoided this.) Presuming that everything man "knows" does not merely fail to satisfy his desires but rather contradicts them and produces a sense of horror, what a divine way out to have the right to seek the responsibility for this not in "desire" but in "knowledge"!

"There is no knowledge: *consequently*—there is a God": what a new *elegantia syllogismi!* [8] what a *triumph* for the ascetic ideal!—

---

[6] Ximénès Doudan (1800–1872), a French critic, contributed to the *Journal des Débats* and was the author of the posthumously published *Mélanges et lettres* (1876–77; Mixed writings and letters), *Lettres* (1879; Letters), and *Pensées et fragments, suivis des révolutions du goût* (1881; Thoughts and fragments, and the revolutions of taste).

[7] The habit of admiring the unintelligible instead of staying quite simply in the unknown.

[8] Elegance of the syllogism.

26

Or does modern historiography perhaps display an attitude more assured of life and ideals? Its noblest claim nowadays is that it is a mirror; it rejects all teleology; it no longer wishes to "prove" anything; it disdains to play the judge and considers this a sign of good taste—it affirms as little as it denies; it ascertains, it "describes" . . . All this is to a high degree ascetic; but at the same time it is to an even higher degree *nihilistic*, let us not deceive ourselves about that! One observes a sad, stern, but resolute glance —an eye that looks far, the way a lonely Arctic explorer looks far (so as not to look within, perhaps? so as not to look back? . . .) Here is snow; here life has grown silent; the last crows whose cries are audible here are called "wherefore?," "in vain!," *"nada!"*— here nothing will grow or prosper any longer, or at the most Petersburg metapolitics and Tolstoian "pity."

As for that other type of historian, an even more "modern" type perhaps, a hedonist and voluptuary who flirts both with life and with the ascetic ideal, who employs the word "artist" as a glove and has today taken sole lease of the praise of contemplation: oh how these sweetish and clever fellows make one long even for ascetics and winter landscapes! No! the devil take this type of "contemplative"! I would even prefer to wander through the gloomy, gray, cold fog with those historical nihilists! Indeed, if I *had* to choose I might even opt for some completely unhistorical, antihistorical person (such as Dühring, whose voice today intoxicates in Germany a hitherto shy and unavowed species of "beautiful soul," the *species anarchistica* within the educated proletariat).

The "contemplatives" are a hundred times worse: I know of nothing that excites such disgust as this kind of "objective" armchair scholar, this kind of scented voluptuary of history, half parson, half satyr, perfume by Renan,[1] who betrays immediately with

---

[1] Ernest Renan (1823–1892), a prolific French scholar and writer, is remembered chiefly for his immensely successful *Life of Jesus*, published in June 1863. Before November 1863, 60,000 copies were in circulation. This was his first volume on the *Origins of Christianity*, followed shortly by

the high falsetto of his applause what he lacks, *where* he lacks it, *where* in this case the Fates have applied their cruel shears with, alas, such surgical skill! This offends my taste; also my patience: let him have patience with such sights who has nothing to lose by them—such a sight arouses my ire, such "spectators" dispose me against the "spectacle" more than the spectacle itself (the spectacle of history, you understand); I fall unawares into an Anacreontic mood. Nature, which gave the bull his horns and the lion his *chasm' odontōn*,[2] why did nature give me my foot? . . . To kick, Holy Anacreon! and not only for running away; for kicking to pieces these rotten armchairs, this cowardly contemplativeness, this lascivious historical eunuchism, this flirting with ascetic ideals, this justice-tartuffery of impotence!

All honor to the ascetic ideal *insofar as it is honest!* so long as it believes in itself and does not play tricks on us! But I do not like all these coquettish bedbugs with their insatiable ambition to smell out the infinite, until at last the infinite smells of bedbugs; I do not like these whited sepulchers who impersonate life; I do not like these weary and played-out people who wrap themselves in wisdom and look "objective"; I do not like these agitators dressed up as heroes who wear the magic cap of ideals on their straw heads; I do not like these ambitious artists who like to pose as ascetics and priests but who are at bottom only tragic buffoons; and I also do not like these latest speculators in idealism, the anti-Semites, who today roll their eyes in a Christian-Aryan-bourgeois manner and exhaust one's patience by trying to rouse up all the horned-beast elements in the people by a brazen abuse of the cheapest of all agitator's tricks, moral attitudinizing (that *no* kind of swindle fails to succeed in

---

The Apostles (1866) and St. Paul (1869). In 1876 the fourth volume appeared, Renan's Antichrist, which dealt with the reign of Nero; and by 1881 two more volumes came out, The Christian Church and Marcus Aurelius. Renan published many other works as well.

Nietzsche's references to him are uniformly hostile: see Beyond Good and Evil, section 48; Twilight, "Skirmishes," sections 2 and 6 (Portable Nietzsche, pp. 513f. and 516); and Antichrist, sections 17, 29, 31, and 32 (ibid., pp. 584, 600, and 604).

[2] "Nature gave horns to the bull . . . to the lion a chasm of teeth" is what Anacreon, the Greek lyrical poet who flourished in 540 B.C., wrote in one of his odes (number 24).

Germany today is connected with the undeniable and palpable stagnation of the German spirit; and the cause of that I seek in a too exclusive diet of newspapers, politics, beer, and Wagnerian music, together with the presuppositions of such a diet: first, national constriction and vanity, the strong but narrow principle *"Deutschland, Deutschland über alles,"* and then the *paralysis agitans*[3] of "modern ideas").

Europe is rich and inventive today above all in means of excitation; it seems to need nothing as much as it needs stimulants and brandy: hence also the tremendous amount of forgery in ideals, this most potent brandy of the spirit; hence also the repulsive, ill-smelling, mendacious, pseudo-alcoholic air everywhere. I should like to know how many shiploads of sham idealism, heroic trappings and grand-word-rattles, how many tons of sugared sympathy-spirits (distillers: *la religion de la souffrance*[4]), how many "noble-indignation" stilts for the aid of the spiritually flatfooted, how many *comedians* of the Christian-moral ideal would have to be exported from Europe today before its air would begin to smell fresh again.

With this overproduction there is obviously a new opening for *trade* here; there is obviously a "business" to be made out of little ideal-idols and the "idealists" who go with them: don't let this opportunity slip! Who has the courage for it?—we have in our *hands* the means to "idealize" the whole earth!

But why am I speaking of courage: only one thing is needed here, the hand, an uninhibited, a very uninhibited hand.—

27

Enough! Enough! Let us leave these curiosities and complexities of the most modern spirit, which provoke as much laughter as chagrin: *our* problem, the problem of the *meaning* of the ascetic ideal, can dispense with them: what has this problem to do with yesterday or today! I shall probe these things more thoroughly and severely in another connection (under the title "On the History of

---

[3] Shaking palsy, *alias* Parkinson's disease.
[4] The religion of suffering.

European Nihilism"; it will be contained in a work in progress: *The Will to Power: Attempt at a Revaluation of All Values*[1]). All I have been concerned to indicate here is this: in the most spiritual sphere, too, the ascetic ideal has at present only *one* kind of real enemy capable of *harming* it: the comedians of this ideal— for they arouse mistrust of it. Everywhere else that the spirit is strong, mighty, and at work without counterfeit today, it does without ideals of any kind—the popular expression for this abstinence is "atheism"—*except for its will to truth.* But this will, this *remnant* of an ideal, is, if you will believe me, this ideal itself in its strictest, most spiritual formulation, esoteric through and through, with all external additions abolished, and thus not so much its remnant as its *kernel.* Unconditional honest atheism (and *its* is the only air we breathe, we more spiritual men of this age!) is therefore *not* the antithesis of that ideal, as it appears to be; it is rather only one of the latest phases of its evolution, one of its terminal forms and inner consequences—it is the awe-inspiring *catastrophe* of two thousand years of training in truthfulness that finally forbids itself the *lie involved in belief in God.*

(The same evolutionary course in India, completely independent of ours, should prove something: the same ideal leads to the same conclusion; the decisive point is reached five centuries before the beginning of the European calendar, with Buddha; more exactly, with the Sankhya philosophy, subsequently popularized by Buddha and made into a religion.)

What, in all strictness, has really *conquered* the Christian God? The answer may be found in my *Gay Science* (section 357): "Christian morality itself, the concept of truthfulness taken more and more strictly, the confessional subtlety of the Christian conscience translated and sublimated into the scientific conscience, into intellectual cleanliness at any price. To view nature as if it were a proof of the goodness and providence of a God; to interpret

---

[1] Nietzsche never finished this work nor any part of it. But many of his notes were published posthumously under the title *The Will to Power: Attempt at a Revaluation of All Values* (1st ed., 1901; 2nd, radically revised ed., 1906), and the second chapter of this collection was entitled "On the History of European Nihilism." (English edition with commentary by Walter Kaufmann, New York, Random House, 1967.)

history to the glory of a divine reason, as the perpetual witness to a moral world order and moral intentions; to interpret one's own experiences, as pious men long interpreted them, as if everything were preordained, everything a sign, everything sent for the salvation of the soul—that now belongs to the *past,* that has the conscience *against* it, that seems to every more sensitive conscience indecent, dishonest, mendacious, feminism, weakness, cowardice: it is this rigor if anything that makes us *good Europeans* and the heirs of Europe's longest and bravest self-overcoming."

All great things bring about their own destruction through an act of self-overcoming:[2] thus the law of life will have it, the law of the necessity of "self-overcoming" in the nature of life—the lawgiver himself eventually receives the call: *"patere legem, quam ipse tulisti."* [3] In this way Christianity *as a dogma* was destroyed by its own morality; in the same way Christianity *as morality* must now perish, too: we stand on the threshold of *this* event. After Christian truthfulness has drawn one inference after another, it must end by drawing its *most striking inference,* its inference *against* itself; this will happen, however, when it poses the question *"what is the meaning of all will to truth?"*

And here I again touch on my problem, on our problem, my *unknown* friends (for as yet I *know* of no friend): what meaning would *our* whole being possess if it were not this, that in us the will to truth becomes conscious of itself as a *problem?*

As the will to truth thus gains self-consciousness—there can be no doubt of that—morality will gradually *perish* now: this is the great spectacle in a hundred acts reserved for the next two centuries in Europe—the most terrible, most questionable, and perhaps also the most hopeful of all spectacles.—

---

[2] *Selbstaufhebung:* cf. the end of section 10 in the second essay, above. Two lines above the footnoted reference and also in the line below it, "self-overcoming" is used to render *Selbstüberwindung.*

[3] Submit to the law you yourself proposed.

28

Apart from the ascetic ideal, man, the human *animal,* had no meaning so far. His existence on earth contained no goal; "why man at all?"—was a question without an answer; the *will* for man and earth was lacking; behind every great human destiny there sounded as a refrain a yet greater "in vain!" *This* is precisely what the ascetic ideal means: that something was *lacking,* that man was surrounded by a fearful *void*—he did not know how to justify, to account for, to affirm himself; he *suffered* from the problem of his meaning. He also suffered otherwise, he was in the main a sickly animal: but his problem was *not* suffering itself, but that there was no answer to the crying question, "*why* do I suffer?"

Man, the bravest of animals and the one most accustomed to suffering, does *not* repudiate suffering as such; he *desires* it, he even seeks it out, provided he is shown a *meaning* for it, a *purpose* of suffering. The meaninglessness of suffering, *not* suffering itself, was the curse that lay over mankind so far—*and the ascetic ideal offered man meaning!* It was the only meaning offered so far; any meaning is better than none at all; the ascetic ideal was in every sense the *"faute de mieux"* par excellence so far. In it, suffering was *interpreted;* the tremendous void seemed to have been filled; the door was closed to any kind of suicidal nihilism. This interpretation—there is no doubt of it—brought fresh suffering with it, deeper, more inward, more poisonous, more life-destructive suffering: it placed all suffering under the perspective of *guilt.*

But all this notwithstanding—man was *saved* thereby, he possessed a meaning, he was henceforth no longer like a leaf in the wind, a plaything of nonsense—the "sense-less"—he could now *will* something; no matter at first to what end, why, with what he willed: *the will itself was saved.*

We can no longer conceal from ourselves *what* is expressed by all that willing which has taken its direction from the ascetic ideal: this hatred of the human, and even more of the animal, and more still of the material, this horror of the senses, of reason itself, this fear of happiness and beauty, this longing to get away from all

appearance, change, becoming, death, wishing, from longing itself
—all this means—let us dare to grasp it—*a will to nothingness,* an
aversion[1] to life, a rebellion against the most fundamental presuppositions of life; but it is and remains a *will!* . . . And, to repeat
in conclusion what I said at the beginning: man would rather will
nothingness than *not* will.[2]—

---

[1] *Widerwillen.*

[2] *Lieber will noch der Mensch* das Nichts *wollen, als* nicht *wollen* . . .

APPENDIX

———◆◦◆———

Seventy-five Aphorisms
from Five Volumes

Human, All-Too-Human (1878)

Dual prehistory of good and evil.— The concept of good and evil has a dual prehistory; *first,* in the soul of the ruling tribes and castes. Whoever has the power to repay good with good, evil with evil, and also actually repays, thus being grateful and vengeful, is called good; whoever is powerless and unable to repay is considered bad. As one who is good, one belongs to the "good," a community that possesses communal feeling because all individuals are knit together by the sense of repayment. As one who is bad, one belongs to the "bad," a group of subjected, impotent human beings who have no communal feeling. The good are a caste, the bad a mass like dust. Good and bad are for a time the same as noble and low, master and slave. But the *enemy* is not considered evil, he can repay. Trojan and Greek are both good in Homer. Not he that does us harm but he that is contemptible is considered bad. In the community of the good, good is inherited; it is impossible that a bad person should grow out of such good soil. If one of the good nevertheless does something unworthy of the good, then one has recourse to excuses; one blames a god, for example, saying that he struck the good man with delusion and madness.

Then, in the soul of the oppressed, the powerless. Here all *other* human beings are considered hostile, ruthless, exploiting, cruel, cunning, whether they be noble or low. Evil is the characteristic word for man, indeed for every living being believed in, for example for a god; human or divine means as much as devilish or evil. The signs of graciousness, helpfulness, pity are taken anxiously as wiles, as preludes to a disastrous conclusion, soporifics and craft, in short, as refined malice. As long as individuals have such an attitude, a community can hardly come into being; at best, only its rudiments: hence, wherever this conception of good and evil rules, the ruination of individuals, their tribes and races, is near.

Our current morality has grown on the soil of the *ruling* tribes and castes.[1]

92

Origin of justice.—Justice (fairness)[2] originates among those who are approximately *equally powerful,* as Thucydides (in the terrible conversation between the Athenian and Melian ambassadors) comprehended correctly: where there is no clearly recognizable predominance and a fight would mean inconclusive mutual damage, there the idea originates that one might come to an understanding and negotiate one's claims: the initial character of justice is the character of a trade. Each satisfies the other inasmuch as each receives what he esteems more than the other does. One gives another what he wants, so that it becomes his, and in return one receives what one wants. Thus justice is repayment and exchange on the assumption of an approximately equal power position; revenge originally belongs in the domain of justice, being an exchange. Gratitude, too.

Justice naturally derives from prudent concern with self-preservation; that means, from the egoism of the consideration: "Why should I harm myself uselessly and perhaps not attain my goal anyway?"

So much on the *origin* of justice. In accordance with their intellectual habits, men have *forgotten* the original purpose of so-called just, fair actions, and for millennia children have been taught to admire and emulate such actions. Hence it has gradually come

---

[1] The theme of this section is taken up again in *Beyond Good and Evil* (1886), section 260, where we gain the distinct impression—though Nietzsche is not as emphatic as in the last sentence above—that our current morality is a mixed type. It would seem that this became his considered view, notwithstanding the widespread misapprehension that he considered modern morality an example of "slave morality." Most important: as the above aphorism makes abundantly clear, Nietzsche is not concerned to divide the men among whom he lives into masters and slaves; he is concerned with the history, the genesis, the genealogy of morals. And in the Preface to the *Genealogy of Morals* (1887), Nietzsche refers to several early aphorisms, including this one.

[2] *Die Gerechtigkeit (Billigkeit)* . . .

to appear as if a just action were unegoistic; but the high esteem for it depends on this appearance, and this esteem, moreover, continues to grow all the time, like all esteem; for whatever is highly esteemed becomes the object of striving, emulation, and multiplication, coupled with many sacrifices, and grows further because the value of the effort and zeal is added by every individual to the value of the thing he esteems.

How little the world would look moral without forgetfulness! A poet might say that God made forgetfulness the guard he placed at the threshold of human dignity.

96

Mores and moral.[3]— Being moral or ethical means obeying ancient established law or custom. Whether one submits to it with difficulty or gladly, that is immaterial; it is enough that one does it. *"Good"* is what one calls those who do what is moral as if they did it by nature, after long heredity—in other words, easily and gladly —whatever may be moral in this sense (practicing revenge, for example, when practicing revenge belongs, as it did among the more ancient Greeks, to good mores). He is called good because he is good "for something"; but because benevolence, pity, and that sort of thing have always been felt to be, through many changes in mores, "good for something" and useful, it has come to pass that now the benevolent and helpful are pre-eminently considered "good."

Being evil is being "not *moral*" (immoral), practicing immorality, resisting tradition, however reasonable or stupid tradition may be. Harming the neighbor, however, has been felt to be pre-eminently harmful in all the moral laws of different ages, until now the word "evil" is associated primarily with the deliberate harming of the neighbor.

---

[3] *Sitte und sittlich:* wherever Nietzsche pairs these words, they are translated as above, and *unsittlich* is rendered as immoral. Elsewhere, Nietzsche often uses such words as *Moral, moralisch, Immoralist*—e.g., in *Beyond Good and Evil* and in the *Genealogy of Morals* (not only in the title of the latter book) —and morality, morals, moral, and immoralist have been used to render them.

Not "egoistic" and "unegoistic" is the fundamental pair of contraries that has led men to distinguish moral and immoral, good and evil, but rather: being tied to a tradition and law, and detachment from them. How the tradition *originated* is indifferent; in any case it was without any regard for good and evil or any immanent categorical imperative, but above all in order to preserve a *community,* a people: every superstitious custom that originated on the basis of some misinterpreted accident involves a tradition that it is moral to follow; for detaching oneself from it is dangerous, even more dangerous for the community than for the individual (because the deity punishes the community—and the individual only indirectly—for the sacrilege and the violation of divine privileges). Now every tradition becomes ever more venerable the more remote its origins are and the more they have been forgotten; the veneration shown it is accumulated, generation upon generation; finally, the tradition becomes holy and inspires reverence; and thus the *morality of pious regard for the old* [4] is certainly a much more ancient morality than that which demands unegoistic actions.

136

On Christian asceticism and holiness.—Strongly as individual thinkers have endeavored to present the rare phenomena of morality that are usually called asceticism and holiness as if they were marvels that it would almost be sacrilege and desecration to illuminate by raising the torch of rational explanation up to their face— the temptation to commit this sacrilege is just as strong. A powerful impulse of nature has led men in all ages to protest against these phenomena as such; science, insofar as it is, as mentioned, an imitation of nature, at least takes the liberty to object to their alleged inexplicability and even unapproachability. To be sure, so far it has not succeeded: these phenomena are still unexplained, much to the delight of the said admirers of moral marvels. For, to speak generally: the unexplained should by all means be unexplainable, the unexplainable by all means unnatural, supernatural, miraculous—

---

[4] *Moral der Pietät* (emphasis in the original).

thus goes the demand in the souls of all the religious and metaphysicians (of artists, too, if they are at the same time thinkers); while the scientific person sees in this demand the "evil principle."

The general first probability one encounters as one contemplates holiness and asceticism is this: their nature is *complicated;* for almost everywhere, in the physical world as well as in the moral world, one has succeeded in reducing the allegedly miraculous to the complicated which depends on many conditions. Let us dare then to begin by isolating single impulses in the souls of holy men and ascetics, and to conclude by thinking of them as grown together.

137

There is a *defiance of oneself* among whose most sublimated expressions some forms of asceticism belong. For certain human beings have such a great need to exercise their force and lust to rule that, lacking other objects, or because they have always failed elsewhere, they finally have recourse to tyrannizing certain parts of their own nature, as it were sections or stages of themselves.

Thus some thinkers profess views that evidently do not serve to increase or improve their reputations; some practically conjure up the disrespect of others for them, although it would be easy for them to remain highly respected, simply by keeping still. Others recant former opinions and are not afraid of henceforth being called inconsistent: on the contrary, they exert themselves to that end and behave like exuberant riders who like their horse best when it has gone wild, is covered with sweat, and shying.

Thus man ascends the highest mountains on dangerous paths, to laugh scornfully at his anxiety and his trembling knees; thus the philosopher professes views of asceticism, humility, and sanctity in whose splendor his own image is made exceedingly ugly. This breaking of oneself, this mockery of one's own nature, this *spernere se sperni*[5] of which religions have made so much, is really a very high degree of vanity. The whole morality of the Sermon on the Mount belongs here: man experiences a veritable voluptuousness

---

[5] Scorn of one's being scorned.

in violating himself by means of exaggerated demands and in then deifying this tyrannically demanding force in his soul.

In every ascetic morality man adores part of himself as God and to that end needs to diabolicize the rest.

142

To sum up what has been said here: that state of the soul which the holy man or the man who is becoming holy enjoys is composed of elements which all of us know quite well; they merely take on a different coloring when they are influenced by nonreligious ideas, and then they are usually reproached by men just as much as they can count—or at least could count in former times— on admiration, even worship, when associated with religion and the ultimate meaning of existence.

Sometimes the holy man practices that defiance against himself which is closely related to the lust to rule at any price and which gives even the loneliest the feeling of power; sometimes his swollen feeling changes from the craving to let his passions run their course into the craving to make them collapse like wild horses under the powerful pressure of a proud soul; sometimes he wants the complete cessation of all feelings that disturb, torment, provoke —a wakeful sleep, an enduring rest in the lap of a dumb, animal- or plant-like indolence; sometimes he seeks a fight and inflames it within himself because boredom fixes him with a yawning countenance: he scourges his self-deification with self-contempt and cruelty, he delights in the wild rebellion of his desires, in the sharp pain of sin, even in the idea that he is lost; he knows how to lay a snare for his affects, that of the most extreme lust to rule, for example, so that it changes into the most extreme humiliation and this contrast completely unbalances his hounded soul; and finally: if he should crave visions or conversation with the dead or with divine beings, this is at bottom a rare kind of voluptuousness that he desires, but perhaps that voluptuousness in which all the others are tied up into one knot. Novalis,[6] one of the authorities on questions

---

[6] Pseudonym of Friedrich von Hardenberg (1772–1801), widely considered the greatest of the early German romantic poets. Cf. *Twenty German Poets: A Bilingual Collection* (New York, Modern Library, 1963), pp. 63–69.

of holiness, both by experience and by instinct, once expressed the whole secret with a naïve joy: "It is marvelous enough that the association of voluptuousness, religion, and cruelty has not long attracted the attention of men to their close kinship and common tendency."

143

Not what the holy man *is* but what he *signifies* in the eyes of those who are not holy gives him his world-historical value. It was because one was *wrong* about him, because one *misinterpreted* the states of his soul and drew as sharp a line as possible between oneself and him, as if he were something utterly incomparable and strangely superhuman—that he gained that extraordinary power with which he could dominate the imagination of whole peoples and ages. He did not know himself; he understood the writing of his moods, inclinations, and actions according to an art of interpretation which was just as extravagant and artificial as the pneumatic interpretation of the Bible. What was eccentric and sick in his nature, with its fusion of spiritual poverty, faulty knowledge, spoilt health, and overexcited nerves remained concealed from his own eyes and from the eyes of those who looked at him. He was not an especially good person, even less an especially wise person; but he *signified* something that exceeded all human measure of goodness and wisdom. The faith in him supported the faith in the divine and miraculous, in a religious meaning of all existence, in an impending final day of judgment. In the evening splendor of the world-end's sunset that illuminated the Christian peoples, the shadowy figure of the holy man grew into something enormous—indeed, to such a height that even in our time, which no longer believes in God, there are still thinkers who believe in the holy man.[7]

144

It scarcely needs saying that this sketch of the holy man, being drawn after the average of the whole species, can be countered with

---

[7] For example—but not only—Schopenhauer.

many sketches that tend to produce a more agreeable feeling. Single exceptions stand out from the species, whether by virtue of great mildness and humanitarianism or by the magic of unusual energy; others are attractive in the highest degree because certain delusions inundate their whole nature with light—as is the case, for example, with the celebrated founder of Christianity who considered himself the inborn son of God and therefore felt he was without sin; thus, by virtue of an illusion—which should not be judged too harshly, for the whole of antiquity was full of sons of gods —he attained the same goal, the feeling of complete freedom from sin, complete lack of responsibility, which is now available to everybody by means of science!

I have also ignored the holy men of India who occupy an intermediate stage between the Christian holy man and the Greek philosopher, and thus do not represent a pure type: knowledge, science—insofar as science existed—raising oneself above other men through the logical discipline and training of thought, were just as much demanded among the Buddhists, as a sign of holiness, as the same qualities were repudiated and pronounced heretical in the Christian world where they were held to be signs of unholiness.

Mixed Opinions
and Maxims (1879)

89

Mores and their victim.— The origin of mores may be found in two thoughts: "society is worth more than the individual," and "enduring advantage is to be preferred to ephemeral advantage"— from which it follows that the enduring advantage of society must be given precedence, unconditionally, over the advantage of the individual, especially over his momentary well-being but also over his enduring advantage and even his continued existence. Whether the individual suffers from an institution that is good for the whole, whether it causes him to atrophy or perish—mores must be preserved, sacrifices must be made. But such an attitude *originates* only in those who are *not* its victims—for they claim in their behalf that the individual may be worth more than many, also that present enjoyment, the moment in paradise, may have to be valued higher than a pallid continuation of painless or complacent states. The philosophy of the sacrificial animal, however, is always sounded too late; and so we retain mores and *morality*[1]—which is no more than the feeling for the whole quintessence of mores under which one lives and has been brought up—brought up not as an individual but as a member of a whole, as a digit of a majority.— Thus it happens constantly that an individual brings to bear upon himself, by means of his morality, the tyranny of the majority.[2]

130

Readers' bad manners.— A reader is doubly guilty of bad manners against the author when he praises his second book at the expense of the first (or vice versa) and then asks the author to be grateful for that.

137

The worst readers.— The worst readers are those who proceed like plundering soldiers: they pick up a few things they can use, soil and confuse the rest, and blaspheme the whole.

145

Value of honest books.— Honest books make the reader honest, at least by luring into the open his hatred and aversion which his sly prudence otherwise knows how to conceal best. But against a book one lets oneself go, even if one is very reserved toward people.

---

[1] *So bleibt es bei der Sitte und der* Sittlichkeit.

[2] *Sich selbst . . .* majorisiert.

157

Sharpest criticism.— One criticizes a person, a book, most sharply when one pictures their ideal.

168

Praise of aphorisms.— A good aphorism is too hard for the tooth of time and is not consumed by all millennia, although it serves every time for nourishment: thus it is the great paradox of literature, the intransitory amid the changing, the food that always remains esteemed, like salt, and never loses its savor, as even that does.

200

Original.— Not that one is the first to see something new, but that one sees *as new* what is old, long familiar, seen and overlooked by everybody, is what distinguishes truly original minds. The first discoverer is ordinarily that wholly common creature, devoid of spirit and addicted to fantasy—accident.

201

Philosophers' error.— The philosopher supposes that the value of his philosophy lies in the whole, in the structure; but posterity finds its value in the stone which he used for building, and which is used many more times after that for building—better. Thus it finds the value in the fact that the structure can be destroyed and *nevertheless* retains value as building material.

206

Why scholars are nobler[3] than artists.— Science requires *nobler* natures than poetry does: they have to be simpler, less ambitious,

---

[3] *Edler.*

more abstinent, quieter, not so concerned about posthumous fame, and forget themselves over matters that rarely seem worthy in the eyes of many of such a sacrifice of one's personality. To this must be added another loss of which they are conscious: the type of their work, the continual demand for the greatest sobriety, weakens their *will;* the fire is not kept as strong as on the hearth of poetic natures—and therefore they often lose their highest strength and bloom at an earlier age than those men do—and, as mentioned, they *realize* this danger. In any case they *appear* less gifted because they shine less, and they will be considered inferior to what they are.

251

In parting.— Not how one soul comes close to another but how it moves away shows me their kinship and how much they belong together.

298

Virtue has not been invented by the Germans.— Goethe's nobility[4] and lack of envy, Beethoven's noble[5] hermit's resignation, Mozart's charm and grace of the heart, Handel's unbendable manliness and freedom under the law, Bach's confident and transfigured inner life that does not even find it necessary to renounce splendor and success—are these in any way *German* qualities?— But if not, it at least shows for what Germans should strive and what they can attain.

309

Siding against oneself.— Our adherents never forgive us if we take sides against ourselves: for in their eyes this means not only rejecting their love but also exposing their intelligence.

---

[4] *Vornehmheit.*
[5] *Edle.*

325

Opinions.— Most people are nothing and are considered nothing until they have dressed themselves up in general convictions and public opinions—in accordance with the tailor philosophy: clothes make people. Of the exceptional person, however, it must be said: *only he that wears it makes the costume;*[6] here opinions cease to be public and become something other than masks, finery, and disguises.

341

Loving the master.— Not as apprentices do, loves a master a master.[7]

346

Being misunderstood.— When one is misunderstood as a whole, it is impossible to remove completely a single misunderstanding. One has to realize this lest one waste superfluous energy on one's defense.

404

How duty acquires splendor.— The means for changing your iron duty to gold in everyone's eyes is this: always keep a little more than you promise.

405

Prayer to men.— "Forgive us our virtues"—thus one should pray to men.

---

[6] *Erst der Träger macht die Tracht.*
[7] Based on Nietzsche's relationship to Wagner.

408

The journey to Hades.— I, too, have been in the underworld, like Odysseus, and shall be there often yet; and not only rams have I sacrificed to be able to speak with a few of the dead, but I have not spared my own blood. Four pairs it was that did not deny themselves to my sacrifice: Epicurus and Montaigne, Goethe and Spinoza, Plato and Rousseau, Pascal and Schopenhauer. With these I must come to terms when I have long wandered alone; they may call me right and wrong; to them will I listen when in the process they call each other right and wrong. Whatsoever I say, resolve, or think up for myself and others—on these eight I fix my eyes and see their eyes fixed on me.

May the living forgive me that occasionally *they* appear to me as shades, so pale and somber, so restless and, alas, so lusting for life—while those men then seem so alive to me as if now, *after* death, they could never again grow weary of life. But *eternal aliveness* is what counts: what matters "eternal life" or any life! [8]

The Wanderer and His Shadow (1880)

33

Elements of revenge.— The word "revenge" is said so quickly, it almost seems as if it could not contain more than one root concept and feeling. And so people are still trying to find this root—just as our economists still have not got tired of smelling such a unity in the

---

[8] This is the final aphorism with which the book, published in 1879, ended. In a later note (*Musarion* edition, 1920–29, vol. XIV, p. 109) Nietzsche jotted down: "My ancestors: *Heraclitus, Empedocles, Spinoza, Goethe.*" And his eyes were much more consistently fixed on Socrates than on Epicurus and Montaigne. His references to Pascal and Rousseau, especially Rousseau, are generally very critical.

word "value" and of looking for the original root concept of value. As if all words were not pockets into which now this and now that has been put, and now many things at once! [1] Thus "revenge," too, is now this and now that, and now something very composite.

Let us distinguish, *first,* that return blow of resistance which is almost an involuntary reflex, executed even against lifeless objects that have harmed us (such as moving machines): the sense of this countermove is to stop the harm by bringing the machine to a halt. Occasionally, the strength of the counterblow must be so strong to succeed in this that it smashes the machine; but where that is too strong to be destructible immediately by an individual, he will nevertheless strike as hard as he can—making, as it were, an all-out-attempt. One behaves the same way against persons who harm one, as long as one feels the harm immediately: if you want to call this action an act of revenge, all right; but consider that it is only *self-preservation* that has here put its rational machinery into motion, and that in the last analysis one does not think at all of the harming person in such a case but only of oneself: we act that way *without* any wish to do harm in return, merely in order to *get away* with life and limb.

Time is needed—when instead of concentrating on oneself one begins to think about one's opponent, asking oneself how one can hurt him the most. This happens in the *second* type of revenge: reflection on the other person's vulnerability and capacity for suffering is its presupposition; one wants to hurt. Protecting oneself against further harm, on the other hand, is so little a consideration for the seeker of such vengeance that he almost regularly brings about further harm to himself and quite often anticipates this in cold blood. In the first type of revenge it was fear of a second blow that made the counterblow as strong as possible; here we find almost total indifference to what the opponent *will* do yet; the strength of the counterblow is determined solely by what he *has*

---

[1] A remarkably clear and vivid statement of a point that is widely held to be one of Ludwig Wittgenstein's major contributions to philosophy; cf. Wittgenstein's *Philosophical Investigations* (1953), sections 65ff. The great antipode of Nietzsche and Wittgenstein is Plato's theory of ideas, which holds that all the instances called by the same name participate in the same idea or form which alone embodies to perfection the quality named.

done to us. But what has he done? And what use is it to us if he now suffers after we have suffered on his account? What matters is a *restoration,* while the act of revenge of the first type serves only *self-preservation.* Perhaps we have lost through our opponent possessions, rank, friends, children: such losses are not brought back by revenge; the restoration concerns solely a *loss incidental* to all these losses. The revenge of restoration does not protect against further harm; it does not make good the harm suffered—except in one case. If our *honor* has suffered from our opponent, then revenge can *restore* it. But this has suffered damage in every instance in which suffering has been inflicted on us deliberately; for our opponent thus demonstrated that he did not *fear* us. By revenge we demonstrate that we do not fear him either: this constitutes the equalization, the restoration. (The intent of showing one's utter lack of *fear* goes so far in some persons that the danger their revenge involves for them—loss of health or life or other damage—is for them an indispensable condition of all revenge. Therefore they choose the means of a duel although the courts offer them help in obtaining satisfaction for the insult: but they do not accept an undangerous restoration of their honor as sufficient, because it cannot demonstrate their lack of fear.)

In the first type of revenge it is fear that strikes the counterblow; here, on the other hand, it is the absence of fear that, as I have tried to show, *wants to prove* itself by means of the counterblow.

Nothing therefore seems more different than the inner motivation of the two ways of action that are called by one name, "revenge." Nevertheless it happens quite frequently that the person seeking revenge is unclear about what really induced him to act: perhaps he delivered the counterblow from fear and in order to preserve himself, but later, when he has time to think about the point of his injured honor, he convinces himself that he avenged himself for his honor's sake—after all, this motive is *nobler* than the other one. Moreover, it is also important whether he believes his honor to have been injured in the eyes of others (the world) or only in the eyes of the opponent who insulted him: in the latter case he will prefer secret revenge, in the former public revenge.

Depending on whether he projects himself strongly or weakly into the soul of his opponent and the spectators, his revenge will be more embittered or tamer; if he lacks this type of imagination entirely, he will not think of revenge at all, for in that case the feeling for "honor" is not present in him and hence cannot be injured. Just so, he will not think of revenge if he *despises* the doer and the spectators of the deed—because they, being despised, cannot accord him any honor and hence also cannot take it away. Finally, he will forgo revenge in the not unusual case in which he loves the doer: to be sure, he thus loses honor in his opponent's eyes and perhaps thus becomes less worthy of being loved in return. But even forgoing all such counterlove is a sacrifice that love is prepared to make if only it does not *have to hurt* the beloved being: that would mean hurting oneself more than this sacrifice hurts.

Thus: everybody will revenge himself unless he is without honor or full of contempt or full of love for the person who has harmed and insulted him. Even when he has recourse to the courts he wants revenge as a private person—but *besides,* being a member of society who thinks further and considers the future, he also wants society's revenge on one who does not *honor* it. Thus judicial punishment *restores* both private honor and the honor of society— which means, punishment is revenge.

Indubitably, it also contains that other element of revenge which we described first, insofar as society uses punishment for its *self-preservation* and deals a counterblow in *self-defense*. Punishment desires to prevent *further* damage; it desires to *deter*. Thus both of these so different elements of revenge are actually *tied together* in punishment, and perhaps this is the main support of that above-mentioned conceptual confusion by virtue of which the individual who revenges himself usually does not *know what* he really *wants*.

194

Dreams.— On the rare occasions when our dreams succeed and achieve perfection—most dreams are bungled—they are symbolic chains of scenes and images in place of a narrative poetic language; they circumscribe our experiences or expectations or situations with such poetic boldness and decisiveness that in the morning we are always amazed at ourselves when we remember our dreams. We use up too much artistry in our dreams—and therefore often are impoverished during the day.

202

Tourists.— They climb mountains like animals, stupid and sweating; one has forgotten to tell them that there are beautiful views on the way up.

203

Too much and too little.— All men now live through too much and think through too little: they suffer at the same time from extreme hunger and from colic, and therefore become thinner and thinner, no matter how much they eat.— Whoever says now, "I have not lived through anything"—is an ass.

204

End and goal.— Not every end is the goal. The end of a melody is not its goal; and yet: as long as the melody has not reached its end, it also hasn't reached its goal. A parable.

208

How to have all men against you.— If anyone dared to say now, "Whoever is not for me, is against me," [2] he would immediately have all men against him.— This does our time honor.

249

Positive and negative.— This thinker needs nobody to refute him: for that he suffices himself.

---

[2] Mat. 12:30; Luke 11:23.

263

Way to equality.— A few hours of mountain climbing turn a villain and a saint into two rather equal creatures. Exhaustion is the shortest way to *equality* and *fraternity*—and *liberty* is added eventually by sleep.

297

Not to wish to see too soon.— As long as one lives through an experience, one must surrender to the experience and shut one's eyes instead of becoming an observer *immediately*. For that would disturb the good digestion of the experience: instead of wisdom one would acquire indigestion.

298

From the practice of wise men.— To become wise, one must *wish* to have certain experiences and run, as it were, into their gaping jaws. This, of course, is very dangerous; many a wise guy has been swallowed.

301

A testimony of love.— Somebody said: "About two persons I have never reflected very thoroughly: that is the testimony of my love for them." [3]

302

How one tries to improve bad arguments.— Some people throw a bit of their personality after their bad arguments, as if that might straighten their paths and turn them into right and good arguments—just as a man in a bowling alley, after he has let go of the ball, still tries to direct it with gestures.

---

[3] Nietzsche may have thought particularly of his mother and sister.

307

When taking leave is needed.— From what you would know and measure, you must take leave, at least for a time. Only after having left town, you see how high its towers rise above the houses.

317

Opinions and fish.— Possessing opinions is like possessing fish, assuming one has a fish pond. One has to go fishing and needs some luck—then one has one's own fish, one's own opinions. I am speaking of live opinions, of live fish. Others are satisfied if they own a cabinet of fossils—and in their heads, "convictions." [4]

322

Death.— The certain prospect of death could sweeten every life with a precious and fragrant drop of levity—and now you strange apothecary souls have turned it into an ill-tasting drop of poison that makes the whole of life repulsive.

323

Remorse.— Never give way to remorse, but immediately say to yourself: that would merely mean adding a second stupidity to the first.— If you have done harm, see how you can do good.— If you are punished for your actions, bear the punishment with the feeling that you *are* doing good—by deterring others from falling prey to the same folly. Every evildoer who is punished may feel that he is a benefactor of humanity.

326

Don't touch!— There are terrible people who, instead of solving a problem, bungle it and make it more difficult for all who come

---

[4] See section 333 below. About convictions, cf. *The Antichrist*, sections 50ff. (*Portable Nietzsche*, pp. 631ff.).

after. Whoever can't hit the nail on the head should, please, not hit it at all.

333

Dying for the "truth."— We should not let ourselves be burnt for our opinions: we are not that sure of them. But perhaps for this: that we may have and change our opinions.

The Dawn (1881)

1

Rationality ex post facto.— Whatever lives long is gradually so saturated with reason that its irrational origins become improbable. Does not almost every accurate history of the origin of something sound paradoxical and sacrilegious to our feelings? Doesn't the good historian *contradict* all the time?

18

The morality of voluntary suffering.— What is the supreme enjoyment for men who live in the state of war of those small, continually endangered communities which are characterized by the strictest mores? In other words, for vigorous, vindictive, vicious, suspicious souls who are prepared for what is most terrible and hardened by deprivations and mores? The enjoyment of *cruelty;* and in these circumstances it is even accounted among the *virtues* of such a soul if it is inventive and insatiable in cruelty. The community feels refreshed by cruel deeds, and casts off for once the gloom of continual anxiety and caution. Cruelty belongs to the most ancient festive joys of mankind. Hence one supposes that the *gods,* too, feel refreshed and festive when one offers them the sight of cruelty; and so the idea creeps into the world that *voluntary suffering,* torture one has chosen oneself, has value and makes good sense.

Gradually, the mores shape a communal practice in accordance with this idea: all extravagant well-being henceforth arouses some mistrust, and all hard and painful states more and more confidence. One supposes that the gods might look upon us ungraciously because of our happiness, and graciously because of our suffering—not by any means with pity. For pity is considered contemptible and unworthy of a strong and terrible soul. Rather, graciously, because it delights them and puts them into good spirits; for those who are cruel enjoy the supreme titillation of the feeling of power.[1]

Thus the concept of the "most moral man" of the community comes to contain the virtue of frequent suffering, deprivation, a hard way of life, and of cruel self-mortification—*not*, to say this again and again, as a means of self-discipline, self-control, and the desire for individual happiness, but as a virtue that makes the community look good to the evil gods, steaming up to them like a continual sacrifice of atonement upon some altar. All those spiritual leaders of peoples who succeeded in stirring something in the inert but fertile mud of their mores, had need not only of madness but also of voluntary torture to engender faith—and most and first of all, as always, their faith in themselves. The more their own spirit moved along novel paths and was therefore tormented by pangs of conscience and anxieties, the more cruelly they raged against their own flesh, their own desires, and their own health—as if they wanted to offer the deity some substitute gratification in case it should perhaps be embittered on account of customs one had neglected and fought against and new goals one had championed.

Let us not believe too quickly that now we have rid ourselves completely of such a logic of feeling. Let the most heroic souls question themselves about this. Every smallest step on the field of free thought and the individually formed life has always been fought for with spiritual and physical torments: not only moving forward, no, above all moving, motion, change have required innumerable martyrs, all through the long path-seeking and basic mil-

---

[1] This was written before Nietzsche developed his conception of the will to power. The function of *The Dawn* in the development of this idea is discussed in detail in Chapter 6 of Kaufmann's *Nietzsche*.

lennia of which, to be sure, people don't think when they talk, as usual, about "world history," that ridiculously small segment of human existence. And even in this so-called world history, which is at bottom much ado about the latest news, there is no really more important theme than the primordial tragedy of the martyrs *who wanted to move the swamps.*

Nothing has been bought more dearly than that little bit of human reason and of a feeling of freedom that now constitutes our pride. But it is this very pride that now makes it almost impossible for us to feel with those vast spans of time characterized by the "morality of mores" [2] which antedate "world history" as the *real and decisive main history that determined the character of humanity*—when suffering was a virtue, cruelty a virtue, dissimulation a virtue, revenge a virtue, the slander of reason a virtue, while well-being was a danger, the craving for knowledge a danger, peace a danger, pity a danger, being pitied ignominy, work ignominy, madness divine, change immoral [3] and pregnant with disaster.

You think that all this has changed, and that humanity must thus have changed its character? You who think you know men, learn to know yourselves better!

112

On the natural history of duty and right.— Our duties—are the rights others have against us. How did the others acquire these rights? By taking us to be capable of contracts and of repayment, as equal and similar to them; by entrusting us with something on this basis and educating, correcting, and supporting us. We do our duty—that means: we justify this idea of our power on the basis of which we have been treated this way; we give back in the same measure in which one has given to us. Thus it is our pride that bids us do our duty—we want to regain our sovereignty when we balance what others have done for us with something we do for them —for in this way they have intruded into the sphere of our power

---

[2] *Sittlichkeit der Sitte.*
[3] *Unsittlich:* practically by definition.

and would keep their hand in it constantly if we did not repay them with our "duty," which means that we intrude into their power. The rights of others can relate only to what is within our power; it would be unreasonable if they wanted something from us that does not belong to us. To be more precise one should say: only to what they suppose is within our power, assuming that it is the same thing we suppose to be within our power. The same error could easily be made on both sides: the sense of a duty depends on our sharing with the others the same *faith* about the extent of our power: namely, that we promise certain things and are *capable* of incurring these duties ("freedom of the will").

My *rights:* they define that part of my power which the others have not only conceded to me but in which they wish to preserve me. What leads the others to do this? First, their prudence and fear and caution—whether they expect something similar in return from us (protection of their rights), or consider a fight with us dangerous or pointless, or see in every diminution of our strength a disadvantage for themselves because it would render us unfit for an alliance with them against a third and hostile power. Then, deeding or ceding. In this case the others have power enough, more than enough, to be able to give some of it away and to guarantee the piece they give away to the person who receives it—in which case a slight feeling of power is assumed in the person who accepts the present. Thus rights originate: recognized and guaranteed degrees of power. If the proportions of power are changed drastically, rights pass away, and new rights come to be—which is apparent in international law with its constant passing away and coming to be. If our power is decreased drastically, the feelings of those who have so far guaranteed our rights change: they consider whether they can restore us to our old full possession—and if they feel incapable of that, then they deny our "rights" henceforth. Just so, when our power is increased drastically, the feelings of those change who have so far recognized it and whose recognition we now no longer need: they may try to reduce our power to its former measure, they may wish to interfere, invoking their "duty"—but this is just a waste of words. Where right *rules,* a state and degree of power is preserved, and a diminution and increase are resisted. The right of others is the concession of our feeling of power to the feeling of power among these others. When our power is proved to have been profoundly shaken and broken, our rights cease; on the other hand, when we have become a great deal more powerful, the rights of others cease for us, at least in the form in which we have so far conceded them.

The "fair person" constantly needs the fine tact of a scale for the degrees of power and right which, in view of the transitory nature of human affairs, will always be balanced only for a short time, while for the most part they either sink or rise: to be fair is therefore difficult and requires much practice, good will, and a great deal of good *spirit*.—

231

Of German virtue.— How degenerate in taste, how slavish before offices, classes, robes, pomp, and splendor must a people have been when it evaluated the simple [*schlicht*] as the bad [*schlecht*], the simple man as the bad man! One should counter the moral arrogance of the Germans with this one little word, *schlecht,* and nothing more.[4]

232

From a disputation.— A: My friend, you have talked yourself hoarse. B: Then I stand refuted. Let us not discuss the matter any further.

236

Punishment.— A strange thing, our punishment! It does not cleanse the criminal, it is no atonement; on the contrary, it pollutes worse than the crime does.

---

[4] The etymology is sound—and the aphorism invites comparison with *Genealogy of Morals,* I, section 4.

The Gay Science (1882)

51

Sense of truth.— I think well of all skepticism to which I may reply: "Let us try it." But I no longer want to hear anything of all those things and questions which do not permit experiments. This is the limit of my "sense of truth": for there courage has lost its rights.

108

New struggles.— After Buddha was dead, his shadow was still shown for centuries in a cave—a tremendous, gruesome shadow. God is dead: but given the way men are, there may still be caves for thousands of years in which his shadow will be shown.— And we—we still have to vanquish his shadow, too.[1]

121

Life no argument.— We have fixed up a world for ourselves in which we can live—assuming bodies, lines, planes, causes and effects, motion and rest, form and content: without these articles of faith, nobody now would endure life. But that does not mean that they have been proved. Life is no argument; the conditions of life could include error.[2]

129

The conditions of God.— "God himself cannot exist without wise men"—Luther said, and was right. But "God can exist even less without unwise men"—that good old Luther did not say.

---

[1] Cf. section 125 (*Portable Nietzsche*, pp. 95f.).
[2] Cf. *Beyond Good and Evil*, section 4.

130

A dangerous resolve.— The Christian resolve to find the world ugly and bad has made the world ugly and bad.

142

Incense.— Buddha said: "Do not flatter your benefactor." This saying should be repeated in a Christian church—right away it clears the air of everything Christian.

163

After a great victory.— What is best about a great victory is that it rids the victor of fear of defeat. "Why not also lose for once?" he says to himself; "now I am rich enough for that."

173

Being deep and appearing deep.— Whoever knows he is deep, strives for clarity; whoever would like to appear deep to the crowd, strives for obscurity. For the crowd considers anything deep if only it cannot see to the bottom: the crowd is so timid and afraid of going into the water.

200

Laughter.— Laughter means: being *schadenfroh*,[3] but with a good conscience.

205

Need.— A need is considered the cause of the origin: in truth, it is often merely an effect of what did originate.

---

[3] The word is famous for being untranslatable: it signifies taking a mischievous delight in the discomfort of another person.

228

Against mediators.— Those who wish to be mediators between two resolute thinkers are marked as mediocre: they lack eyes to see the unparalleled; seeing things as similar and making them the same is the mark of weak eyes.

231

"Thorough."— Those slow in knowledge suppose that slowness belongs to knowledge.[4]

232

Dreams.— We have no dreams at all or interesting ones. We should learn to be awake the same way—not at all or in an interesting manner.

258

Those who deny chance.— No victor believes in chance.

273

Whom do you call bad?— Those who always want to put to shame.

274

What do you consider most humane?— To spare someone shame.

275

What is the seal of attained freedom?— No longer being ashamed in front of oneself.

---

[4] Cf. section 381, below, and *Beyond Good and Evil*, section 27.

292

To the preachers of morals.— I have no wish to establish morals, but I have this advice for those who do: if you want to do the best things and states out of all honor and worth, then continue to talk about them as you have been doing. Place them at the head of your morality and talk from morning till night of the happiness of virtue, of peace of soul, of justice and immanent retribution: the way you are carrying on, all these good things finally acquire a popularity and are shouted about in the streets; but at the same time all of their gold will be worn off, and even worse—all the gold that was *in* them will have been changed to lead. Truly, you are masters of inverse alchemy, of the devaluation of the most valuable things. Why don't you reach, experimentally, for another recipe, lest you keep attaining the opposite of what you seek: *deny* these good things, deprive them of the mob's acclaim and their constant currency; restore them to the concealed bashfulness of solitary souls; say that *morality is something forbidden.* Perhaps you will in that way gain the support for these things of the only type of men that matter—those who are *heroic.* But then they must have a quality that inspires fear, and not, as hitherto, nausea. Should we not say of morality today what Master Eckhart[5] said: "I ask God that he rid me of God."

312

My dog.— I have given a name to my pain and call it "dog": it is just as faithful, just as obtrusive and shameless, just as entertaining, just as clever as any other dog—and I can scold it and vent my bad moods on it, as others do with their dogs, servants, and wives.

---

[5] Meister Eckhart (1260–1327) was the greatest German mystic of the Middle Ages.

316

Prophetic men.— You have no feeling for the fact that prophetic men are men who suffer a great deal: you merely suppose that they have been granted a beautiful "gift," and you would even like to have it yourself. But I shall express myself in a parable. How much may animals suffer from the electricity in the air and clouds! We see how some species have a prophetic faculty regarding the weather; monkeys, for example (as may be observed even in Europe, and not only in zoos—namely, on Gibraltar). But we do not heed that it is their *pains* that make them prophets. When a strong positive electrical charge, under the influence of an approaching cloud that is as yet far from visible, suddenly changes into negative electricity, these animals behave as if an enemy were drawing near and prepare for defense or escape; most often they try to hide: they do not understand bad weather as a kind of weather but as an enemy whose hand they already *feel*.

322

Parable.— Those thinkers in whom all stars move in cyclic orbits are not the most profound: whoever looks into himself as into vast space and carries galaxies in himself also knows how irregular all galaxies are; they lead into the chaos and labyrinth of existence.

325

What belongs to greatness.— Who will attain anything great if he does not possess the strength and the will to *inflict* great suffering? Being able to suffer is the least thing: weak women and even slaves often attain mastery in that. But not to perish of inner distress and uncertainty when one inflicts great suffering and hears the cry of this suffering—that is great, that belongs to greatness.[6]

---

[6] This aphorism is surely quite as much prompted by personal experience as the three that precede it: Nietzsche is thinking of the suffering that his ideas

327

Taking seriously.— In the great majority, the intellect is a clumsy, gloomy, creaking machine that is difficult to start. They call it "taking the matter seriously," when they work with this machine and want to think well: how onerous they must find thinking well! The lovely beast, man, seems to lose its good spirits every time it thinks well: it becomes "serious." And "where laughter and gaiety are found, the quality of thought is poor"—that is the prejudice of this serious beast against all "gay science."— Well, then, let us prove that it is a prejudice.[7]

332

The bad hour.— Every philosopher has probably had a bad hour when he thought: what do I matter if one does not accept my bad arguments, too?— And then some mischievous[8] little bird flew past him and twittered: "What do you matter? What do you matter?"

381 [9]

On the question of being understandable.— One does not only wish to be understood when one writes; one wishes just as surely *not* to be understood. It is not by any means necessarily an objection to a book when anybody finds it impossible to understand: perhaps that was part of the author's intention—he did not want to be understood by just "anybody." Every more noble spirit

---

and books inflict on his mother, the Wagner circle, and those whose pieties he offends.

[7] This aphorism, and the whole conception of the "gay science," should be recalled in connection with Nietzsche's inquiry concerning "ascetic ideals" in the *Genealogy*. Science and scholarship, he argues there, involve variations of asceticism. But his solution does not consist in renouncing reason: he wants to develop a "gay science."

[8] *Schadenfrohes.*

[9] From the Fifth Book, added in 1887.

and taste selects its audience when it wishes to communicate itself; and choosing them, it at the same time erects barriers against "the others." All the more subtle laws of any style have their origin at this point: they at the same time keep away, create a distance, forbid "entrance," understanding, as said above—while they open the ears of those whose ears are related to ours.

And let me say this among ourselves and about my own case: I don't want either my ignorance or the liveliness of my temperament to keep me from being understandable for *you,* my friends— not the liveliness, however much it compels me to tackle a matter swiftly to tackle it at all. For I approach deep problems like cold baths: quickly into them and quickly out again. That one does not get to the depths that way, not deep enough down, is the superstition of those afraid of the water, the enemies of cold water; they speak without experience. The freezing cold makes one swift.

And to ask this incidentally: does a matter necessarily remain ununderstood and unfathomed merely because it has been touched only in flight, glanced at, in a flash? Is it absolutely imperative that one settles down on it? that one has brooded over it as over an egg? *Diu noctuque incubando,* as Newton said of himself? At least there are truths that are singularly shy and ticklish and cannot be caught except suddenly—that must be *surprised* or left alone.

Finally, my brevity has yet another value: given such questions as concern me, I must say many things briefly in order that they may be heard still more briefly. For, being an immoralist, one has to take steps against corrupting innocents—I mean, asses and old maids of both sexes whom life offers nothing but their innocence. Even more, my writings should inspire, elevate, and encourage them to be virtuous. I cannot imagine anything on earth that would be a merrier sight than inspired old asses and maids who feel excited by the sweet sentiments of virtue; and "this I have seen"— thus spoke Zarathustra.

So much regarding brevity. Matters stand worse with my ignorance which I do not try to conceal from myself. There are hours when I feel ashamed of it—to be sure, also hours when I feel ashamed of feeling ashamed. Perhaps all of us philosophers are in a bad position nowadays regarding knowledge: science keeps growing, and the most scholarly among us are close to discovering that they know too little. But it would be still worse if it were different —and we knew *too much;* our task is and remains above all not to mistake ourselves for others. We *are* something different from scholars, although it is unavoidable for us to be also, among other things, scholarly. We have different needs, grow differently, and also have a different digestion: we need more, we also need less. How much a spirit needs for its nourishment, for this there is no formula; but if its taste is for independence, for quick coming and going, for roaming, perhaps for adventures for which only the swiftest are a match, it is better for such a spirit to live in freedom with little to eat than unfree and stuffed. It is not fat but the greatest possible suppleness and strength that a good dancer desires from his nourishment—and I would not know what the spirit of a philosopher might wish more to be than a good dancer. For the dance is his ideal, also his art, and finally also his only piety, his "service of God."

ECCE HOMO

Editor's Introduction

1

Ecce Homo is one of the treasures of world literature. Written in 1888 and first published in 1908, it has been largely ignored or misunderstood. Yet it is Nietzsche's own interpretation of his development, his works, and his significance; and we should gladly trade the whole vast literature on Nietzsche for this one small book. Who would not rather have Shakespeare on Shakespeare, including the poet's own reflections on his plays and poems, than the exegeses and conjectures of thousands of critics and professors?

Socrates said in the *Apology* that the poets are among the worst interpreters of their own works: they create without understanding, on the wings of inspiration; but when they discuss their works they rely on their uninspired reason and falter. But *Ecce Homo* is clearly not the work of a pedant whose genius has quit him. It is itself a work of art and marks one of the high points of German prose.

There are those who like Nietzsche's early works best—especially *The Birth of Tragedy* and the "untimely" meditation on historiography; but they are few by now and no longer a force to reckon with. Others have always preferred the aphoristic works in which Nietzsche emerged as Germany's greatest master of prose. By far the larger number of his readers have most admired *Zarathustra*. And the rest, including the greater part of the Anglo-American philosophers who take him seriously at all, have little doubt that *Beyond Good and Evil* and the *Genealogy of Morals* are his finest books. I am assuredly in a minority—perhaps of one—when I confess that I love best the five books Nietzsche wrote during his last productive year, 1888—not least because they are such brilliant works of art.

The Case of Wagner, The Twilight of the Idols, The Antichrist, and *Ecce Homo* present a crescendo without equal in prose. Then comes the final work, *Nietzsche contra Wagner,* Nietzsche's briefest and most beautiful book—a selection of passages from his earlier works, admittedly very slightly revised and improved in a few places—an attempt to approximate perfection. The preface to that book was dated Christmas 1888. A few days later, during the first week of January, he collapsed on the street, recovered sufficient lucidity to dispatch a few mad but strangely beautiful letters[1] —and then darkness closed in and extinguished passion and intelligence. He suffered and thought no more. He had burnt himself out.

Was the vegetating body that survived another decade and more, until August 1900, still the poet and philosopher, artist and Antichrist? Socrates gently ridiculed disciples who thought that the body that remained after his death would still be Socrates. But reproductions of portraits of Nietzsche in the eighteen-nineties, commissioned by his sister who let his mustache grow as he himself never had, who clad him in white robes and fancied his vacant stare—portraits that show no glimpse of Nietzsche's vanished spirit —these appear with his books to this day.

Of Nietzsche's last works, none has proved harder to understand than *Ecce Homo*. The self-portrait is not naturalistic; hence, it was widely felt, it is clearly insane and to be disregarded. This prevalent view is doubly false. The lack of naturalism is not proof of insanity but a triumph of style—of a piece with the best paintings of that time. And even if what might be interpreted as signs of madness do occasionally flicker in a passage, that does not mean that the portrait can therefore be ignored. In both respects Nietzsche should be compared with Van Gogh.

Ecce Homo does not fit any ordinary conception of philosophers. It is not only remote from the world of professorial or donnish philosophy, from tomes and articles, footnotes and jargon—in brief, from the modern image. It is equally far from the popular notion of the wise man: serene, past passion, temperate, and Apollinian. But this is plainly part of Nietzsche's point: to offer a new image—a philosopher who is not an Alexandrian academician, nor an Apollinian sage, but Dionysian.

While Van Gogh, having fled his native north, burnt himself

---

[1] See, e.g., *Portable Nietzsche* (New York, Viking, 1954), pp. 684–87.

out in southern France, creating an incredible number of works without any public recognition, fighting time till 1890, when madness could no longer be held off and he shot himself, Nietzsche spent himself with comparable passion just a few miles further east, writing feverishly—not even pausing, as in keeping with his own ideas he ought to have done, to take his life before his spirit quit it. Freud used to say of him that "he had a more penetrating knowledge of himself than any other man who ever lived or was ever likely to live";[2] yet Nietzsche was not aware of his impending madness and therefore, unable to forestall it.

In his first book Nietzsche had traced the "birth of tragedy" to the creative fusion of the Apollinian and the Dionysian, and the death of tragedy to the imperious rationalism for which he found the most impressive symbol in Socrates. Then he had found a rebirth of tragedy in Wagner's work and had looked forward to the advent of an "artistic Socrates"—Nietzsche himself. The critical passion, the revolt against hallowed pieties, the demand for clarity, and the fusion of life and thought need not always remain opposed to the spirit of art and need not inspire such confidence in the unaided reason that one's heir would proceed to proscribe all tragedy, as Plato did; rather, all this might be merged with a vision of the world that would be closer to Sophocles, and with a poetic temperament partaking more of Pindar than of Plato, more of Dionysus than Apollo. *Ecce Homo* is the *Apology* of this "artistic Socrates."

Plato's Socrates had claimed in his *Apology* that he was the wisest of men, not because he was so wise but because his fellow men were so stupid, especially those who were considered the wisest—for they thought they knew what in fact they did not know. And Socrates, accused of impiety and corrupting the youth of Athens, argued that he was actually the city's greatest benefactor and deserving of the highest honors. Thus, *Ecce Homo* could have been entitled "Variations on a Theme by Socrates." That would have been an artistic title, but out of the question for a writer who had just finished *The Antichrist*. *Ecce Homo*—the words Pilate had, according to John (19:5), spoken of Jesus: "Behold the man!"—

---

[2] Ernest Jones, *The Life and Work of Sigmund Freud*, Vol. II, (New York, Basic Books, 1953), p. 344.

seemed more to the point. But that point was not to suggest any
close similarity between himself and Jesus; more nearly the opposite. *Here* is a man! Here is a new, a different image of humanity:
not a saint or holy man any more than a traditional sage, but a
modern version.

In the text Nietzsche said he wished to prevent any mischievous use of himself—*dass man Unfug mit mir treibt.* Our knowledge that two months after finishing the first draft of the book, and
less than four weeks after he had gone over the whole work once
more, he became insane gives the book a tragic dimension that is
heightened almost intolerably if we bear in mind how he failed to
prevent the mischief he feared. The first section of the Preface
ends: "Above all, do not mistake me for someone else!" He underlined this cry—but soon his sister imposed her exceedingly unsub-
tle notion of hero and prophet on a mindless invalid—and in her
sign he triumphed.

That was but the beginning. Far worse mischief followed.
Nietzsche's voice was drowned out as misinterpretations that he
had explicitly repudiated with much wit and malice were accepted
and repeated, and repeated and accepted, until most readers knew
what to expect before they read Nietzsche, and so read nothing but
what they had long expected.

2

What of Nietzsche's comments on his own works? Can his interpretations really be taken seriously?

The very question smacks of an obscene revaluation of all
values, through which, soon after the book was written, everything
was turned upside down. Nietzsche's sister had mocked her brother's claims to fame, but then, switching to his cause after her hus-
band's suicide, she took private lessons in Nietzsche's philosophy
from Rudolf Steiner, a Goethe scholar who later became famous as
the founder of anthroposophy. Soon Steiner gave her up as simply
incapable of understanding Nietzsche. Meanwhile she became her
brother's official exegete and biographer, tampered with his letters
—and was taken seriously by almost everyone. And who was *not*
taken seriously? Even the most unscrupulous Nazi interpretations

were taken seriously not only inside Germany, but by a host of foreign scholars who did not bother to check Nazi quotations.

Earlier, Ernst Bertram had frankly subtitled his interpretation "Attempt at a Mythology": but who checked *his* quotations? And whose Nietzsche image, except the sister's, was taken more seriously from 1918, when Bertram's *Nietzsche* appeared, until 1933 when Hitler broke out? Or who checked Jaspers' quotations *in their context?* (The English translation of his *Nietzsche* omits all source references, as Bertram had done.)

It would be pointless to rescue from their imminent oblivion many lesser figures who have also associated their names with Nietzsche's, writing about him without having read carefully the works they discuss, or editing him by selecting passages from hopeless mistranslations that these professors lacked the German or the patience to check. Yet such publications are taken seriously and used as the basis for many discussions in colleges and universities.

While some of Nietzsche's self-interpretations are much less persuasive than others, all of them have several inestimable advantages over almost everything that passes as serious literature about him: he did not discuss any of his works without having read them carefully, more than once; indeed, he did not discuss any without knowing all of them, in the sequence in which they were written—and, of course, in the original. He also knew all of his letters, as well as his unpublished fragments and notes. And he wrote about his *oeuvre* with singular penetration, wit, and style.

Let us be specific: Do his comments on *The Birth of Tragedy* make sense? Very little written on that book is as illuminating, and most discussions of the book are dated by Nietzsche's own discussion, which long antedates them.

Yet *Ecce Homo* has its faults. It contains all too many references to *Zarathustra*—most of them embarrassing—and the numerous long quotations from that book are almost rendered pointless by *Zarathustra*'s great posthumous success: the quotations were intended for readers who did not know that book. And although Nietzsche has often been linked with German nationalism, his remarks about the Germans are open to criticism for being too extreme in stressing what he finds abominable.

We return to the question of naturalism. Nietzsche's portrait

of the Germans is not meant to be objective. It partakes more
nearly of the spirit of George Grosz, who, after World War I, entitled a collection of his graphic attacks on his countrymen, *Ecce
Homo*. But we also hear the anguished cry of one who sees—fore-
sees—himself mistaken for a writer he is not: for an apostle of
military power and empire, a nationalist, and even a racist. In
order to define himself emphatically, Nietzsche underlines (too
often) and shrieks—to no avail. Those who construe the overman
in evolutionary terms he calls "oxen"—in vain. Respected professors *still* write books in which Nietzsche's ethics is presented as "evolutionary."

The break with Wagner? Nietzsche's picture is stylized, not
false. There is, of course, hindsight in it; but readers of Sartre
should know, if they have not learned it firsthand from Nietzsche
himself, that an act is one event, and the way we interpret it afterward and relate ourselves to it is another. Looking back on the year
in which he resigned from the university, published *Human, All-
Too-Human* with a dedication to Voltaire—turning from German
romanticism to the French enlightenment, and from Wagner to independence—he felt, more clearly than he had felt it at the time,
that this had been his Rubicon, the turning point in his life. Can
one deny that it was?

For all that, is Wagner represented in a Manichaean spirit, as
the force of evil, as a dragon? On the contrary, the portrait is im-
bued with gratitude and love—with *amor fati,* love of fate. *There is
no "if only" in this autobiography, and there are no excuses.* A
man who was in physical agony much of his adult life and warned
by his doctors not to read or write much lest he strain his half-blind
eyes, does not once complain. He is thankful for his illness and tells
us how it made his life better.

The philosophical and religious literature of the world does
not contain many sayings that equal the wisdom and nobility of
Zarathustra's challenge: "If you have an enemy, do not requite
him evil with good, for that would put him to shame. Rather prove
that he did you some good." [3] In *Ecce Homo* Nietzsche embodies

---

[3] Part One, "On the Adder's Bite" (*Portable Nietzsche*, p. 180).

this attitude, this triumph over *ressentiment*. Instead of bearing a grudge toward the world that treated him so cruelly, instead of succumbing to the rancor of sickness, he relates the story of his life and work in a spirit of gratitude—and goes out of his way to pay his respects to Paul Rée and Lou Salomé,[4] with whom he had fallen out.

Ecce Homo, "Dionysus versus the Crucified": the contrast with the Jesus of the Gospels is central. The Jesus of the Gospels— who, Nietzsche argued in *The Antichrist,* is different in this respect from the historic Jesus—is far from being above resentment: not only does he obsessively slander his enemies, he stands opposed to this world and this life, and neither takes nor teaches any joy in small pleasures and beauties. The strange emphasis on little things, material factors generally thought beneath the notice of philosophers and sages, that distinguishes the first two chapters of *Ecce Homo* has to be seen in this light, too. This theme was picked up by Camus, also with an anti-Christian pathos, but restrained by lyricism and his distinctive charm. Nietzsche, like Socrates who was said to look like a satyr, disdains charm and embraces irony and sarcasm: he is not ingratiating, but wants to give offense. Is there no resentment in that?

In the case of Socrates, Nietzsche emphasized the element of rancor in his sarcasm—what he called *Bosheit,* malice. And in that case many did not wish to see Socrates in this light and, because Socrates was felt to be ideal, tranquil, the perfect sage, took offense at Nietzsche's portrait. Only the safe distance of more than twenty centuries could make the hero of the *Apology* look saintly. No doubt, those who had *heard* his apology, felt what Nietzsche saw— and had smarted under it for years. After all, what Socrates boasted of was perfectly true: he had taken pleasure in engaging men of reputation in the marketplace to humiliate them before the crowd that gathered—often (assuming, as is surely fair, that Plato did not

---

[4] Both are discussed briefly in my *Nietzsche: Philosopher, Psychologist, Antichrist* (1950; 2nd rev. ed., 1956; 3rd rev. ed., 1968). Chapter 1, section III. For a much more comprehensive treatment that embodies a vast amount of original research, see Rudolph Binion's *Frau Lou* (Princeton, N.J.: Princeton University Press, 1968).

mean to slander Socrates) by using clever debater's tricks. He had
a wicked sense of humor and found all this very funny; those he
bested certainly did not.

Goethe, too, possessed not only the serenity of *amor fati*[5] but
also an Olympian malice. But even if Nietzsche is in noble company, was there not after all resentment in him, even in *Ecce
Homo?* It is a matter of what Nietzsche called in *The Gay Science*
"giving style to one's character." The negative feelings, he taught,
should not be suppressed, much less extirpated; they should be sublimated. And in *Ecce Homo* he discusses how he was both a No-
saying and a Yes-saying spirit. The negative feelings are not vented
on individuals or directed against life or the world; they are mobi-
lized in the service of life and creativity against obstructions, movements, causes.

Ultimate nobility must rise above rancor and must yet be capable of echoing Voltaire's cry, *écrasez l'infâme.*[6] Resentment is
reprehensible, but so is the failure to engage in the fight against
infamy. It is only when the infamy to be crushed turns out to be
Christianity that most readers recoil. But Nietzsche's attack, of
course, depends on his conception of Christianity and—as he himself insists—cannot be understood at all except as a part of his
campaign against resentment.

Indeed, this attack seems to me much more successfully stylized than Nietzsche's denunciations of the Germans. Since World
War II the Germans may seem fair game, but Nietzsche's indict-
ments are sometimes stained by his own wounds: in more than one
passage he falls short of his own standards, and resentment clings
to him like a leech.

Nietzsche's ties to the pre-Christian world are stronger than is
usually supposed, though this should not surprise us in a classical
philologist who, even in his teens, nourished his spirit and emotions
on Greek literature and thought. This is not the place for a lengthy
survey of classical inspirations, but in addition to Socrates' *Apology* we must mention Aristotle's portrait of the great-souled man in
the *Nicomachean Ethics.* It is a commonplace that Aristotle's eth-

---

[5] Cf. p. 258, note 4.
[6] Crush the infamy.

ics was based in large measure on the morality of Athenian gentlemen, and that the man described in this passage represents not
merely Aristotle's ideal but a type very much admired in Athens. It
has not been widely noticed—and for all I know, I may have been
the first to point this out some years ago—that Aristotle's portrait
was probably inspired in part by Socrates' *Apology*. In any case,
both left their mark on *Ecce Homo*.

"A person is thought to be great-souled if he claims much and
deserves much." Aristotle's words—antithetical as they are to the
Christian influence on modern morality—represent *one* of the leit-
motifs of *Ecce Homo*. "He does not bear a grudge" represents another. That he does not speak evil "even of his enemies, except
when he deliberately intends to give offense," is a third. But Aristotle's whole portrait is relevant.[7] And to Nietzsche's central contrast of the New Testament and the Greeks, Greek tragedy, Thucydides, and the *Iliad* are relevant, too. And so is Greek comedy;
so are the satyrs, the companions of Dionysus; so are Greek laughter and Socratic irony. It should not be assumed that the chapter
titles of *Ecce Homo* are devoid of all humor. Neither, of course, is
Nietzsche *only* speaking in jest when he explains, "Why I Write
Such Good Books"—any more than George Bernard Shaw was
only jesting when he spoke in a similar vein.

Looking for a pre-Christian, Greek symbol that he might oppose to "the Crucified," Nietzsche found Dionysus. His "Dionysus" is neither the god of the ancient Dionysian festivals nor the
god Nietzsche had played off against Apollo in *The Birth of Tragedy,* although he does, of course, bear some of the features of
both. In the later works of Nietzsche, "Dionysus" is no longer the
spirit of unrestrained passion, but the symbol of the affirmation of
life with all its suffering and terror. "The problem," Nietzsche explained in a note that was later included in the posthumous *Will to
Power* (section 1052), "is that of the meaning of suffering: whether
a Christian meaning or a tragic meaning. . . . The tragic man
affirms even the harshest suffering." And *Ecce Homo* is, not least
of all, Nietzsche's final affirmation of his own cruel life.

---

[7] *Nicomachean Ethics,* IV.3. Most of the description is quoted in my
Nietzsche, Chapter 12, section VI; much of it also in my note on *Beyond
Good and Evil* (New York, Vintage Books, 1966), section 212.

A Note on the Publication of Ecce Homo

Many who have never carefully read any of Nietzsche's works have read *about* two German editions of the works that elicited some sensational but uninformed comments in print. The first was Karl Schlechta's edition of all of Nietzsche's books and a selection from his notes, fragments, and letters, in three volumes. But Schlechta simply reprinted the previously published versions of *Ecce Homo* and need not be considered here.

The second was Erich F. Podach's book, *Friedrich Nietzsches Werke des Zusammenbruchs* (1961),[1] which offered texts of *Nietzsche contra Wagner, The Antichrist, Ecce Homo,* and the so-called *Dionysus Dithyrambs* that were said to supersede all previous editions. I have shown elsewhere[2] how ill-founded Podach's strident claims are. Here we need only consider his handling of *Ecce Homo.* He aims to show that "The hitherto familiar *Ecce Homo* does not exist" (p. 208). This sensational charge has to be met here, even if some readers should prefer to skim the next six paragraphs.

Podach prints the manuscript with Nietzsche's editorial directions, such as requests to insert or move passages; he reproduces alternative versions of the same passages, including pages that had been pasted over; and he admits that he has "not indicated where whole sections in the manuscript sent to the printer are crossed out. Here some of the texts show plainly that they are variants or preliminary versions, while in other cases [very few] it cannot be decided whether N or Gast [Nietzsche's young friend who helped him with editorial chores and proofs] has deleted them" (p. 408).

In fact, *Ecce Homo* was begun October 15, 1888, on Nie-

---

[1] "The Works of Friedrich Nietzsche's Collapse" (or, literally, "Friedrich Nietzsche's Works of the Collapse"), Heidelberg, Wolfgang Rothe, 1961.

[2] "Nietzsche in the Light of His Suppressed Manuscripts," *Journal of the History of Philosophy,* II (October 1964), 205–25. This is included in the revised third edition of my *Nietzsche* (1968).

tzsche's forty-fourth birthday, and finished November 4. A few days later Nietzsche sent the manuscript to his publisher, Naumann; but on November 20 he mentioned some additions in a letter to Georg Brandes, the Danish critic who was the first to lecture on Nietzsche at a university (Copenhagen); and then he also mentioned additions to Naumann. On a postcard, November 27, he asked Naumann to return "the second part of the MS . . . because I still want to insert some things," and explained that he meant "the whole second half of the MS, beginning with the section entitled 'Thus Spoke Zarathustra.' I assume that this won't delay the printing for even a moment as I shall send back the MS immediately." On December 1 he acknowledged receipt of the second half but requested the return of the whole MS, including the additions: "I want to give you a MS as good as the last one, at the risk that I have to be a copier for another week." On December 3 Naumann replied that he was returning the MS, but "copying it once more I do not consider necessary; I merely should especially recommend that you read the proofs carefully although I shall make a point of doing likewise." This shows plainly how wrong Podach's claims are: *the publisher found the manuscript finished, clear, and printable.*

Nor did Nietzsche keep it long. On December 6, he telegraphed Naumann: "MS back. Everything reworked [*umgearbeitet*]." And on the eighth, Nietzsche wrote Gast: "I sent *Ecce Homo* back to C. G. Naumann day before yesterday after laying it once more on the gold scales from the first to the last word to set my conscience finally at rest."

All this information was given by Professor Raoul Richter in his long postscript to the first edition of 1908, and Richter also described the manuscript: "The manuscript is written clearly and cleanly from beginning to end, so that even every untrained person can read it quickly on the whole, without trouble. Changes have been made either by striking things out (with pencil or ink) or by pasting things over. In both cases the editor [Richter] has copied the original version in order to help provide a basis for a later critical edition. For that, ample use would also have to be made of the drafts and variants found in the three octavo notebooks

(. . .) [3] and some separate sheets. Nietzsche's corrections in the manuscript have been entered with scrupulous exactness; where, owing to lack of space, some additions had to be written in minia-ture script, they are little graphic masterpieces: so readable is every letter, and so exactly is the bracket of insertion drawn above the line . . . Slips that affect the spelling or grammar are very rare and probably rarer than in the average manuscript submitted to a printer" (p. 146).

Neither Richter's probity nor the authenticity of the letters I have cited, and of any number of others that corroborate them, has ever been questioned. Podach simply ignores all of this. Still, two departures of his version from the traditional ones ought to be mentioned here. First, he omits section 7 of the second chapter, which contains Nietzsche's well-known poem that is sometimes called "Venice," sometimes "Gondola Song." Podach prints this section under the title "Intermezzo," after the second section of *Nietzsche contra Wagner*. This is understandable, for that is where it appeared in the unpublished first printing of the latter book (1889; I have a copy of that), though not in any published version. But on December 20 Nietzsche sent his publisher a postcard: "I have sent you a single sheet with the title 'Intermezzo,' with the request to insert it in *N. contra W.* Now let us rather insert it in *Ecce,* for which it was intended originally[!]—in the *second* chap-ter (Why I am so clever), as *section 5* [*sic*]. The following num-bers will have to be changed accordingly. The title 'Intermezzo,' of course, goes." Two days later Nietzsche wrote Gast similarly. But a few days later he received proofs of *Nietzsche contra Wagner* that naturally still included this section, and he did not delete it but made some slight corrections in it. Richter printed it in his edition of *Ecce Homo,* with the corrections Nietzsche had made in the proofs. Podach mentions none of this but says simply that Gast, "for his own glory and the enhancement of *Ecce Homo,* embodied the 'Intermezzo' printed in *Nietzsche contra Wagner* in the manu-script" (p. 188; cf. also p. 201). While this is in keeping with the tenor of Podach's book, it seems sensible to me to include this

---

[3] Identified in parentheses by their Archive numbers.

section in *Ecce Homo,* in keeping with all previous editions except Podach's.

Finally, at the end of *Ecce Homo,* Podach prints a three-page poem entitled "Ruhm und Ewigkeit" (fame and eternity). Here he follows Richter's edition, while all subsequent editions have omitted the poem. This did not involve any suppression, although Podach is very scornful of all who have omitted it at this point: the poem has usually been included in the so-called *Dionysus Dithyrambs* and is readily available in volumes containing Nietzsche's poems. Podach considers it important—it is not clear why or for what—that Nietzsche wanted to conclude all of his last works with poems. But as a matter of fact, the last two books he saw through the press, *The Case of Wagner* and *The Twilight of the Idols,* did not end with poems; neither did *The Antichrist;* and as for *Nietzsche contra Wagner* and *Ecce Homo,* in his last communications to his publisher, Nietzsche asked Naumann January 1, 1889, to return one final poem, and January 2, 1889, to return both. That he did not want them published in their present form at the end of these books seems clear; that he would have revised them, if he had not collapsed on January 3, is possible. But it is no less possible and actually more likely, I think, that he realized that the books would be better without these poems.

After Nietzsche's collapse, his family decided not to publish any further books by him. *The Twilight of the Idols* did appear, as scheduled, in January 1889, but the three books written after that were held up. In 1891 the fourth part of *Thus Spoke Zarathustra* was printed, together with the *Dionysus Dithyrambs*—and published in 1892. By 1895 there was sufficient interest in Nietzsche to include both *The Antichrist* and *Nietzsche contra Wagner* in volume VIII of a new edition of Nietzsche's works. But *Ecce Homo* was held back, perhaps partly because it might compromise Nietzsche, partly because his sister found it useful to quote from Nietzsche's self-interpretations when she wrote prefaces for new editions of his books. As long as she knew *Ecce Homo* and the public did not, her biographies of her brother as well as her occasional journalistic pieces had a special authority.

Finally, in 1908 the book appeared in an expensive limited

edition of 1250 copies. It was not brought out by a publisher who had been previously associated with Nietzsche, but by the Insel Verlag; and the title, binding, and ornaments had all been designed by Henry van de Velde in the *Jugendstil* of that time. There is no English word for that style: one uses the French phrase *art nouveau*. Nietzsche, who had written Gast, November 26, 1888, that he wanted *Ecce* to be designed just like *Twilight*—that is, very simply, with clear print and wide margins and nothing to distract the eye from the text—would surely have found the book hideous. But Richter's postscript was dignified and informative.

Two years later, in 1910, *Ecce Homo* was included in the new volume XV of Nietzsche's works, which along with volume XVI (1911) contained a greatly enlarged and entirely remodeled version of the *Will to Power* and replaced the old volume XV (1901), which had contained the first edition of the *Will to Power*. Many libraries acquired only volume XVI, adding it to their old sets: as a result, many sets of the so-called Grossoktav edition[4] of Nietzsche's works lack *Ecce Homo*. But henceforth *Ecce* was included in editions of the works and no longer hard to come by. And all editions of the book, except for Podach's, followed the first edition, except that they omitted the poem at the end.

The present translation follows the standard editions, but the notes and Appendix also offer previously untranslated variants and passages from drafts, along with other information and comments not previously found in any edition in any language. In a way, all this apparatus weighs down a book written with light feet; but *Ecce* is not easily accessible, and on a first or second reading the commentary may prove helpful. The form in which it is offered should make it easy to reread *Ecce Homo* straight through, without any editorial interruptions.

Perhaps one or another reader of the book will react in a manner similar to "Napoleon's surprise when he came to see Goethe: it shows what people had associated with the 'German spirit' for centuries. '*Voilà un homme!*'"[5]

---

[4] See Bibliography in my translation of *The Birth of Tragedy* and *The Case of Wagner* (one vol., New York, Vintage Books, 1967), p. 200.
[5] *Beyond Good and Evil,* section 209.

ECCE HOMO

How One Becomes What One Is

Preface

1

Seeing that before long I must confront humanity with the most difficult demand ever made of it, it seems indispensable to me to say *who I am*. Really, one should know it, for I have not left myself "without testimony." But the disproportion between the greatness of my task and the *smallness* of my contemporaries has found expression in the fact that one has neither heard nor even seen me. I live on my own credit; it is perhaps a mere prejudice that I live.

I only need to speak with one of the "educated" who come to the Upper Engadine[1] for the summer, and I am convinced that I do *not* live.

Under these circumstances I have a duty against which my habits, even more the pride of my instincts, revolt at bottom—namely, to say: *Hear me! For I am such and such a person. Above all, do not mistake me for someone else.*

2

I am, for example, by no means a bogey, or a moralistic monster—I am actually the very opposite of the type of man who so far has been revered as virtuous. Between ourselves, it seems to me that precisely this is part of my pride. I am a disciple of the philosopher Dionysus; I should prefer to be even a satyr to being a saint. But one should really read this essay. Perhaps I have succeeded; perhaps this essay had no other meaning than to give expression to this contrast in a cheerful and philanthropic manner.

The last thing *I* should promise would be to "improve" mankind.[2] No new idols are erected by me; let the old ones learn what

---

[1] The Alpine valley in Switzerland where Nietzsche spent almost every summer from 1879 to 1888.

[2] Cf. the chapter "The 'Improvers' of Mankind" in *Twilight of the Idols*.

feet of clay mean. *Overthrowing idols* (my word for "ideals")—that comes closer to being part of my craft. One has deprived reality of its value, its meaning, its truthfulness, to precisely the extent to which one has mendaciously invented an ideal world.

The "true world" and the "apparent world"—that means: the mendaciously invented world and reality.

The *lie* of the ideal has so far been the curse on reality; on account of it, mankind itself has become mendacious and false down to its most fundamental instincts—to the point of worshiping the *opposite* values of those which alone would guarantee its health, its future, the lofty *right* to its future.

3

Those who can breathe the air of my writings know that it is an air of the heights, a *strong* air. One must be made for it. Otherwise there is no small danger that one may catch cold in it. The ice is near, the solitude tremendous—but how calmly all things lie in the light! How freely one breathes! How much one feels *beneath* oneself!

Philosophy, as I have so far understood and lived it, means living voluntarily among ice and high mountains—seeking out everything strange and questionable in existence, everything so far placed under a ban by morality. Long experience, acquired in the course of such wanderings *in what is forbidden,* taught me to regard the causes that so far have prompted moralizing and idealizing in a very different light from what may seem desirable: the *hidden* history of the philosophers, the psychology of the great names, came to light for me.

How much truth does a spirit *endure,* how much truth does it *dare?* More and more that became for me the real measure of value. Error (faith in the ideal) is not blindness, error is *cowardice.*

Every attainment, every step forward in knowledge, *follows* from courage, from hardness against oneself, from cleanliness in relation to oneself.

I do not refute ideals, I merely put on gloves before them.

Nitimur in vetitum:[3] in this sign my philosophy will triumph one day, for what one has forbidden so far as a matter of principle has always been—truth alone.

4

Among my writings my *Zarathustra* stands to my mind by itself. With that I have given mankind the greatest present that has ever been made to it so far. This book, with a voice bridging centuries, is not only the highest book there is, the book that is truly characterized by the air of the heights—the whole fact of man lies *beneath* it at a tremendous distance—it is also the *deepest,* born out of the innermost wealth of truth, an inexhaustible well to which no pail descends without coming up again filled with gold and goodness. Here no "prophet" is speaking, none of those gruesome hybrids of sickness and will to power whom people call founders of religions. Above all, one must *hear* aright the tone that comes from this mouth, the halcyon tone, lest one should do wretched injustice to the meaning of its wisdom.

"It is the stillest words that bring on the storm. Thoughts that come on doves' feet guide the world." [4]

> The figs are falling from the trees; they are good and sweet; and, as they fall, their red skin bursts. I am a north wind to ripe figs.
>
> Thus, like figs, these teachings fall to you, my friends: now consume their juice and their sweet meat. It is fall around us, and pure sky and afternoon.[5]

It is no fanatic that speaks here; this is not "preaching"; no *faith* is demanded here: from an infinite abundance of light and depth of happiness falls drop upon drop, word upon word: the tempo of these speeches is a tender adagio. Such things reach only

---

[3] "We strive for the forbidden": Ovid, *Amores,* III, 4, 17. Cf. *Beyond Good and Evil,* section 227.

[4] *Thus Spoke Zarathustra,* Second Part, last chapter: *The Portable Nietzsche,* tr. Walter Kaufmann (New York, Viking, 1954), p. 258.

[5] *Ibid.,* second chapter.

the most select. It is a privilege without equal to be a listener here. Nobody is free to have ears for Zarathustra.

Is not Zarathustra in view of all this a *seducer*?— But what does he himself say, as he returns again for the first time to his solitude? Precisely the opposite of everything that any "sage," "saint," "world-redeemer," or any other decadent would say in such a case.— Not only does he speak differently, he also *is* different.—

Now I go alone, my disciples, You, too, go now, alone. Thus I want it.

Go away from me and resist Zarathustra! And even better: be ashamed of him! Perhaps he deceived you.

The man of knowledge must not only love his enemies, he must also be able to hate his friends.

One repays a teacher badly if one always remains nothing but a pupil. And why do you not want to pluck at my wreath?

You revere me; but what if your reverence *tumbles* one day? Beware lest a statue slay you.

You say that you believe in Zarathustra? But what matters Zarathustra? You are my believers—but what matter all believers?

You had not yet sought yourselves; and you found me. Thus do all believers; therefore all faith amounts to so little.

Now I bid you lose me and find yourselves; and only *when you have all denied me* will I return to you.[6]

Friedrich Nietzsche

---

[6] *Ibid.*, First Part, last chapter.

On this perfect day, when everything is ripening and not only the grape turns brown, the eye of the sun just fell upon my life: I looked back, I looked forward, and never saw so many and such good things at once. It was not for nothing that I buried my forty-fourth year today; I had the *right* to bury it; whatever was life in it has been saved, is immortal. The first book of the *Revaluation of All Values*,[1] the *Songs of Zarathustra*,[2] the *Twilight of the Idols,* my attempt to philosophize with a hammer[3]—all presents of this year, indeed of its last quarter! *How could I fail to be grateful to my whole life?*—and so I tell my life to myself.

---

[1] *The Antichrist.*

[2] Published, after Nietzsche's collapse, under the title *Dionysus Dithyrambs,* in the same volume with *Zarathustra IV*.

[3] This image is explained in the preface of *Twilight:* ". . . idols, which are here touched with a hammer as with a tuning fork."

Why I Am So Wise

1

The good fortune of my existence, its uniqueness perhaps, lies in its fatality: I am, to express it in the form of a riddle, already dead as my father, while as my mother I am still living and becoming old. This dual descent, as it were, both from the highest and the lowest rung on the ladder of life, at the same time a *decadent* and a *beginning*—this, if anything, explains that neutrality, that freedom from all partiality in relation to the total problem of life, that perhaps distinguishes me. I have a subtler sense of smell for the signs of ascent and decline than any other human being before me; I am the teacher *par excellence* for this—I know both, I am both.

My father died at the age of thirty-six: he was delicate, kind, and morbid, as a being that is destined merely to pass by—more a gracious memory of life than life itself. In the same year in which his life went downward, mine, too, went downward: at thirty-six, I reached the lowest point of my vitality—I still lived, but without being able to see three steps ahead. Then—it was 1879—I retired from my professorship at Basel, spent the summer in St. Moritz like a shadow, and the next winter, than which not one in my life has been poorer in sunshine, in Naumburg *as* a shadow. This was my minimum: the *Wanderer and His Shadow* originated at this time. Doubtless, I then knew about shadows.

The following winter, my first one in Genoa, that sweetening and spiritualization which is almost inseparably connected with an extreme poverty of blood and muscle, produced *The Dawn*. The perfect brightness and cheerfulness, even exuberance of the spirit, reflected in this work, is compatible in my case not only with the most profound physiological weakness, but even with an excess of pain. In the midst of the torments that go with an uninterrupted three-day migraine, accompanied by laborious vomiting of phlegm, I possessed a dialectician's clarity *par excellence* and thought through with very cold blood matters for which under healthier circumstances I am not mountain-climber, not subtle, not *cold* enough. My readers know perhaps in what way I consider dialectic as a symptom of decadence; for example in the most famous case, the case of Socrates.

All pathological disturbances of the intellect, even that half-numb state that follows fever, have remained entirely foreign to me to this day; and I had to do research to find out about their nature and frequency. My blood moves slowly. Nobody has ever discovered any fever in me. A physician who treated me for some time as if my nerves were sick finally said: "It's not your nerves, it is rather I that am nervous." There is altogether no sign of any local degeneration; no organically conditioned stomach complaint, however profound the weakness of my gastric system may be as a consequence of over-all exhaustion. My eye trouble, too, though at times dangerously close to blindness, is only a consequence and not a cause: with every increase in vitality my ability to see has also increased again.

A long, all too long, series of years signifies recovery for me; unfortunately it also signifies relapse, decay, the periodicity of a kind of decadence. Need I say after all this that in questions of decadence I am *experienced?* I have spelled them forward and backward. Even that filigree art of grasping and comprehending in general, those fingers for *nuances,* that psychology of "looking around the corner," and whatever else is characteristic of me, was learned only then, is the true present of those days in which everything in me became subtler—observation itself as well as all organs of observation. Looking from the perspective of the sick toward *healthier* concepts and values and, conversely, looking again from the fullness and self-assurance of a *rich* life down into the secret work of the instinct of decadence—in this I have had the longest training, my truest experience; if in anything, I became master in *this.* Now I know how, have the know-how, to *reverse perspectives:* the first reason why a "revaluation of values" is perhaps possible for me alone.

2

Apart from the fact that I am a decadent, I am also the opposite. My proof for this is, among other things, that I have always instinctively chosen the *right* means against wretched states; while the decadent typically chooses means that are disadvantageous for him. As *summa summarum*,[1] I was healthy; as an angle, as a specialty, I was a decadent. The energy to choose absolute solitude and leave the life to which I had become accustomed; the insistence on not allowing myself any longer to be cared for, waited on, and *doctored*—that betrayed an absolute instinctive certainty about *what* was needed above all at that time. I took myself in hand, I made myself healthy again: the condition for this—every physiologist would admit that—is *that one be healthy at bottom*. A typically morbid being cannot become healthy, much less make itself healthy. For a typically healthy person, conversely, being sick can even become an energetic *stimulus* for life, for living *more*. This, in fact, is how that long period of sickness appears to me *now:* as it were, I discovered life anew, including myself; I tasted all good and even little things, as others cannot easily taste them—I turned my will to health, to *life,* into a philosophy.

For it should be noted: it was during the years of my lowest vitality that I *ceased* to be a pessimist; the instinct of self-restoration *forbade* me a philosophy of poverty and discouragement.

What is it, fundamentally, that allows us to recognize *who has turned out well?* That a well-turned-out person pleases our senses, that he is carved from wood that is hard, delicate, and at the same time smells good. He has a taste only for what is good for him; his pleasure, his delight cease where the measure of what is good for him is transgressed. He guesses what remedies avail against what is harmful; he exploits bad accidents to his advantage; what does not kill him makes him stronger.[2] Instinctively, he collects from everything he sees, hears, lives through, *his* sum: he is a principle of selection, he discards much. He is always in his own company,

---

[1] Over-all.

[2] Cf. *Twilight*, Chapter I, section 8 (*Portable Nietzsche*, p. 467).

whether he associates with books, human beings, or landscapes: he honors by *choosing,* by *admitting,* by *trusting.* He reacts slowly to all kinds of stimuli, with that slowness which long caution and deliberate pride have bred in him: he examines the stimulus that approaches him, he is far from meeting it halfway. He believes neither in "misfortune" nor in "guilt": he comes to terms with himself, with others; he knows how to *forget*—he is strong enough; hence everything *must* turn out for his best.

Well then, I am the *opposite* of a decadent, for I have just described *myself.*

3

This *dual* series of experiences, this access to apparently separate worlds, is repeated in my nature in every respect: I am a *Doppelgänger,* I have a "second" face in addition to the first. *And* perhaps also a third.

Even by virtue of my descent, I am granted an eye beyond all merely local, merely nationally conditioned perspectives; it is not difficult for me to be a "good European." On the other hand, I am perhaps more German than present-day Germans, mere citizens of the German *Reich,* could possibly be—I, the last *anti-political* German. And yet my ancestors were Polish noblemen: I have many racial instincts in my body from that source—who knows? In the end perhaps even the *liberum veto.*[1]

When I consider how often I am addressed as a Pole when I travel, even by Poles themselves, and how rarely I am taken for a German, it might seem that I have been merely externally *sprinkled* with what is German. Yet my mother, Franziska Oehler, is at any rate something very German; ditto, my grandmother on my father's side, Erdmuthe Krause. The latter lived all her youth in the middle

---

[1] Unrestricted veto—one of the traditional privileges of the members of the Polish Diet.

During the Nazi period, one of Nietzsche's relatives, Max Oehler, a retired major, went to great lengths to prove that Nietzsche had been racially pure: "Nietzsches angebliche polnische Herkunft" (N's alleged Polish descent) in *Ostdeutsche Monatshefte,* 18 (1938), 679–82, and *Nietzsches Ahnentafel* (N's pedigree), Weimar, 1938.

of good old Weimar, not without some connection with the circle of
Goethe. Her brother, the professor of theology Krause in Königs-
berg, was called to Weimar as general superintendent after
Herder's death. It is not impossible that her mother, my great-
grandmother, is mentioned in the diary of the young Goethe under
the name of "Muthgen." Her second marriage was with the superintendent Nietzsche in Eilenburg; and in the great war year of
1813, on the day that Napoleon entered Eilenburg with his general
staff, on the tenth of October, she gave birth. As a Saxon, she was a
great admirer of Napoleon; it could be that I still am, too. My
father, born in 1813, died in 1849. Before he accepted the pastor's
position in the parish of Röcken, not far from Lützen, he lived for a
few years in the castle of Altenburg and taught the four princesses
there. His pupils are now the Queen of Hanover, the Grand Duchess Constantine, the Grand Duchess of Altenburg, and the Princess
Therese of Saxe-Altenburg. He was full of deep reverence for the
Prussian king Frederick William IV, from whom he had also received his pastoral position; the events of 1848 grieved him beyond
all measure. I myself, born on the birthday of the above named
king, on the fifteenth of October, received, as fitting, the Hohenzol-
lern name *Friedrich* Wilhelm. There was at least one advantage to
the choice of this day: my birthday was a holiday throughout my
childhood.

I consider it a great privilege to have had such a father: it
even seems to me that this explains whatever else I have of privileges—*not* including life, the great Yes to life. Above all, that it
requires no resolve on my part, but merely biding my time, to enter
quite involuntarily into a world of lofty and delicate things: I am at
home there, my inmost passion becomes free only there. That I
have almost paid with my life for this privilege is certainly no un-
fair trade.

In order to understand anything at all of my *Zarathustra* one
must perhaps be similarly conditioned as I am—with one foot *beyond* life.

4

I have never understood the art of predisposing people against me—this, too, I owe to my incomparable father—even when it seemed highly desirable to me. However un-Christian this may seem, I am not even predisposed against myself. You can turn my life this way and that, you will rarely find traces, and actually only once, that anybody felt ill will toward me—but perhaps rather too many traces of *good* will.

Even my experiences with people with whom everybody has bad experiences bear witness, without exception, in their favor: I tame every bear, I make even buffoons behave themselves. During the seven years that I taught Greek in the senior class in the *Pädagogium* in Basel, I never had occasion to punish anyone; the laziest boys worked hard. I am always equal to accidents; I have to be unprepared to be master of myself. Let the instrument be what it may, let it be as out of tune as only the instrument "man" can be—I should have to be sick if I should not succeed in getting out of it something worth hearing. And how often have I been told by the "instruments" themselves that they had never heard themselves like that.— Most beautifully perhaps by Heinrich von Stein,[1] who died so unpardonably young. Once, after he had courteously requested permission, he appeared for three days in Sils Maria, explaining to everybody that he had *not* come to see the Engadine. This excellent human being, who had walked into the Wagnerian morass with all the impetuous simplicity of a Prussian Junker (and in addition even into that of Dühring![2]), acted during these three days like one transformed by a tempest of freedom, like one who has suddenly been lifted to his own height and acquired wings. I always said to him that this was due to the good air up here, that this happened to everybody, that one was not for nothing six thousand feet above Bayreuth[3]—but he would not believe me.

---

[1] For Nietzsche's relation to this young man, see my note on the "Aftersong" that concludes *Beyond Good and Evil* (New York, Vintage Books, 1966).

[2] See my note in *Genealogy* II, section 11.

[3] The capital of the Wagner cult. Stein admired Wagner as well as Nietzsche.

If, in spite of that, some small and great misdemeanors have been committed against me, "the will" cannot be blamed for this, least of all any *ill* will: sooner could I complain, as I have already suggested, of the good will that has done no small mischief in my life. My experiences entitle me to be quite generally suspicious of the so-called "selfless" drives, of all "neighbor love" that is ready to give advice and go into action. It always seems a weakness to me, a particular case of being incapable of resisting stimuli: *pity* is considered a virtue only among decadents. I reproach those who are full of pity for easily losing a sense of shame, of respect, of sensitivity for distances; before you know it, pity begins to smell of the mob and becomes scarcely distinguishable from bad manners—and sometimes pitying hands can interfere in a downright destructive manner in a great destiny, in the growing solitude of one wounded, in a privileged right to heavy guilt.

The overcoming of pity I count among the *noble* virtues: as "Zarathustra's temptation" I invented a situation in which a great cry of distress reaches him, as pity tries to attack him like a final sin that would entice him away from *himself*.[4] To remain the master at this point, to keep the eminence of one's task undefiled by the many lower and more myopic impulses that are at work in so-called selfless actions, that is the test, perhaps the ultimate test, which a Zarathustra must pass—his real *proof* of strength.

5

At another point as well, I am merely my father once more and, as it were, his continued life after an all-too-early death. Like everyone who has never lived among his equals and who finds the concept of "retaliation" as inaccessible as, say, the concept of "equal rights," I forbid myself all countermeasures, all protective measures, and, as is only fair, also any defense, any "justification," in cases when some small or *very great* folly is perpetrated against me. My kind of retaliation consists in following up the stupidity as fast as possible with some good sense: that way one may actually

---

4 *Zarathustra IV*, Chapter 2.

catch up with it.[1] Metaphorically speaking, I send a box of confections to get rid of a painful story.

One needs only to do me some wrong, I "repay" it—you may be sure of that: soon I find an opportunity for expressing my gratitude to the "evil-doer" (at times even for his evil deed)—or to *ask* him for something, which can be more obliging than giving something.

It also seems to me that the rudest word, the rudest letter are still more benign, more decent than silence. Those who remain silent are almost always lacking in delicacy and courtesy of the heart. Silence is an objection; swallowing things leads of necessity to a bad character—it even upsets the stomach. All who remain silent are dyspeptic.

You see, I don't want rudeness to be underestimated: it is by far the *most humane* form of contradiction and, in the midst of effeminacy, one of our foremost virtues.

If one is rich enough for this, it is even a good fortune to be in the wrong. A god who would come to earth must not *do* anything except wrong: not to take the punishment upon oneself but the *guilt* would be divine.[2]

6

Freedom from *ressentiment*, enlightenment about *ressentiment*—who knows how much I am ultimately indebted, in this respect also, to my protracted sickness! This problem is far from simple: one must have experienced it from strength as well as from weakness. If anything at all must be adduced against being sick and being weak, it is that man's really remedial instinct, his *fighting*

---

[1] Cf. the chapter "On The Adder's Bite" in *Zarathustra I:* "If you have an enemy, do not requite him evil with good, for that would put him to shame. Rather prove that he did you some good. And rather be angry than put to shame. . . ."

[2] Cf. *ibid.,* "Would that you might invent for me the love that bears not only all punishment but also all guilt!" This theme is developed in Sartre's *Flies*. For Nietzsche's immense influence on *The Flies*, see my article on "Nietzsche Between Homer and Sartre" in *Revue internationale de philosophie,* 1964.

instinct[1] wears out. One cannot get rid of anything, one cannot get over anything, one cannot repel anything—everything hurts. Men and things obtrude too closely; experiences strike one too deeply; memory becomes a festering wound. Sickness itself *is* a kind of *ressentiment.*

Against all this the sick person has only one great remedy: I call it *Russian fatalism,* that fatalism without revolt which is exemplified by a Russian soldier who, finding a campaign too strenuous, finally lies down in the snow. No longer to accept anything at all, no longer to take anything, no longer to absorb anything—to cease reacting altogether.

This fatalism is not always merely the courage to die; it can also preserve life under the most perilous conditions by reducing the metabolism, slowing it down, as a kind of will to hibernate. Carrying this logic a few steps further, we arrive at the fakir who sleeps for weeks in a grave.

Because one would use oneself up too quickly if one reacted in *any* way, one does not react at all any more: this is the logic. Nothing burns one up faster than the affects of *ressentiment.* Anger, pathological vulnerability, impotent lust for revenge, thirst for revenge, poison-mixing in any sense—no reaction could be more disadvantageous for the exhausted: such affects involve a rapid consumption of nervous energy, a pathological increase of harmful excretions—for example, of the gall bladder into the stomach. *Ressentiment* is what is forbidden *par excellence* for the sick —it is their specific evil—unfortunately also their most natural inclination.

This was comprehended by that profound physiologist, the Buddha. His "religion" should rather be called a kind of *hygiene,* lest it be confused with such pitiable phenomena as Christianity: its effectiveness was made conditional on the victory over *ressentiment.* To liberate the soul from this is the first step toward recovery. "Not by enmity is enmity ended; by friendliness enmity is ended": these words stand at the beginning of the doctrine of the

---

[1] *Wehr- und Waffen-Instinkt* (emphasized in the original) alludes to Luther's famous hymn, "A mighty fortress is our God, a good defense and weapons [*ein' gute Wehr und Waffen*]."

Buddha.[2] It is *not* morality that speaks thus; thus speaks physiology.

Born of weakness, *ressentiment* is most harmful for the weak themselves. Conversely, given a rich nature, it is a *superfluous* feeling; mastering this feeling is virtually what proves riches. Whoever knows how seriously my philosophy has pursued the fight against vengefulness and rancor, even into the doctrine of "free will" [3]— the fight against Christianity is merely a special case of this—will understand why I am making such a point of my own behavior, my *instinctive sureness* in practice. During periods of decadence I forbade myself such feelings as harmful; as soon as my vitality was rich and proud enough again, I forbade myself such feelings as *beneath* me. I displayed the "Russian fatalism" I mentioned by tenaciously clinging for years to all but intolerable situations, places, apartments, and society, merely because they happened to be given by accident: it was better than changing them, than *feeling* that they could be changed—than rebelling against them.

Any attempt to disturb me in this fatalism, to awaken me by force, used to annoy me mortally—and it actually was mortally dangerous every time.

Accepting oneself as if fated, not wishing oneself "different" —that is in such cases *great reason* itself.

7

War[1] is another matter. I am warlike by nature. Attacking is one of my instincts. Being *able* to be an enemy, *being* an enemy— perhaps that presupposes a strong nature; in any case, it belongs to every strong nature. It needs objects of resistance; hence it *looks*

---

[2] Cf. *The Dhammapada*, tr. Max Müller: "Hatred does not cease by hatred at any time: hatred ceases by love" (Chapter 1). Given the original context, Nietzsche's comments are not at all far-fetched.

[3] Cf. *Twilight*, "The Four Great Errors," section 7 (*Portable Nietzsche*, pp. 499ff.). Nietzsche's attack on Christianity cannot be understood apart from the point made in the sentence above.

[1] This section throws a great deal of light on some of Nietzsche's other writings—especially the chapter "On War and Warriors" in *Zarathustra I*. Cf. also below, "Human, All-Too-Human," section 1, and "Dawn," section 1.

for what resists: the *aggressive* pathos belongs just as necessarily to strength as vengefulness and rancor belong to weakness. Woman, for example, is vengeful: that is due to her weakness, as much as is her susceptibility to the distress of others.

The strength of those who attack can be measured in a way by the opposition they require: every growth is indicated by the search for a mighty opponent—or problem; for a warlike philosopher challenges problems, too, to single combat. The task is *not* simply to master what happens to resist, but what requires us to stake all our strength, suppleness, and fighting skill—opponents that are our *equals.*

Equality before the enemy: the first presupposition of an *honest* duel. Where one feels contempt, one *cannot* wage war; where one commands, where one sees something beneath oneself, one has no business waging war.

My practice of war can be summed up in four propositions. First: I only attack causes that are victorious; I may even wait until they become victorious.[2]

Second: I only attack causes against which I would not find allies, so that I stand alone—so that I compromise myself alone.— I have never taken a step publicly that did not compromise me: that is *my* criterion of doing right.

Third: I never attack persons; I merely avail myself of the person as of a strong magnifying glass that allows one to make visible a general but creeping and elusive calamity. Thus I attacked David Strauss—more precisely, the *success* of a senile book with the "cultured" people in Germany: I caught this culture in the act.

Thus I attacked Wagner—more precisely, the falseness, the half-couth instincts of our "culture" which mistakes the subtle for the rich, and the late for the great.

Fourth: I only attack things when every personal quarrel is excluded, when any background of bad experiences is lacking. On the contrary, attack is in my case a proof of good will, sometimes

---

[2] Nietzsche's first great polemic was directed against the tremendous success of David Friedrich Strauss' book, *The Old Faith and The New,* and he broke with Wagner only after Wagner had returned to Germany and triumphed in Bayreuth.

even of gratitude. I honor, I distinguish by associating my name
with that of a cause or a person: pro or con—that makes no difference to me at this point. When I wage war against Christianity I am
entitled to this because I have never experienced misfortunes and
frustrations from that quarter—the most serious Christians have
always been well disposed toward me. I myself, an opponent of
Christianity *de rigueur*,[3] am far from blaming individuals for the
calamity of millennia.

8

May I still venture to sketch one final trait of my nature that
causes me no little difficulties in my contacts with other men? My
instinct for cleanliness is characterized by a perfectly uncanny sensitivity so that the proximity or—what am I saying?—the inmost
parts, the "entrails" of every soul are physiologically perceived by
me—*smelled*.

This sensitivity furnishes me with psychological antennae with
which I feel and get a hold of every secret: the abundant *hidden*
dirt at the bottom of many a character—perhaps the result of bad
blood, but glossed over by education—enters my consciousness almost at the first contact. If my observation has not deceived me,
such characters who offend my sense of cleanliness also sense from
their side the reserve of my disgust—and this does not make them
smell any better.

As has always been my wont—extreme cleanliness in relation
to me is the presupposition of my existence; I perish under unclean
conditions—I constantly swim and bathe and splash, as it were, in
water—in some perfectly transparent and resplendent element.
Hence association with people imposes no mean test on my patience: my humanity does *not* consist in feeling with men how they
are, but in *enduring* that I feel with them.[1]

My humanity is a constant self-overcoming.

But I need *solitude*—which is to say, recovery, return to myself, the breath of a free, light, playful air.

---

[3] In accordance with good manners.
[1] Nietzsche's critique of pity should be considered in this light.

My whole *Zarathustra* is a dithyramb on solitude or, if I have been understood, on *cleanliness.*—Fortunately not on *pure foolishness.*[2]— Those who have eyes for colors will compare it to a diamond.— *Nausea* over man, over the "rabble," was always my greatest danger.— Do you want to hear the words in which Zarathustra speaks of the *redemption* from nausea?

What was it that happened to me? How did I redeem myself from nausea? Who rejuvenated my sight? How did I fly to the height where no more rabble sits by the well? Was it my nausea itself that created wings for me and water-divining powers? Verily, I had to fly to the highest spheres that I might find the fount of pleasure again.

Oh, I found it, my brothers! Here, in the highest spheres the fount of pleasure wells up for me! And here is a life of which the rabble does not drink.

You flow for me almost too violently, fountain of pleasure. And often you empty the cup again by wanting to fill it. And I must still learn to approach you more modestly: all too violently my heart still flows toward you—my heart, upon which my summer burns, short, hot, melancholy, overblissful: how my summer heart craves your coolness!

Gone is the hesitant gloom of my spring! Gone the snowflakes of my malice in June![3] Summer have I become entirely, and summer noon! A summer in the highest spheres with cold wells and blissful silence: oh, come, my friends, that the silence may become still more blissful!

For this is *our* height and our home: we live here too high and steep for all the unclean and their thirst. Cast your pure eyes into the well of my pleasure, friends! How should that make it muddy? It shall laugh back at you in its own purity.

On the tree, Future, we build our nest; and in our solitude eagles shall bring us nourishment in their beaks. Verily, no nourishment that the unclean might share: they would think

---

[2] Wagner himself had characterized his Parsifal as the pure fool.

[3] This long passage is quoted from the chapter "On The Rabble" in *Zarathustra II.* But in *Zarathustra,* Nietzsche had "the malice of my snowflakes in June!"

they were devouring fire, and they would burn their mouths. Verily, we keep no homes here for the unclean: our pleasure would be an ice cave to their bodies and their spirits.

And we want to live over them like strong winds, neighbors of the eagles, neighbors of the snow, neighbors of the sun: thus live strong winds. And like a wind I yet want to blow among them one day, and with my spirit take away the breath of their spirit: thus my future wills it.

Verily, a strong wind is Zarathustra for all who are low; and this counsel I give to all his enemies and all who spit and spew: Beware of spitting *against* the wind! . . .

Why I Am So Clever

1

Why do I know a few things *more?* Why am I altogether so clever? I have never reflected on questions that are none—I have not wasted myself.

Really *religious* difficulties, for example, I don't know from experience. It has escaped me altogether in what way I was supposed to be "sinful." Likewise, I lack any reliable criterion for recognizing the bite of conscience: according to what one *hears* about it, the bite of conscience does not seem respectable to me.

I do not want to leave an action in the lurch *afterward;*[1] I should prefer to exclude the bad result, the *consequences,* from the question of value as a matter of principle. Faced with a bad result, one loses all too easily the *right* perspective for what one has done: the bite of conscience seems to me a kind of *"evil eye."* To hold in honor in one's heart even more what has failed, *because* it failed—that would go better with my morality.

"God," "immortality of the soul," "redemption," "beyond"—without exception, concepts to which I never devoted any attention, or time; not even as a child. Perhaps I have never been childlike enough for them?

I do not by any means know atheism as a result; even less as an event: it is a matter of course with me, from instinct. I am too inquisitive, too *questionable,* too exuberant to stand for any gross answer.[2] God is a gross answer, an indelicacy against us thinkers—

---

[1] Cf. *Twilight,* Chapter I, section 10: "Not to perpetrate cowardice against one's own acts! Not to leave them in the lurch afterwards! The bite of conscience is indecent." And *The Will to Power,* section 234: *"The bite of conscience:* a sign that the character is no match for the deed." Also Sartre's *The Flies* and Walter Kaufmann, "Nietzsche Between Homer and Sartre," *Revue internationale de philosophie,* 1964.

[2] *Ich bin zu neugierig, zu* fragwürdig, *zu übermütig, um mir eine faustgrobe Antwort gefallen zu lassen.* Nietzsche's atheism is not a "result"; it is a cor-

at bottom merely a gross prohibition for us: you shall not think!

I am much more interested in a question on which the "salvation of humanity" depends far more than on any theologians' curio: the question of *nutrition.* For ordinary use, one may formulate it thus: "how do *you,* among all people, have to eat to attain your maximum of strength, of *virtù* in the Renaissance style, of moraline-free[3] virtue?"

My experiences in this matter are as bad as possible; I am amazed how late I heard this question, how late I learned "reason" from these experiences. Only the complete worthlessness of our German education—its "idealism"—explains to me to some extent why at precisely this point I was backward to the point of holiness. This "education" which teaches one from the start to ignore *realities* and to pursue so-called "ideal" goals—a "classical education," for example—as if it were not hopeless from the start to unite "classical" and "German" into a single concept! More, it is amusing: only imagine a "classically educated" man with a Leipzig dialect! [4]

Indeed, till I reached a very mature age I always ate *badly:* morally speaking, "impersonally," "selflessly," "altruistically"— for the benefit of cooks and other fellow Christians. By means of Leipzig *cuisine,* for example, I very earnestly denied my "will to life" at the time when I first read Schopenhauer (1865). To upset one's stomach for the sake of inadequate nutrition—this problem seemed to me to be solved incredibly well by the aforementioned

---

rolary of his commitment to question every conviction, including his own convictions.

In a sense, of course, he does know atheism "as an event"; namely, as a cultural event which he designated with the words, "God is dead" (*Gay Science,* section 125; *Zarathustra,* Prologue, section 2: *Portable Nietzsche,* pp. 95f., 124). What he means above is that he did not experience the loss of faith in God as an event in his own life: he did not pass through any crisis of faith. Cf. *Genealogy* III, section 27, and Kaufmann's *Nietzsche,* Chapter 3, section I.

[3] The coinage of a man who neither smoked nor drank coffee. Cf. *Antichrist,* section 2 (*Portable Nietzsche,* p. 570).

[4] Leipzig, about a hundred miles south-southwest of Berlin, is one of the two major cities of Saxony and renowned for its exceptionally broad dialect. It is also the seat of a university at which Nietzsche studied classical philology.

cuisine. (It is said that 1866 brought about a change in this respect.)[5] But German cuisine quite generally—what doesn't it have on its conscience! Soup *before* the meal (in Venetian cookbooks of the sixteenth century this is still called *alla tedesca*);[6] overcooked meats, vegetables cooked with fat and flour; the degeneration of pastries and puddings into paperweights! Add to this the virtually bestial prandial drinking habits of the ancient, and by no means only the *ancient* Germans, and you will understand the origin of the *German spirit*—from distressed intestines.

The German spirit is an indigestion: it does not finish with anything.

But *English* diet, too—which is, compared to the German and even to the French, a kind of "return to nature," meaning to cannibalism—is profoundly at odds with my instincts: it seems to me that it gives the spirit *heavy* feet—the feet of English women.

The best *cuisine* is that of *Piedmont*.[7]

Alcohol is bad for me: a single glass of wine or beer in one day is quite sufficient to turn my life into a vale of misery—the people of Munich are my antipodes. Assuming that I did not comprehend this until rather late, I really *experienced* it from childhood. As a boy I believed that drinking wine was, like smoking, to begin with merely a vanity of young men, and later on a bad habit. Perhaps this *harsh* judgment should be blamed in part on the wine of Naumburg.[8] To believe that wine *exhilarates* I should have to be a Christian—believing what is for me an absurdity. Strangely enough, in spite of this extreme vulnerability to *small*, strongly diluted doses of alcohol, I almost become a sailor when it is a matter of *strong* doses. Even as a boy, my fortitude appeared at that point. Writing a long Latin essay in a single night, and copying it over, too, with the ambition in my pen to emulate my model, Sallust, in

---

[5] In June 1866, during the war with Austria, the Prussians marched into Saxony and occupied Dresden (the capital).

[6] After the German manner.

[7] The north-westermost province of Italy, which borders on France and Switzerland. Its biggest city is Turin, where Nietzsche lived for two months in the spring of 1888, and again from September 21, 1888, until his collapse in January, 1889.

[8] The city, thirty miles southwest of Leipzig, where Nietzsche had grown up.

severity and compactness, and to pour some grog of the heaviest caliber over my Latin—even when I was a student at the venerable Schulpforta,[9] that did not in any way disagree with my physiology, nor perhaps with that of Sallust—however it disagreed with the venerable Schulpforta.

Later, around the middle of life, to be sure, I decided more and more strictly *against* all "spirits": I, an opponent of vegetarianism from experience, just like Richard Wagner, who converted me, cannot advise all *more spiritual* natures earnestly enough to abstain entirely from alcohol. *Water* is sufficient.

I prefer towns in which opportunities abound for dipping from running wells (Nizza, Turin, Sils); a small glass accompanies me like a dog.[10] *In vino veritas:*[11] it seems that here, too, I am at odds with all the world about the concept of "truth"—in my case, the spirit moves over water.[12]

A few more hints from my morality. A hearty meal is easier to digest than one that is too small. That the stomach as a whole becomes active is the first presupposition of a good digestion. One has to know the size of one's stomach. For the same reason one should be warned against those long-drawn-out meals which I call interrupted sacrificial feasts—those at a *table d'hôte.*

No meals between meals, no coffee: coffee spreads darkness. *Tea* is wholesome only in the morning. A little, but strong: tea is very unwholesome and sicklies one o'er the whole day if it is too weak by a single degree. Everybody has his own measure, often between the narrowest and most delicate limits. In a climate that is very *agaçant,*[13] tea is not advisable for a beginning: one should begin an hour earlier with a cup of thick, oil-less cocoa.

Sit as little as possible; give no credence to any thought that

---

[9] Perhaps the most famous boarding school in Germany.

[10] This is surely the meaning intended, although *ein kleines Glas läuft mir nach wie ein Hund* means literally: a small glass runs after me like a dog. This sentence has been adduced—very unreasonably—as evidence that Nietzsche was suffering from hallucinations and no longer sane when he wrote *Ecce Homo.*

[11] In wine there is truth.

[12] Allusion to Genesis 1.2.

[13] Provocative.

was not born outdoors while one moved about freely—in which the muscles are not celebrating a feast, too. All prejudices[14] come from the intestines.

The sedentary life—as I have said once before[15]—is the real *sin* against the holy spirit.

2

The question of *place* and *climate* is most closely related to the question of nutrition. Nobody is free to live everywhere; and whoever has to solve great problems that challenge all his strength actually has a very restricted choice in this matter. The influence of climate on our *metabolism,* its retardation, its acceleration, goes so far that a mistaken choice of place and climate can not only estrange a man from his task but can actually keep it from him: he never gets to see it. His animal *vigor* has never become great enough for him to attain that freedom which overflows into the most spiritual regions and allows one to recognize: *this* only I can do.

The slightest sluggishness of the intestines is entirely sufficient, once it has become a bad habit, to turn a genius into something mediocre, something "German." The German climate alone is enough to discourage strong, even inherently heroic, intestines. The *tempo* of the metabolism is strictly proportionate to the mobility or lameness of the spirit's *feet;* the "spirit" itself is after all merely an aspect of this metabolism. List the places where men with *esprit*[1] are living or have lived, where wit, subtlety, and malice belonged to happiness, where genius found its home almost of necessity: all of them have excellent dry air. Paris, Provence, Florence, Jerusalem, Athens—these names prove something: genius *depends* on dry air, on clear skies—that is, on a rapid metabolism, on the possibility of drawing again and again on great, even tre-

---

14 *Vorurteile. Vorteile* (advantages) in Karl Schlechta's edition is a misprint.
15 *Twilight,* Chapter I, section 34 (*Portable Nietzsche,* p. 471).
1 *Geistreiche Menschen. Geistreich,* literally rich in spirit, means ingenious, witty, intelligent, bright.

mendous quantities of strength. I know of a case in which a spirit of generous predisposition, destined for greatness, became, merely because he lacked any delicate instinct for climate, narrow, withdrawn, a peevish specialist. And I myself might ultimately have become just such a case, if my sickness had not forced me to see reason, to reflect on reason in reality. Now that the effects of climate and weather are familiar to me from long experience and I take readings from myself as from a very subtle and reliable instrument—and even during a short journey, say, from Turin to Milan, my system registers the change in the humidity—I reflect with horror on the *dismal* fact that my life, except for the last ten years, the years when my life was in peril, was spent entirely in the wrong places that were nothing short of *forbidden* to me. Naumburg, Schulpforta, the province of Thuringia quite generally, Leipzig, Basel, Venice—so many disastrous places for my physiology.

Altogether, I have no welcome memories whatever from my whole childhood and youth; but it would be folly to drag in so-called "moral" reasons, such as the undeniable lack of adequate company: for this lack persists today as it has always persisted, without preventing me from being cheerful and brave. Rather it was the ignorance *in physiologicis*—that damned "idealism"—that was the real calamity in my life, totally superfluous and stupid, something of which nothing good ever grew, for which there is no compensation, no counterbalance. The consequences of this "idealism" provide my explanation of all blunders, all great instinctual aberrations and "modesties" that led me away from the *task* of my life; for example, that I became a philologist—why not at least a physician or something else that opens one's eyes?

During my Basel period [2] my whole spiritual diet, including the way I divided up my day, was a completely senseless abuse of extraordinary resources, without any new supply to cover this consumption in any way, without even any thought about consumption and replenishment. Any refined self-concern, any protection by some commanding instinct was lacking; I simply posited myself as

---

[2] The ten years when Nietzsche was a professor of classical philology at the University of Basel, Switzerland.

equal to any nobody; it was a "selflessness," an oblivion of all distance between myself and others that I shall never forgive myself. When I was close to the end, *because* I was close to the end, I began to reflect on this fundamental unreason of my life—this "idealism." Only my sickness brought me to reason.

3

The choice of nutrition; the choice of climate and place: the third point at which one must not commit a blunder at any price is the choice of *one's own kind of recreation.* Here, too, depending on the degree to which a spirit is *sui generis,*[1] the limits of what is permitted to him, that is, profitable for him, are narrow, quite narrow. In my case, every kind of reading belongs among my recreations—hence among the things that liberate me from myself, that allow me to walk about in strange sciences and souls—that I no longer take seriously. Reading is precisely my recreation from my own seriousness. During periods when I am hard at work you will not find me surrounded by books: I'd beware of letting anyone near me talk, much less think. And that is what reading would mean.

Has it been noted that in that profound tension to which pregnancy condemns the spirit, and at bottom the whole organism, chance and any kind of stimulus from the outside have too vehement an effect and strike[2] too deep? One must avoid chance and outside stimuli as much as possible; a kind of walling oneself in belongs among the foremost instinctive precautions of spiritual pregnancy. Should I permit an *alien* thought to scale the wall secretly?— And that is what reading would mean.

The periods of work and fertility are followed by periods of recreation: come to me, pleasant, brilliant, clever books!

Will it be German books?

I must count back half a year before catching myself with a book in my hand. What was it?— A superb study by Victor Bro-

---

[1] Unique.

[2] *"Einschlägt"* (placed in quotes by Nietzsche) suggests lightning.

chard, *Les Sceptiques Grecs*,[3] in which my *Laertiana*[4] are also put
to good use. The skeptics, the only honorable type among the
equivocal, quinquivocal tribe of philosophers!

Otherwise I almost always seek refuge with the same books—
actually, a small number—books *proved to me*. Perhaps it is not
my way to read much, or diverse things: a reading room makes me
sick. Nor is it my way to love much, or diverse things. Caution,
even hostility against new books comes closer to my instincts than
"tolerance," *"largeur du coeur,"* [5] and other "neighbor love." [6]

It is a small number of old Frenchmen to whom I return again
and again: I believe only in French culture[7] and consider everything else in Europe today that calls itself "culture" a misunderstanding—not to speak of German culture.

The few cases of high culture that I have encountered in Germany have all been of French origin, especially Frau Cosima Wagner, by far the first voice in matters of taste that I have ever heard.

The fact that I do not read but *love* Pascal, as the most instructive victim of Christianity, murdered slowly, first physically,
then psychologically—the whole logic of this most gruesome form of
inhuman cruelty; that I have in my spirit—who knows? perhaps
also in my body—something of Montaigne's sportiveness; that my
artist's taste vindicates the names of Molière, Corneille, and Ra-
cine, not without fury, against a wild genius like Shakespeare—all
that does not preclude in the end that I find even the most recent
Frenchmen charming company. I do not see from what century of
the past one could dredge up such inquisitive and at the same time
such delicate psychologists as in contemporary Paris: tentatively—
for their number is far from small—I name Messieurs Paul Bourget, Pierre Loti, Gyp, Meilhac, Anatole France, Jules Lemaître, or,

---

[3] The Greek skeptics.

[4] Nietzsche's early philological studies of Diogenes Laertius: *De Laertii
Diogenis fontibus* (On Diogenes Laertius' sources, 1868 and 1869) and
Beiträge zur Quellenkunde und Kritik des Laertius Diogenes (contributions
to the critique and the study of the sources of Diogenes Laertius, 1870).

[5] Largeness of heart.

[6] Nietzsche had corrected printer's proofs and given his *imprimatur* up to
this point in the book, before he collapsed.

[7] The word here rendered several times as "culture" is *Bildung*.

to single out one of the strong race, a genuine Latin toward whom I am especially well disposed, Guy de Maupassant.[8] Between ourselves, I prefer *this* generation even to their great teachers who, without exception, have been corrupted by German philosophy (M. Taine, for example, by Hegel, to whom he owes his misunderstanding of great men and ages). As far as Germany extends, she *corrupts* culture. Only the war[9] "redeemed" the spirit in France.

Stendhal, one of the most beautiful accidents of my life—for whatever marks an epoch in it came my way by accident, never through someone's recommendation—is truly invaluable with his anticipatory psychologist's eye, with his knack for the facts which is reminiscent of the greatest of factual men (*ex ungue Napoleonem*),[10] and finally not least as an *honest* atheist—a species that is rare in France and almost impossible to find—with all due respect for *Prosper Mérimée.*[11]

Perhaps I am even envious of Stendhal? He took away from me the best atheistical joke that precisely I might have made: "God's only excuse is that he does not exist."

---

[8] Paul Bourget (1852–1935), a critic and novelist, wrote, among other things, *Essais de psychologie contemporaine,* of which the first volume (1883) contains a chapter *"Théorie de la décadence."* On the question of Bourget's influence on Nietzsche see the first footnote in Chapter 2 of my *Nietzsche.*

Pierre Loti was the pen name of Louis Marie Julien Viaud (1850–1923) who wrote, e.g., *Pêcheur d'Islande* (the Iceland fisherman; 1886).

Gyp was the pen name of Sibylle Gabrielle Marie Antoinette Riqueti de Mirabeau, Comtesse de Martel de Janville (1850–1932), a very prolific writer.

Henri Meilhac (1831–1897) was a dramatist and collaborated with Ludovic Halévy (1834–1908) on a large number of operettas, farces, and comedies, including librettos for Offenbach; e.g., *La Belle Hélène* (1864).

Anatole France was the pen name of Jacques Anatole Thibault (1844–1924), generally regarded as one of the leading French writers of his time.

François Elie Jules Lemaître (1853–1914) was a critic and dramatist.

Guy de Maupassant (1850–1893), though also a poet and novelist, is remembered chiefly for his magnificent short stories. He died in an insane asylum.

[9] The Franco-Prussian War of 1870–71.

[10] From the claw (you can tell) Napoleon. Nietzsche's variation of *ex ungue leonem* (from the claw, a lion).

[11] Novelist, essayist, and archaeologist (1803–1870), now best remembered for his *Carmen* (1847), which became the basis of the libretto for Georges Bizet's opera.

I myself have said somewhere: what has been the greatest objection to existence so far? *God*.[12]

4

The highest concept of the lyrical poet was given to me by *Heinrich Heine*. I seek in vain in all the realms of history for an equally sweet and passionate music. He possessed that divine malice without which I cannot imagine perfection: I estimate the value of men, of races, according to the necessity by which they cannot conceive the god apart from the satyr.

And how he handles his German! One day it will be said that Heine and I have been by far the foremost artists of the German language—at an incalculable distance from everything mere Germans have done with it.[1]

I must be profoundly related to *Byron's* Manfred: all these abysses I found in myself; at the age of thirteen I was ripe for this work. I have no word, only a glance, for those who dare to pronounce the word "Faust" in the presence of Manfred.[2] The Germans are *incapable* of any notion of greatness; proof: Schumann. Simply from fury against this sugary Saxon, I composed a counteroverture for *Manfred* of which Hans von Bülow said that he had

---

[12] *Twilight*, "The Four Great Errors," section 8 (*Portable Nietzsche*, p. 501).

[1] *Ecce Homo* was published in 1908. The same year Thomas Mann penned a "Note on Heine" (*Notiz über Heine*) in which he said: "Of his works I have long loved the book on Börne most. . . . His psychology of the Nazarene type anticipates Nietzsche. . . . And incidentally no German prose prior to Nietzsche's matches its genius" (*Rede und Antwort* [speech and reply], 1922, p. 382). Nietzsche's reference to "mere Germans" makes a point of the fact that Heine was a Jew (and very widely resented), and Nietzsche took himself to be of Polish descent.

[2] Nietzsche neither emphasizes book titles nor usually places them in quotes after the German manner; but the comparison Nietzsche intends is presumably between the two heroes, Faust and Manfred. Nietzsche's tremendous admiration for Goethe was not primarily based on *Faust*. Cf. *Portable Nietzsche*, pp. 69f. and 553ff., and for further quotations Kaufmann's *Nietzsche*, the final pages of Chapter 4.

never seen anything like it on paper, and he called it rape of Euterpe.[3]

When I seek my ultimate formula for *Shakespeare,* I always find only this: he conceived of the type of Caesar. That sort of thing cannot be guessed: one either is it, or one is not. The great poet dips *only* from his own reality—up to the point where afterward he cannot endure his work any longer.

When I have looked into my *Zarathustra,* I walk up and down in my room for half an hour, unable to master an unbearable fit of sobbing.

I know no more heart-rending reading than Shakespeare: what must a man have suffered to have such a need of being a buffoon! [4]

Is Hamlet *understood?* Not doubt, *certainty* is what drives one insane.[5]— But one must be profound, an abyss, a philosopher to feel that way.— We are all *afraid* of truth.

And let me confess it: I feel instinctively sure and certain that Lord Bacon was the originator, the self-tormentor[6] of this uncanniest kind of literature: what is the pitiable chatter of American flat- and muddle-heads to *me?* But the strength required for the vision of the most powerful reality is not only compatible with the most powerful strength for action, for monstrous action, for crime—it even presupposes it.[7]

We are very far from knowing enough about Lord Bacon, the first realist in every great sense of that word, to know everything he did, wanted, and experienced in himself.

---

[3] The muse of music. Bülow (1830–1894) was a pianist and conductor. In 1857 he married Cosima Liszt, who later left him for Richard Wagner, whom she married in 1870.

[4] A hint for readers of *Ecce Homo.*

[5] Cf. *The Birth of Tragedy,* end of section 7.

[6] *Selbsttierquäler:* literally, self-animal-tormentor. Incidentally, Freud believed that the Earl of Oxford had written "Shakespeare's" plays.

[7] Presumably Nietzsche means that he has been persuaded not by American Baconians but by considerations of his own. Bacon was Lord Chancellor, and the "crime" to which he pleaded guilty in 1621 was bribery. He explained: "I was the justest judge that was in England these fifty years; but it was the justest censure in Parliament that was these two hundred years." In accordance with the general practice of the age, he said, he had accepted gifts from litigants; but his judgment had never been swayed by a bribe.

And damn it, my dear critics! Suppose I had published my *Zarathustra* under another name—for example, that of Richard Wagner—the acuteness of two thousand years would not have been sufficient for anyone to guess that the author of *Human, All-Too-Human* is the visionary of *Zarathustra*.

5

Speaking of the recreations of my life, I must say a word to express my gratitude for what has been by far the most profound and cordial recreation of my life. Beyond a doubt, that was my intimate relationship with Richard Wagner. I'd let go cheap the whole rest of my human relationships; I should not want to give away out of my life at any price the days of Tribschen[1]—days of trust, of cheerfulness, of sublime accidents, of *profound* moments.

I do not know what experiences others have had with Wagner: *our* sky was never darkened by a single cloud.

And with that I return once more to France—I have no reasons but merely a contemptuous corner of the mouth for Wagnerians *et hoc genus omne*[2] who think they are honoring Wagner by finding him similar to *themselves*.

The way I am, so alien in my deepest instincts to everything German that the mere proximity of a German retards my digestion, the first contact with Wagner was also the first deep breath of my life: I experienced, I revered him as a *foreign* land, as an antithesis, as an incarnate protest against all "German virtues."

We who were children in the swamp air of the fifties are of necessity pessimists concerning the concept "German"; we simply cannot be anything but revolutionaries—we shall not come to terms with any state of affairs in which the *bigot*[3] is at the top. It is a matter of total indifference to me whether today he dons different

---

[1] The place in Switzerland where Wagner had lived and Nietzsche had often visited him.

[2] And all that tribe. Wagner *was* a Francophobe and Teutomaniac, but Nietzsche insists that he was very different indeed from his nationalist followers.

[3] *Mucker.*

colors, clothing himself in scarlet and putting on a hussar's uni-form.[4]

Well then! Wagner was a revolutionary—he ran away from the Germans.[5]

As an *artist* one has no home in Europe, except Paris: the *délicatesse* in all five artistic senses that is presupposed by Wagner's art, the fingers for *nuances,* the psychological morbidity are found only in Paris. Nowhere else does one have this passion in questions of form, this seriousness in *mise en scène*[6]—which is Parisian seriousness *par excellence.* In Germany people simply lack any notion of the tremendous ambition that lives in the soul of a Parisian artist. Germans are good-natured—Wagner was anything but good-natured.

But I have long said adequately (in *Beyond Good and Evil,* section 256)[7] where Wagner belongs and who are his closest relatives: the late French romantics, that high-flying and yet rousing manner of artists like Delacroix, like Berlioz, with a characteristic *fond*[8] of sickness, of incurability—all of them fanatics of *expression,* virtuosos through and through.

Who was the first *intelligent* adherent of Wagner anywhere? Charles Baudelaire, who was also the first to understand Delacroix—that typical decadent in whom a whole tribe of artists recognized themselves—and perhaps he was also the last.[9]

What did I never forgive Wagner? That he *condescended* to the Germans—that he became *reichsdeutsch.*[10]

As far as Germany extends, she corrupts culture.[11]

---

[4] The allusion is primarily to Kaiser Wilhelm II, who had ascended to the throne in June 1888, but is also aimed at the German *Reich* in which Wagner had become a national—and nationalist—hero.

[5] During the time of their friendship Wagner was quite literally living in voluntary exile in Switzerland.

[6] Staging.

[7] Pp. 256f. in the MS is a slip.

[8] Core.

[9] That is, the last *intelligent* adherent of Wagner.

[10] That is, made common cause with the new German Empire.

[11] Quoting section 3 above.

6

All things considered, I could not have endured my youth without Wagner's music. For I was *condemned* to Germans. If one wants to rid oneself of an unbearable pressure, one needs hashish. Well then, I needed Wagner. Wagner is the antitoxin against everything German *par excellence*—a toxin, a poison, that I don't deny.

From the moment when there was a piano score of *Tristan*— my compliments, Herr von Bülow—I was a Wagnerian.[1] Wagner's

---

[1] This would take us back to the spring of 1861 when Nietzsche was sixteen. Indeed, the text of one of Nietzsche's own compositions, dated June 1861, "included an unmistakable token of the proximity of *Tristan und Isolde:* 'Wild wogt der Wahn, wo durch bewegt, das Wunder wollend mein Gemüth? [*sic*]'" (Frederick R. Love, *Young Nietzsche and the Wagnerian Experience,* Chapel Hill, N. C., University of North Carolina Press, 1963, p. 22; reviewed by Walter Kaufmann in *Journal of the History of Philosophy,* October 1965, pp. 284–86). The quoted passage reads like a parody of Wagner and makes little sense: "Wildly illusion surges, whereby moves the wonder wishing my bosom?"

Nevertheless, Love, making use of unpublished materials, including Nietzsche's compositions, argues convincingly that Nietzsche never was "a passionate devotee of Wagnerian music" (p. viii). He finds "nothing whatever Wagnerian" in Nietzsche's songs between 1862 and 1865 (p. 28); he cites a letter of the winter 1865–66 in which Nietzsche, then a student, wrote, "Three things are my recreations, but rare recreations, my Schopenhauer, Schumann's music, finally long walks"; and he cites a list Nietzsche made around the same time of his musical favorites: Schumann, Beethoven, and Schubert are most prominent, "two choral works by Bach are mentioned, 'ein paar' [a couple of] Lieder of Brahms, and of Wagner only the early opera *Tannhäuser,* listed indiscriminately next to a work by Meyerbeer" (p. 35).

Love argues further: "As for Wagner's music, it can be stated unequivocally that *Die Meistersinger* was the only one of the mature works which Nietzsche acquired fully on his own and the one which he knew best from actual performance" (p. 63). *Tristan* he heard only twice, in June 1872, in Munich, where "Hans von Bülow gave the European musical public its second chance to experience a production of *Tristan*" (p. 64). Love thinks that *Tristan* "became for Nietzsche the permanent symbol of his unforgettable Tribschen experience" because "Wagner himself must have opened his mind to the deeper meaning of his most radical work" (p. 65).

Love fails to note that Nietzsche's tribute to von Bülow in the text above evidently conflates two events: the one in 1861 to which Nietzsche alludes, and the other in 1872. Love also refers to (p. 69) but does not quote von Bülow's scathing letter to Nietzsche about one of Nietzsche's compositions. It is noteworthy that Nietzsche cites this letter in section 4 above, humor-

older works I deemed beneath myself—still too vulgar, too "German."

But to this day I am still looking for a work that equals the dangerous fascination and the gruesome[2] and sweet infinity of *Tristan*—and look in all the arts in vain. All the strangenesses of Leonardo da Vinci emerge from their spell at the first note of *Tristan*. This work is emphatically Wagner's *non plus ultra;* with the *Meistersinger* and the *Ring* he recuperated[3] from it. Becoming healthier—is a retrogression, given a nature like Wagner's.

I take it for a good fortune of the first order that I lived at the right time and among Germans, of all peoples, so that I was *ripe* for this work: that is how far the psychologist's inquisitiveness extends in my case. The world is poor for anyone who has never been sick enough for this "voluptuousness of hell": it is permitted, it is almost imperative, to employ a formula of the mystics at this point.

I think I know better than anyone else of what tremendous things Wagner is capable—the fifty worlds of alien ecstasies for which no one besides him had wings; and given the way I am, strong enough to turn even what is most questionable and dangerous to my advantage and thus to become stronger, I call Wagner the great benefactor of my life. That in which we are related—that

---

ously, without any trace of *ressentiment,* and that he goes out of his way in the text above to voice his gratitude to von Bülow.

Regarding Nietzsche's relationship to Wagner's music, Love is surely right in not regarding Nietzsche's break with Wagner as an act of self-betrayal (as many Wagnerians have done), concluding instead that "Nietzsche's infatuation with Wagnerian music . . . may indeed be regarded as an aberration" from his own line. But again it is noteworthy that Nietzsche makes a point of speaking of Wagner without *ressentiment* and with gratitude; and it is obviously possible to have *more opportunities* to hear *Die Meistersinger* and even, whether this is true in Nietzsche's case or not, to know and in some sense like this opera especially well, while yet considering *Tristan* "Wagner's *non plus ultra.*"

Nietzsche's judgments in *Ecce Homo* are plainly highly stylized: he loves Wagner—in spite of his Teutonomania, in spite of his ideas and his self-image, in spite of everything that eventually endeared him to his countrymen; he loves Wagner as the ultimate in decadence, as a kind of apotheosis of *French* romanticism, as fascinatingly sick—and *Tristan* fits into that picture a thousand times better than *Die Meistersinger.*

[2] *Schauerlich:* etymologically, what makes one shudder.

[3] *Er erholte sich.* Above, *Erholung* has been rendered several times as recreation.

we have suffered more profoundly, also from each other, than men of this century are capable of suffering—will link our names again and again, eternally; and as certainly as Wagner is merely a misunderstanding among Germans, just as certainly I am and always shall be.

Two centuries of psychological and artistic discipline must come first, my dear Teutons!— But with that one does not catch up.

7

I shall say another word for the most select ears: what I really want from music. That it be cheerful and profound like an afternoon in October. That it be individual, frolicsome, tender, a sweet small woman full of beastliness and charm.

I shall never admit that a German *could* know what music is. Those who are called German composers—the greatest above all —are *foreigners:* Slavs, Croats, Italians, Dutchmen—or Jews; otherwise, Germans of the strong race, *extinct* Germans, like Heinrich Schütz, Bach, and Handel. I myself am still enough of a Pole to surrender the rest of music for Chopin, excepting, for three reasons, Wagner's Siegfried Idyll, perhaps also a few things by Liszt, who surpasses all other musicians in his noble orchestral accents, and, finally, everything that grew beyond the Alps—*this* side.[1]

I should not know how to get along without Rossini; even less, without my own south in music, the music of my Venetian *maëstro Pietro Gasti.*[2] And when I say beyond the Alps, I really

---

[1] Nietzsche spent his summers in Switzerland, his winters in Italy, and wrote *Ecce Homo* in Turin.

[2] Heinrich Köselitz, a young composer who vastly admired Nietzsche, helped him prepare copies of his manuscripts for the printer, read proofs for him, and assisted him very devotedly. Nietzsche called him Peter Gast, and this became his pen name when he later became one of the editors of Nietzsche's works. His opera, "The Lion of Venice," never made a reputation for him as a composer, but Nietzsche's letters to Gast (1908) made him famous. His own letters to Nietzsche (2 vols., 1923–24) are much less interesting and not at all widely known. The passage in the text is plainly inspired by gratitude and to that extent offers a clue to some of Nietzsche's other judgments in *Ecce Homo:* he is often more concerned with his own attitudes and their fittingness, their style, than with their literal content.

merely say Venice. When I seek another word for music, I always find only the word Venice. I do not know how to distinguish between tears and music—I do not know how to think of happiness, of the *south,* without shudders of timidity.

> *At the bridge I stood*
> *lately in the brown night.*
> *From afar came a song:*
> *as a golden drop it welled*
> *over the quivering surface.*
> *Gondolas, lights, and music—*
> *drunken it swam out into the twilight.*
>
> *My soul, a stringed instrument,*
> *sang to itself, invisibly touched,*
> *a secret gondola song,*
> *quivering with iridescent happiness.*
> *—Did anyone listen to it?*

8

In all these matters—in the choice of nutrition, of place and climate, of recreation—an instinct of self-preservation issues its commandments, and it gains its most unambiguous expression as an instinct of *self-defense.* Not to see many things, not to hear many things, not to permit many things to come close—first imperative of prudence, first proof that one is no mere accident but a necessity. The usual word for this instinct of self-defense is *taste.* It commands us not only to say No when Yes would be "selfless" but also to say *No as rarely as possible.* To detach oneself, to separate oneself from anything that would make it necessary to keep saying No. The reason in this is that when defensive expenditures, be they ever so small, become the rule and a habit, they entail an extraordinary and entirely superfluous impoverishment. Our *great* expenses are composed of the most frequent small ones. Warding off, not letting things come close, involves an expenditure—let nobody deceive himself about this—energy *wasted* on negative ends. Merely through the constant need to ward off, one can become weak enough to be unable to defend oneself any longer.

Suppose I stepped out of my house and found, instead of quiet, aristocratic Turin, a small German town: my instinct would have to cast up a barrier to push back everything that would assail it from this pinched and flattened, cowardly world. Or I found a German big city—this built-up vice where nothing grows, where everything, good or bad, is imported. Wouldn't this compel me to become a *hedgehog?*

But having quills is a waste, even a double luxury when one can choose not to have quills but *open* hands.

Another counsel of prudence and self-defense is to *react as rarely as possible,* and to avoid situations and relationships that would condemn one to suspend, as it were, one's "freedom" and initiative and to become a mere reagent. As a parable I choose association with books. Scholars who at bottom do little nowadays but thumb books—philologists, at a moderate estimate, about 200 a day—ultimately lose entirely their capacity to think for themselves. When they don't thumb, they don't think. They *respond* to a stimulus (a thought they have read) whenever they think—in the end, they do nothing but react. Scholars spend all of their energies on saying Yes and No, on criticism of what others have thought—they themselves no longer think.

The instinct of self-defense has become worn-out in them; otherwise they would resist books. The scholar—a decadent.

I have seen this with my own eyes: gifted natures with a generous and free disposition, "read to ruin" in their thirties—merely matches that one has to strike to make them emit sparks—"thoughts."

Early in the morning, when day breaks, when all is fresh, in the dawn of one's strength—to *read a book* at such a time is simply depraved!

9

At this point the real answer to the question, *how one becomes what one is,* can no longer be avoided. And thus I touch on the masterpiece of the art of self-preservation—of *selfishness.*

For let us assume that the task, the destiny, the fate of the task transcends the average very significantly: in that case, nothing could be more dangerous than catching sight of oneself *with* this task. To become what one is, one must not have the faintest notion *what* one is. From this point of view even the *blunders* of life have their own meaning and value—the occasional side roads and wrong roads, the delays, "modesties," seriousness wasted on tasks that are remote from *the* task. All this can express a great prudence, even the supreme prudence: where *nosce te ipsum*[1] would be the recipe for ruin,[2] forgetting oneself, *misunderstanding* oneself, making oneself smaller, narrower, mediocre, become reason itself. Morally speaking: neighbor love, living for others, and other things *can* be a protective measure for preserving the hardest self-concern. This is the exception where, against my wont and conviction, I side with the "selfless" drives: here they work in the service of *self-love, of self-discipline*.[3]

The whole surface of consciousness—consciousness *is* a surface[4]—must be kept clear of all great imperatives. Beware even of every great word, every great pose! So many dangers that the instinct comes too soon to "understand itself"——. Meanwhile the organizing "idea" that is destined to rule keeps growing deep down —it begins to command; slowly it leads us *back* from side roads and wrong roads; it prepares *single* qualities and fitnesses that will one day prove to be indispensable as means toward a whole—one by one, it trains all *subservient* capacities before giving any hint of the dominant task, "goal," "aim," or "meaning."

Considered in this way, my life is simply wonderful. For the task of a *revaluation of all values* more capacities may have been needed than have ever dwelt together in a single individual—above all, even contrary capacities that had to be kept from disturbing, destroying one another. An order of rank among these capacities; distance; the art of separating without setting against one another; to mix nothing, to "reconcile" nothing; a tremendous variety that is nevertheless the opposite of chaos—this was the precondition, the long, secret work and artistry of my instinct. Its *higher protection*

---

[1] Know thyself.

[2] *Untergang.*

[3] *Selbstsucht, Selbstzucht.*

[4] This anti-Cartesian epigram anticipates Freud.

manifested itself to such a high degree that I never even suspected what was growing in me—and one day all my capacities, suddenly ripe, *leaped forth* in their ultimate perfection.[5] I cannot remember that I ever tried hard [6]—no trace of *struggle* can be demonstrated in my life; I am the opposite of a heroic nature. "Willing" something, "striving"[7] for something, envisaging a "purpose," a "wish"—I know none of this from experience. At this very moment I still look upon my future—an *ample* future!—as upon calm seas: there is no ripple of desire. I do not want in the least that anything should become different than it is; I myself do not want to become different.

But that is how I have always lived. I had no wishes. A man over forty-four who can say that he never strove[8] for *honors,* for *women,* for *money!*

Thus it happened, for example, that one day I was a university professor—no such idea had ever entered my mind, for I was barely twenty-four years old. Thus it happened two years earlier that one day I was suddenly a philologist—insofar as my *first* philological essay, my beginning in every sense, was requested by my teacher, Ritschl, for publication in his *Rheinisches Museum.*[9] (*Ritschl*—I say it with reverence—the only scholar of genius on whom I have laid eyes to this day. He was characterized by that agreeable corruption which distinguishes us Thuringians and which makes even Germans sympathetic: even to reach truth, we still prefer furtive paths. These words are not meant to underestimate my close compatriot, the *clever* Leopold von Ranke——.)[10]

---

[5] An allusion to the birth of Pallas Athene who was said to have sprung, fully armed, from the head of Zeus.

[6] *Dass ich mich je bemüht hätte.* Deliberately or not, Nietzsche pictures himself as the antithesis of Goethe's Faust who speaks of his ardent *Bemühn* in the first sentence of his first speech (line 357); and Faust's redemption after his death is explained by the angels in two of the most famous lines of German literature: "Who ever strives with all his power,/ We are allowed to save"; *Wer immer strebend sich bemüht,/ Den können wir erlösen* (lines 11936-37).

[7] *Streben:* see the preceding note.

[8] *Dass er sich nie . . . bemüht hat!*

[9] One of the leading professional journals.

[10] The great historian (1795–1886) was born in Wiehe, in Thuringia,

10

One will ask me why on earth I've been relating all these small things which are generally considered matters of complete indifference: I only harm myself, the more so if I am destined to represent great tasks. Answer: these small things—nutrition, place, climate, recreation, the whole casuistry of selfishness—are inconceivably more important than everything one has taken to be important so far. Precisely here one must begin to *relearn*. What mankind has so far considered seriously have not even been realities but mere imaginings—more strictly speaking, *lies* prompted by the bad instincts of sick natures that were harmful in the most profound sense —all these concepts, "God," "soul," "virtue," "sin," "beyond," "truth," "eternal life."— But the greatness of human nature, its "divinity," was sought in them.— All the problems of politics, of social organization, and of education have been falsified through and through because one mistook the most harmful men for great men—because one learned to despise "little" things, which means the basic concerns of life itself.[1]

When I now compare myself with the men who have so far

---

roughly thirty miles west of Röcken (near Lützen), where Nietzsche was born. And Ranke, like Nietzsche, got his secondary school education at Schulpforta.

[1] Podach (*Friedrich Nietzsches Werke*, 1961) reproduces a photograph of section 10 (plate XV) and points out that the spiral scribble used to delete the following passage at this point was characteristic of Nietzsche's sister and never employed by him (p. 408; cf. also pp. 245f.).

"Our present culture is ambiguous in the highest degree.— The German emperor making a pact with the pope, as if the pope were not the representative of deadly hostility to life!— What is being built today will no longer stand in three years.— When I measure myself against my *ability*, not to speak of what will come after me, a collapse, a construction without equal, then I more than any other mortal have a claim to the epithet of greatness."

In the first edition of *Ecce Homo* (1908) this paragraph was printed in a footnote in Raoul Richter's postscript (pp. 147f.) and introduced with the following comment: "There are only two passages of any length where the peculiarity of the crossing out and Peter Gast's testimony, based on his recollection, make it merely *probable* that the deletion was Nietzsche's own." The other passage will be found at the end of the discussion of "The Case of Wagner," below.

been honored as the *first,* the difference is palpable. I do not even count these so-called "first" men among men in general: for me they are the refuse of humanity, monsters of sickness and vengeful instincts; they are inhuman, disastrous, at bottom incurable, and revenge themselves on life.

I want to be their opposite: it is my privilege to have the subtlest sensitivity for all signs of healthy instincts. There is no pathological trait in me; even in periods of severe sickness I never became pathological; in vain would one seek for a trait of fanaticism in my character. There is not a moment in my life to which one could point to convict me of a presumptuous and pathetic[2] posture. The pathos of poses does *not* belong to greatness; whoever needs poses at all is *false.*— Beware of all picturesque men!

Life was easy for me—easiest when it made the hardest demands on me. Whoever saw me during the seventy days this fall when, without interruption, I did several things of the first rank the like of which nobody will do after me—or impose on me[3]—with a

---

[2] *Pathetisch* in German is closer in meaning to bombastic than it is to pitiful. The word is readily associated with an actor's style and with highly idealistic passages in drama—in Schiller's plays, for example—where big words are used freely and a laugh would puncture the whole effect. The same consideration applies to *Pathos* in the next sentence.

One may wonder whether this whole paragraph is starkly ironical or, on the contrary, totally lacking in self-awareness. Without denying that both alternatives contain a grain of truth, one may insist that Nietzsche's central point is important. He never lost the ability to laugh, and his self-image was the very antithesis of his sister's later image of him which, at her bidding, was translated into pictures and sculptures that she commissioned and for which she posed her brother who was by then a helpless invalid.

Finally, if we take seriously Nietzsche's words, "not a moment in my life"—as distinguished from "not a line in this book"—he is incontestably right. Consider how Dr. Paneth, one of Freud's friends, described Nietzsche of whom he saw a great deal in Nizza from December 26, 1883, until March 26, 1884: "There is not a trace of false pathos or the prophet's pose in him, as I had rather feared after his last work. Instead his manner is completely inoffensive and natural. . . . He told me, but without the least affectation or conceit, that he always felt himself to have a task . . ." For further quotations from his letters and some discussion, see Walter Kaufmann, *From Shakespeare to Existentialism* (Garden City, N.Y., Doubleday Anchor Books, 1960) pp. 323f.

[3] *Die kein Mensch mir nachmacht—oder vormacht* . . . If Nietzsche meant —and this possibility cannot be ruled out—"or has done before me," the text ought to read: *oder mir vorgemacht hat.*

responsibility for all millennia after me, will not have noticed any trace of tension in me; but rather an overflowing freshness and cheerfulness. I never ate with more pleasant feelings; I never slept better.

I do not know any other way of associating with great tasks than *play:* as a sign of greatness, this is an essential presupposition. The least compulsion, a gloomy mien, or any harsh tone in the throat are all objections to a man; how much more against his work!— One must not have any nerves.— *Suffering* from solitude is also an objection—I have suffered only from "multitudes."

At an absurdly early age, at seven, I already knew that no human word would ever reach me: has anyone ever seen me saddened on that account?

To this day I still have the same affability for everyone; I even treat with special respect those who are lowliest: in all of this there is not one grain of arrogance or secret contempt. If I despise a man, he *guesses* that I despise him: by my mere existence I outrage everything that has bad blood in its veins.

My formula for greatness in a human being is *amor fati:*[4] that one wants nothing to be different, not forward, not backward, not in all eternity. Not merely bear what is necessary, still less conceal it—all idealism is mendaciousness in the face of what is necessary— but *love* it.

---

[4] Love of fate. It should be noted how *Ecce Homo* exemplifies this attitude. As long as one overlooks this, as well as the fact that Nietzsche's life for the preceding decade, and more, had been troubled by continued ill health and excruciating physical pain, and that his books were, without exception, totally "unsuccessful," one does not begin to understand *Ecce Homo.*

Why I Write Such Good Books

1

I am one thing, my writings are another matter.— Before I discuss them, one by one, let me touch on the question of their being understood or *not* understood. I'll do it as casually as decency permits; for the time for this question certainly hasn't come yet. The time for me hasn't come yet: some are born posthumously.

Some day institutions will be needed in which men live and teach as I conceive of living and teaching; it might even happen that a few chairs will then be set aside for the interpretation of *Zarathustra*. But it would contradict my character entirely if I expected ears and hands for my truths today: that today one doesn't hear me and doesn't accept my ideas is not only understandable, it even seems right to me. I don't want to be confounded with others —not even by myself.

To repeat, one cannot find many traces of ill will in my life; and of literary ill will, too, I could scarcely relate a single case. But only too many of pure foolishness!

To me it seems one of the rarest distinctions that a man can accord himself if he takes one of my books into his hands—I even suppose that he first takes off his shoes,[1] not to speak of boots.

When Dr. Heinrich von Stein once complained very honestly that he didn't understand a word of my *Zarathustra*, I told him that this was perfectly in order: having understood six sentences from it—that is, to have really experienced them—would raise one to a higher level of existence than "modern" men could attain. Given this feeling of distance, how could I possibly wish to be read by those "moderns" whom I know!

My triumph is precisely the opposite of Schopenhauer's: I say, *"non legor, non legar."* [2]

---

[1] Allusion to Exodus 3:5.

[2] I am not read, I *will* not be read.

Not that I should like to underestimate the pleasure I have felt on several occasions at the *innocence* of people who said No to my writings. Only this past summer, at a time when I may have upset the balance of the whole rest of literature with my weighty, too weighty, literature, a professor from the University of Berlin suggested very amiably that I ought to try another form: nobody read such things.

In the last analysis, it was not Germany but Switzerland that produced the two extreme cases. An essay by Dr. V. Widmann in the *Bund,* about *Beyond Good and Evil,* under the title "Nietzsche's Dangerous Book," and a comprehensive report about my books in general by Karl Spitteler,[3] also in the *Bund,* represent a maximum in my life—I refrain from saying, of what.

The latter treated my *Zarathustra,* for example, as an advanced exercise in style, and expressed the wish that later on I might provide some content as well. Dr. Widmann expressed his respect for the courage I had shown in my attempt to abolish all decent feelings.[4]

---

[3] J. V. Widmann (1842–1911) published his review in the *Berner Bund* on September 16–17, 1888. In the *Encyclopedia of Poetry and Poetics,* ed. Alex Preminger (Princeton, N. J., Princeton University Press, 1965), Henri de Ziègler, former President of the University of Geneva, says of him in the article on "Swiss Poetry" (p. 830): "A fascinating grace of expression—rare in German-Swiss literature—distinguishes the anachronistic verse-idylls of Spitteler's friend J. V. Widmann."

Carl Spitteler (1845–1924) published the "comprehensive report," mentioned in the text, in the New Year's Supplement, 1888, of the *Bund.* On November 8, 1888, he published a very favorable review of *The Case of Wagner* in the *Bund.* This book he also reviewed in *Basler Nachrichten.* Nietzsche was so pleased with Spitteler's reaction to *The Case of Wagner* that he asked him to publish, with a preface, the passages from Nietzsche's earlier books that Nietzsche *then* decided—even before Spitteler had had time to decline—to publish himself: *Nietzsche contra Wagner.* In 1908 Spitteler published a small fifty-page pamphlet, *Meine Beziehungen zu Nietzsche* (my relations—or contacts—with Nietzsche; Munich, *Süddeutsche Monatshefte*). In Peter Gast's notes on Nietzsche's letters to him, February 26, 1888, and December 16, 1888, Gast took issue with Spitteler (*Friedrich Nietzsches Briefe an Peter Gast,* Leipzig, 1908, pp. 503, 517f.). In 1919 Spitteler received the Nobel Prize for literature.

See also note 4 below.

[4] At this point Nietzsche himself deleted the following passage in his MS: "Not that there was any lack of 'good will' in either case; even less, of intelligence. Indeed, I consider Herr Spitteler one of the most welcome and refined of all who write criticism today; his work on the French drama—not published yet—may be of the first rank. That much more do I seek

As the petty spite of accident would have it, every sentence in this latter piece was, with a consistency I admired, some truth stood on its head: one really had to do no more than "revalue all values" in order to hit the nail on the head about me in a truly remarkable manner—instead of hitting my head with a nail.— That makes an explanation only more desirable.

Ultimately, nobody can get more out of things, including books, than he already knows. For what one lacks access to from experience one will have no ear. Now let us imagine an extreme case: that a book speaks of nothing but events that lie altogether beyond the possibility of any frequent or even rare experience— that it is the first language for a new series of experiences. In that case, simply nothing will be heard, but there will be the acoustic illusion that where nothing is heard, nothing is there.

This is, in the end, my average experience and, if you will, the originality of my experience. Whoever thought he had understood something of me, had made up something out of me after his own image—not uncommonly an antithesis to me; for example, an "idealist"—and whoever had understood nothing of me, denied that I need be considered at all.

The word "overman," as the designation of a type of supreme achievement, as opposed to "modern" men, to "good" men, to Christians and other nihilists—a word that in the mouth of a Zarathustra, the annihilator of morality, becomes a very pensive word —has been understood almost everywhere with the utmost innocence in the sense of those very values whose opposite Zarathustra was meant to represent—that is, as an "idealistic" type of a higher kind of man, half "saint," half "genius."

Other scholarly oxen have suspected me of Darwinism on that account. Even the "hero worship" of that unconscious and involuntary conterfeiter, Carlyle, which I have repudiated so maliciously, has been read into it. Those to whom I said in confidence that they should sooner look even for a Cesare Borgia than for a Parsifal, did not believe their own ears.[5]

---

some explanation" (see Podach, *Friedrich Nietzsches Werke,* p. 249; and for Nietzsche's instructions to delete these sentences, p. 250).

[5] All of Nietzsche's references to Cesare Borgia are discussed in Kaufmann's *Nietzsche,* Chapter 7, section III.

That I feel no curiosity at all about reviews of my books, especially in newspapers, should be forgiven me. My friends and my publishers know this and do not speak to me about such things. In one particular case I once did get to see all the sins that had been committed against one of my books—it was *Beyond Good and Evil*—and I could make a pretty report about that. Would you believe it? The *Nationalzeitung*—a Prussian newspaper, as I might explain for the benefit of my foreign readers—I myself read, if I may say so, only the *Journal des Débats*—actually managed to understand the book as a "sign of the times," as the real and genuine Junker philosophy for which the *Kreuzzeitung*[6] merely lacked the courage.

2

This was said for the benefit of Germans; for everywhere else I have readers—nothing but first-rate intellects and proven characters, trained in high positions and duties; I even have real geniuses among my readers. In Vienna, in St. Petersburg, in Stockholm, in Copenhagen, in Paris, in New York—everywhere I have been discovered; but not in the shallows of Europe, Germany.[1]

And let me confess that my nonreaders delight me even more —those who have never heard my name, nor the word "philosophy." But wherever I go, here in Turin, for example, everybody's face lights up and looks pleased at my sight. What has flattered me most so far is that old costermonger women won't relax until they have found their sweetest grapes for me. That is the extent to which one should be a philosopher.

It is not for nothing that the Poles are called the Frenchmen among the Slavs. A charming Russian woman would not doubt for

---

[6] An ultra-right newspaper.

[1] In a discarded draft for this passage we find the following (Podach, pp. 254f.): "Whoever reads me in Germany today has first *de-Germanized* himself thoroughly, as I have done: my formula is known, 'to be a good German means to de-Germanize oneself'; or he is—no small distinction among Germans—of Jewish descent.— Jews among Germans are always the higher race—more refined, spiritual, kind.— *L'adorable* Heine, they say in Paris."

a moment where I belong. I cannot be solemn, at most I become embarrassed.

To think German, to feel German—I can do anything, but not that.

My old teacher, Ritschl, actually claimed that I planned even my philological essays like a Parisian *romancier*—absurdly exciting. Even in Paris they are amazed by *"tout mes audaces et finesses"*—this is M. Taine's expression.[2] I fear that even into the highest forms of the dithyramb one finds in my case some admixture of that salt which never loses its savor and becomes flat— "German"—namely, *esprit*.— I cannot do otherwise. God help me! Amen.[3]

All of us know, some even know from experience, which animal has long ears. Well then, I dare assert that I have the smallest ears. This is of no small interest to women—it seems to me that they may feel I understand them better.— I am the *anti-ass par excellence* and thus a world-historical monster—I am, in Greek, and not only in Greek, the *Antichrist*.

3

I have some notion of my privileges as a writer; in a few instances I have been told, too, how getting used to my writings "spoils" one's taste. One simply can no longer endure other books, least of all philosophical works. It is a distinction without equal to enter this noble and delicate world—one must not by any means be a German; it is after all a distinction one must have earned. But whoever is related to me in the height of his aspirations will experience veritable ecstasies of learning; for I come from heights that no bird ever reached in its flight, I know abysses into which no foot ever strayed. I have been told that it is impossible to put down one of my books—that I even disturb nightly rest.

Altogether, there is no prouder and at the same time subtler

---

2 "All my audacities and finesses." Nietzsche's correspondence with Hippolyte Taine has been published in *Friedrich Nietzsches Gesammelte Briefe*, vol. III, Berlin and Leipzig, Schuster & Loeffler, 1905.

3 Luther's famous words at the Diet of Worms.

type of book: here and there they achieve the highest thing achievable on earth, cynicism; they have to be conquered with the most delicate fingers as well as the bravest fists. Every frailty of the soul excludes one once and for all, even every kind of dyspepsia: one must not have any nerves, one needs a cheerful digestion. Not only the poverty, also the nook air of a soul excludes one; even more, any cowardice, uncleanliness, secret vengefulness in the entrails: a single word from me drives all his bad instincts into a man's face. My acquaintances include several guinea pigs who illustrate for me different reactions to my writings—different in a very instructive manner. Those who want no part of the contents, my so-called friends, for example, become "impersonal": they congratulate me for having got "that far" again—and find some progress in the greater cheerfulness of the tone.

Utterly depraved "spirits," "beautiful souls," being mendacious through and through, simply do not know where they are with these books—hence they consider them *beneath* themselves, the beautiful consistency of all "beautiful souls." The oxen among my acquaintances—mere Germans, if I may say so—suggest that one cannot always agree with my opinions, but at times— This I have been told even about *Zarathustra*.

All "feminism," too—also in men—closes the door: it will never permit entrance into this labyrinth of audacious insights. One must never have spared oneself, one must have acquired hardness as a habit to be cheerful and in good spirits in the midst of nothing but hard truths. When I imagine a perfect reader, he always turns into a monster of courage and curiosity; moreover, supple, cunning, cautious; a born adventurer and discoverer. In the end, I could not say better to whom alone I am speaking at bottom than Zarathustra said it: to whom alone will he relate his riddle?

"To you, the bold searchers, researchers, and whoever embarks with cunning sails on terrible seas—to you, drunk with riddles, glad of the twilight, whose soul flutes lure astray to every whirlpool, because you do not want to grope along a thread with cowardly hand; and where you can *guess,* you hate to *deduce*." [1]

---

[1] Part III, "On the Vision and the Riddle," section 1.

4

This is also the point for a general remark about my art of style. To communicate a state, an inward tension of pathos, by means of signs, including the tempo of these signs—that is the meaning of every style;[1] and considering that the multiplicity of inward states is exceptionally large in my case, I have many stylistic possibilities—the most multifarious art of style that has ever been at the disposal of one man. Good is any style that really communicates an inward state, that makes no mistake about the signs, the tempo of the signs, the gestures—all the laws about long periods are concerned with the art of gestures.[2] Here my instinct is infallible.

Good style in itself—a pure folly, mere "idealism," on a level with the "beautiful in itself," the "good in itself," the "thing in itself."

Always presupposing that there are ears—that there are those capable and worthy of the same pathos, that there is no lack of those to whom one may communicate oneself.— My Zarathustra, for example, is still looking for those—alas, it will have to keep looking for a long time yet!— One must be worthy of hearing him.

And until then there will be nobody to understand the art that has been squandered here: nobody ever was in a position to squander more new, unheard-of artistic devices that had actually been created only for this purpose. That this was possible in German, of all languages, remained to be shown: I myself would have rejected any such notion most unhesitatingly before. Before me, it was not known what could be done with the German language—what could be done with language in general. The art of the great rhythm, the great style of long periods to express a tremendous up and down of sublime, of superhuman passion, was discovered only by me; with a dithyramb like the last one in the third part of Zarathustra, enti-

---

[1] For the importance of tempo, cf. Beyond Good and Evil, sections 27, 28, and 246.

[2] See ibid., section 247. This sentence suggests some of the difficulties faced by a translator of Nietzsche.

tled "The Seven Seals," I soared a thousand miles beyond what was called poetry hitherto.

5

That a psychologist without equal speaks from my writings, is perhaps the first insight reached by a good reader—a reader as I deserve him, who reads me the way good old philologists read their Horace. Those propositions on which all the world is really agreed —not to speak of the world's common run of philosophers, the moralists and other hollow pots, cabbage heads[1]—appear in my books as naïve blunders: for example, the belief that "unegoistic" and "egoistic" are opposites, while the ego itself is really only a "higher swindle," an "ideal."— There are neither egoistic nor un-egoistic acts: both concepts are psychological absurdities. Or the proposition: "man strives for happiness."— Or the proposition: "happiness is the reward of virtue."— Or the proposition: "pleasure and displeasure are opposites."— The Circe of humanity, morality, has falsified all *psychologica* through and through—*moralizing* them—down to that gruesome nonsense that love is supposed to be something "unegoistic."— One has to sit firmly upon *oneself*, one must stand bravely on one's own two legs, otherwise one is simply *incapable* of loving. Ultimately, women know that only too well: they don't give a damn about selfless, merely objective men.

May I here venture the surmise that I *know* women? That is part of my Dionysian dowry. Who knows? Perhaps I am the first psychologist of the eternally feminine. They all love me—an old story—not counting *abortive* females, the "emancipated" who lack the stuff for children.— Fortunately, I am not willing to be torn to pieces: the perfect woman tears to pieces when she loves.— I know these charming maenads.— Ah, what a dangerous, creeping, sub-terranean little beast of prey she is! And yet so agreeable!— A little woman who pursues her revenge would run over fate itself.— Woman is indescribably more evil than man; also cleverer: good nature is in a woman a form of degeneration.— In all so-called

---

[1] *Den Allerwelts-Philosophen, den Moralisten und andren Hohltöpfen, Kohlköpfen.*

"beautiful souls" something is physiologically askew at bottom; I do not say everything, else I should become medi-cynical. The fight for equal rights is actually a symptom of a disease: every physician knows that.— Woman, the more she is a woman, resists rights in general hand and foot: after all, the state of nature, the eternal war between the sexes, gives her by far the first rank.

Has my definition of love been heard? It is the only one worthy of a philosopher. Love—in its means, war; at bottom, the deadly hatred of the sexes.

Has my answer been heard to the question how one *cures* a woman—"redeems" her? One gives her a child. Woman needs children, a man is for her always only a means: thus spoke *Zarathustra*.

"Emancipation of women"—that is the instinctive hatred of the abortive[2] woman, who is incapable of giving birth, against the woman who is turned out well [3]—the fight against the "man" is always a mere means, pretext, tactic. By raising themselves higher, as "woman in herself," as the "higher woman," as a female "idealist," they want to lower the level of the general rank of woman; and there is no surer means for that than higher education, slacks, and political voting-cattle rights. At bottom, the emancipated are anarchists in the world of the "eternally feminine," the underprivileged whose most fundamental instinct is revenge.

One whole species of the most malignant "idealism"—which, incidentally, is also encountered among men; for example, in Henrik Ibsen, this typical old virgin—aims to *poison* the good conscience, what is natural in sexual love.[4]

And lest I leave any doubt about my very decent and strict views in these matters, let me still cite a proposition against vice from my moral code: I use the word "vice" in my fight against

---

2 *Missraten.*

3 *Wohlgeraten.*

4 It seems plain that Nietzsche did not know most of Ibsen's plays. Cf. my edition of *The Will to Power* (New York, Random House, 1967), sections 86 (including my long note) and 747, and for some parallels between Ibsen and Nietzsche also my translation of *Beyond Good and Evil* (New York, Vintage Books, 1966)—the last section of my Preface to that volume as well as my note on section 213. Nietzsche would have loved *The Wild Duck.*

every kind of antinature or, if you prefer pretty words, idealism.
The proposition reads: "The preaching of chastity amounts to a
public incitement to antinature. Every kind of contempt for sex,
every impurification of it by means of the concept 'impure,' is the
crime *par excellence* against life—is the real sin against the holy
spirit of life."

6

To give an idea of me as a psychologist, I choose a curious bit
of psychology from *Beyond Good and Evil;* incidentally, I forbid
any surmise about whom I am describing in this passage:[1]

> The genius of the heart, as that great concealed one pos-
> sesses it, the tempter god and born pied piper of consciences
> whose voice knows how to descend into the netherworld of ev-
> ery soul; who does not say a word or cast a glance in which
> there is no consideration and ulterior enticement; whose mas-
> tery includes the knowledge of how to seem—not what he is
> but what is to those who follow him one *more* constraint to
> press ever closer to him in order to follow him even more in-
> wardly and thoroughly—the genius of the heart who silences
> all that is loud and self-satisfied, teaching it to listen; who
> smooths rough souls and lets them taste a new desire—to lie
> still as a mirror, that the deep sky may mirror itself in them—
> the genius of the heart who teaches the doltish and rash hand
> to hesitate and reach out more delicately; who guesses the con-
> cealed and forgotten treasure, the drop of graciousness and
> sweet spirituality under dim and thick ice, and is a divining rod
> for every grain of gold that has long lain buried in the dungeon
> of much mud and sand; the genius of the heart from whose
> touch everyone walks away richer, not having received grace
> and surprised, not as blessed and oppressed by alien goods, but

---

[1] Section 295. In a footnote for that section (in my translation of *Beyond
Good and Evil*) I have brought together materials that show how much this
portrait owes to Socrates; also how Nietzsche came to see *himself* this way.
"I forbid any surmise . . ." surely suggests that the description seems to
Nietzsche to fit himself.

richer in himself, newer to himself than before, broken open, blown at and sounded out by a thawing wind, perhaps more unsure, tenderer, more fragile, more broken, but full of hopes that as yet have no name, full of new will and currents, full of new dissatisfaction and undertows . . .

The Birth of Tragedy

1

To be fair to *The Birth of Tragedy* (1872), one has to forget a few things. Its effect and fascination were due to what was wrong with it—its practical application to Wagnerism, as if that were a symptom of *ascent*. In this respect, this essay was an event in the life of Wagner: it was only from that moment on that Wagner's name elicited high hopes. People still remind me of this today, sometimes even in the context of *Parsifal*—how I am the one who has it on his conscience that such a high opinion of the. *cultural value* of this movement gained prevalence.

Several times I saw this book cited as "The Re-Birth of Tragedy Out of the Spirit of Music": what people had ears for was only a new formula for the art, the intentions, the task of *Wagner*—and what was really valuable in the essay was ignored. "Hellenism and Pessimism" would have been a less ambiguous title—suggesting the first instruction about how the Greeks got over their pessimism, how they *overcame* it.

Precisely their tragedies prove that the Greeks were *not* pessimists: Schopenhauer went wrong at this point, as he went wrong everywhere.

Taken up with some degree of neutrality, *The Birth of Tragedy* looks quite untimely: one would never dream that it was begun amid the thunder of the battle of Wörth. Before the walls of Metz, in cold September nights, while on duty as a medical orderly, I thought through these problems. One might sooner believe that the essay was fifty years older.[1] It is indifferent toward politics—"un-German," to use the language of the present time—it smells offensively Hegelian, and the cadaverous perfume of Schopenhauer sticks

---

[1] That would take us back to the time of Hegel, 1820.

only to a few formulas. An "idea" [2]—the antithesis[3] of the Dionysian and the Apollinian—translated into the realm of metaphysics;
history itself as the development of this "idea"; in tragedy this antithesis is sublimated [4] into a unity; and in this perspective things
that had never before faced each other are suddenly juxtaposed,
used to illuminate each other, and comprehended [5]—opera, for
example, and the revolution.

The two decisive innovations of the book are, first, its understanding of the Dionysian phenomenon among the Greeks: for the
first time, a psychological analysis of this phenomenon is offered,
and it is considered as one root of the whole of Greek art. Secondly, there is the understanding of Socratism: Socrates is recognized for the first time as an instrument of Greek disintegration, as
a typical decadent. "Rationality" *against* instinct. "Rationality" at
any price as a dangerous force that undermines life.[6]

Profound, hostile silence about Christianity throughout the
book. That is neither Apollinian nor Dionysian; it negates all aesthetic values—the only values recognized in *The Birth of Tragedy:*
it is nihilistic in the most profound sense, while in the Dionysian
symbol the ultimate limit of affirmation is attained. There is one
allusion to Christian priests as a "vicious kind of dwarfs" who are
"subterranean." [7]

2

This beginning is exceedingly strange. I had discovered the
only parable and parallel in history for my own inmost experience

---

[2] *Idee:* one of the key terms of Hegel's philosophy.

[3] *Gegensatz:* the word Hegel generally uses where English translations have
"antithesis."

[4] *Aufgehoben:* a term Hegel liked especially because in ordinary German it
can mean canceled, preserved, and lifted up. For this whole passage, cf.
Kaufmann's *Nietzsche,* Chapter 13, section I, including note 7.

[5] *Begriffen:* another term Hegel used frequently.

[6] For a comprehensive discussion of Nietzsche's complex attitude toward
Socrates and its development from *The Birth of Tragedy* to *Ecce Homo,* see
Kaufmann's *Nietzsche,* Chapter 13.

[7] At the end of section 24. But the quotation is inexact, and the interpretation—that priests were meant—is questionable.

—and thus became the first to comprehend the wonderful phenomenon of the Dionysian. At the same time my discovery that Socrates was a decadent proved unequivocally how little the sureness of my psychological grasp would be endangered by any moral idiosyncrasy: seeing morality itself as a symptom of decadence is an innovation and a singularity of the first rank in the history of knowledge. How high had I jumped with these two insights above the wretched and shallow chatter about optimism versus pessimism!

I was the first to see[1] the real opposition: the degenerating instinct that turns against life with subterranean vengefulness (Christianity, the philosophy of Schopenhauer, in a certain sense already the philosophy of Plato, and all of idealism as typical forms) versus a formula for the highest affirmation, born of fullness, of overfullness, a Yes-saying without reservation, even to suffering, even to guilt, even to everything that is questionable and strange in existence.

This ultimate, most joyous, most wantonly extravagant Yes to life represents not only the highest insight but also the *deepest,* that which is most strictly confirmed and born out by truth and science. Nothing in existence may be subtracted, nothing is dispensable—those aspects of existence which Christians and other nihilists repudiate are actually on an infinitely higher level in the order of rank among values than that which the instinct of decadence could approve and call good.[2] To comprehend this requires courage and, as a condition of that, an excess of strength: for precisely as far as courage may venture forward, precisely according to that measure of strength one approaches the truth. Knowledge, saying Yes to reality, is just as necessary for the strong as cowardice and the flight from reality—as the "ideal" is for the weak, who are inspired by weakness.

They are not free to know: the decadents *need* the lie—it is one of the conditions of their preservation.

Whoever does not merely comprehend the word "Dionysian"

---

[1] Except for the context, this could well mean: First I saw . . .

[2] *Gutheissen, gut heissen.*

but comprehends *himself* in the word "Dionysian" needs no refutation of Plato or Christianity or Schopenhauer—he *smells the decay.*

3

How I had thus found the concept of the "tragic" and at long last knowledge of the psychology of tragedy, I have explained most recently in *Twilight of the Idols,* p. 139:[1]

"Saying Yes to life even in its strangest and hardest problems; the will to life rejoicing over its own inexhaustibility even in the very sacrifice of its highest types—that is what I called Dionysian, that is what I understood as[2] the bridge to the psychology of the tragic poet. Not in order to get rid of terror and pity, not in order to purge oneself of a dangerous affect by its vehement discharge—Aristotle misunderstood[3] it that way—but in order to be oneself the eternal joy of becoming, beyond all terror and pity—that joy which includes even joy in destroying."

In this sense I have the right to understand myself as the first *tragic philosopher*—that is, the most extreme opposite and antipode of a pessimistic philosopher. Before me this transposition of the Dionysian into a philosophical pathos did not exist: *tragic wisdom* was lacking; I have looked in vain for signs of it even among the *great* Greeks in philosophy, those of the two centuries *before* Socrates.[4] I retained some doubt in the case of *Heraclitus,* in whose proximity I feel altogether warmer and better than anywhere else. The affirmation of passing away *and destroying,* which is the decisive feature of a Dionysian philosophy; saying Yes to opposition and war; *becoming,* along with a radical repudiation of the very concept of *being*—all this is clearly more closely related to me than anything else thought to date. The doctrine of the "eternal recurrence," that is, of the unconditional and infinitely repeated circular

---

[1] In the final section of the book (*Portable Nietzsche,* pp. 562f.).

[2] In *Twilight:* guessed to be.

[3] In *Twilight:* understood. Nietzsche is referring to Aristotle's conception of catharsis (*Poetics* 6, 1449b).

[4] Nietzsche's extremely high valuation of the pre-Socratics was taken up by Karl Jaspers and Martin Heidegger.

course of all things—this doctrine of Zarathustra *might* in the end have been taught already by Heraclitus. At least the Stoa has traces of it, and the Stoics inherited almost all of their principal notions from Heraclitus.

4

A tremendous hope speaks out of this essay. In the end I lack all reason to renounce the hope for a Dionysian future of music. Let us look ahead a century; let us suppose that my attempt to assassinate two millennia of antinature and desecration of man were to succeed. That new party of life which would tackle the greatest of all tasks, the attempt to raise humanity higher, including the relentless destruction of everything that was degenerating and parasitical, would again make possible that excess of life on earth from which the Dionysian state, too, would have to awaken again. I promise a tragic age: the highest art in saying Yes to life, tragedy, will be reborn when humanity has weathered the consciousness of the hardest but most necessary wars *without suffering from it.*

A psychologist might still add that what I heard as a young man listening to Wagnerian music really had nothing to do with Wagner; that when I described Dionysian music I described what *I* had heard—that instinctively I had to transpose and transfigure everything into the new spirit that I carried in me. The proof of that, *as strong as any proof can be,* is my essay on *Wagner in Bayreuth:* in all psychologically decisive places I alone am discussed— and one need not hesitate to put down my name or the word "Zarathustra" where the text has the word "Wagner." The entire picture of the dithyrambic artist is a picture of the pre-existent poet of *Zarathustra,* sketched with abysmal profundity and without touching even for a moment the Wagnerian reality. Wagner himself had some notion of that; he did not recognize himself in this essay.

Similarly, "the idea of Bayreuth" was transformed into something that should not puzzle those who know my *Zarathustra:* into that great noon at which the most elect consecrate themselves for the greatest of all tasks. Who could say? The vision of a feast that I shall yet live to see.

The pathos of the first pages is world-historical; the glance spoken of on the seventh page is Zarathustra's distinctive glance; Wagner, Bayreuth, the whole wretched German pettiness are a cloud in which an infinite mirage of the future is reflected. Even psychologically all decisive traits of my own nature are projected into Wagner's—the close proximity of the brightest and the most calamitous forces, the will to power as no man ever possessed it,[5] the ruthless courage in matters of the spirit, the unlimited power to learn without damage to the will to act. Everything in this essay points to the future: the impending return of the Greek spirit, the necessity of counter-Alexanders who will retie the Gordian knot of Greek culture.

Listen to the world-historical accent with which the concept of the tragic attitude is introduced at the end of section 4: this essay is full of world-historical accents. This is the strangest "objectivity" possible: the absolute certainty about what I am was projected on some accidental reality—the truth about me spoke from some gruesome depth. At the beginning of section 9 the *style* of *Zarathustra* is described with incisive certainty and anticipated; and no more magnificent expression could be found for the *event* of *Zarathustra,* the act of a tremendous purification and consecration of humanity, than was found in section 6.[6]

---

[5] This striking confession of the philosopher of the will to power has been ignored although, quite apart from its human and psychological interest, it helps to illuminate his conception of the will to power.

[6] All these references are to *Richard Wagner in Bayreuth,* and that is the book discussed in the last four paragraphs of this section. Nietzsche, as usual, furnishes page references—which Karl Schlechta, in his edition of the works, misconstrues as referring to *The Birth of Tragedy:* whoever looks up Schlechta's page references won't find any of the passages discussed by Nietzsche.

The Untimely Ones[1]

1

The four Untimely Ones are certainly warlike. They prove that I was no Jack the Dreamer, that I take pleasure in fencing—perhaps also that I am dangerously quick at the draw. The *first* attack (1873) was directed against German "culture"[2] on which I looked down even then with ruthless contempt. Without meaning, without substance, without aim: mere "public opinion." There is no more malignant misunderstanding than to believe that the great military success[3] of the Germans proved anything in favor of this "culture"—or, of all things, *its* triumph over France.

The *second* Untimely One (1874) brings to light what is dangerous and gnaws at and poisons life in our kind of traffic with science and scholarship[4]—how life is made sick by this dehumanized and mechanical grinding of gears, the "impersonality" of the laborer, the false economy of the "division of labor." The aim is lost, genuine culture—and the means, the modern traffic with science, *barbarized*. In this essay the "historical sense" of which this century is proud was recognized for the first time as a disease, as a typical symptom of decay.

---

[1] *Die Unzeitgemässen:* the four essays in question were published as *Unzeitgemässe Betrachtungen* (untimely meditations), one by one, with separate titles: *David Strauss, The Confessor and Writer; On the Use and Disadvantage of History for Life; Schopenhauer as Educator;* and *Richard Wagner in Bayreuth.*

[2] *Bildung* has no exact equivalent in English: *Bild* means picture or image; *bilden,* to shape or form, but also to educate; *ungebildet,* uneducated, uncultured. In this section, *Bildung* has been rendered by "culture" (in quotes), *Kultur* by culture (without quotes).

[3] In the Franco-Prussian War of 1870–71.

[4] Science and scholarship: *Wissenschaft.* After this, science has been used to render *Wissenschaft,* but it should be kept in mind that the reference is not primarily to the natural sciences. Cf. *Beyond Good and Evil,* Part Six ("We Scholars," sections 204–13): the concept of the laborer is used similarly in section 211. See also *Genealogy,* III, sections 23ff.

In the *third* and *fourth* Untimely Ones, two images of the hardest self-love, self-discipline[5] are put up against all this, as pointers to a higher concept of culture, to restore the concept of culture—untimely types *par excellence,* full of sovereign contempt for everything around them that was called "Empire," "culture," [6] "Christianity," "Bismarck," "success"—Schopenhauer and Wagner *or,* in one word, Nietzsche.

2

Of these four attempts at assassination the first had an extraordinary success. The noise it evoked was in every sense splendid. I had touched the sore spot of a victorious nation—that its victory was *not* a cultural event but perhaps, perhaps something altogether different.

The response came from all sides and by no means only from the old friends of David Strauss whom I had made ridiculous as a type of the German "cultural" philistine and *satisfait,*[1] in short as the author of his beer-hall gospel of *The Old and the New Faith* (the word *Bildungsphilister* has survived in the German language from my essay).[2] These old friends, Württembergers and Swabians whom I had wounded deeply when I found their prodigy, Strauss, funny, replied in such a foursquare and rude manner that I could not have asked for more; the replies from Prussia were more prudent—they had more Prussian, Berlin blue in them. It was a news-

---

[5] *Selbstsucht, Selbstzucht.* On the former, see the chapter "On the Three Evils" in *Zarathustra III* (*Portable Nietzsche,* pp. 298ff., especially 302): the word used there is also *Selbstsucht.* ⌣ also Aristotle's *Nicomachean Ethics,* 1169a: "the good man ought to be a lover of self since he will then act nobly, and so both benefit himself and aid his fellows; but the bad man ought not to be a lover of self, since he will follow his base passions, and so injure both himself and his neighbours" (trans. Rackham, Loeb Classical Library).

[6] *"Reich," "Bildung"* . . .

[1] *Smug.*

[2] The word had actually been used earlier by Gustav Teichmüller (1832–1888), a professor at Basel from 1868 to 1871; but Nietzsche's claim (*ist von meiner Schrift her in der Sprache übriggeblieben*) is literally true. For all that, he would hardly have said this if he had remembered that the coinage was Teichmüller's.

paper in Leipzig, the notorious *Grenzboten,* that became most indecent; I found it difficult to restrain the indignant Baselers from taking action. The only ones who decided unconditionally in my favor were a few old gentlemen, from mixed and in part undiscoverable motives. Ewald in Göttingen was among them;[3] he suggested my attempt had been fatal for Strauss. Also the old Hegelian, Bruno Bauer,[4] who was henceforth one of my most attentive readers. During his last years he liked to refer to me; for example, by giving Herr von Treitschke, the Prussian historiographer, a hint whom he might ask for some information about the concept of culture which had escaped him. Nothing written about this essay and its author was more thought-provoking or longer than what an old disciple of the philosopher von Baader[5] said, a Professor Hoffmann in Würzburg.[6] On the basis of this essay he predicted a great destiny for me—bringing about a kind of crisis and ultimate

[3] Heinrich Ewald (1803–1875), a very eminent Old Testament scholar and orientalist, was one of the celebrated "Göttingen Seven" who in 1837 were expelled from the university because they had signed a liberal manifesto; he went to Tübingen, but returned to Göttingen in 1848—and was pensioned off in 1867 because he refused to swear an oath of allegiance to the king of Prussia.

[4] Bruno Bauer (1809–82) started out as a right-wing, conservative Hegelian and became a professor of theology at Bonn in 1839. In 1840 and 1841 he published two volumes of New Testament criticism, and in 1842 he was deprived of the right to teach. Now he was accounted a "Young" or left-wing Hegelian, and he has been called "the most radical of the New Testament critics of his age." He attacked David Friedrich Strauss's ideas about the origins of Christianity and emphasized Hellenistic influences. Albert Schweitzer praised him highly in his *Geschichte der Leben Jesu Forschung* (Tübingen 1921, p. 161; *The Quest of the Historical Jesus*) for having assembled the most brilliant and complete summary of the difficulties presented by the life of Jesus. Marx's and Engels' attacks on Bauer, as "St. Bruno," written in 1845/46, are included in *Die Deutsche Ideologie* (published posthumously in 1932; The German Ideology). Bauer's ideas are also discussed by Karl Löwith in *Von Hegel bis Nietzsche* (Europa Verlag, Zürich and New York 1941; *From Hegel to Nietzsche,* Holt, Rinehart and Winston, New York 1964).

[5] Franz Xaver von Baader (1765–1841), who became a professor at Munich in 1826, influenced Schelling and other romantics.

[6] Franz Hoffmann, *Philosophische Schriften,* vol. V (Erlangen, 1878), pp. 410–47. See also J. Haefner, *Leben und Schaffen des Würzburger Philosophen F. K. Hoffmann* (The life and work of the Würzburg philosopher F. K. Hoffmann; dissertation, 1941, 112 pp.).

decision in the problem of atheism whose most instinctive and relentless type he divined in me. It was atheism that led me to Schopenhauer.

Nothing was heard as well or experienced as bitterly as an extraordinarily strong and courageous plea by the usually mild Karl Hillebrand, this last *humane* German who knew how to write. His piece was read in the *Augsburger Zeitung;* today it can be read, in a somewhat more cautious form, in his collected essays.[7] Here the essay was considered as an event, a turning point, a first self-examination, the very best sign, as a real *return* of German seriousness and German passion in matters of the spirit. Hillebrand was full of high praise for the form of the essay, for its mature taste, for its perfect tact in distinguishing between the person and the issue: he designated it as the best polemical essay written in German—in the art of polemics which is so dangerous and inadvisable for Germans. Saying Yes unconditionally, even sharpening the points I had dared to make against the galloping slovenliness of the German language[8] (today they play the purists and can no longer form a sentence), with equal contempt for the "foremost writers" of this nation, he concluded with an expression of his admiration for my *courage*—that "supreme courage which prefers charges precisely against the favorites of a people."

The aftereffects of this essay upon my life are virtually inestimable. Nobody so far has picked quarrels with me; in Germany I am treated with gloomy caution: for years I have made use of an unconditional freedom of speech for which nobody today, least of all in the *Reich,* has sufficient liberty. My paradise lies "in the shadow of my sword."

At bottom, I had put into practise one of Stendhal's maxims:

---

[7] Karl Hillebrand, "Einiges über den Verfall der deutschen Sprache und der deutschen Gesinnung" (some thoughts about the decay of the German language and the German mind) in *Zeiten, Völker und Menschen* (periods, peoples, and persons), vol. II (Berlin, 1875; 2nd ed., Strassburg, 1892), pp. 291–310. Hillebrand also reviewed Nietzsche's second and third "untimely meditations": "Über Wissen und historischen Sinn" (on knowledge and the historical sense) and "Schopenhauer und das deutsche Publikum" (Schopenhauer and the German public), *ibid.,* pp. 314–38 and 353–66.

[8] *Sprach-Verlumpung in Deutschland.*

he advises men to make their entry into society with a *duel*. And how I had picked my opponent! the foremost German free spirit!

Indeed, an altogether new type of free spirit thus gained his first expression: to this day nothing is more foreign and less related to me than the whole European and American species of *libres penseurs*.[9] I am much more profoundly at odds with them, as incorrigible blockheads and buffoons of "modern ideas," than with any of their opponents. They also want in their own way to "improve" mankind, in their own image; against what I am, what I *want,* they would wage an irreconcilable war if they understood me: all of them still believe in the "ideal."— I am the first *immoralist*.

3

That the two Untimely Ones distinguished by the names of Schopenhauer and Wagner contribute much to the understanding of, or even to the formulation of the proper psychological questions about, these two cases, I should not wish to assert—excepting, as seems fair, some details. Thus, for example, the elementary fact in Wagner's character is already designated with a profound sureness of instinct as an actor's talent that merely explicates itself in his means and intentions.

What I was fundamentally trying to do in these essays was something altogether different from psychology: an unequaled problem of education, a new concept of self-discipline, self-defense to the point of hardness, a way to greatness and world-historical tasks was seeking its first expression. Broadly speaking, I caught hold of two famous and as yet altogether undiagnosed types, as one catches hold of an opportunity, in order to say something, in order to have at hand a few more formulas, signs, means of language. This is really suggested with a perfectly uncanny sagacity near the end of section 7 in the third Untimely One. Plato employed Socrates in this fashion, as a [sign language for Plato].[1]

---

[9] Cf. *Beyond Good and Evil,* Part Two, "The Free Spirit," especially section 44.

[1] The words placed in brackets are not in Nietzsche's hand and were added

Now that I am looking back from a certain distance upon the conditions of which these essays bear witness, I do not wish to deny that at bottom they speak only of me. The essay *Wagner in Bayreuth* is a vision of my future, while in *Schopenhauer as Educator* my innermost history, my *becoming,* is inscribed. Above all, my promise!

What I am today, where I am today—at a height where I speak no longer with words but with lightning bolts—ah, how remote from this I still was at that time!— But I beheld the land—I did not deceive myself for a moment about the way, the sea, the danger—and success. The great calm in promising, this happy gaze into a future that is not to remain a mere promise!

Here every word is experienced, is deep, is inward; what is most painful is not lacking: there are words in it that are virtually bloodthirsty. But a wind of the great freedom blows over everything; even wounds do not have the effect of objections.

How I understand the philosopher—as a terrible explosive, endangering everything—how my concept of the philosopher is worlds removed from any concept that would include even a Kant, not to speak of academic "ruminants" and other professors of philosophy—this essay gives inestimable information about that, although at bottom it is admittedly not "Schopenhauer as Educator" that speaks here, but his opposite, "Nietzsche as Educator."

Considering that in those days I practiced the scholar's craft, and perhaps *knew* something about this craft, the harsh psychology of the scholar that suddenly emerges in this essay is of some significance: it expresses the *feeling of distance,*[2] the profound assurance

---

by a German editor—presumably Gast. What Nietzsche claims may sound farfetched, but actually the *first* section of *Schopenhauer as Educator* makes this point very plainly. The question is raised how we can realize our true self, and the prescription is that we should ask ourselves: "What have you really loved till now?" For "your true self does not lie deeply concealed within you but immeasurably high above you, or at least above what you usually take for your ego. Your real educators, those who formed you, reveal to you what is the true primary meaning and fundamental substance of your being . . ." The meditation on Schopenhauer is thus introduced as Nietzsche's attempt to discover his own true self; and Nietzsche's praise not only of Schopenhauer's honesty but also—of all things—of his "cheerfulness" (in section 2) points in the same direction.

[2] Cf. the *pathos of distance* in section 257 of *Beyond Good and Evil.*

about what could be my *task* and what could only be means, *entr'acte,* and minor works. It shows my prudence that I was many things and in many places in order to be able to become one thing —to be able to attain one thing. I *had* to be a scholar, too, for some time.[3]

_____

[3] Cf. *ibid.,* section 211: "It may be necessary for the education of a genuine philosopher that he himself has also once stood on all these steps on which his servants, the scientific laborers of philosophy, remain standing . . ."

Human, All-Too-Human
With Two Sequels

1

Human, All-Too-Human is the monument of a crisis. It is subtitled "A Book for *Free* Spirits": almost every sentence marks some victory—here I liberated myself from what in my nature did not belong to me. Idealism, for example; the title means: "where *you* see ideal things, *I* see what is—human, alas, all-too-human!"—I know man better.

The term "free spirit" here is not to be understood in any other sense; it means a spirit that has *become free,*[1] that has again taken possession of itself. The tone, the voice, is completely changed: you will find the book clever, cool, perhaps hard and mocking. A certain spirituality of noble *taste* seems to be fighting continually against a more passionate current in order to stay afloat. In this connection it makes sense that it was actually the hundredth anniversary of the death of *Voltaire* that the book pleaded, as it were, as an excuse for coming out in 1878.[2] For Voltaire was above all, in contrast to all who wrote after him, a *grandseigneur*[3] of the spirit—like me.— The name of Voltaire on one of my essays —that really meant progress—*toward me.*

On closer inspection you discover a merciless spirit that knows all the hideouts where the ideal is at home—where it has its secret dungeons and, as it were, its ultimate safety. With a torch whose light never wavers, an incisive light is thrown into this *underworld* of the ideal. This is war, but war without powder and smoke, without warlike poses, without pathos and strained limbs:[4] all that

---

[1] Cf. *Twilight,* section 49 (*Portable Nietzsche,* p. 554).

[2] The first edition bore the following dedication: "To the memory of Voltaire, in commemoration of his death, May 30, 1878."

[3] Nobleman.

[4] Cf. section 7 of the first chapter, above; also the first footnote for that section.

would still be "idealism." One error after another is coolly placed
on ice; the ideal is not refuted—it *freezes* to death.— Here, for
example, "the genius" freezes to death; at the next corner, "the
saint"; under a huge icicle, "the hero"; in the end, "faith," so-
called "conviction"; "pity" also cools down considerably—and almost everywhere "the thing in itself" freezes to death.

2

The beginnings of this book belong right in the midst of the
first *Bayreuther Festspiele;*[1] a profound alienation from everything
that surrounded me there is one of its preconditions. Whoever has
any notion of the visions I had encountered even before that, may
guess how I felt when one day I woke up in Bayreuth. As if I were
dreaming!

Wherever was I? There was nothing I recognized; I scarcely
recognized Wagner. In vain did I leaf through my memories. Tribschen—a distant isle of the blessed: not a trace of any similarity.
The incomparable days when the foundation stone was laid, the
small group of people that had belonged, had celebrated, and did
not need first to acquire fingers for delicate matters—not a trace of
any similarity. *What had happened?*— Wagner had been translated
into German! The Wagnerian had become master over Wagner.—
German art. The *German* master. *German* beer.

We others, who know only too well to what subtle artists and
what cosmopolitanism of taste Wagner's art speaks, exclusively,
were beside ourselves when we found Wagner again, draped with
German "virtues."

I think I know the Wagnerians; I have experienced three generations, beginning with the late Brendel [2] who confounded Wagner
and Hegel, down to the "idealists" of the *Bayreuther Blätter*[3] who

---

[1] The Wagner opera festivals at Bayreuth.

[2] Karl Franz Brendel (1811–1868) was editor of the *Neue Zeitschrift für
Musik* (new journal for music), 1845–1868, and of *Anregungen für Kunst,
Leben und Wissenschaft* (stimulations for art, life and science), 1856–61.
He became a champion of Wagner in 1851.

[3] Wagner's new periodical.

confound Wagner and themselves—I have heard every kind of confession of "beautiful souls" about Wagner. A kingdom for one sensible word!— In truth, a hair-raising company! Nohl, Pohl, *Kohl—*
droll with charm, *in infinitum!* [4] Not a single abortion is missing
among them, not even the anti-Semite.— Poor Wagner! Where had
he landed!— If he had at least entered into swine! [5] But to descend
among Germans!

Really, for the instruction of posterity one ought to stuff a
genuine Bayreuther or, better yet, preserve him in spirits, for spirits
are lacking—with the label: that is how the "spirit" looked on
which the *Reich* was founded.

Enough; in the midst of it I left for a couple of weeks,[6] very
suddenly, although a charming Parisienne tried to console me; the

---

[4] Karl Friedrich Ludwig Nohl (1831–1885) was a professor of music at the
universities of Munich and Heidelberg, a prolific writer, especially on
Mozart and Beethoven, and a dedicated Wagnerian. His publications include
R. Wagners Bedeutung für die nationale Kunst (R. Wagner's significance for
national art; Vienna, 1883) and *Das moderne Musikdrama* (the modern
music drama; Vienna, 1884).

Richard Pohl (1826–1896) became co-editor (with Brendel) of *Anregungen für Kunst, Leben und Wissenschaft,* in 1857. A Wagnerian since
1846, he was sometimes called "the oldest Wagnerian."

Kohl, emphasized by Nietzsche, means drivel or twaddle as well as cabbage, and "drivel" is clearly the primary meaning intended here ("droll"
represents an attempt to capture something of the spirit of the passage). This
does not preclude the possibility that there may also have been some individual with this unfortunate name; e.g., a young man named Otto Kohl was a
member of a small circle of philology students to which Nietzsche and Erwin
Rohde had belonged in Leipzig.

A superseded draft for this section contains two short passages worth
quoting here: "Typical was the old Kaiser [i.e., Wilhelm I] who applauded
with his hands while saying loudly to his adjutant, Count Lehndorf: 'Hideous!
hideous!' [*scheusslich! scheusslich!*]" And: "In the music of Wagner, which
persuaded by means of its secret sexuality, one found a bond for a society in
which everybody pursued his own *plaisirs* [pleasures]. The rest and, if you
will, also the innocence of the matter, its 'idealists' were the idiots, the Nohl,
Pohl, *Kohl*—the latter, known to me, the *genius loci* [minor local deity] in
Bayreuth . . ." (Podach, *Friedrich Nietzsches Werke,* 1961, p. 276).

[5] Luke 8:33.

[6] Podach's vitriolic attack on Nietzsche's account of his break with Wagner,
and on *Ecce Homo* generally, is often out of touch with the facts—as when
he says of Nietzsche's sister, ignoring these words: "After all, it was
scarcely feasible to blow down the story in *Ecce Homo* like a house of cards,
by stating that her brother, in spite of financial difficulties, had soon returned
to Bayreuth . . ." (p. 196).

only excuse I offered Wagner was a fatalistic telegram. In Klingen-brunn, a small town concealed in the woods of the *Böhmerwald,* I dragged around my melancholy and contempt for Germans like a disease—and from time to time I'd write a sentence into my note-book, under the general title "The Plowshare"—*hard psychologica* that can perhaps still be found in *Human, All-Too-Human.*

3

What reached a decision in me at that time was not a break with Wagner: I noted a total aberration of my instincts of which particular blunders, whether Wagner or the professorship at Basel, were mere symptoms. I was overcome by *impatience* with myself; I saw that it was high time for me to recall and reflect on myself. All at once it became clear to me in a terrifying way how much time I had already wasted—how useless and arbitrary my whole existence as a philologist appeared in relation to my task. I felt ashamed of this *false* modesty.

Ten years lay behind me in which the nourishment of my spirit had really come to a stop; I had not learned anything new that was useful; I had forgotten an absurd amount for the sake of dusty scholarly gewgaws. Crawling scrupulously with bad eyes through ancient metrists—that's what I had come to!— It stirred my com-passion to see myself utterly emaciated, utterly starved: my knowl-edge simply failed to include *realities,* and my "idealities" were not worth a damn.

A truly burning thirst took hold of me: henceforth I really pursued nothing *more*[1] than physiology, medicine, and natural sciences—and I did not return even to properly historical studies until my *task* compelled me to, imperiously. It was then, too, that I first guessed how an activity chosen in defiance of one's instincts, a so-called "vocation" for which one does not have the least voca-tion, is related to the need for *deadening* the feeling of desolation

---

[1] . . . *nichts mehr getrieben als* . . . : if the accent falls on *nichts,* the meaning is "pursued nothing any more except," which is palpably false as a matter of biographical fact. If the accent falls on *mehr,* the meaning is that suggested above, which may still be considered a rhetorical exaggeration.

and hunger by means of a narcotic art—for example, Wagnerian art.

Looking about me cautiously, I have discovered that a large number of young men experience the same distress: one antinatural step virtually compels the second. In Germany, in the *Reich*— to speak unambiguously—all too many are condemned to choose vocations too early, and then to waste away under a burden they can no longer shake off.— These people require Wagner as an *opiate:* they forget themselves, they are rid of themselves for a moment.— What am I saying? For *five or six hours!*

4

It was then that my instinct made its inexorable decision against any longer yielding, going along, and confounding myself. Any kind of life, the most unfavorable conditions, sickness, poverty—anything seemed preferable to that unseemly "selflessness" into which I had got myself originally in ignorance and *youth* and in which I had got stuck later on from inertia and so-called "sense of duty." [1]

Here it happened in a manner that I cannot admire sufficiently that, precisely at the right time, my father's *wicked* heritage came to my aid—at bottom, predestination to an early death.[2] Sickness *detached me slowly:* it spared me any break, any violent and offensive step. Thus I did not lose any good will and actually gained not a little. My sickness also gave me the right to change all my habits completely; it permitted, it *commanded* me to forget; it bestowed on me the necessity of lying still, of leisure, of waiting and being patient.— But that means, of thinking.— My eyes alone put an end to all bookwormishness—in brief, philology: I was delivered from the "book"; for years I did not read a thing—the greatest benefit I ever conferred on myself.— That nethermost self which had, as it

---

[1] This splendid sentence illuminates Nietzsche's ideas about "self-love" and "selflessness."

[2] Nietzsche collapsed a few weeks after writing this. This paragraph illustrates beautifully what Nietzsche says about *amor fati,* freedom from *ressentiment,* and saying Yes even to suffering.

were, been buried and grown silent under the continual pressure of
having to listen to other selves (and that is after all what reading
means) awakened slowly, shyly, dubiously—but eventually it
spoke again. Never have I felt happier with myself than in the sick-
est and most painful periods of my life: one only need look at *The
Dawn* or perhaps *The Wanderer and His Shadow* to comprehend
what this "return to myself" meant—a supreme kind of recovery.
— The other kind merely followed from this.

5

Human, All-Too-Human, this monument of rigorous self-
discipline with which I put a sudden end to all my infections with
"higher swindle," "idealism," "beautiful feelings," and other effem-
inacies, was written in the main in Sorrento; it was finished and
received its final form during a winter in Basel, under conditions
incomparably less favorable than those in Sorrento. Ultimately,
Herr *Peter Gast,* who was then studying at the University of Basel
and very devoted to me, has this book on his conscience. I dictated,
my head bandaged and in pain; he wrote and also corrected: fundamentally, he was really the writer while I was merely the author.

When the book was finally finished and in my hands—a profound surprise for one so seriously ill—I also sent two copies,
among others, to Bayreuth. By a miraculously meaningful coinci-
dence, I received at the very same time a beautiful copy of the text
of *Parsifal,* with Wagner's inscription for me, "for his dear friend,
Friedrich Nietzsche, Richard Wagner, Church Councilor."— This
crossing of the two books—I felt as if I heard an ominous sound—
as if two swords had crossed.— At any rate, both of us felt that
way; for both of us remained silent.— Around that time the first
Bayreuther Blätter appeared: I understood for *what* it was high
time.— Incredible! Wagner had become pious.

6

How I thought about myself at this time (1876), with what
tremendous sureness I got hold of my task and its world-historical

aspect—the whole book bears witness to that, above all a very explicit passage. Only, with my instinctive cunning, I avoided the little word "I" once again and bathed in world-historical glory—not Schopenhauer or Wagner this time but one of my friends, the excellent Dr. Paul Rée—fortunately far too refined a creature to—[1]

Others were less refined: I have always recognized who among my readers was hopeless—for example, the typical German professor—because on the basis of this passage they thought they had to understand the whole book as higher Réealism.— In fact, the contents contradicted five or six propositions of my friend—a point discussed in the Preface to my *Genealogy of Morals*.

The passage reads: "What is after all the main proposition that one of the boldest and coldest thinkers, the author of the book *On the Origin of Moral Feelings* [read: Nietzsche, the first *immoralist*] has reached on the basis of his incisive and penetrating analyses of human activity? 'The moral man is no closer to the intelligible world than the physical man—for there is no intelligible world . . .' This proposition, grown hard and sharp under the hammer blow of historical insight [read: *revaluation of all values*], may perhaps one day, in some future—1890!—serve as the ax swung against the 'metaphysical need' of mankind—but whether that will be more of a blessing or a curse for mankind, who could say? But in any case as a proposition of immense consequences, fruitful and terrible at the same time, looking into the world with that Janus face which all great insights share . . ." [2]

---

[1] Presumably: to have misunderstood and taken this literally.

[2] In the various German editions of *Ecce Homo* this quotation is not printed in quotation marks, and Nietzsche's insertions are placed in parentheses rather than brackets; nor is there any reference to the source of the quotation: *Human, All-Too-Human*, section 37. As a result, it is left unclear what exactly is quoted and what is not. Of course, "—1890!—" is also an insertion not found in the text of 1878. Nietzsche's other deviations from the original text are so slight that they are not worth listing here, except that the quotation from Rée's book originally read as follows: "The moral man," says he, "is no closer to the intelligible (metaphysical) world than the physical man." The next six words were not quoted in *Human, All-Too-Human*.

Dawn
Thoughts About Morality as a Prejudice

1

With this book my campaign against morality begins. Not that it smells in the least of powder: you will smell far different and much lovelier scents in it, assuming your nostrils have some sensitivity. Neither big nor small guns: if the effect of the book is negative, its means are anything but that—these means from which the effect issues like an inference, not like a cannon shot. If one takes leave of the book with a cautious reserve about everything that has so far attained honor and even worship under the name of morality, this in no way contradicts the fact that the whole book contains no negative word, no attack, no spite—that it lies in the sun, round, happy, like some sea animal basking among rocks.

Ultimately, I myself was this sea animal: almost every sentence in this book was first thought, *caught* among that jumble of rocks near Genoa where I was alone and still had secrets with the sea. Even now, whenever I accidentally touch this book, almost every sentence turns for me into a net that again brings up from the depths something incomparable: its entire skin trembles with tender thrills of memory. The art that distinguishes it is not inconsiderable when it comes to fixing to some extent things that easily flit by, noiselessly—moments I call divine lizards—but not with the cruelty of that young Greek god who simply speared the poor little lizard, though, to be sure, with something pointed—a pen.

"There are so many dawns that have not yet glowed"—this Indian inscription marks the opening of this book. Where does its author seek that new morning, that as yet undiscovered tender red that marks the beginning of another day—ah, a whole series, a whole world of new days? In a *revaluation of all values,* in a liberation from all moral values, in saying Yes to and having confidence in all that has hitherto been forbidden, despised, and damned. This

Yes-saying book pours out its light, its love, its tenderness upon ever so many wicked things; it gives back to them their "soul," a good conscience, the lofty right and privilege of existence. Morality is not attacked, it is merely no longer in the picture.

This book closes with an "Or?"—it is the only book that closes with an "Or?"

2

My task of preparing a moment of the highest self-examination for humanity, a *great noon* when it looks back and far forward, when it emerges from the dominion of accidents and priests and for the first time poses, *as a whole,* the question of Why? and For What?—this task follows of necessity from the insight that humanity is *not* all by itself on the right way, that it is by no means governed divinely, that, on the contrary, it has been precisely among its holiest value concepts that the instinct of denial, corruption, and decadence has ruled seductively. The question concerning the origin of moral values is for me a question of the very first rank because it is crucial for the future of humanity. The demand that we should believe that everything is really in the best of hands, that a book, the Bible, offers us definitive assurances about the divine governance and wisdom in the destiny of man, is—translated back into reality—the will to suppress the truth about the pitiable opposite of all this; namely, that humanity has so far been in the *worst* of hands and that it has been governed by the underprivileged, the craftily vengeful, the so-called "saints," these slanderers of the world and violators of man.

The decisive symptom that shows how the priest (including those *crypto*-priests, the philosophers) has become master quite generally and not only within a certain religious community, and that the morality of decadence, the will to the end has become accepted as morality itself, is the fact that what is unegoistic is everywhere assigned absolute value while what is egoistic is met with hostility. Whoever is at odds with me about that is to my mind *infected*.— But all the world is at odds with me.

For a physiologist such a juxtaposition of values simply leaves no doubt. When the least organ in an organism fails, however slightly, to enforce with complete assurance its self-preservation, its "egoism," restitution of its energies—the whole degenerates. The physiologist demands *excision* of the degenerating part; he denies all solidarity with what degenerates; he is worlds removed from pity for it. But the priest desires precisely the degeneration of the whole, of humanity: for that reason, he *conserves* what degenerates —at this price he rules.

When seriousness is deflected from the self-preservation and the enhancement of the strength of the body—*that is, of life*— when anemia is construed as an ideal, and contempt for the body as "salvation of the soul"—what else is this if not a *recipe* for decadence?

The loss of the center of gravity, resistance to the natural instincts—in one word, "selflessness"—that is what was hitherto called *morality*.— With the *Dawn* I first took up the fight against the morality that would unself man.[1]

---

[1] *Die Entselbstungs-Moral: Entselbstung* is Nietzsche's coinage; "unself" is inspired by Lady Macbeth's "unsex me."

The Gay Science
("la gaya scienza")

The *Dawn* is a Yes-saying book, deep but bright and gracious. The same is true also and in the highest degree of the *gaya scienza:* in almost every sentence profundity and high spirits go tenderly hand in hand. Some verses that express my gratitude for the most wonderful month of January I ever experienced—this whole book was its present—reveals sufficiently from what depths this "science" emerged to gaiety:

> *With a flaming spear you parted*
> *All its ice until my soul*
> *Hurries roaring toward the ocean*
> *Of its highest hope and goal:*
>
> *Ever healthier and brighter,*
> *In most loving constraint, free—*
> *Thus it praises your great wonders,*
> *Fairest month of January!* [1]

What is here called "highest hope"—who could have any doubt about that when he sees the diamond beauty of the first words of *Zarathustra* flashing at the end of the fourth book?— Or when at the end of the third book he reads the granite words in which a destiny finds for the first time a formula for itself, for *all* time? [2]

---

[1] *Der du mit dem Flammenspeere*
Meiner Seele Eis zerteilt,
Dass sie brausend nun zum Meere
Ihrer höchsten Hoffnung eilt:

Heller stets und stets gesunder,
Frei im liebevollsten Muss—
Also preist sie deine Wunder,
Schönster Januarius!

[2] The last three aphorisms of Book III, numbered 273–75, are included in this volume.

The "Songs of Prince Free-as-a-Bird," [3] written for the most part in Sicily, are quite emphatically reminiscent of the Provençal concept of *gaya scienza*—that unity of *singer, knight,* and *free spirit* which distinguishes the wonderful early culture of the Provençals from all equivocal cultures. The very last poem above all, "To the Mistral," [4] an exuberant dancing song in which, if I may say so, one dances right over morality, is a perfect Provençalism.

---

[3] An appendix of poems, added along with Book V (sections 343–83) to the second edition, in 1887. *Vogelfrei,* rendered literally above, also means: declared an outlaw whom anybody may shoot at sight.

[4] This poem is included in my *Twenty German Poets: A Bilingual Edition* (New York, Modern Library, 1963).

Thus Spoke Zarathustra
A Book for All and None

1

Now I shall relate the history of *Zarathustra*. The fundamental conception of this work, the idea of the eternal recurrence, this highest formula of affirmation that is at all attainable, belongs in August 1881: it was penned on a sheet with the notation underneath, "6000 feet beyond man and time." That day I was walking through the woods along the lake of Silvaplana; at a powerful pyramidal rock not far from Surlei I stopped.[1] It was then that this idea came to me.

If I reckon back a few months from this day, I find as an omen a sudden and profoundly decisive change in my taste, especially in music. Perhaps the whole of *Zarathustra* may be reckoned as music; certainly a rebirth of the art of *hearing* was among its preconditions. In a small mountain spa not far from Vicenza, Recoaro, where I spent the spring of 1881, I discovered together with my maestro and friend, Peter Gast, who was also "reborn," that the phoenix of music flew past us with lighter and more brilliant feathers than it had ever displayed before. But if I reckon forward from that day to the sudden birth that occurred in February 1883 under the most improbable circumstances—the *finale* from which I have quoted a few sentences in the Preface was finished exactly in that sacred hour in which Richard Wagner died in Venice—we get eighteen months for the pregnancy. This figure of precisely eighteen months might suggest, at least to Buddhists, that I am really a female elephant.

---

[1] Clearly, the rock is not the one on the Chasté, a peninsula in the Silser See, on which a tablet with the text of the "Drunken Song" from *Zarathustra IV* (section 12) has been fastened. A photograph of the right rock illustrates a small booklet of 44 pages put out by and entitled *Nietzsche-Haus in Sils-Maria*.

My *gaya scienza* belongs in the interval and contains a hundred signs of the proximity of something incomparable; in the end it even offers the beginning of *Zarathustra,* and in the penultimate section of the fourth book the basic idea of *Zarathustra.*[2]

Something else also belongs in this interval: that *Hymn to Life* (for mixed choir and orchestra) whose score was published two years ago by E. W. Fritzsch in Leipzig—a scarcely trivial symptom of my condition during that year when the Yes-saying pathos *par excellence,* which I call the tragic pathos/ was alive in me to the highest degree. The time will come when it will be sung in my memory.[3]

The text, to say this expressly because a misunderstanding has gained currency, is not by me: it is the amazing inspiration of a young Russian woman who was my friend at that time, Miss Lou von Salomé.[4] Whoever can find any meaning at all in the last words

---

[2] Section 341 (*Portable Nietzsche,* pp. 101f.). The idea meant is that of the eternal recurrence.

[3] The manuscript sent to the printer (*Druckmanuskript*) was preserved in the Nietzsche Archive and characterized as follows by Hans Joachim Mette: "Autograph composition for a solo voice with piano accompaniment,* written in August/September 1882, based on a stanza of the poem *Prayer to Life* by Lou Salomé: this very Lied was reworked by Peter Gast, who also took into account the second stanza, which Nietzsche presumably communicated to him—and was turned, in the summer of 1887, into a *Hymn to Life: Composition for Mixed Choir and Orchestra* and published by him under this title over Nietzsche's name, in the form of a first edition, E 39 (cf. *Friedrich Nietzsches Gesammelte Briefe,* III.2, 2nd ed., 1919, pp. 366–68); music sheet written upon on both sides." Mette's footnote reads: "*The melody had been found already in 1873/74 for the *Hymn to Friendship*" (*Der Literarische Nachlass Friedrich Nietzsches,* Hadl, Leipzig 1932, pp. 12f.; the same report was included a year later in the first volume of Nietzsche's *Werke und Briefe: Historisch-Kritische Gesamtausgabe; Werke,* vol. I, Munich, Beck, 1933).

Cf. Podach, *Ein Blick in Notizbücher Nietzsches* (a glance into Nietzsche's notebooks; Heidelberg, Wolfgang Rothe, 1963), p. 132: ". . . Gast had reworked the score so often that it . . . really was his. Nietzsche knew this very well and suggested that the composer's name should appear on the title page. A correspondence on this point ensued, not only with Gast who protested modestly but also with the publisher . . ."

See also Frederick R. Love, *Young Nietzsche and the Wagnerian Experience* (Chapel Hill, N.C., University of North Carolina Press, 1963).

[4] In the MS, Nietzsche's sister crossed out the last eleven words of this sentence, but they were printed nevertheless in 1908, and in all subsequent editions (cf. Podach, *Friedrich Nietzsches Werke,* pp. 200 and 285).

of this poem will guess why I preferred and admired it: they attain greatness. Pain is *not* considered an objection to life: "If you have no more happiness to give me, well then! *you still have suffering.*" Perhaps my music, too, attains greatness at this point. (Last note of the A-clarinet, c flat, not c: misprint.)

The following winter I stayed in that charming quiet bay of Rapallo which, not far from Genoa, is cut out between Chiavari and the foothills of Portofino. My health could have been better; the winter was cold and excessively rainy; my small *albergo,*[5] situated right at the sea so that the high sea made it impossible to sleep at night, was in just about every way the opposite of what one might wish for. In spite of this and almost in order to prove my proposition that everything decisive comes into being "in spite of," it was that winter and under these unfavorable circumstances that my *Zarathustra* came into being.

Mornings I would walk in a southerly direction on the splendid road to Zoagli, going up past pines with a magnificent view of the sea; in the afternoon, whenever my health permitted it, I walked around the whole bay from Santa Margherita all the way to Portofino. This place and this scenery came even closer to my heart because of the great love that Emperor Frederick III felt for them; by chance, I was in this coastal region again in the fall of 1886 when he visited this small forgotten world of bliss for the last time.[6]

---

[5] Hotel.

[6] Nietzsche originally wrote, "the unforgettable German Emperor" but then crossed out three words (Podach, p. 286). When the first Emperor of the Second *Reich,* Wilhelm I, had died at ninety-one on March 9, 1888, his much more liberal son, Friedrich III, had succeeded him; but Friedrich died of cancer after a hundred days, June 15, and was succeeded by his son, the last German Kaiser, Wilhelm II. It has often been surmised that European history might have taken a different turn if Friedrich III had lived longer.

On June 20 Nietzsche had written Gast: "The death of Kaiser Friedrich has moved me: in the end he was a small glimmering light of *free* thought, the last hope for Germany. Now the rule of *Stöcker* begins: I project the consequence and already *know* that now my *Will to Power* will be confiscated in Germany first of all."

Hofprediger (Court Chaplain) Stöcker was the leading German anti-Semite of that period. *The Will to Power* was then no more than a project for which Niezsche had accumulated a great deal of material, and the work now known under this striking title is merely a posthumously published col-

— It was on these two walks that the whole of *Zarathustra I* occurred to me,[7] and especially Zarathustra himself as a type: rather, he *overtook me*.[8]

2

To understand this type, one must first become clear about his physiological presupposition: this is what I call the *great health*. I don't know how I could explain this concept better, more *personally,* than I have done it in one of the last sections of the fifth book of my *gaya scienza*.[1]

Being new, nameless, self-evident, we premature births of an as yet unproven future, we need for a new goal also a new means—namely, a new health, stronger, more seasoned, tougher, more audacious, and gayer than any previous health. Whoever has a soul that craves to have experienced the whole range of values and desiderata to date, and to have sailed around all the coasts of this ideal "mediterranean"; whoever wants to know from the adventures of his own most authentic experience how a discoverer and conqueror of the ideal feels, and also an artist, a saint, a legislator, a sage, a scholar, a pious man,[2] and one who stands divinely apart in the old style—needs one thing above everything else: the *great health*—that one does not merely have but also acquires continually, and must acquire because one gives it up again and again, and must give it up.

And now, after we have long been on our way in this manner, we argonauts of the ideal, with more daring perhaps

---

lection of many of Nietzsche's most interesting notes. Still, this letter shows —along with a lot of other evidence—how the title was *not* meant, and how thoroughly Nietzsche's intentions and spirit differed from those of the last Kaiser.

[7] *Fiel mir . . . ein.*

[8] *Überfiel mich.*

[1] The last section but one, number 382.

[2] At this point, the original text of 1887 still had "a soothsayer" in addition to the others enumerated above.

than is prudent, and have suffered shipwreck and damage often enough, but are, to repeat it, healthier than one likes to permit us, dangerously healthy, ever again healthy—it will seem to us as if, as a reward, we now confronted an as yet undiscovered country whose boundaries nobody has surveyed yet, something beyond all the lands and nooks of the ideal so far, a world so overrich in what is beautiful, strange, questionable, terrible, and divine that our curiosity as well as our craving to possess it has got beside itself—alas, now nothing will sate us any more!

After such vistas and with such a burning hunger in our conscience and science,[3] how could we still be satisfied with *present-day man?* It may be too bad but it is inevitable that we find it difficult to remain serious when we look at his worthiest goals and hopes, and perhaps we do not even bother to look any more.

Another ideal runs ahead of us, a strange, tempting, dangerous ideal to which we should not wish to persuade anybody because we do not readily concede *the right to it* to anyone: the ideal of a spirit who plays naïvely—that is, not deliberately but from overflowing power and abundance—with all that was hitherto called holy, good, untouchable, divine; for whom those supreme things that the people naturally accept as their value standards, signify danger, decay, debasement, or at least recreation, blindness, and temporary self-oblivion; the ideal of a human, superhuman well-being and benevolence[4] that will often appear *inhuman*—for example, when it confronts all earthly seriousness so far, all solemnity in gesture, word, tone, eye, morality, and task so far, as if it were their most incarnate and involuntary parody—and in spite of all of this, it is perhaps only with him that *great seriousness* really begins, that the real question mark is posed for the first time, that the destiny of the soul changes, the hand moves forward, the tragedy *begins.*[5]

---

[3] *In Wissen und Gewissen.*

[4] *Wohlseins und Wohlwollens.*

[5] The last aphorism of Book IV, which concluded the first edition of *The*

3

Has anyone at the end of the nineteenth century a clear idea of what poets of strong ages have called *inspiration?* If not, I will describe it.— If one had the slightest residue of superstition left in one's system, one could hardly reject altogether the idea that one is merely incarnation, merely mouthpiece, merely a medium of over-powering forces. The concept of revelation—in the sense that suddenly, with indescribable certainty and subtlety, something becomes *visible,* audible, something that shakes one to the last depths and throws one down—that merely describes the facts. One hears, one does not seek; one accepts, one does not ask who gives; like lightning, a thought flashes up, with necessity, without hesitation regarding its form—I never had any choice.

A rapture whose tremendous tension occasionally discharges itself in a flood of tears—now the pace quickens involuntarily, now it becomes slow; one is altogether beside oneself, with the distinct consciousness of subtle shudders and of one's skin creeping[1] down to one's toes; a depth of happiness in which even what is most painful and gloomy does not seem something opposite but rather conditioned, provoked, a *necessary* color in such a superabundance of light; an instinct for rhythmic relationships that arches over wide spaces of forms—length, the need for a rhythm with wide arches,[2] is almost the measure of the force of inspiration, a kind of compensation for its pressure and tension.

Everything happens involuntarily in the highest degree but as in a gale of a feeling of freedom, of absoluteness, of power, of

---

Gay Science, had been entitled *Incipit tragoedia* (the tragedy begins) and was reused as the first section of the Prologue of *Zarathustra.*

The reference to "parody" in the sentence above is a reminder that Nietzsche's occasional pathos in *Zarathustra* and *Ecce Homo* is not devoid of irony: cf. the opening paragraph of section 4 of "Why I Am So Clever."

[1] "One's skin creeping": *Überrieselungen* conjures up a slightly different image—as if water trickled over us.

[2] "Arches over" and "wide arches" are in the original *überspannt* and *weit-gespannt,* and the word for tension at the end of the sentence and also a little earlier is *Spannung.*

divinity.— The involuntariness of image and metaphor is strangest of all; one no longer has any notion of what is an image or a metaphor: everything offers itself as the nearest, most obvious, simplest expression. It actually seems, to allude to something Zarathustra says, as if the things themselves approached and offered themselves as metaphors ("Here all things come caressingly to your discourse and flatter you; for they want to ride on your back. On every metaphor you ride to every truth. . . . Here the words and word-shrines of all being open up before you; here all being wishes to become word, all becoming wishes to learn from you how to speak").[3]

This is *my* experience of inspiration; I do not doubt that one has to go back thousands of years in order to find anyone who could say to me, "it is mine as well." [4]

4

Afterwards I was sick for a few weeks in Genoa. Then came a melancholy spring in Rome where I put up with life—it was not easy. Fundamentally, this most indecent place on earth for the poet of *Zarathustra* distressed me exceedingly, and I had not chosen it voluntarily. I wanted to go to *Aquila*,[1] Rome's counterconcept, founded from hostility against Rome, as I shall one day found a place, in[2] memory of an atheist and enemy of the church *comme il faut*,[3] one of those most closely related to me, the great Hohenstaufen Emperor Frederick II.[4] But some fatality was at work: I had to

---

[3] *Zarathustra III*, "The Return Home." The German editions do not have the three dots inserted above to mark Nietzsche's omission of almost one page; and instead of "you" (twice) after the three dots, *Zarathustra* has "me."

[4] This conclusion is criticized by Kaufmann, *Critique of Religion and Philosophy* (New York, Harper, 1958; Garden City, N.Y., Doubleday Anchor Books, 1961), section 75.

[1] A town 50 miles northeast of Rome, 2360 feet above sea level, founded as a bulwark against the power of the papacy by Conrad, son of Emperor Frederick II, about 1250, the year Frederick II died.

[2] Reading *zur* (in) where the German editions have *die* (the). The German reading makes no sense and presumably represents an error due to haste.

[3] As he should be.

[4] Cf. *Beyond Good and Evil*, section 200.

go back again.[5] In the end I resigned myself to the Piazza Barberini, after my exertions to go to an *anti-Christian* environment had wearied me. I fear that in order to avoid bad odors as far as possible I once inquired at the Palazzo del Quirinale itself [6] whether they did not have a quiet room for a philosopher.

It was on a *loggia* high above that Piazza, from which one has a fine view of Rome and hears the *fontana* splashing far below, that the loneliest song was written that has ever been written, the "Night Song." [7] Around that time a melody of indescribable melancholy was always about me, and I found its refrain in the words, "dead from immortality."

That summer, back home at the holy spot where the first lightning of the *Zarathustra* idea had flashed for me, I found *Zarathustra II*. Ten days sufficed; in no case, neither for the first nor for the third and last,[8] did I require more. The next winter, under the halcyon sky of Nizza, which then shone into my life for the first time, I found *Zarathustra III*—and was finished. Scarcely a year for the whole of it.

Many concealed spots and heights in the landscape around Nizza are hallowed for me by unforgettable moments; that decisive passage which bears the title "On Old and New Tablets" [9] was composed on the most onerous ascent from the station to the marvelous Moorish eyrie, Eza—the suppleness of my muscles has always been greatest when my creative energies were flowing most abundantly. The *body* is inspired; let us keep the "soul" out of it.—

---

[5] Here the following words in the MS were deleted, I do not know by whom —but Nietzsche himself might well have struck them out on rereading them: "In Rome I had the experience that *Parsifal* was praised to my face: twice I had attacks of laughter at that" (Podach, p. 289).

[6] Before 1870 this had been a papal residence; since 1870 it was the residence of the king of Italy. One of Nietzsche's last letters (December 31, 1888, to Gast) ends: "My address I do not know any more: let us suppose that at first it may be the *Palazzo del Quirinale*. N."

[7] The ninth chapter of *Zarathustra II*.

[8] Nietzsche had published only Parts I, II, and III, at first separately and then, in 1887, also in one volume. Part IV, written in Nizza and Mentone the next winter (early in 1885) was printed privately in 1885 (only forty copies), and only seven copies were distributed among close friends.

[9] The twelfth chapter of *Zarathustra III*.

Often one could have seen me dance; in those days I could walk in the mountains for seven or eight hours without a trace of weariness. I slept well, I laughed much—my vigor and patience were perfect.

5

Except for these ten-day works, the years during and above all *after* my *Zarathustra* were marked by distress without equal. One pays dearly for immortality: one has to die several times while still alive.

There is something I call the *rancune*[1] of what is great: everything great—a work, a deed—is no sooner accomplished than it turns *against* the man who did it. By doing it, he has become *weak;* he no longer endures his deed, he can no longer face it. Something one was never permitted to will lies *behind* one, something in which the knot in the destiny of humanity is tied—and now one labors *under* it!— It almost crushes one.— The *rancune* of what is great.

Then there is the gruesome silence one hears all around one. Solitude has seven skins; nothing penetrates them any more. One comes to men, one greets friends—more desolation, no eye offers a greeting. At best, a kind of revolt. Such revolts I experienced, very different in degree but from almost everybody who was close to me. It seems nothing offends more deeply than suddenly letting others feel a distance;[2] those *noble* natures who do not know how to live without reverence are rare.

Thirdly, there is the absurd sensitivity of the skin to small stings, a kind of helplessness against everything small.[3] This seems

---

[1] Rancor.

[2] Cf. the "pathos of distance," *Beyond Good and Evil,* section 257; also above, "The Untimely Ones," section 3, the last paragraph.

[3] In a discarded draft we find the following passage: "The psychologist still adds that there are no conditions in which one's defenselessness and lack of protection are greater. If there are any means at all for destroying [*umzubringen*] men who *are destinies,* the instinct of poisonous flies discerns these means. For one who has greatness there is no fight with the small: hence the small become masters" (Podach, pp. 291f.). Cf. also "The Flies of the Market Place" in *Zarathustra I* and, of course, Sartre's *The Flies.*

to me to be due to the tremendous squandering of all defensive
energies which is a presupposition of every *creative* deed, every
deed that issues from one's most authentic, inmost, nethermost regions. Our *small* defensive capacities are thus, as it were, suspended; no energy is left for them.

I still dare to hint that one digests less well, does not like to
move, is all too susceptible to feeling chills as well as mistrust—
mistrust that is in many instances merely an etiological blunder. In
such a state I once sensed the proximity of a herd of cows even
before I saw it, merely because milder and more philanthropic
thoughts came back to me: *they* had warmth.

6

This work stands altogether apart. Leaving aside the poets:
perhaps nothing has ever been done from an equal excess of
strength. My concept of the "Dionysian" here became a *supreme
deed;* measured against that, all the rest of human activity seems
poor and relative. That a Goethe, a Shakespeare, would be unable
to breathe even for a moment in this tremendous passion and
height, that Dante is, compared with Zarathustra, merely a believer
and not one who first *creates* truth, a *world-governing* spirit, a destiny—that the poets of the Veda are priests and not even worthy of
tying the shoelaces of a Zarathustra—that is the least thing and
gives no idea of the distance, of the *azure* solitude in which this
work lives. Zarathustra possesses an eternal right to say: "I draw
circles around me and sacred boundaries; fewer and fewer men
climb with me on ever higher mountains: I am building a mountain
range out of ever more sacred mountains." [1]

Let anyone add up the spirit and good nature of all great
souls: [2] all of them together would not be capable of producing
even one of Zarathustra's discourses. The ladder on which he ascends and descends [3] is tremendous; he has seen further, willed fur-

---

[1] *Zarathustra III*, "On Old and New Tablets," section 19.

[2] Cf. Aristotle's conception of *megalopsychia*, cited in the Editor's Introduction, section 2.

[3] Genesis 28:12.

ther, been *capable* further than any other human being. In every word he contradicts, this most Yes-saying of all spirits; in him all opposites are blended into a new unity. The highest and the lowest energies of human nature, what is sweetest, most frivolous, and most terrible wells forth from one fount with immortal assurance. Till then one does not know what is height, what depth; one knows even less what truth is. There is no moment in this revelation of truth that has been anticipated or guessed by even *one* of the greatest. There is no wisdom, no investigation of the soul, no art of speech before Zarathustra; what is nearest and most everyday, here speaks of unheard-of things. Epigrams trembling with passion, eloquence become music, lightning bolts hurled forward into hitherto unfathomed futures. The most powerful capacity for metaphors that has existed so far is poor and mere child's play compared with this return of language to the nature of imagery.

And how Zarathustra descends and says to everyone what is most good-natured! How gently he handles even his antagonists, the priests, and suffers of them *with* them!— Here man has been overcome at every moment; the concept of the "overman" has here become the greatest reality—whatever was so far considered great in man lies beneath him at an infinite distance. The halcyon, the light feet, the omnipresence of malice and exuberance, and whatever else is typical of the type of Zarathustra—none of this has ever before been dreamed of as essential to greatness. Precisely in this width of space and this accessibility for what is contradictory, Zarathustra experiences himself as the *supreme type of all beings;* and once one hears how he defines this, one will refrain from seeking any metaphor for it.[4]

"The soul that has the longest ladder and reaches down deepest—the most comprehensive soul, which can run and stray and roam farthest within itself; the most necessary soul that plunges joyously into chance; the soul that, having being, dives into becoming; the soul that *has,* but *wants* to want and will; the soul that flees itself and catches up with itself in the widest circles; the wisest soul that folly exhorts most sweetly; the soul that loves itself most, in

---

[4] *Nach seinem Gleichnis zu suchen.* This makes little sense; Nietzsche probably meant: *nach seinesgleichen zu suchen,* i.e.: seeking his equal.

which all things have their sweep and countersweep and ebb and
flood——" [5]

But that is the concept of Dionysus himself.— Another consideration leads to the very same result. The psychological problem
in the type of Zarathustra is how he that says No and *does* No to an
unheard-of degree, to everything to which one has so far said Yes,
can nevertheless be the opposite of a No-saying spirit; how the
spirit who bears the heaviest fate, a fatality of a task, can nevertheless be the lightest and most transcendent—Zarathustra is a dancer
—how he that has the hardest, most terrible insight into reality,
that has thought the "most abysmal idea," nevertheless does not
consider it an objection to existence, not even to its eternal recurrence—but rather one reason more for being himself the eternal
Yes to all things, "the tremendous, unbounded saying Yes and
Amen." [6]— "Into all abysses I still carry the blessings of my saying
Yes."— *But this is the concept of Dionysus once again.*

7

What language will such a spirit speak when he speaks to himself? The language of the *dithyramb*. I am the inventor of the dithyramb. Listen to how Zarathustra speaks to himself before sunrise:
such emerald happiness, such divine tenderness did not have a
tongue before me. Even the deepest melancholy of such a Dionysus
still turns into a dithyramb. To give some indication of this, I
choose the "Night Song," the immortal lament at being condemned
by the overabundance of light and power, by his sun-nature, not to
love.

> Night has come; now all fountains speak more loudly.
> And my soul, too, is a fountain.

---

[5] "On Old and New Tablets," section 19. The first dash, after "deepest," is
not found in the original but has been inserted above to mark Nietzsche's
omission of the words: "how should the most parasites not sit on that?" And
where Nietzsche has a double dash, Zarathustra concludes: "oh, how should
the highest soul not have the worst parasites?"

[6] Cf. *Zarathustra III,* the last chapter, which is entitled "The Seven Seals
(Or: The Yes and Amen Song)."

Night has come; only now all the songs of lovers awaken. And my soul, too, is the song of a lover.

Something unstilled, unstillable is within me; it wants to be voiced. A craving for love is within me; it speaks the language of love.

Light am I; ah, that I were night! But this is my loneliness that I am girt with light. Ah, that I were dark and nocturnal! How I would suck at the breasts of light! And even you would I bless, you little sparkling stars and glowworms up there, and be overjoyed with your gifts of light.

But I live in my own light; I drink back into myself the flames that break out of me. I do not know the happiness of those who receive; and I have often dreamed that even stealing must be more blessed than receiving. This is my poverty, that my hand never rests from giving; this is my envy, that I see waiting eyes and the lit-up nights of longing. Oh, wretchedness of all givers! Oh, darkening of my sun! Oh, craving to crave! Oh, ravenous hunger in satiation!

They receive from me, but do I touch their souls? There is a cleft between giving and receiving; and the narrowest cleft is the last to be bridged. A hunger grows out of my beauty: I should like to hurt those for whom I shine; I should like to rob those to whom I give; thus do I hunger for malice. To withdraw my hand when the other hand already reaches out to it; to linger like the waterfall, which lingers even while it plunges: thus do I hunger for malice. Such revenge my fullness plots: such spite wells up out of my loneliness. My happiness in giving died in giving; my virtue tired of itself in its overflow.

The danger of those who always give is that they lose their sense of shame; and the heart and hand of those who always mete out become callous from always meting out. My eye no longer wells over at the shame of those who beg; my hand has grown too hard for the trembling of filled hands. Where have the tears of my eyes gone and the down of my heart? Oh, the loneliness of all givers! Oh, the taciturnity of all who shine!

Many suns revolve in the void: to all that is dark they

speak with their light—to me they are silent. Oh, this is the enmity of the light against what shines: merciless it moves in its orbit. Unjust in its heart against all that shines, cold against suns—thus moves every sun.

The suns fly like a storm in their orbits: that is their motion. They follow their inexorable will: that is their coldness.

Oh, it is only you, you dark ones, you nocturnal ones, who create warmth out of that which shines. It is only you who drink milk and refreshment out of the udders of light.

Alas, ice is all around me, my hand is burned by the ice. Alas, thirst is within me that languishes after your thirst.

Night has come: alas, that I must be light! And thirst for the nocturnal! And loneliness!

Night has come: now my craving breaks out of me like a well; to speak I crave.

Night has come; now all fountains speak more loudly. And my soul, too, is a fountain.

Night has come; now all the songs of lovers awaken. And my soul, too, is the song of a lover.

8

Nothing like this has ever been written, felt, or *suffered:* thus suffers a god, a Dionysus. The answer to such a dithyramb of solar solitude in the light would be Ariadne.— Who besides me knows what Ariadne is!— For all such riddles nobody so far had any solution; I doubt that anybody even saw any riddles here.

Zarathustra once defines, quite strictly, his task—it is mine, too—and there is no mistaking his meaning: he says Yes to the point of justifying, of redeeming even all of the past.

"I walk among men as among the fragments of the future—that future which I envisage. And this is all my creating and striving, that I create and carry together into One what is fragment and riddle and dreadful accident. And how could I bear to be a man if man were not also a creator and guesser of riddles and redeemer of accidents? *To redeem those who lived in the past* and to turn every 'it was' into a 'thus I willed it'—that alone should I call redemption." [1]

In another passage he defines as strictly as possible what alone "man" can be for him—*not* an object of love or, worse, pity —Zarathustra has mastered the *great nausea* over man, too: man is for him an un-form, a material, an ugly stone that needs a sculptor.

"Willing no more and *esteeming* no more and *creating* no more—oh, that this great weariness might always remain far from me! In knowledge, too, I feel only my will's joy in begetting and becoming; and if there is innocence in my knowledge, it is because the *will to beget* is in it. Away from God and gods this will has lured me; what could one create if gods—were there?

"But my fervent will to create impels me ever again toward man; thus is the hammer impelled toward the stone. O men, in the stone an image is sleeping, the image of images! Alas, that it has to sleep in the hardest, ugliest stone! *Now my hammer rages cruelly against its prison.* Pieces of rock rain from the stone: what is that to me? I want to perfect it; for a shadow came to me—the stillest and lightest of all things once came to me. The beauty of the overman came to me as a shadow. O my brothers, what are gods to me now?" [2]

I stress a final point: the verse in italics furnishes the occasion. Among the conditions for a *Dionysian* task are, in a decisive way, the hardness of the hammer, the *joy even in destroying.* The imperative, "become hard!" the most fundamental certainty *that all creators are hard,* [3] is the distinctive mark of a Dionysian nature.

---

1 *Zarathustra II,* "On Redemption." The lines after the phrase in italics should be compared with "Human, All-Too-Human," section 4, above: *Ecce Homo* voices Nietzsche's own *amor fati.*

2 *Zarathustra II,* "Upon the Blessed Isles."

3 *Zarathustra III,* "On Old and New Tablets," 29, as quoted at the end of *Twilight (Portable Nietzsche,* pp. 326 and 563). *Zarathustra:* "For creators are hard." *Twilight:* "For all creators are hard." And "Become hard!" is emphasized in *Zarathustra* but not in *Twilight.*

Beyond Good and Evil
Prelude to a Philosophy of the Future

1

The task for the years that followed now was indicated as clearly as possible. After the Yes-saying part of my task had been solved, the turn had come for the No-saying, *No-doing* part: the revaluation of our values so far, the great war—conjuring up a day of decision. This included the slow search for those related to me, those who, prompted by strength, would offer me their hands for *destroying*.

From this moment forward all my writings are fish hooks: perhaps I know how to fish as well as anyone?— If nothing was caught, I am not to blame. *There were no fish.*

2

This book (1886) is in all essentials a *critique of modernity*, not excluding the modern sciences, modern arts, and even modern politics, along with pointers to a contrary type that is as little modern as possible—a noble, Yes-saying type. In the latter sense, the book is a school for the *gentilhomme*,[1] taking this concept in a more spiritual and radical sense than has ever been done. One has to have guts merely to endure it; one must never have learned how to be afraid.

All those things of which our age is proud are experienced as contradictions to this type, almost as bad manners; our famous "objectivity," for example; "pity for all that suffers"; the "historical sense" with its submission to foreign tastes, groveling on its belly before *petits faits*,[2] and "being scientific."

When you consider that this book followed *after Zarathustra*,

---

[1] Nobleman, gentleman.
[2] Small facts.

you may perhaps also guess the dietetic regimen to which it owes its origin. The eye that had been spoiled by the tremendous need for seeing *far*—Zarathustra is even more far-sighted than the Tsar —is here forced to focus on what lies nearest, the age, the around-us. In every respect, above all also in the form, you will find the same *deliberate* turning away from the instincts that had made possible a Zarathustra. The refinement in form, in intention, in the art of *silence* is in the foreground; psychology is practiced with admitted hardness and cruelty—the book is devoid of any good-natured word.

All this is a recuperation: who would guess after all *what* sort of recuperation such a squandering of good-naturedness as Zarathustra represents makes necessary?

Theologically speaking—listen closely, for I rarely speak as a theologian—it was God himself who at the end of his days' work lay down as a serpent under the tree of knowledge: thus he recuperated from being God.— He had made everything too beautiful.[3] — The devil is merely the leisure of God on that seventh day.

---

[3] Or: too beautifully.

Genealogy of Morals
A Polemic

Regarding expression, intention, and the art of surprise, the three inquiries which constitute this *Genealogy* are perhaps uncannier than anything else written so far. Dionysus is, as is known, also the god of darkness.

Every time a beginning that is *calculated* to mislead: cool, scientific, even ironic, deliberately foreground, deliberately holding off. Gradually more unrest; sporadic lightning; very disagreeable truths are heard grumbling in the distance—until eventually a *tempo feroce* is attained in which everything rushes ahead in a tremendous tension. In the end, in the midst of perfectly gruesome detonations, a *new* truth becomes visible every time among thick clouds.

The truth of the *first* inquiry is the birth of Christianity: the birth of Christianity out of the spirit of *ressentiment,* not, as people may believe, out of the "spirit"—a countermovement by its very nature, the great rebellion against the dominion of *noble* values.

The *second* inquiry offers the psychology of the *conscience*—which is not, as people may believe, "the voice of God in man": it is the instinct of cruelty that turns back after it can no longer discharge itself externally. Cruelty is here exposed for the first time as one of the most ancient and basic substrata of culture that simply cannot be imagined away.

The *third* inquiry offers the answer to the question whence the ascetic ideal, the priests' ideal, derives its tremendous *power* although it is the *harmful* ideal *par excellence,* a will to the end, an ideal of decadence. Answer: not, as people may believe, because God is at work behind the priests but *faute de mieux*[1]—because it was the only ideal so far, because it had no rival. "For man would

---

[1] Lacking something better.

rather will even nothingness than *not* will." [2]— Above all, a *counterideal* was lacking—*until Zarathustra*.

I have been understood. Three decisive preliminary studies by a psychologist for a revaluation of all values.— This book contains the first psychology of the priest.

---

[2] An almost but not quite exact quotation of the last words of the book, found also—again a little differently—near the end of the first section of the third inquiry.

Twilight of the Idols
How One Philosophizes with a Hammer[1]

1

This essay of less than 150 pages,[2] cheerful and ominous in tone, a demon that laughs—the work of so few days that I hesitate to mention how many, is an exception among books: there is none richer in substance, more independent, more subversive[3]—more evil. If you want a quick idea how before me everything stood on its head,[4] begin with this essay. What is called *idol* on the title page is simply what has been called truth so far. *Twilight of the Idols*— that is: the old truth is approaching its end.

2

There is no reality, no "ideality" that is not touched in this essay (touched: what a cautious euphemism!). Not only *eternal* idols, also the youngest which are therefore feeblest on account of their age. "Modern ideas," for example. A great wind blows among the trees, and everywhere fruit fall down—truths. The squandering of an all-too-rich autumn: one stumbles over truths, one steps on and kills a few—there are too many.

But what we get hold of is no longer anything questionable but rather decisions. I am the first to hold in my hands the measure for "truths"; I am the first who is *able* to decide. Just as if a second

---

[1] For the meaning of this famous phrase, see the Preface to the book: ". . . not just idols of the age, but eternal idols, which are here touched with a hammer as with a tuning fork: there are . . . none more hollow."

[2] *Portable Nietzsche,* pp. 465–563.

[3] *Umwerfenderes:* literally, more overthrowing.

[4] Nietzsche's revaluation, like Marx's correction of Hegel, represents an attempt to put things right-side up again. Yet Nietzsche and Marx have usually been misrepresented as if they had boasted that *they* had stood everything on its head.

consciousness had grown in me; just as if "the will" had kindled a light for itself in me so that it might see the inclined plane, the *askew* path[5] on which it went down so far.— The *askew* path— people called it the way to "truth."

It is all over with all "darkling aspiration"; precisely the *good* man was least aware of the right way.[6]— And in all seriousness: nobody before me knew the right way, the way *up;* it is only beginning with me that there are hopes again, tasks, ways that can be prescribed for culture—*I am he that brings these glad tidings.*— And thus I am also a destiny.—

3

Immediately upon finishing this work, without losing even one day, I attacked the tremendous task of the *Revaluation,*[1] with a sovereign feeling of pride that was incomparable, certain at every moment of my immortality, engraving sign upon sign on bronze tablets with the sureness of a destiny. The Preface was written on September 3, 1888: when I stepped outdoors the morning after, I saw the most beautiful day that the Upper Engadine ever showed me—transparent, the colors glowing, including all opposites, everything that lies between ice and south.

It was only on September 20 that I left Sils Maria, detained by floods—in the end by far the only guest of this wonderful place on which my gratitude wants to bestow an immortal name. After a journey with incidents, including some danger to my life in Como, which was flooded—I got there only late at night—I reached Turin on the afternoon of the 21st—my *proven* place, my residence from now on. I took the same apartment I had occupied in the spring, Via Carlo Alberto 6, fourth floor, opposite the imposing Palazzo

---

[5] Here six words have been used to render *die schiefe Bahn;* in the next sentence, only three words. The ordinary German reader would assume at first that an inclined plane was meant; then, coming to the second occurrence of *schiefe,* emphasized by Nietzsche, he would interpret it as askew, crooked.

[6] Allusion to Goethe's *Faust,* lines 328f.

[1] That is, *The Antichrist,* which Nietzsche conceived as the first of the four parts of the *Revaluation of All Values.* Cf. the Preface (*Portable Nietzsche,* pp. 568f.).

Carignano in which Vittorio Emanuele[2] was born, with a view of
the Piazza Carlo Alberto and of the hills beyond. Without hesitation and without permitting myself to be distracted for a moment, I
went back to work: only the final quarter of the work remained to
be done. On the 30th of September, great victory; seventh day; the
leisure of a god walking along the Po river.[3] On the same day I
wrote the Preface for *Twilight of the Idols:* [4] correcting the printer's proofs of that book had been my recreation in September.

Never have I experienced such an autumn, nor considered
anything of the sort possible on earth—a Claude Lorrain[5] projected into the infinite, every day of the same indomitable perfection.

---

[2] Born 1820, King of Sardinia 1849–1861, the first King of Italy from 1861
until his death in 1878.

[3] *Müssiggang eines Gottes am Po entlang.*

[4] When he wrote the Preface he still intended to call the book *Müssiggang
eines Psychologen* (a psychologist's leisure). A letter from Peter Gast (cited
in *Portable Nietzsche,* p. 464), asking for a less unassuming title, changed
Nietzsche's mind. The book appeared with the new title in January 1889, a
few days after Nietzsche's collapse. *The Case of Wagner,* on the other hand,
had appeared in the fall of 1888: with respect to these two books, Nietzsche
does not adhere to the chronological order. *The Antichrist,* which is not reviewed here by Nietzsche, and *Nietzsche contra Wagner,* which was composed after *Ecce Homo,* were first published in 1895.

[5] French painter (1600–1682). His real name was Claude Gelée (also
spelled Gellée), but he is remembered as Claude Lorrain.

The Case of Wagner
A Musician's Problem

1

To do justice to this essay, one has to suffer of the fate of music as of an open wound.— Of *what* do I suffer when I suffer of the fate of music? That music has been done out of its world-transfiguring, Yes-saying character, so that it is music of decadence and no longer the flute of Dionysus.

Assuming, however, that a reader experiences the cause of music in this way as his own cause, as the history of his own sufferings, he will find this essay full of consideration and exceedingly mild. To be cheerful in such cases, genially mocking oneself, too— *ridendo dicere severum*[1] when the *verum dicere* would justify any amount of hardness—is humanity itself. Does anyone really doubt that I, as the old artillerist I am,[2] could easily bring up my *heavy* guns against Wagner?— Everything decisive in this matter I held back—I have loved Wagner.

Ultimately, an attack on a subtler "unknown one," whom nobody else is likely to guess, is part of the meaning and way of my task—oh, I can uncover "unknown ones" who are in an altogether different category from a Cagliostro[3] of music—even more, to be sure, an attack on the German nation which is becoming ever lazier

---

[1] The motto of the book: "Through what is laughable say what is somber"— a variation of Horace's *ridentem dicere verum, quid vetat* (what forbids us to tell the truth, laughing?), *Satires* I.24.

[2] Nietzsche had done his compulsory military service with an artillery regiment, beginning in October 1867; but his actual service was cut short by an accident in which he was hurt, and he was bedridden and then convalescing until his discharge in October 1868. During the Franco-Prussian War of 1870–71, he was a Swiss subject, being a Swiss professor, but volunteered and served briefly as a medical orderly—for less than a month. Sick with dysentery and diphtheria, he was discharged.

[3] An impostor or charlatan, after Count Alessandro di Cagliostro (1743–1795; really Giuseppe Balsamo).

and more impoverished in its instincts, ever more *honest,* and
which continues with an enviable appetite to feed on opposites,
gobbling down without any digestive troubles "faith" as well as
scientific manners,[4] "Christian love" as well as anti-Semitism, the
will to power (to the *Reich*) as well as the *évangile des humbles.*[5]
— Such a failure to take sides among opposites! Such neutrality
and "selflessness" of the stomach! This sense of justice of the German palate that finds all causes just and accords all equal rights[6]—
that finds everything tasty.— Beyond a doubt, the Germans are
idealists.

When I visited Germany last, I found the German taste exert-
ing itself to concede equal rights to Wagner and to the *Trumpeter
of Säkkingen;*[7] I myself witnessed how a Liszt Society was founded
in Leipzig, for the cultivation and propagation of insidious[8] church
music, ostensibly in honor of one of the most genuine and German
musicians—German in the old sense of that word, no mere *Reichs-
deutscher*—the old master Heinrich Schütz.— Beyond a doubt, the
Germans are idealists.[9]

---

4 *Wissenschaftlichkeit.*

5 Gospel of the humble.

6 *. . . Gaumens, der allem gleiche Rechte gibt . . .*

7 An immensely popular epic poem by Josef Viktor Scheffel (1826–1886)
that had gone through about 140 editions by 1886. In an earlier draft for this
passage Nietzsche had considered pairing "Goethe and Scheffel" the way the
will to power and the gospel of the humble are paired above (see Podach,
Friedrich Nietzsches Werke, p. 309).

    Richard M. Meyer says of Scheffel in *Die deutsche Literatur des Neun-
zehnten Jahrhunderts* (German literature of the nineteenth century, Berlin,
Bondi, 1900): "No poet of our time has been glorified with so many monuments, memorial stones, and memorial tablets"; also, *"The Trumpeter of Säkkingen* (1854) belongs among those books which have made popularity
unpopular among us" (pp. 523, 528).

8 *Listiger.* Franz Liszt (1811–1886), the composer and pianist—and father
of Cosima, then Wagner's widow—was born in Raiding, Hungary; retired to
Rome in 1861 and joined the Franciscan order in 1865; he died in Bayreuth
in 1886.

9 In the sense made popular by Schelling and Hegel: men who seek syn-
theses of opposites.

2

But here nothing shall keep me from becoming blunt and telling the Germans a few hard truths: *who else would do it?*

I speak of their indecency *in historicis.* Not only have the German historians utterly lost the *great perspective* for the course and the values of culture; nor are they merely, without exception, buffoons of politics (or the church)—but they have actually *proscribed* this great perspective. One must first be "German" and have "race," then one can decide about all values and disvalues *in historicis*—one *determines* them.

"German" has become an argument, *Deutschland, Deutschland über alles*[1] a principle; the Teutons represent the "moral world order" in history—the carriers of freedom versus the *imperium Romanum,* and the restoration of morality and the "categorical imperative" [2] versus the eighteenth century.— There is now a historiography that is *reichsdeutsch;* there is even, I fear, an anti-Semitic one—there is a *court* historiography, and Herr von Treitschke is not ashamed—[3]

Recently an idiotic[4] judgment *in historicis,* a proposition of the fortunately late aesthetic Swabian, Vischer,[5] was repeated in one German newspaper after another, as a "truth" to which every German has to say Yes: "The Renaissance *and* the Reformation—

---

1 "Germany, Germany above everything": the beginning of the German national anthem.

2 The unconditional and universal imperative that Kant considered the core of morality.

3 For Nietzsche's thoughts on Heinrich von Treitschke (1834–1896) and the German historians of that time see also *Beyond Good and Evil,* section 251, along with my long footnote (22). None of this kept Ernest Barker, an eminent British scholar, from publishing a tract on *Nietzsche and Treitschke: The Worship of Power in Modern Germany,* Oxford Pamphlets, Number 20, London, Oxford University Press, 1914; 4th impression, 1914!

4 The words "idiot" and "idiotic" figure prominently in Nietzsche's writings, beginning in 1887: see Kaufmann's *Nietzsche,* Chapter 12, note 2.

5 Friedrich Theodor Vischer (1807–1887) wrote *Aesthetik,* 6 volumes (1846–57); also a parody of Goethe's *Faust II,* entitled *Faust: Der Tragödie dritter Teil* (i.e., Faust III; 1862, under the pseudonym Mystifizinski), and a very popular novel, *Auch Einer* (another one; 1879).

only the two together make a whole: the aesthetic rebirth *and* the moral rebirth."

When I read such sentences, my patience is exhausted and I feel the itch, I even consider it a duty, to tell the Germans for once how many things they have on their conscience by now.[6] *All great crimes against culture for four centuries they have on their conscience.*— And the reason is always the same: their innermost *cowardice* before reality, which is also cowardice before the truth; their untruthfulness which has become instinctive with them; their "idealism."

The Germans did Europe out of the harvest, the meaning, of the last *great* age, the age of the Renaissance, at a moment when a higher order of values, the noble ones, those that say Yes to life, those that guarantee the future, had triumphed at the seat of the opposite values, those of *decline—even in the very instincts of those who were sitting there.* Luther, this calamity of a monk, restored the church and, what is a thousand times worse, Christianity, at the very moment *when it was vanquished.*— Christianity, this denial of the will to life become religion!— Luther, an impossible monk who, on account of his own "impossibility," attacked the church and—consequently—restored it.— The Catholics would have good reasons to celebrate Luther festivals, to write Luther plays.— Luther—and the "moral rebirth"! To hell with psychology! [7]— Beyond a doubt, the Germans are idealists.

Twice, when an honest, unequivocal, perfectly scientific way of thinking had just been attained with tremendous fortitude and self-overcoming, the Germans managed to find devious paths to the old "ideal," reconciliations of truth and "ideal"—at bottom, formulas for a right to repudiate science, a right to *lie.* Leibniz and Kant—these two greatest brake shoes of intellectual integrity in Europe!

---

[6] The remainder of this section is quite similar to *The Antichrist*, section 61 (*Portable Nietzsche*, pp. 653ff.).

[7] *Zum Teufel mit aller Psychologie:* presumably, Nietzsche means that those who associate Luther with a "moral rebirth" have no regard whatever for psychology. Cf. *The Antichrist*, section 39 (*Portable Nietzsche*, p. 613), *The Will to Power*, section 192, and Kaufmann's *Nietzsche*, Chapter 12, section II.

Finally, when on the bridge between two centuries of decadence, a *force majeure*[8] of genius and will became visible, strong enough to create a unity out of Europe, a political and *economic* unity for the sake of a world government—the Germans with their "Wars of Liberation" did Europe out of the meaning, the miracle of meaning in the existence of Napoleon; hence they have on their conscience all that followed, that is with us today—this most *anti-cultural* sickness and unreason there is, nationalism, this *névrose nationale*[9] with which Europe is sick, this perpetuation of European particularism, of *petty* politics:[10] they have deprived Europe itself of its meaning, of its reason—they have driven it into a dead-end street.[11]— Does anyone besides me know the way out of this dead-end street?— A task that is great enough to *unite* nations again?

3

And in the end, why should I not voice my suspicion? In my case, too, the Germans will try everything to bring forth from a tremendous destiny—a mouse. So far they have compromised themselves in my case; I doubt that they will do any better in the future.— Ah, how I wish I were a *bad* prophet in this case!— My natural readers and listeners are even now Russians, Scandinavians, and Frenchmen—will it always be that way?

In the history of the quest for knowledge the Germans are inscribed with nothing but ambiguous names; they have always brought forth only "unconscious" counterfeiters (Fichte, Schelling, Schopenhauer, Hegel, and Schleiermacher deserve this epithet as well as Kant and Leibniz: they are all mere veil makers):[1] they shall never enjoy the honor that the first *honest* spirit in the history

---

[8] Superior force.

[9] National neurosis.

[10] *Der Kleinstaaterei Europas, der* kleinen *Politik.*

[11] *Sie haben Europa selbst um seinen Sinn, um seine* Vernunft—*sie haben es in eine Sackgasse gebracht.*

[1] The name of Schleiermacher (1768–1834), the leading Protestant theologian of the German romantic movement, means literally veil maker.

of the spirit, the spirit in whom truth comes to judgment over the counterfeiting of four millennia, should be counted one with the German spirit.

The "German spirit" is for me bad air: I breathe with difficulty near the by now instinctive uncleanliness *in psychologicis* which every word, every facial expression of a German betrays. They have never gone through a seventeenth century of hard self-examination, like the French—a La Rochefoucauld and a Descartes are a hundred times superior in honesty to the foremost Germans—to this day they have not had a psychologist. But psychology is almost the measure of the *cleanliness* or *uncleanliness* of a race.

And if one is not even cleanly, how should one have *depth*? It is with Germans almost as it is with women: one never fathoms their depths; they don't have any, that is all. They aren't even shallow.[2]— What is called "deep" in Germany is precisely this instinctive uncleanliness in relation to oneself of which I have just spoken: one does not *want* to gain clarity about oneself. Might I not propose the word "German" as an international coinage for this psychological depravity?— At this very moment, for example, the German Kaiser calls it his "Christian duty" to liberate the slaves in Africa: among us other Europeans this would then simply be called "German."

Have the Germans produced even one book that has depth? They even lack the *idea* of depth in a book. I have met scholars who considered Kant deep; at the Prussian court, I fear, Herr von Treitschke is considered deep. And when I occasionally praise Stendhal as a deep psychologist, I have encountered professors at German universities who asked me to spell his name.

4

And why should I not go all the way? I like to make a clean sweep of things. It is part of my ambition to be considered a de-

---

[2] Nietzsche here uses one of the "Maxims and Arrows" (number 27) from *Twilight* and applies it to the Germans. The last sentence is crossed out in the MS—presumably not by Nietzsche, and therefore printed in the German editions.

spiser of the Germans *par excellence.* My mistrust of the German character I expressed even when I was twenty-six (in the third Untimely One, section 6)[1]—the Germans seem impossible to me. When I imagine a type of man that antagonizes all my instincts, it always turns into a German.[2]

The first point on which I "try the reins" is to see whether a man has a feeling for distance in his system, whether he sees rank, degree,[3] order between man and man everywhere, whether he makes *distinctions:* with that one is a *gentilhomme;* otherwise one belongs hopelessly in the broad-minded—ah, so good-natured—concept of canaille. But the Germans are canaille—ah, they are so good-natured.— One lowers oneself when one associates with Germans: the German puts others on a par.— Except for my association with a few artists, above all with Richard Wagner, I have not spent one good hour with a German.[4]—

If the most profound spirit of all millennia appeared among Germans, some savioress of the capitol [5] would suppose that her very unbeautiful soul deserved at least equal consideration.— I cannot endure this race among whom one is always in bad company, that has no fingers for nuances—alas, I am a nuance—that has no *esprit* in its feet and does not even know how to walk.— The Germans ultimately have no feet at all, they have only legs.— The Germans have no idea how vulgar they are; but that is the superlative of vulgarity—they are not even *ashamed* of being merely Germans.— They join in every discussion; they consider

---

[1] Just before the middle of the section: ". . . Certainly, one who has to live among Germans suffers badly from the notorious grayness of their life and senses, their crudity, their dullness and doltishness, their clumsiness in delicate relationships, and even more their envy and a certain slyness and uncleanliness in their character; one is pained and offended by their deeply rooted pleasure in the false and inauthentic . . ." *Schopenhauer as Educator* was written and published in 1874, the year Nietzsche turned thirty. And he was twenty-seven when his first book appeared. Thus "twenty-six" in the text is an error; but it is noteworthy how early he attributed "uncleanliness" to the Germans.

[2] There is no period in the MS, which continued: "—or an anti-Semite." These words were struck out, presumably not by Nietzsche.

[3] Cf. Ulysses' great speech in Shakespeare's *Troilus and Cressida,* Act I, scene 3, about "degree."

[4] See Appendix, section 3.

[5] That is, some goose.

themselves decisive; I fear they have reached a decision even about me.

My whole life is the demonstration *de rigueur*[6] of these propositions. In vain do I seek among them for some sign of tact, of *délicatesse* in relation to me. From Jews, yes; never yet from Germans.

It is part of my nature to be gentle and benevolent toward everybody—I have the *right* not to make distinctions—but that does not prevent me from keeping my eyes open. I except no one, least of all my friends; in the end I hope that this has not diminished my humanity in relation to them. There are five or six things that have always been a point of honor with me.—- Nevertheless it is true that almost every letter that has reached me for years now strikes me as a piece of cynicism: there is more cynicism in being kind to me than in any hatred.

I tell every one of my friends to his face that he has never considered it worth while to *study* any of my writings: I infer from the smallest signs that they do not even know what is in them. As for my *Zarathustra*: who among my friends saw more in it than an impermissible but fortunately utterly inconsequential presumption?

Ten years—and nobody in Germany has felt bound in conscience to defend my name against the absurd silence under which it lies buried: it was a foreigner, a Dane, who first possessed sufficient refinement of instinct *and courage* for this, who felt outraged by my alleged friends.—- At what German university would it be possible today to have lectures on my philosophy, such as were given last spring in Copenhagen by Dr. Georg Brandes who thus proved himself once again as a psychologist?

I myself have never suffered from all this; what is *necessary* does not hurt me; *amor fati*[7] is my inmost nature. But this does not preclude my love of irony, even world-historical irony. And thus I have sent into the world, about two years before the shattering lightning bolt of the *Revaluation* that will make the earth convulse —*The Case of Wagner*: let the Germans commit one more immortal blunder in relation to me that will stand in all eternity. There is

---

[6] According to strict form.

[7] Cf. the conclusion of Chapter 2, above.

barely enough time left for that.— Has it been accomplished?—
Most delightfully, my dear Teutons! My compliments! [8]

---

[8] According to Podach (p. 410) the following passage (*ibid.*, p. 315) is
crossed out in the MS with a colored pencil, meaning that it was deleted by
the printer: "Just now, lest my friends be left out, an old friend writes me
that she is now *laughing* at me.— And that at a moment when an indescribable responsibility weighs on me—when no word can be delicate and no eye
respectful enough towards me. For I bear the destiny of humanity on my
shoulders."

Raoul Richter included this passage in a footnote to his postscript to the
first edition of *Ecce Homo* (1908) but said he considered it *"probable"* that
the deletion was Nietzsche's own" (p. 147). Cf. note 1 to Chapter 2, section
10, above.

The reference to the *Revaluation*, in the text, should be compared with
section 3 of "Twilight of the Idols," above: Nietzsche is speaking of his
forthcoming book. He is not implying that the earth will be convulsed by his
revelation of new values; as he explains in the first section of "Beyond
Good and Evil," above, the revaluation is a "No-saying"—a critique of
faith and morals. This point is developed further on the following pages.

Why I Am a Destiny

1

I know my fate. One day my name will be associated with the memory of something tremendous—a crisis without equal on earth, the most profound collision of conscience, a decision that was conjured up *against* everything that had been believed, demanded, hallowed so far. I am no man, I am dynamite.[1]— Yet for all that, there is nothing in me of a founder of a religion—religions are affairs of the rabble; I find it necessary to wash my hands after I have come into contact with religious people.— I *want* no "believers"; I think I am too malicious to believe in myself; I never speak to masses.— I have a terrible fear that one day I will be pronounced *holy:* you will guess why I publish this book *before;* it shall prevent people from doing mischief with me.[2]

I do not want to be a holy man; sooner even a buffoon.— Perhaps I am a buffoon.— Yet in spite of that—or rather *not* in spite of it, because so far nobody has been more mendacious than holy men—the truth speaks out of me.— But my truth is *terrible;* for so far one has called *lies* truth.

Revaluation of all values: that is my formula for an act of supreme self-examination on the part of humanity, become flesh and genius in me. It is my fate that I have to be the first *decent* human being; that I know myself to stand in opposition to the mendaciousness of millennia.— I was the first to *discover* the truth by being the first to experience lies as lies—smelling them out.— My genius is in my nostrils.

---

[1] This had been said of Nietzsche in the *Berner Bund*, in J. V. Widmann's review of *Beyond Good and Evil*, September 16–17, 1886. The passage is quoted at length in Nietzsche's letter to Malwida von Meysenbug, September 24, 1886 (*Werke*, ed. Karl Schlechta, vol. III, p. 1245).

[2] But *Ecce Homo* was not published until 1908, and at Nietzsche's funeral in 1900 Peter Gast proclaimed: "Holy be thy name to all coming generations." Even after it was published, *Ecce Homo* failed to prevent far worse mischief.

I contradict as has never been contradicted before and am nevertheless the opposite of a No-saying spirit. I am a bringer of glad tidings like no one before me; I know tasks of such elevation that any notion of them has been lacking so far; only beginning with me are there hopes again. For all that, I am necessarily also the man of calamity. For when truth enters into a fight with the lies of millennia, we shall have upheavals, a convulsion of earthquakes, a moving of mountains and valleys, the like of which has never been dreamed of. The concept of politics will have merged entirely with a war of spirits; all power structures of the old society will have been exploded—all of them are based on lies: there will be wars the like of which have never yet been seen on earth. It is only beginning with me that the earth knows *great politics*.

2

You want a formula for such a destiny *become man?* That is to be found in my *Zarathustra:*

"And whoever wants to be[1] a creator in good and evil, must first be an annihilator and break values. Thus the highest evil belongs to the greatest goodness: but this is—being creative."

I am by far the most terrible human being that has existed so far; this does not preclude the possibility that I shall be the most beneficial. I know the pleasure in destroying to a degree that accords with my powers to destroy—in both respects I obey my Dionysian nature which does not know how to separate doing No from saying Yes. I am the first immoralist: that makes me the annihilator *par excellence.*

3

I have not been asked, as I should have been asked, what the name of Zarathustra means in my mouth, the mouth of the first immoralist: for what constitutes the tremendous historical uniqueness of that Persian is just the opposite of this. Zarathustra was the first to consider the fight of good and evil the very wheel in the

---

[1] In *Zarathustra II,* "On Self-Overcoming," the text reads "must be"; and "evil" is followed by "verily."

machinery of things: the transposition of morality into the meta-physical realm, as a force, cause, and end in itself, is *his* work. But this question itself is at bottom its own answer. Zarathustra created this most calamitous error, morality; consequently, he must also be the first to recognize it. Not only has he more experience in this matter, for a longer time, than any other thinker—after all, the whole of history is the refutation by experiment of the principle of the so-called "moral world order"—what is more important is that Zarathustra is more truthful than any other thinker. His doctrine, and his alone, posits truthfulness as the highest virtue; this means the opposite of the cowardice of the "idealist" who flees from real-ity; Zarathustra has more intestinal fortitude than all other thinkers taken together. To speak the truth and to *shoot well with arrows,* that is Persian virtue.[2]— Am I understood?— The self-overcoming of morality, out of truthfulness; the self-overcoming of the moral-ist, into his opposite—into me—that is what the name of Zarathus-tra means in my mouth.

4

Fundamentally, my term *immoralist* involves two negations. For one, I negate a type of man that has so far been considered supreme: the good, the benevolent, the beneficent. And then I ne-gate a type of morality that has become prevalent and predominant as morality itself—the morality of decadence or, more concretely, *Christian* morality. It would be permissible to consider the second contradiction the more decisive one, since I take the overestimation of goodness and benevolence on a large scale for a consequence of decadence, for a symptom of weakness, irreconcilable with an ascending, Yes-saying life: negating *and destroying* are conditions of saying Yes.[1]

---

[2] Cf. *Zarathustra I,* "On the Thousand and One Goals": ". . . 'To speak the truth and to handle bow and arrow well'—that seemed both dear and diffi-cult to the people who gave me my name . . ."

[1] Although Nietzsche associates this with Dionysus, cf. also Jer. 1:10: "See, I have this day set thee over the nations and over the kingdoms, to root out, and to pull down, and to destroy, and to throw down, to build and to plant." But Jeremiah felt no pleasure in destruction.

Let me tarry over the psychology of the good human being. To estimate what a type of man is worth, one must calculate the price paid for his preservation—one must know the conditions of his existence. The condition of the existence of the good is the *lie:* put differently, not *wanting* to see at any price how reality is constituted fundamentally—namely, not in such a way as to elicit benevolent instincts at all times, and even less in such a way as to tolerate at all times the interference of those who are myopically good-natured. To consider distress of all kinds as an objection, as something that must be abolished, is the *niaiserie*[2] *par excellence* and, on a large scale, a veritable disaster in its consequences, a nemesis[3] of stupidity—almost as stupid as would be the desire to abolish bad weather—say, from pity for poor people.

In the great economy of the whole, the terrible aspects of reality (in affects, in desires, in the will to power) are to an incalculable degree more necessary than that form of petty happiness which people call "goodness"; one actually has to be quite lenient to accord the latter any place at all, considering that it presupposes an instinctive mendaciousness. I shall have a major occasion to demonstrate how the historical consequences of *optimism,* this abortion of the *homines optimi,*[4] have been uncanny beyond measure. Zarathustra, who was the first to grasp that the optimist is just as decadent as the pessimist, and perhaps more harmful, says: *"Good men never speak the truth."* [5]

"False coasts and assurances the good have taught you; in the lies of the good you were hatched and huddled. Everything has been made fraudulent and has been twisted through and through by the good." [6]

Fortunately, the world has not been designed with a view to such instincts that only good-natured herd animals could find their narrow happiness in it: to demand that all should become "good

---

[2] Folly, stupidity, silliness.

[3] *Schicksal.*

[4] Best men.

[5] Quoted from *Zarathustra III,* "On Old and New Tablets," section 7. There are no quotation marks in the German text.

[6] *Ibid.,* section 28. Again, no quotation marks.

human beings," herd animals, blue-eyed, benevolent, "beautiful souls"—or as Mr. Herbert Spencer[7] would have it, altruistic—would deprive existence of its *great* character and would castrate men and reduce them to the level of desiccated Chinese stagnation. — *And this has been attempted!*— *Precisely this has been called morality.*

In this sense, Zarathustra calls the good, now "the last men," [8] now the "beginning of the end"; above all, he considers them the most harmful type of man because they prevail at the expense of *truth* and at the expense of the *future*.[9]

"The good are unable to *create*; they are always the beginning of the end; they crucify him who writes new values on new tablets; they sacrifice the future to *themselves*—they sacrifice all man's future.

"The good have always been the beginning of the end."

"And whatever harm those do who slander the world, the harm done by the good is the most harmful harm." [10]

5

Zarathustra, the first psychologist of the good, is—consequently—a friend of the evil. When a decadent type of man ascended to the rank of the highest type, this could only happen at the expense of its countertype, the type of man that is strong and sure of life. When the herd animal is irradiated by the glory of the purest virtue, the exceptional man must have been devaluated into evil. When mendaciousness at any price monopolizes the word "truth" for its perspective, the really truthful man is bound to be branded with the worst names. Zarathustra leaves no doubt at this

---

[7] English philosopher (1820–1903).

[8] In the "Prologue," section 5. Indeed, that section, along with the whole Prologue, may be the best commentary on the above section—though it would be more accurate to say that the above is a commentary on *Zarathustra*.

[9] Those who want to abolish all hardships because they themselves are not up to them are like sick people who wish to abolish rain, no matter what the consequences might be to others and to the earth generally. Cf. Nietzsche's own remark about "bad weather" above.

[10] Both quotations are from section 26 of "On Old and New Tablets"; but the second quotation occurs earlier in that section.

point: he says that it was his insight precisely into the good, the "best," that made him shudder at man in general; that it was from *this* aversion that he grew wings "to soar off into distant futures"; he does not conceal the fact that *his* type of man, a relatively superhuman type, is superhuman precisely in its relation to the *good* —that the good and the just would call his overman *devil*.

"You highest men whom my eyes have seen, this is my doubt about you and my secret laughter: I guess that you would call my overman—devil."

"What is great is so alien to your souls that the overman would be terrifying to you in his goodness." [1]

It is here and nowhere else that one must make a start to comprehend what Zarathustra wants: this type of man that he conceives, conceives reality *as it is,* being strong enough to do so; this type is not estranged or removed from reality but is reality itself and exemplifies all that is terrible and questionable in it—*only in that way can man attain greatness.*

6

There is yet another sense, however, in which I have chosen the word *immoralist* as a symbol and badge of honor for myself; I am proud of having this word which distinguishes me from the whole of humanity. Nobody yet has felt *Christian* morality to be *beneath* him: that requires a height, a view of distances, a hitherto altogether unheard-of psychological depth and profundity. Christian morality has been the Circe of all thinkers so far—they stood in her service.— Who before me climbed into the caverns from which the poisonous fumes of this type of ideal—slander of the world—are rising? Who even dared to suspect that they are caverns? Who among philosophers was a *psychologist* at all before me, and not rather the opposite, a "higher swindler" and "idealist"? There was no psychology at all before me.— To be the first here may be a curse; it is at any rate a destiny: *for one is also the first to despise.*— *Nausea* at man is my danger.

---

[1] All three quotations, beginning with "to soar off . . ." come from *Zarathustra II,* "On Human Prudence."

7

Have I been understood?— What defines me, what sets me apart from the whole rest of humanity is that I *uncovered* Christian morality. That is why I needed a word that had the meaning of a provocation for everybody. That they did not open their eyes earlier at this point, I regard as the greatest uncleanliness that humanity has on its conscience; as self-deception become instinctive; as a fundamental will *not* to see any event, any causality, any reality; as counterfeiting *in psychologicis* to the point of criminality. Blindness to Christianity is the crime *par excellence*—the crime against life.

The millennia, the nations, the first and the last, the philosophers and old women—excepting five, six moments in history, and me as the seventh—at this point all of them are worthy of each other. The Christian has so far been *the* "moral being"—a matchless curiosity—and *as* the "moral being" he was more absurd, mendacious, vain, frivolous, and more disadvantageous for himself than even the greatest despiser of humanity could imagine in his dreams. Christian morality—the most malignant form of the will to lie, the real Circe of humanity—that which *corrupted* humanity. It is *not* error as error that horrifies me at this sight—not the lack, for thousands of years, of "good will," discipline, decency, courage in matters of the spirit, revealed by its victory: it is the lack of nature, it is the utterly gruesome fact that *antinature* itself received the highest honors as morality and was fixed over humanity as law and categorical imperative.— To blunder to such an extent, not as individuals, not as a people, but as humanity!— That one taught men to despise the very first instincts of life; that one mendaciously invented a "soul," a "spirit" to ruin the body; that one taught men to experience the presupposition of life, sexuality, as something unclean; that one looks for the evil principle in what is most profoundly necessary for growth, in *severe* self-love[1] (this very word

---

[1] *Selbstsucht:* the word is pejorative, like "selfishness." Cf. note 5, section 1 of "The Untimely Ones," above; also the beginning of section 4 on "Human, All-Too-Human."

constitutes slander); that, conversely, one regards the typical signs of decline and contradiction of the instincts, the "selfless," the loss of a center of gravity, "depersonalization" and "neighbor love" (*addiction* to the neighbor) as the *higher* value—what am I saying?—the *absolute* value!

What? Is humanity itself decadent? Was it always?— What is certain is that it has been *taught* only decadence values as supreme values. The morality that would un-self man is the morality of decline *par excellence*—the fact, "I am declining," transposed into the imperative, "all of you *ought* to decline"—and not only into the imperative.— This only morality that has been taught so far, that of un-selfing, reveals a will to the end; fundamentally, it negates life.

This would still leave open the possibility that not humanity is degenerating but only that parasitical type of man—that of the *priest*—which has used morality to raise itself mendaciously to the position of determining human values—finding in Christian morality the means to come to *power*.— Indeed, this is *my* insight: the teachers, the leaders of humanity, theologians all of them, were also, all of them, decadents: *hence* the revaluation of all values into hostility to life,[2] *hence* morality—

Definition of morality: Morality—the idiosyncrasy of decadents, with the ulterior motive of revenging oneself against life—successfully. I attach value to this definition.

8

Have I been understood?— I have not said one word here that I did not say five years ago through the mouth of Zarathustra.

The uncovering of Christian morality is an event without parallel, a real catastrophe. He that is enlightened about that, is a *force majeure,* a destiny—he breaks the history of mankind in two. One lives before him, or one lives after him.

The lightning bolt of truth struck precisely what was highest

---

[2] Nietzsche's revaluation is meant to undo the damage done by a previous revaluation: values have been stood on their head and are now to be turned right-side up again.

so far: let whoever comprehends *what* has here been destroyed see whether anything is left in his hands. Everything that has hitherto been called "truth" has been recognized as the most harmful, insidious, and subterranean form of lie; the holy pretext of "improving" mankind, as the ruse for sucking the blood of life itself. Morality as vampirism.

Whoever uncovers morality also uncovers the disvalue of all values that are and have been believed; he no longer sees anything venerable in the most venerated types of man, even in those pronounced holy; he considers them the most calamitous type of abortion—calamitous because they exerted such fascination.

The concept of "God" invented as a counterconcept of life—everything harmful, poisonous, slanderous, the whole hostility unto death against life synthesized in this concept in a gruesome unity! The concept of the "beyond," the "true world" invented in order to devaluate the only world there is[1]—in order to retain no goal, no reason, no task for our earthly reality! The concept of the "soul," the "spirit," finally even *"immortal* soul," invented in order to despise the body,[2] to make it sick, "holy"; to oppose with a ghastly levity everything that deserves to be taken seriously in life, the questions of nourishment, abode, spiritual diet, treatment of the sick, cleanliness, and weather.[3]

In place of health, the "salvation of the soul"—that is, a *folie circulaire*[4] between penitential convulsions and hysteria about redemption. The concept of "sin" invented along with the torture instrument that belongs with it, the concept of "free will," in order to confuse the instincts, to make mistrust of the instincts second nature. In the concept of the "selfless," the "self-denier," the distinctive sign of decadence, feeling attracted by what is harmful, being unable to find any longer what profits one, self-destruction is turned into the sign of value itself, into "duty," into "holiness," into what is "divine" in man. Finally—this is what is most terrible of all—the concept of the *good* man signifies that one sides

---

[1] Cf. *Twilight*, Chapters III and IV.
[2] Cf. *Zarathustra I*, "On The Despisers of the Body."
[3] Cf. "Why I am So Clever," above.
[4] Manic-depressive insanity.

with all that is weak, sick, failure, suffering of itself—all that ought to perish: the principle of selection is crossed [5]—an ideal is fabricated from the contradiction against the proud and well-turned-out human being who says Yes, who is sure of the future, who guarantees the future—and he is now called *evil*.— And all this was believed, *as morality!*— *Ecrasez l'infâme!* [6]——

9

Have I been understood?— *Dionysus versus the Crucified.*—[1]

---

[5] Cf. *The Antichrist*, section 7.

[6] Voltaire's motto—crush the infamy—in his fight against the church.

[1] The best commentary is section 1052 of *The Will to Power*.

APPENDIX

Variants from Nietzsche's Drafts

Part of a discarded draft for section 3 of "Why I Am So Clever" (Podach, *Friedrich Nietzsches Werke*, pp. 236f.):

Emerson with his essays has been a good friend and cheered me up even in black periods: he contains so much skepsis, so many "possibilities" that even virtue achieves esprit in his writings. A unique case! Even as a boy I enjoyed listening to him. *Tristram Shandy* also belongs to my earliest favorites; how I experienced Sterne may be seen from a very pensive passage in *Human, All-Too-Human* [Part II, section 113]. Perhaps it was for related reasons that I preferred Lichtenberg[1] among German books, while the "idealist" Schiller was more than I could swallow even when I was thirteen.— I don't want to forget Abbé Galiani,[2] this most profound buffoon that ever lived.

Of *all* books, one of my strongest impressions is that exuberant Provençal, Petronius, who composed the last *Satura Menippea*.[3] Such sovereign freedom from "morality," from "seriousness," from his own sublime taste; such subtlety in his mixture of vulgar and "educated" Latin; such indomitable good spirits that leap with grace and malice over all anomalies of the ancient "soul"

---

[1] Georg Christoph Lichtenberg (1742–1799), professor of physics at Göttingen, was perhaps the greatest German aphorist and satirist of his century.

[2] A writer (1728–1787) often mentioned by Nietzsche. See my note (6) in *Beyond Good and Evil* (New York, Vintage Books, 1966), section 26.

[3] The relevant information has been put most succinctly by William Arrowsmith, in his Introduction to his own translation of *The Satyricon of Petronius* (Ann Arbor, Mich., University of Michigan Press, 1959), p. x: "Formally . . . the *Satyricon* . . . belongs to that genre we call Menippean satire, the curious blending of prose with verse and philosophy with realism invented by the Cynic philosopher Menippus of Gadara [third century B.C.] and continued by his Roman disciple, Varro [116–27 B.C.]." The identity and dates of Petronius have been disputed, but he probably committed suicide when Nero was Emperor. Cf. *Beyond*, section 28.

—I could not name any book that makes an equally liberating impression on me: the effect is Dionysian. In cases in which I find it necessary to recuperate quickly from a base impression—for example, because for the sake of my critique of Christianity I had to breathe all too long the swampy air of the apostle Paul—a few pages of Petronius suffice me as a *heroic* remedy, and immediately I am well again.

2

Part of a discarded draft for section 3 of "Why I Write Such Good Books" (Podach, *Friedrich Nietzsches Werke*, pp. 251f.):

My writings are difficult; I hope this is not considered an objection? To understand the most *abbreviated* language ever spoken by a philosopher—and also the one poorest in formulas, most alive, most artistic—one must follow the *opposite* procedure of that generally required by philosophical literature. Usually, one must *condense,* or upset one's digestion; I have to be diluted, liquefied, mixed with water, else one upsets one's digestion.

Silence is as much of an instinct with me as is garrulity with our dear philosophers. I am *brief;* my readers themselves must become long and comprehensive in order to bring up and together all that I have thought, and thought deep down.

On the other hand, there are prerequisites for "understanding" here, which very few can satisfy: one must be able to see a problem in its proper place—that is, in the context of the other problems that *belong with it;* and for this one must have at one's finger tips the topography of various nooks and the difficult areas of whole sciences and above all of philosophy.

Finally, I speak only of what I have lived through, not merely of what I have thought through; the opposition of thinking and life is lacking in my case. My "theory" grows from my "practice"—oh, from a practice that is not by any means harmless or unproblematic!

3

In his postscript to the first edition, 1908, Raoul Richter said: "A page that, according to information received from Frau Förster-Nietzsche, was mailed to Paraguay, with a notation regarding its insertion in *Ecce Homo*, survives in a copy and contains invective against his brother-in-law and friends, but has been excluded from publication here as something not belonging to the authentic Nietzsche. This is presumably one of those violent outpourings of which several have been found in the Förster papers, some of them long destroyed, with uninhibited attacks on Bismarck, the Kaiser, and others. The fact alone that an addition to *Ecce Homo* was sent to South America [where the sister and brother-in-law were then living], instead of being sent to the publisher in Leipzig, shows that this is presumably a page that belongs to the first days of the collapse. Possibly, a similar but no longer extant note sent to the publisher was also intended for *Ecce*." Podach's criticism of Richter for not publishing this note (*Friedrich Nietzsches Werke*, pp. 198f.) seems highly unreasonable; but the text (p. 314) deserves inclusion in this Appendix. Nietzsche's notation read: "To be inserted in the chapter 'The Case of Wagner,' section 4, after the words: 'Except for my association with a few artists, above all with Richard Wagner, I have not spent one good hour with a German'" (*ibid.*, p. 410). The text itself reads:

Shall I here divulge my "German" experiences?—Förster: long legs, blue eyes, blond (straw head!), a "racial German" who with poison and gall attacks everything that guarantees spirit and future: Judaism, vivisection, etc.—but for his sake my sister left those nearest her[1] and plunged into a world full of dangers and evil accidents.

Köselitz:[2] Saxon, weak, at times awkward, immovable, an embodiment of the law of gravity—but his music is of the first rank and runs on light feet.

Overbeck[3] dried up, become sour, subject to his wife, hands me,

---

[1] *Ihre "Nächsten"*: The word used in the Bible for neighbor.

[2] Heinrich Köselitz was the real name of Peter Gast.

[3] Franz Overbeck was professor of church history at Basel, but an unbeliever. For accounts of Förster, Gast, and Overbeck see Kaufmann's *Nietzsche*, Chapter 1, sections I and III, or—for a much fuller account, in German—Podach's *Gestalten um Nietzsche* (figures around Nietzsche; Weimar, Lichtenstein, 1932).

like Mime,[4] the poisoned draft of doubt and mistrust of myself—but he shows how he is full of good will toward me and worried about me and calls himself my "indulgent friend."

Look at them—these are three German types! Canaille!

And if the most profound spirit of all millennia appeared among Germans

4

All of the paragraphs in this section come from three discarded drafts for the attack on the Germans in the chapter "The Case of Wagner." (a) and (b) constitute the beginning and end of the same draft (Podach, *Friedrich Nietzsches Werke*, p. 316); (c) comes from another attempt (*ibid.*, p. 317); (d) from the last (*ibid.*, pp. 318f.).

(a)

And from what side did all *great* obstructions, all calamities in my life emanate? Always from Germans. The damnable German anti-Semitism, this poisonous boil of *névrose nationale*, has intruded into my existence almost ruinously during that decisive time when not my destiny but the destiny of humanity was at issue. And I owe it to the same element that my *Zarathustra* entered this world as *indecent* literature—its publisher being an anti-Semite. In vain do I look for some sign of tact, of *délicatesse*, in relation to me: from Jews, yes; never yet from Germans.

(b)

The Germans are by far the worst experience of my life; for sixteen years now one has left me in the lurch, not only concerning my philosophy but also in regard to my honor. What respect can I have for the Germans when even my friends cannot discriminate between me and a liar like Richard Wagner? In one extreme case, one even straddles the fence between me and anti-Semitic canaille. — And this at a moment when an indescribable responsibility weighs on me—[1]

---

[4] In Wagner's *Ring*.

[1] The passage ends like the one cited in the final footnote for that chapter, above. The "extreme case" is presumably that of Nietzsche's sister.

(c)

It seems to be that association with Germans even corrupts one's character. I lose all mistrust; I feel how the fungus of neighbor-love spreads in me—it has even happened, to my profound humiliation, that I have become *good-natured.* Is it possible to sink any lower?— For with me, malice belongs to happiness—I am no good when I am not malicious[2]—I find no small justification of existence in provoking tremendous stupidities against me.

(d)

I am *solitude* become man.[3]— That no word ever reached me, forced me to reach myself.— I should not be possible without a countertype of race, without Germans, without *these* Germans, without Bismarck, without 1848, without "Wars of Liberation," without Kant, even without Luther.— The great crimes committed against culture by the Germans are justified in a *higher* economy of culture.— I want nothing differently, not backward either—I was not permitted to want anything differently.— *Amor fati.*— Even Christianity becomes necessary: only the highest form, the most dangerous, the one that was most seductive in its No to life, provokes its highest affirmation—me.— What in the end are these two millennia? Our most instructive experiment, a vivisection of life itself.— Merely two millennia!—

5

For a time, Nietzsche thought of concluding *Ecce Homo* with two sections that are included in a table of contents reproduced photographically by Podach (*Friedrich Nietzsches Werke,* plate XIV); but then he wrote on a separate sheet (*ibid.,* p. 332): "The section *Declaration of War* is to be omitted— Also *The Hammer Speaks.*" The latter he moved to the end of *Twilight* (*Portable Nietzsche,* p. 563); the former is lost, except for the following paragraph on a sheet with the notation: "At the end, after the Declaration of War" (*ibid.,* p. 332).

---

2 *Ich tauge Nichts, wenn ich nicht boshaft bin.* "Malice": *Bosheit.*
3 *Ich bin die* Einsamkeit *als Mensch.*

Final Consideration

If we could dispense with wars, so much the better. I can imagine more profitable uses for the twelve billion now paid annually for the armed peace we have in Europe; there are other means of winning respect for physiology than field hospitals.— Good; *very good even*: since the old God is abolished, I am prepared *to rule the world*—

INDEX

On the Genealogy of Morals

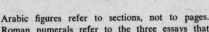

Arabic figures refer to sections, not to pages. Roman numerals refer to the three essays that comprise the *Genealogy*. **E** refers to the editor's Introduction, **P** to Nietzsche's Preface, **n** to the editor's notes. For references to Nietzsche's works, see Nietzsche.

A separate Index for the Appendix follows this Index.

INDEX

Seventy-five Aphorisms

Arabic figures refer to sections, not pages. The following abbreviations have been employed:

D: *Dawn;* **GS:** *Gay Science;* **H:** *Human, All-Too-Human;* **MM:** *Mixed Opinions and Maxims;* **S:** *The Wanderer and His Shadow.*

For references to Nietzsche's works, see Nietzsche.

INDEX

Ecce Homo

Arabic numerals refer to sections, not to pages. The following abbreviations have been used:

I:	Why I Am So Wise
II:	Why I Am So Clever
III:	Why I Write Such Good Books
IV:	Why I Am a Destiny
BT:	Birth of Tragedy
U:	Untimely Ones
H:	Human, All-Too-Human
D:	Dawn
GS:	Gay Science
Z:	Thus Spoke Zarathustra
B:	Beyond Good and Evil
GM:	Genealogy of Morals
T:	Twilight of the Idols
W:	The Case of Wagner
A:	Appendix
E:	Editor's Introduction
NP:	Note on the Publication of *Ecce Homo*
P:	Nietzsche's Preface
n:	Editor's notes

For reference to Nietzsche's works, see Nietzsche: works.

FRIEDRICH NIETZSCHE was born in 1844 in Röcken (Saxony), Germany. He studied classical philology at the universities of Bonn and Leipzig, and in 1869 was appointed to the chair of classical philology at the University of Basel, Switzerland. Ill health led him to resign his professorship ten years later. His works include *The Birth of Tragedy, Thus Spoke Zarathustra, Beyond Good and Evil, On the Genealogy of Morals, The Case of Wagner, Twilight of the Idols, The Antichrist, Nietzsche contra Wagner,* and *Ecce Homo.* He died in 1900. *The Will to Power,* a selection from his notebooks, was published posthumously.

WALTER KAUFMANN was born in Freiburg, Germany, in 1921, came to the United States in 1939, and studied at Williams College and Harvard University. In 1947 he joined the faculty of Princeton University, where he is now Professor of Philosophy. He has held many visiting professorships, including Fulbright grants at Heidelberg and Jerusalem. His books include *Nietzsche, Critique of Religion and Philosophy, From Shakespeare to Existentialism, The Faith of a Heretic, Cain and Other Poems,* and *Hegel,* as well as verse translations of Goethe's *Faust* and *Twenty German Poets.* He has also translated all of the books by Nietzsche listed above. In addition to *On The Genealogy of Morals* and *Ecce Homo,* the following appear in Vintage Books: *Beyond Good and Evil* and, in one volume, *The Birth of Tragedy* and *The Case of Wagner.* Mr. Kaufmann's edition of *The Will to Power* is available from Random House.

R. J. HOLLINGDALE is an English writer, best known for his book *Nietzsche: The Man and His Philosophy.*